SO-BBT-006

The Northwest Coast

OR, THREE YEARS' RESIDENCE IN WASHINGTON TERRITORY

The Northwest Coast

OR, THREE YEARS' RESIDENCE IN WASHINGTON TERRITORY

By JAMES G. SWAN

Introduction by Norman H. Clark

UNIVERSITY OF WASHINGTON PRESS

SEATTLE AND LONDON

First published by Harper & Brothers, Publishers, 1857
Introduction by Norman H. Clark copyright © 1969 by
     Harper & Row Publishers, Incorporated
University of Washington Press paperback edition, 1972
Fifth printing, 1992

Library of Congress Catalog Card Number 70–90378
ISBN 0–295–95190–7
Printed in the United States of America

All rights reserved. No part of this publication may be
reproduced or transmitted in any form or by any means,
electronic or mechanical, including photocopying, recording,
or any information storage or retrieval system, without
permission in writing from the publisher.

The paper used in this publication meets the minimum
requirements of American National Standard for Information
Sciences—Permanence of Paper for Printed Library Materials,
ANSI Z39.48–1984. ∞

Cover illustrations courtesy of Special Collections Division,
University of Washington Libraries.

INTRODUCTION

By Norman H. Clark

James Gilchrist Swan was a moral refugee disguised as a businessman when, in 1852, he found shelter and solace in the wilderness of the Northwest Coast. He had chosen a shallow harbor, bound by rock and sand and dark cedar forests, in a season of heavy winds and relentless rains. He was one of perhaps two dozen white Americans then on the Pacific Coast north of the Columbia River. Yet he settled there and built a cedar cabin, happily turning his back on the polite and predictable world of commerce he had left in Boston and on the larger implications of middle-class life in the United States during the days of Daniel Webster and Franklin Pierce. Learned in geography and history, trained in admiralty law, experienced in trade, elegantly schooled in social graces, Swan had nevertheless kicked against the apparently secure and rewarding circumstances of his thirty-four years as a proper New Englander. He had fled from a wife and two children, a prosperous ship-fitting business, and an immeasurable and forever private burden of frustration or remorse or regret. To Swan the West meant the opportunity to shape his life again under circumstances of his own choice. How he did this is one of the subtle dimensions of his narrative of physical and intellectual adventure called *The Northwest Coast.*

Swan escaped under cover of the California gold rush, which, like war, allowed a man to take leave of his obligations and in doing so accept the best wishes of his

neighbors and friends. Folded into the anonymous army
—more than 10,000 from New England alone—Swan
shipped out of Boston in 1849. While the younger men
may have talked hysterically of gold and sung "O California! That's the Land for Me," Swan brooded over the
richly connotative geography he had learned as a boy
at the feet of his seafaring relatives: the Columbia, Destruction Island, Cape Flattery, the Strait of Juan de
Fuca, Nootka Sound, Vancouver Island. His interest in
gold was at most indifferent, and though he dutifully
marched out to the mines that spring, he was back in
San Francisco within three months, sick of California
and its bonanza society. He took the first ship he could
find to the Crown Colony of Vancouver Island, where
in an area much larger than that of Massachusetts there
were maybe 1,000 white subjects of Great Britain and
30,000 native Indians. He had every intention of staying,
but he found himself excluded by the rigid British re-
quirement that immigrants bring servants. Before returning to California, he sailed across the strait to the
small sawmill village of Port Townsend, where he
thoughtfully filed a claim for free land.

Back in San Francisco, Swan outfitted ships for two
years while he again tried to balance the scope of his
freedom against the strength of his discretion. During
this period he met Charles Russell, then a resident of
Shoalwater Bay, just north of the Columbia River, who
encouraged Swan to come up the coast. Besides Russell,
and under circumstances he never made clear, he also
found a strong friendship with the bold and notoriously
boozy Clallam Indian named Chetzamakha, better
known as the Duke of York. (The Duke's brother was
named King George. Swan once described a fishing trip
with the Duke of York, whose relatives in the canoe

included Jenny Lind, General Gaines, Mrs. Gaines, Queen Victoria, and General Walker.) The Duke was from the Northwest Coast near Port Townsend, and he ignited in Swan a latent but powerful interest in Northwest Indians. With invitations from both the Duke and Russell, Swan now turned his back on California. He eagerly took passage aboard a two-masted squarerigger —and here his book begins—"bound up the Bay for a cargo of piles and spruce-timber," to Shoalwater harbor and the fringes of American influence in a yet unspoiled land.

For an earlier generation of Americans, on the edge of an earlier treasure of natural abundance in the Ohio Valley, it was said that between April and October each year Indian corn made the penniless immigrant into a proud capitalist. With less patience, the gold-rush generation dug up the Sacramento Valley from January to December while a few of the more imaginative adventurers found attractive treasure in the forests of the Northwest Coast. North of the Columbia after 1850 a man could make himself well-to-do in a season by chopping trees with a hand ax, felling them in tide water, then cutting them into logs and firewood to sell to San Francisco. If he had a steam-powered saw—and Swan noted sawdust thirty miles out to sea from the mouth of the Columbia—he could make himself wealthy. If he wanted to farm, he could ship to the fantastic prices in San Francisco for potatoes, butter, or wheat. California would buy almost anything that was for sale, and along the Northwest Coast shrewd men were looking for almost anything.

The men Swan met there were all newcomers to the region, free spirits in no way cramped by the history or traditions of the missionary-ridden society of pioneer

viii INTRODUCTION

farmers that had since 1834 nourished American loyal-
ties in the Willamette Valley of Oregon. Oregon was to
them irrelevant. They would have been appalled by
the thought of enduring the rigors of the Oregon Trail,
the Oregon Temperance Society, or the Methodist
Church. They had never been to Oregon City, nor did
they know the famous Jessie Applegate, leader of wagon
trains and pioneers, or General Joseph Lane, former
governor of Oregon Territory and in 1852 their own
delegate to Congress. Nor did they care. They had come
not to farm but to cut gold out of the sea and the forest,
to plunder timber from lands they did not own, to pack
salmon and shellfish from the seemingly endless rivers
and bays, or simply to sell whiskey to the Indians.

But their ambitions were not always consistent, and
there was relief here from the California frenzy. The
oysters of Shoalwater Bay, just as the Indian corn of
the Ohio Valley, could make more than a few of the
immigrants into incorrigible slobs. The "oyster boys"
of Swan's retreat were taking the brightest nuggets from
the top of a fabulous abundance, and they could do it
with a minimum of labor. Swan's host, Charles Russell,
had Indians and their slaves raking up piles of shellfish
and loading them aboard the California schooners. This
was capitalism in the grand manner: he and Swan sitting in the comfort of a rough cabin before the warmth
of a bottle and a blazing fire, savoring the depth of their
own insights while the Indians labored to make them
rich.

But as a way of life, oyster picking was so directly
bound to the uncertainties of wind and tide that the
man accepting them could not be impatient. What he
made in one raking he might lose with the next. The
Indians would work only spasmodically and according

to their own inclinations, not those of the San Francisco market. Given these conditions, and the adversity of weather and communications, grand plans were the essence of folly.

Yet the affluence was there for the daily taking—fish, clams, oysters, crabs, fowl, game—and one could live very well. And there was also the genial fellowship that Swan found among "generous and noble-hearted men." The drunks and the Indians had found a more or less satisfactory cultural mutuality of some advantage to both. In this wet and miserable forest—which could sometimes be gloriously fresh and crisp in green woods, brown sand, white waves and blue sea—there was a sense of community. In its relationship to American values and energies in the 1850's, it was not an alien community, but it was an alienated one, and Swan eagerly became a part of it. For a brief moment before the Civil War, the railroads, the machines and the factories, Shoalwater Bay sheltered a leisurely society of boozy white loafers and boozy but friendly Indians who lived untroubled by the currents of progress and naturally protected from any windy convictions about the perfectibility of man.

Swan's achievement in this community was that he soon had more influence among the Indians than any other American. This seems to have come almost naturally to him—from his real interest in the Indians and his way of letting them know he was interested, from his ability to accept them as individuals of importance and integrity. He studied their languages and soon spoke them fluently. He ate their food, walked the beaches with them, learned to feel secure when rolled up in a blanket in an Indian lodge. He approached the deeply human problem of cross-cultural communication with humility and intelligence, and the rapport he found brought him a deeply personal fulfillment. This is not to say that Swan went native, for he was much too thoroughly New England and Anglo-Saxon to suspend his basic assumptions about nature and man. But for an American in the 1850's, even for one with serious intellectual and artistic needs, Swan had a degree of tolerance, of curiosity, of broad-mindedness, and of sensitivity that was indeed remarkable. It may have been the truest measure of his alienation from his own society.[1]

[1] The facts and even the essential chronology of James Swan's biography are not easy to come by. There is a biographical sketch of Swan by Glen Adams of Fairfield, Washington, in his facsimile edition of *The Northwest Coast* (Fairfield, Washington: Ye Galleon Press, 1966); but Adams found his material in Guy Allison, *Forgotten Great Man of Washington History* (Longview, Washington: Longview *Daily News*, 1951), which is a very brief appreciation based mostly on Hubert Howe Bancroft's typically long footnote of amplification and glorification in his *History of Washington, Idaho, and Montana* (San Francisco: History Company, 1890), which Bancroft lifted from what Swan told him in "Washington Sketches: Statement of James G. Swan," a manuscript in the Bancroft Library at Berkeley. This can be supplemented with another Bancroft manuscript called "Olympia Club Conversations," which is a transcription made in Olympia by Bancroft's secretary while the historian primed Swan with Olympia beer and encouraged him to talk about himself and about the early years in Washington Territory. These manuscripts are on microfilm at the Suzzallo Library of the University of Washington in Seattle. The Northwest Collection there also contains a Swan Biography File which has a few bits of manuscript and newspaper information. This library also has a rich archival collection of Swan papers that includes 73 volumes of manuscript diaries and account books, films of his correspondence with officials of the Smithsonian Institution, copies of some of his newspaper articles, of correspondence between friends and relatives after Swan's death, and of most of his published work. There is a useful bibliography of Swan's works done by W. A. Katz and published in the Fairfield facsimile edition mentioned above. My quotations are from *The Northwest Coast*, or, where indicated, from the diaries. Bancroft's account of his visit with Swan in 1878, noted below, is in his *Literary Industries*.

Because he could appreciate the difference of Indian cultural values without denying their integrity for Indians, Swan could feel the terrible threat that white Americans raised to Indian culture with their guns and machines, their whiskey, theft, competition, and unequal justice. He could see enough of himself in the Indians to know that they should regard most Americans as casual vanguards of a foreign horde that would force upon them a foreign language, unintelligible customs, and a meaningless religion, and in doing so destroy their identity as Indians. In his moments of solemn clarity—and this is his greatest achievement for readers today—he could see himself as both observer of and participant in a barbaric invasion.

The Indians of the Northwest Coast that Swan came to know were then passing between the twilight of their tranquility and the night of their most desperate affliction. The hour was late: smallpox, measles, and syphilis had already swept grimly over a bewildered people. Since their first contact with Europeans in the eighteenth century, the mortality among some groups was as high as 90 percent. And thereafter the demoralized remnants of a strong and vigorous society fell easily to the debauchery of drunkenness and to the social confusion of new wealth as they took rum, metal, and blankets from the maritime fur traders.

As early as 1805 the Chinook Indians at the mouth of the Columbia River were, as Lewis and Clark found them, decorated with foreign tatoos and beads, dressed in manufactured blankets and sailors' clothes, addicted to whoredom and theft, and suffering from "Venerious and pustelus disorders."[2] But they were still a "mild

[2] Clark, in Bernard DeVoto, ed., *The Journals of Lewis and Clark* (1953).

and inoffensive"[3] people with great reserves of character and stability. They took the fevers in the 1830's, and twenty years later Swan saw them as "a miserable, whiskey-drinking set of vagabonds," a people whose "race is nearly run." At the time of Lewis and Clark they had numbered maybe 5,000. Swan counted fewer than 100.[4]

The natives Swan lived with north of the river had seen fewer whites and fewer calamities. When he knew them in the 1850's, the diseases were among them, but they could still present clear features of an affluent and sophisticated culture. They were rich, first of all, in salmon and cedar. And having an abundance of the necessities of life, they enriched themselves in life's satisfactions. In their fishing, hunting, and gathering, they drew a deep emotional security from mutual participation. In the wide circles of their extended-family relationships, as Swan observed, they cared for their old people with sympathy and dignity, and they honored their children with affection and respect.

They were rich also in leisure and aesthetic sensibility. The artistry of the song and dance Swan recorded touched every individual. Almost every aspect of their lives, in fact, was invested with aesthetic significance. The coming of salmon in the spring inspired an elaborate and delicate ritual, and the fish clubs used daily by the men could be refined into a reflection of grace and pleasure. The baby's cradle sketched by Swan shows a natural integration of utility and beauty.

They were rich, furthermore, in the harmony of their

[3] Lewis, in his *Lewis and Clark Expedition*, ed. Archibald Hanna (1961).

[4] Population statistics from Swan, *Northwest Coast*, and from Herbert C. Taylor, Jr., "Aboriginal Populations of the Lower Northwest Coast," *Pacific Northwest Quarterly*, October, 1963.

interpersonal relationships. A coastal village might have several families whose personal wealth and consequent social status brought them high esteem. These rich people, whom Swan saw as "chiefs," might advise or encourage others to do their will, but seldom did they have the power or authority to coerce individuals or to commit the group collectively to any course of action. Law and order was a matter of praise or ridicule from influential individuals like Swan's friend Old Toke. Violence was seldom if ever a part of social discipline. This tranquility was in striking contrast to the snarling and brawling, whipping and hanging among the whites of Swan's society from whom the Indians were even then learning.[5]

Even so, the Indians north of the Columbia had for years lived peacefully with the employees of Hudson's Bay Company, the powerful British monopoly whose Columbia Department was so intelligently administered. In the 1820's the company had built Fort Vancouver, and from this cedar castle by the wide river it brought sanity and stability to an entire region. Through its rocklike policies of fairness for the natives, discipline for the whites, an end to cutthroat competition in the fur trade, prohibition of liquor, and the conservation of fur resources, the company became an institutional force for law and order and church and state. Under the leadership of the wise and imperious Dr. John McLoughlin—a giant of a man with flowing white hair and a gold-headed cane—the company came not to wreck the native culture but to understand it. Hudson's

[5] Tom McFeat, ed., *Indians of the North Pacific Coast* (1966); Philip Drucker, *Cultures of the North Pacific Coast* (1965) and *Indians of the Northwest Coast* (1955); George I. Quimby, "James Swan among the Indians," *Pacific Northwest Quarterly*, October 1970.

Bay Company men worked with the Indians, mingled freely with them, gained their confidence by learning how to appeal to their sense of private property and by teaching them to be of service both to themselves and to London. Gentlemen and men of the marching brigades took Indian wives and raised famlies. As a bridge between two very different cultures, the Hudson's Bay Company was perhaps the most humane and effective ever conceived by Europeans for North America. It was by far superior to either slavery or war.

It is a tragedy of American history that American values in the 1840's and 1850's were so consistent with slavery and war. Brutally racist and piously arrogant, the United States brought war to Mexico in 1846 so that Americans could seize the promised land of California. And threatening this same belligerence—with wild talk of 54-40 or Fight or of taking all of Canada—James Polk's government forced the British into the Oregon Treaty that same year and into withdrawing to lands beyond the Strait of Juan de Fuca. Though the treaty allowed Hudson's Bay Company to retain certain rights to its properties, the blatant outlawry of American squatters was making the company's position untenable by the time Swan arrived in 1849. For the Indians, the Oregon Treaty meant the collapse of a system that had sustained them with honor for a generation, and it meant the coming of men who held the system and the Indians themselves in ugly contempt. Americans validated their own greed with land laws which provided invaders like Swan with free land before they ever thought of Indian treaties. Most Americans who came with Swan regarded the Indians quite simply as a public menace, free targets for any treachery or for wanton murder. Even before 1850 the United States Government of Oregon Territory had brought war to the Rogues and to the Cayuse and driven both groups relentlessly toward extermination.

A terrible insight into their future could not long escape the others. If they protested sometimes with violence, it was not without terrifying cause. During the "wars" of the 1850's in the new governmental division of Washington Territory, Americans ruthlessly crushed these protests with search-and-destroy missions that were consistent with the treatment that barbarians have usually accorded civilized populations: rape, concentration camps, hostages, arbitrary and summary execution, and outright murder. Thus it was that Colonel George Wright, in 1858 having destroyed the Indians' winter supply of food, ordered the young Yakima leader Qualchin to appear before him and warned that refusal would mean death for hostages, among whom was the leader's aged father. Wright reported that "Qualchin came to me at 9 o'clock and at 9¼ A.M. he was hung." And thus it was that Charles Grainger, a simpleminded deputy sheriff, was ordered the same year to a lonely prairie east of Fort Steilacoom to hang Leschi, the respected leader of Puget Sound Indians, because the 36 rapacious men of the Territorial Legislature wanted to rob these Indians of their finest intelligence and teach them more terror. Even the United States Army and the same Colonel Wright refused to recognize that the government had any legitimate grievance against so noble a man. Leschi in his last words said that he would not be the first man to lose his life on false evidence. If he was dying for his people, he said, he was "willing to die. Christ died for others." Grainger later told a friend that "I felt that I was executing an innocent man."[6]

It was during the rush of this violence that Swan was preparing his book, and one must note that his explanations of "war" in the 1850's are not distinguished by their moral authority. He wanted, on the one hand, to have his readers see the Indians as he had come to know them. He wanted to say why he felt a peaceful and productive coexistence between the two races was possible. For the Indians to survive, he believed, they must be free to nurture their own cultural identity and free to resist the cultural tyranny of white Americans. He knew that the system of forcing the Indians to live on reservations was not conceived in this belief. He knew too of trickery, deceit, and murder, for even his friend the Duke of York was taken hostage. Swan wanted to make it clear that he would be no apologist for American outrages.

Yet at the same time he was serving as secretary to Isaac Stevens, the delegate to Congress and former governor of Washington Territory who had designed the treaties, imposed them upon the Indians, and first called for war. Swan had been an interpreter for Stevens and apparently held him in high regard. Part of Swan's assignment, in fact, was to help Stevens win Congressional approval for the treaties. The result, in Chapter XX of *The Northwest Coast*, is a combination of significant anthropological insight with an absurdly ethnocentric polemic in which Swan seemed to blame Hud-

---

[6] See also, for Colonel Wright, Dorothy Johansen, *Empire of the Columbia* (1967); for Leschi, Ezra Meeker, *Pioneer Reminiscences of Puget Sound: The Tragedy of Leschi* (1905); for Leschi, Qualchin, Wright, the Duke of York, and others, Edmond S. Meany, *History of the State of Washington* (1924).

son's Bay Company and the American army leaders more than he blamed American farmers, lumber pirates, and Governor Stevens.

Clearly, Swan never saw himself as a social critic. He did, however, want a reputation as an ethnologist, but he never attained any generous measure of it from a society not yet awakened to social science. Whatever fame or personal glory Swan knew—and this was never enough to keep him in security or confidence—was almost entirely local fame as a local colorist, a man who had written a book about vivid episodes of the pioneer past.

Swan could spin a good story. His opening sentence of the *Northwest Coast* has a crisp Victorian ring that promises excitement, mystery, or humor, and the chapters that follow are built on sturdy paragraphs, occasionally bright with the flash of a perfect metaphor. His readers have felt quickly at home in the quiet tide pools of Shoalwater society. Swan's careful descriptions have helped readers to imagine the Indians and to picture the whites, like Big Charley, the good-natured, lazy constable, who, "like some stray spar or loose kelp, had been washed up into the Bay without exactly knowing when, where, or how." Or Champ, the Justice of the Peace, who "although he could sign his name, could not see to read very well, having smashed his spectacles on a frolic." And Swan could sometimes reach beyond local color to the deep and even prophetic sadness of men like Old Toke, the lonely Indian who had known high status and prestige but whom whiskey had reduced to contempt and ridicule.

Swan could also focus on the exuberant absurdities of frontier life. In the infinity of space and natural abundance, dozens of Americans creep out of the woods to seek shelter from a storm and gather themselves in an eight-by-ten house to suffer discomforts considerably more profuse than those of the wind and rain without. A fantastic skipper of a San Francisco schooner, to whom people entrust their lives and fortunes, makes trip after trip with a lordly vanity that causes him to wear green goggles which render him practically blind. In the story of the frightful storm that brought chaos and destruction to Swan's house and properties, there is enough humor in pure misery to move the reader toward laughter as well as pain.

Besides pathos and absurdity, Swan sometimes fixed unknowingly upon the apocalyptic. There is a scene in which the enflamed oyster boys roared to the climax of a Fourth of July by setting afire an entire forest that burned until the winter rains came—a scene of such thoughtless folly and impulsive madness that it could stand as a profoundly allegorical comment on the history of the American West.

Swan's most profound comment, however, lies in the imbalance of serious and foolish matters that marked his life after he left Shoalwater Bay. He went east again, to see to the publication of his book and to serve Isaac Stevens for two years in Washington, D.C. Then on Stevens' advice he returned to the Olympic Peninsula and settled near his land claim at Port Townsend, where he waited for the railroads to come and convert his land into his belated bonanza.

It was hard waiting. He did pieces for newspapers of Boston and San Francisco (their "correspondent in Washington Territory") and began a law practice, which in Port Townsend was more a hobby than a profession. The diaries he kept during these years are voluminous records of his day-to-day events and observations, even temperatures and tides, all of them neat, methodical, and literate. One wonders if he wrote all this with any conviction that his life in a muddy saw-mill village glowed with a message or a vision that he would somehow, someday, cast into words and books. In these thousands of pages there is no hint that he did. Nor is there any implicit thrust or spirit, any insights, questions, or indignations. They are not the work of a dedicated artist or scholar or even of a self-consciously literary man.

The waiting aroused other passions. In 1864 Swan stood for election to the territoral legislature, but he was decisively defeated. Even then his surest instincts were to refine his sensitivities to Indian culture and do with this what he could. He spent four years with the Makah Indians at Neah Bay, learning their language, observing their customs, and helping these people do a thousand things, from administering medicines to building houses and discouraging drunken mayhem. In 1868 he produced a small volume of observation, scholarship, and drawings about the Makahs for the Smithsonian Institution. One can say of this book, *The Indians of Cape Flattery*, that the government got its money's worth, whatever it paid for it. The work was probably as perceptive as any work being done in anthropology by any American at that time. If it is disappointing today, it is because the study lacks discipline and because Swan always choked on matters of interpersonal relationships. But at that time anthropology was not a discipline and no American scholar was articulate about such matters. Had Swan been able to conceptualize a science and practice it as we know it a century later, we would indeed regard him as a very great man, just as we would if he had cried out against the wars and treaties a full generation before the Indian Rights Association or Helen Hunt Jackson's *A Century of Dishonor*.

But Swan was not then seeking greatness. He wrote, he waited. He tried to do what as a younger man he had said was impossible—to make whites of the Indians by organizing and teaching school at Neah Bay. This was, the diary recorded, "the most unsatisfactory thing I ever tried." He quit it and spent the rest of his long life in Port Townsend, living precariously from his gift for a felicitous phrase and his sure touch for the sinecure: customs agent, secretary to the Puget Sound Pilots' Commission, "teacher and dispenser of medicine" for the Indians, correspondent for the Smithsonian, occasional counselor in admiralty law, surveyor of boats, ticket agent for a steamship company, notary public, probate judge, and, in his very old age—it sounds like a cruel joke—"Counsel for Hawaii at Port Townsend." In all, he lived from hand to mouth, using his land claim as an annuity by selling small pieces, and performing odd jobs of simple literacy in a society where simple literacy was in demand. In the 1870's he received a small grant to do a study for the Smithsonian. *The Haidah Indians of Queen Charlotte's Island, British Columbia* was the last and most superficial of his books.

He was then deeply involved in elaborate fantasies inspired by the transcontinental railroads, for he really believed that Port Townsend was the natural terminal for the Northern Pacific, that the railroad would make Port Townsend into a metropolis, the gateway to the Orient, the storehouse for the riches of the Pacific Northwest. Swan had even ingratiated himself with the directors of that railroad, having since 1868 offered them detailed, literate, and warmly impractical advice about their best interest on Puget Sound and the Northwest Coast. These directors apparently encouraged him to believe that his advice was being taken seriously. He once accompanied a party of railroad capitalists and bankers on a trip down sound aboard the steamer *Cyrus Walker* and soberly read for them his paper entitled "The Amoor River: The Countries Drained By The Amoor River And Its Tributaries And the Imminent Trade Now Lying Dormant In Siberia, Mongolia, Manchooria, Northern China, Korea, And Japan Which Will Be Brought Into Active Life And Diverted To The American Shore Of The North Pacific Ocean By The Great Continental Railroads Which Will Have The Outlet Of Their Commerce Through The Straits Of Fuca To The Great Ocean Of The West."

In the late 1870's Swan was presenting himself as an agent of the Northern Pacific, which he may in some minor way have been, though there is no evidence that he ever enjoyed any of the railroad's prosperity. During these years Judge Swan became a monument of sorts in the sawmill town and in the territory. He knew the charity of his friends, who in turn knew Swan as an increasingly alcoholic "character"—a handsome, white-haired and neatly bearded gentleman in his sixties, the unofficial intellectual who, it was rumored, would some-day write a great history of Washington Territory. The next generation remembered him as a "picturesque figure" who took no part in the commercial life of the city but who was always ready to accept a drink or a dinner, ready to suffer the deliberations of the local pioneer clubs and moral reform societies, to march in a parade, or to deliver a speech on any public occasion.

Toward the end of that decade the wealthy Hubert Howe Bancroft came north from San Francisco to gather raw materials for the books of western history that made him famous. He stopped in Port Townsend to see "Judge James G. Swan, ethnologist, artist, author..." Bancroft was distressed to find so distinguished a gentleman, scholar, and pioneer-adventurer living behind a translucent alcoholic curtain. Swan was so drunk that day that he refused to see Bancroft until he could sober up, and Bancroft waited, lamenting for the "poor fellow" whom "demon Drink had long held...in his terrible toils." At length, however, Swan was his gracious best, and he happily unloaded upon the historian thirty years' notes and artifacts and long conversations about his early experiences. Bancroft footnoted this generosity with his observation that Judge Swan had "occupied many public places of more honor than profit."

Swan must have been utterly demoralized by 1887 when it was clear that Tacoma, and not Port Townsend, would get the Northern Pacific. The dream of two decades was gone, and he was suddenly an old man. Then, most cruelly, the remaining value of his land was washed away by the depression that hit in 1893. Port Townsend thereafter became a hollow shell of a community. Some of its brick buildings, built for the coming of the railroads, have gone without tenants ever since. Swan stayed on. At the age of 75, he had no place to go and no desire to find one. He stayed in a smoky one-room house, living like the Indians, cooking for himself, sinking into total obscurity—a patriarch in a ghost town, a master of poverty, a sometime poet of the frontier forgotten on the edge of an industrial world.

At his death in 1900 at the age of 82, Swan had nothing but a room full of grease-covered books, his meticulous diaries, and a few minor debts. His life had been a confusion of goals, sensitivities, and values, a drama of quiet desperation played out in a dark and deep wilderness that was the Northwest Coast. In his thirties he had broken like a prisoner from the chains of middle-class securities, free to find his own truth in his own way. In his forties he had abandoned his ex-

periment in freedom among the oyster pickers; for, like
Henry Thoreau, he had other lives to lead. In his fifties
he had turned away from serious scholarship and from
his twenty-years' investment in rapport with the Indians. In his sixties he tried to make money; but in his
seventies he gave this up also, and along with it, perhaps, any hope for recognition, or dignity, or even fellowship. His joys were his energy, curiosity, and intel-
lectuality that would have been admirable in any man,
especially one so friendly and generous. Whatever his
anxieties, his spiritual wounds or griefs, he did not commit them to record. His great misfortune was to live in a
society so merciless in its judgment of those whose broad
and multipurposed talents led them in many directions
and excluded them from the rewards of single-minded
men.

In this century Swan's Shoalwater Bay has been
known as Willapa Bay. Its great forests are gone, but
its shallow water has kept it from becoming the commercial port that Swan once imagined. It is still a quiet
region, a delight to the eye, not everywhere clattering
with people and machines. Opening westward to the
Pacific, the land can still suggest the deeply sensuous
experiences that James Swan so happily embraced. The
Shoalwater Indian Reservation rims the north shore,
and Tokeland, named after Old Toke, is as wind-swept
and drunken-gray in the rain and as magnificently blue
and green and salty pure in the sunshine as Swan described it. North of the bay and beyond Gray's Harbor
there are wilderness strips of beach protected by the
Olympic National Park that remain just as Swan knew
them, with miles of sand, a million tide pools in the
rocks, storm-shaped headlands, impenetrable forests,
and the soft silence of woods and sea.

The Northwest Coast

OR, THREE YEARS' RESIDENCE IN WASHINGTON TERRITORY

ENCAMPMENT OF LIEUTENANT PUGET ON PUGET SOUND.

THE

NORTHWEST COAST;

OR,

THREE YEARS' RESIDENCE IN WASHINGTON
TERRITORY.

By JAMES G. SWAN.

WITH NUMEROUS ILLUSTRATIONS.

NEW YORK:

HARPER & BROTHERS, PUBLISHERS,

FRANKLIN SQUARE.

1857.

TO

THE HON. J. PATTON ANDERSON,

THE FIRST UNITED STATES MARSHAL AND SECOND DELEGATE TO
CONGRESS FROM

WASHINGTON TERRITORY,

𝔗𝔥𝔦𝔰 𝔚𝔬𝔯𝔨 𝔦𝔰 𝔯𝔢𝔰𝔭𝔢𝔠𝔱𝔣𝔲𝔩𝔩𝔶 𝔍𝔫𝔰𝔠𝔯𝔦𝔟𝔢𝔡

BY HIS FRIEND,

JAMES G. SWAN.

INTRODUCTION.

THE intention of this volume is to give a general and concise account of that portion of the Northwest Coast lying between the Straits of Fuca and the Columbia River—a region which has never attracted the explorers and navigators of the Northwest, since the times of Meares and Vancouver, sufficiently for them to give it more than a passing remark.

The fine bay north of the Columbia (Shoal-water Bay), which was discovered and named by Meares in 1789, and surveyed by Lieutenant Alden, of the United States Coast Survey, in 1852, was actually passed through by the boats of Wilkes's Exploring Expedition, who merely mentions the fact, without considering the bay of sufficient importance either to give it a passing notice or even place it on his chart.

At the present time, when every thing relating to the Northwest frontier is looked upon with interest, and particularly the country around the Columbia River, Gray's Harbor, and Puget Sound, it was thought that some later information than can be found in the works of Ross Cox, Lewis and Clarke, and Irving, would be acceptable, both to those persons desirous of emigration to the region west of the Rocky Mountains, as well as those who already have friends in the Territory.

To make the work of interest to the general reader, I have been obliged, while endeavoring to bring forward each subject worthy of interest, to condense and confine myself within certain limits, so as not to elaborate too much any one topic.

I have, so far as possible, only related such circumstances as have come under my immediate observation; and, whenever I have been obliged to deviate from this rule, I have invariably given credit to the proper source, and have been particularly careful to endeavor to be accurate as to date in matters of historical information, narrating all facts, whether as regards my own personal adventures, or tales of the Indians, or anecdotes of the settlers, in a simple manner, and in the order of their occurrence; consequently, most of the narrative will be confined to the immediate Pacific coast, and to descriptions of Shoal-water Bay during my residence of three years.

In all matters relating to the Indians, I only give an account of those *I have lived with*, the Chenooks, Chehalis, and one or two tribes north of Gray's Harbor.

Having lost a valuable collection of notes, made during my residence among the Coast tribes, I am unable to give the interesting legends and mythological tales I should have done, and which might have been of interest to many persons; still, enough has been written to give a general idea of facts concerning the Indians of the Bay which have not before been mentioned, with vocabularies of their language and specimens of their music.

I take this opportunity to acknowledge my obligations to the Hon. J. Patton Anderson, Delegate to Congress from Washington Territory; Henry R. Schoolcraft, LL.D., of Washington City; J. Carson Brevoort, Esq., and Professor W. Gibbs, of New York; John M'Mullen, Esq., Librarian of New York Society Library; Dr. J. G. Cogswell, Librarian of the Astor Library, and Mr. Poole, Librarian of the Boston Athenæum; also, Hon. William Sturgis, and William Tufts, Esq., of Boston, for valuable information, and assistance in enabling me to refer to such works of history, voyages, or statistics as were necessary while writing.

CONTENTS.

CHAPTER I.

Voyage from San Francisco to Shoal-water Bay.—Brig Oriental.—
Passengers on board the Brig.—Ship a heavy Sea.—Mouth of the
Columbia.—Quantities of Drift-wood.—Cross the Bar at Shoal-water
Bay.—Heavy Sea ....Page 17

CHAPTER II.

Discovery of Shoal-water Bay by Meares in 1788.—His Description of
it.—Indians come out of the Bay in a Canoe.—Thick Fog.—Meares's
Long-boat Expedition to the Bay.—Attack by Indians.—Vancouver's Description.—Alden's Survey.—First Settlers.—Description of
Shoal-water Bay 20

CHAPTER III.

Russell's House.—Description of Toke and Suis.—Russell tells the Indians I am a Doctor.—Style of Medicine.—Salmon Fishing on the
Palux.—Old Cartumhays.—Our Reception at his Lodge.—Camp on
the Palux.—Duck Shooting.—Great Quantities of Salmon.—Falls of
the Palux.—The Devil's Walking-stick.—Singular Superstition of
the Indians.. 33

CHAPTER IV.

Wreck of the Willemantic.—Joe the Steward and his curry Stews.—
Climate of the Pacific.—Causes of the Mildness of Temperature.—
Quantities of Rain.—Early Spring.—Method of learning the Indian
Language.—Captain Purrington clearing Land.—Immense Trees.—
Indians' Small-pox.—Indians die.—Russell sick.—Tomhays sick.—
Queaquim dies.—Solemn Scene 43

CHAPTER V.

Arrival of Indians from the North.—Description of the Oysters and
Oyster-fishers of Shoal-water Bay.—Hospitality of early Settlers.—
Joel L. Brown.—Captain Weldon.—Winter in Oregon.............. 59

CHAPTER VI.

Stony Point.—Visit of Walter and myself to the *Memelose Tillicums*, or
Dead People.—Basaltic Boulders.—Indian Tradition respecting them.

—Legend of the Doctor and his Brother.—The Giants build a great
Fire to heat Stones.—They boil out the Bay.—The Doctor finds his
Brother in a Fish's Belly.—Bear-hunt on Stony Point.—Bartlett kills
the Bear.—Method of burying the Dead.—We find a Mummy.—Russell sends the Mummy to San Francisco.—Opinions of scientific Persons respecting the Mummy.—An instance of another Body being
preserved.—I get capsized at Stony Point.—Take a Claim on the
Querquelin River.—Description of the Claim and our mode of Living.—Method of Canoe-making.—Seal-catching.—Method of catching Fish.—Indian Food.—Description of the Roots and Berries.—Sea
Otter.—River Otter.—Beaver.—Furs....................Page 67

CHAPTER VII.

Visit to the Columbia River.—Our Troubles while crossing the Portage.—Description of the Beach around Baker's Bay to Chenook.—
Scarborough's Hill.—Captain Scarborough.—The Priest's House at
Chenook.—Bill M'Carty or Brandywine.—Salmon-fishing at Chenook.—Splendid View of Mount Saint Helen's.—Description of the
Salmon and of the Fishery.—Indian Customs on the first Appearance of Salmon.—The present Remnant of the Chenook Tribe.—
Description of Chenook Village.—Its favorable Location.—Washington Hall, Esq., the Postmaster.—Indian Lodges.—A Description of
the method of building them.—Our Return home, and the funny
Scenes we passed through.—Old Champ and his Fish.............. 97

CHAPTER VIII.

The Country of the Columbia.—Discovery of the Columbia.—Gray's
Harbor.—The Coast north of the Columbia.—Fuca Strait.—Puget
Sound.—Geographical Errors in naming Places.—Excellent Harbors.
—Mount Olympus.—Separation of Washington from Oregon.—The
Columbia and its Tributaries.—The Dalles.—Wappatoo Island.—
Heceta's Voyage.—Attack by Savages.—Point Grenville and De-
struction Island.—River St. Roc.—Vancouver.—Sloop Washington
and Ship Columbia.—Captain Gray.—Lieutenant Broughton and the
Brig Chatham.—Account of the Outfit of the Ship Columbia in 1787.
—Captain John Kendrick.—Gray discovers the Columbia.—Building
of the Adventure at Clyoquot... 117

CHAPTER IX.

The Oystermen celebrate the 4th of July.—A Speech and a great Bonfire.—Arrival of Emigrants.—Colonel H. K. Stevens.—Fishing-party
on the Nasal River.—We go up the River to an Indian Camp.—Method of catching Salmon.—We catch rotten Logs.—The Colonel falls
overboard. — A Chase after a Salmon. — Indian Style of catching
Trout.—Their Medicine to allure Fish.—Immense Quantities of Salmon in Shoal-water Bay.—Wreck of Brig Palos.—Description of my

House.—High Tides.—Quantities of Wild-fowl.—A Gale of Wind.
—Heavy Rain.—The Gale increases, and blows down our Chimney.
—Damage done by the Storm.—Narrow Escape from being killed by
a falling Precipice.—Arrival of Indians.—Pepper Coffee.—Ludicrous
Plight of the Natives.—Their Superstition.—They try to shoot a
Ghost.—They are scared by a Pumpkin Lantern.—Poisoning Crows.
—Method of preserving Cabbages from the Indians..........Page 133

CHAPTER X.

Old Suis relates about the Indians of the Bay.—A Description of the
Coast Indians.—Writers apt to confuse the Reader in Accounts of
Indians.—General Appearance.—Dress of Women.—Dress of Men.
—Smoking.—Fondness for Ardent Spirits.—Whom they received the
first from.—Gambling.—A Description of gambling Games.—Orna-
ments.—Description of the Howqua or Wampum.—Method of ob-
taining the Shells.—Evidences of Wealth.—Great Weight of Ear Or-
naments.—Position of Females among the Coast Tribes.—Duties of
Women. — Various Manufactures. — Lodge Furniture. — Ancient
Method of Cooking. — Bread-making. — Peter's Method of making
Bread.—Time of Eating.— Slaves.—Fondness of Indians for their
Children.—Method of flattening the Head.—Flat Head a mark of
Aristocracy.—Reception of Strangers.—Reception of Friends.—Singular Custom.—Great Newsmongers.—Polygamy.—Customs toward
young Girls.—Singular Superstition.—Fasts.—Religion.—Heathen-
ism 151

CHAPTER XI.

Doctors, or Medicine-men.—Simples used as Medicine.—Polypodium.
—Wild-cat Hair.—An excellent Salve.—Disinclination of Indians to
impart Information in regard to their Medicines.—Necromancy of
the Doctors.—Sickness of Suis.—Sacodlye, the Doctor, and his Mag-
ic. — Old John, the Doctor, and his Method.— John removes the
Devil and Suis recovers.—Old Sal-tsi-mar's Sickness and Death.—
Description of the Burial.—Funeral Ceremonies.—Death Songs.—
Change of Names on the Death of a Friend.—Meaning of Indian
Names.—Superstitions and Ceremonies.—Effects of Christianity.—
Missionaries.—The Indian Idea of the Christian Religion........ 176

CHAPTER XII.

Amusements.—Games.—Children's Amusements.—Imitate the Priest.
—Readily learn Needle-work.—Fond of Singing.—Songs.—History
of the Chenooks and Chehalis.—Difficulty of understanding the Legends.—Creation of Man.—Origin of Coast Tribes.—Evidences of
Emigration.—Tradition of a Junk wrecked at Clatsop Beach.—Beeswax found on the Beach.—Remarks on the various Theories respect-

ing the Origin of the Indians.—Lewis and Clarke's Names of Tribes.
—The correct Names of the Tribes.—Former Tribes of Shoal-water
Bay.—Evidences of great Mortality among the Coast Tribes.—The
Feeling of the Indians respecting the Dead.—Meares's Account of
the Nootkans being Cannibals.—Vancouver doubts the Truth of
Meares. — Indian Dread of Skulls. — Anecdote respecting their
Fears..Page 197

                       CHAPTER XIII.

Trip to San Francisco.—Captain Smith and his Goggles.—We get near-
ly wrecked by reason of the Fog on Captain Smith's "Specks."—Ar-
rive safe at last.—Return to the Columbia in Steamer Peytona.—
Port Orford.—Captain Tichenor.—Cedar of Port Orford.—Mouth of
the Columbia.—Not so terrible as generally represented.—Arrival at
Astoria.—History of Astoria.—Captain Smith, of the Ship Albatross.
—John Jacob Astor.—Ship Tonquin, Captain Thorne.—Ship Beaver,
Captain Sowles.—Ross Cox's Description of Astoria.—Loss of the
Tonquin.—Ship Lark.—Astoria sold to the Northwest Company.—
The Raccoon Sloop-of-war.—Brig Peddler.—Ship Isaac Todd and her
Passengers.—First white Woman.—Death of Mr. M'Tavish.—Resto-
ration of Astoria to the Americans.—H. B. M. Frigate Blossom sa-
lutes the Flag.—Various Expeditions, &c.—First Emigration.—Jes-
uits.—Present Appearance of Astoria.—Military Road, &c....... 215

                       CHAPTER XIV.

Cross the Columbia to Chenook.—Meet Fiddler Smith.—We start for
Shoal-water Bay with Captain Johnson.—Johnson falls overboard.
—John Edmands.—Ox-team Express.—Get stuck in the Swamp.—
Captain Nichols and his Whale-boat.—The Fiddler and myself take
Passage.—Safe Arrival.—Another Start for Astoria.—Detention by
Storm.—General Adair, of Astoria.—Canoe Adventure with Peter.—
Sturgeon-fishing. — Salleel and his Sturgeons' Heads. — Johnson's
Lake.—A hard Walk.—Toke in the Mud.—Brook Navigation.—In-
dian Method of making Fire.—Rate of Speed home.—Strawberry
Expedition 239

                       CHAPTER XV.

Visit to the Queniūlt Indians with Winant and Roberts.—Cross the Bay
and camp with the Indians.—Carcowan and Tleyuk.—Trouble on
starting.—Arrival at Gray's Harbor.—Armstrong's Point.—Difficulty
with Caslahhan.—Sam fires at Caslahhan.—A Settlement.—Swarms
of Fleas.—Our Camp.—We proceed up the Beach.—Adventure with
a Bear.—Reach the Copalis River.—Wreck of the Steamer General
Warren.—The Current north of the Columbia.—Appearance of the
Coast.—Point Grenville.—Arrive at Queniūlt.—Peculiar Variety of
Salmon.—Indian Tricks.—I am taken sick.—Old Carcowan wishes

to have me killed.—Description of the Queniũlts.—Start for Shoal-
water Bay.—Indian Hospitality.—Bird Feast at Point Grenville.—
Style of Cooking.—Heavy Surf and a Capsize.—We proceed through
the Breakers.—Arrive at Gray's Harbor.—A Feast.—Fine View.—
Reach Home .... Page 250

CHAPTER XVI.

Arrival of Winant and Roberts.—An Election.—Our first Justice,
Squire Champ.—Big Charley.—First Court in the Bay.—Constable
Charley makes an Arrest.—A Trial, and a celebrated Verdict.—
Another Arrest and Trial.—Joe locked up in a Hen-house.—First
Vessel built in the Bay.—Bruce Company.—Uncle Ned.—Captain
John Morgan.—Monument of Oyster Shells to Russell.—Hay-e-mar.
—A Trip up the Whil-a-pah for Salmon.—Walter's Point.—Sam
Woodward's Claim.—Roaring Bill.—Ancient Mariners.—Old Chille-
wit.—Night Fishing.—Lively Time.—Start for Home.—Shoot a
Lynx.—Otter Shooting.—Charley sees the *Memelose* or dead Folks.
—Singular Occurrence.—We get rid of Charley.—First Trail from
the Cowlitz.—Lime-kiln for burning Shells 277

CHAPTER XVII.

County Line.—Jury Duty.—United States Court at Chenook.—The
Court-house.—Grand Jury.—Trial of Lamley for killing an Indian.
—Grand Jury Room very Fishy.—Witnesses.—Captain Johnson.—
His funny Address to the Court.—He throws himself on the Mercy
of the Court.—Captain Scarborough.—Bill Martindill.—The Cap-
tain's Advice to Bill.—The District Attorney and his Address.—
The Counsel for the Defense quotes from the "Arabian Nights."—
He gains the Case.—Captain Johnson's Vinegar Speculation.—
Johnson's Death.—Death of Captain Scarborough.—Fidelity of an
Indian Squaw.—Return home.—Sharp Work in a Canoe.—Adven-
ture with Caslahhan 292

CHAPTER XVIII.

Language of the Indians.—The Jargon.—Different Methods of spelling
Words by Writers.—Difficulty of rightly understanding the Jargon.
—How a Language can be formed.—Origin of the Indian Language.
—Remarks of Mr. Squier.—Irish-sounding Words in the Chehalis
Tongue.—An amusing Parable.—Views of Mr. Duponceau.—Re-
marks of Gliddon.—Resemblance between Chehalis and Aztec
Words.—Facts relative of Indian Journeys south.—Mrs. Ducheney's
Narrative.—Difficulty of Indians in pronouncing certain Letters.—
Cause of the chuckling Sound of the Northwest Languages.—Per-
sons apt to misunderstand Indian Words.—Dislike of Indians to
learn English.—Winter Amusements.—Tomhays and the Geese.—
Arrival of Settlers.—Doctor Johnson.—The Doctor and myself act

as Lawyers in Champ's Court.—Strong Medicine.—Kohpoh mistaken for a 'Coon.—Visit of the Klickatats.—Christmas Dinner on Crow.—Baked Skunk.—Fisherman's Pudding......................... Page 306

CHAPTER XIX.

Indian Treaties.—Invitation to be present at a Treaty on the Chehalis River.—Journey to the Chehalis.—Various Adventures.—We reach the River and encamp.—A lively Scene going up to the Treaty-ground. —Description of the Encampment. — Governor Stevens. —Whites present.—Indians.—Uniform of the Governor.—Colonel Simmons.—Story-telling.—The Governor backs up my Stories.—Judge Ford.—Commissary Cushman.—The Treaty.—Indians will not agree to it.—Number of Indians in the Coast Tribes.—Tleyuk.—Governor takes away Tleyuk's "Paper."—Indians have no Faith in the Americans.—The Conduct of the Hudson Bay Company contrasted with that of the Americans.—We start for Home and encounter a Storm.—Chehalis River.—Adventures on our Journey home.—Colonel Anderson's Adventures 327

CHAPTER XX.

The Whale.—Toke in the Whale's Belly.—Blubber Feast.—Doctor Johnson and myself as Counsel.—Higher Law.—Champ's Decision. —Loss of Schooner Empire.—Captain Davis.—Captain Eben P. Baker.—M'Carty's Child among the Indians.—Her Rescue.—Feelings of the Indians toward Whites.—Remarks on the Indian Character.—They can live peaceably with Whites.—Course adopted by the Hudson Bay Company toward Indians.—Suggestions about a System of Sub-agencies.—Correct Views of the Hudson Bay Company respecting Indians.—The Conduct of the Company toward Americans.—They do not wish Americans among them.—History of the Hudson Bay Company and their Proceedings toward Americans.—Cause of the Outbreak among the Indians.—Gold Mines.—General Palmer.—General Wool.—Remarks, &c... 360

CHAPTER XXI.

Description of Washington Territory.—Face of the Country.—Mountains, Minerals, Rivers, Bays, and Lakes.—Objects of Interest to the Tourist.—Falls of the Snoqualmie.—Colonel Anderson's Description. —Anecdote of Patkanim.—He forms an Alliance with Colonel Mike Simmons.—Constructive Presence of Colonel Simmons at a Fight.—Productions of the Territory.—Governor Stevens's Remarks.—Northern Pacific Rail-road.—Military Roads.—Public Spirit.—Appropriations by Congress.—Judge Lancaster.—Population.—Advantages to Emigrants.—Whale Fishery.—Russian Trade.—Amoor River.—Vancouver's Views on Climate.—Winter of 1806 in Latitude 56° North,—Salmon, 1807.—Closing Remarks.—Letter from Colonel Anderson. —Advice to Emigrants 392

LIST OF ILLUSTRATIONS.

1. Map of the Western Part of Washington Territory, compiled by the Author from the U. S. Coast Survey Charts, and from the Map of the Surveyor General at Washington.

2. Frontispiece. An Encampment of Lieutenant Peter Puget, while making his Exploration of Puget Sound. From an original Sketch by John Sykes, one of Vancouver's Draughtsmen.

3. Vignette on Title-page. Territorial Seal. The Motto, *Al-ki*, is an Indian word, meaning hereafter, or by-and-by.

4. C. J. W. Russell's House and Indian Lodge. From an original Sketch by the Author...Page 32

5. Camp on the Palux. From an original Sketch by the Author 37

6. Indian Implements.   "   "   "   "   "   39

7 and 8. Flowers. These are drawn one third their natural size 47, 48

9. Forests in Oregon 52

10. Oystermen waiting for the Tide 61

11. Bear-fight on Stony Point. Sketch by Author.................. 71

12. Querquelin River, and Residence of J. G. Swan. Sketch by Author. Toke's Lodge on the right of the Cut.......................... 75

13 and 14. Canoes. From the Original in Possession of the Author. The Head or Bows of all these Canoes are to the *left* hand on the Cuts...79, 80

15. Otter Hunt 93

16. Salmon Fishing at Chenook. Sketch by Author............... 106

17. Medal of Ship Columbia 131

18. Indian Cradle. The Child in this Cut is elevated from the cradle, so as to show the method of compressing the Head, which would not be seen in its real Position, where nothing of the Infant is visible but its Face.. 163

19. Method of Burial. Sketch by Author............................. 187

20. Port Orford Rock... 218

21. Fight on Battle Rock... 221

22. Queniūlt Village. Sketch by Author.............................. 262

23. Point Grenville.   "   "   "   269

24. Inside of Indian Lodge.   "   "   331

25. Camp on the Treaty Ground. Sketch by Author.............. 336

26. Outside of Indian Lodge.   "   "   "   339

27. Blubber Feast 361

28. Medal of Lewis and Clarke... 407

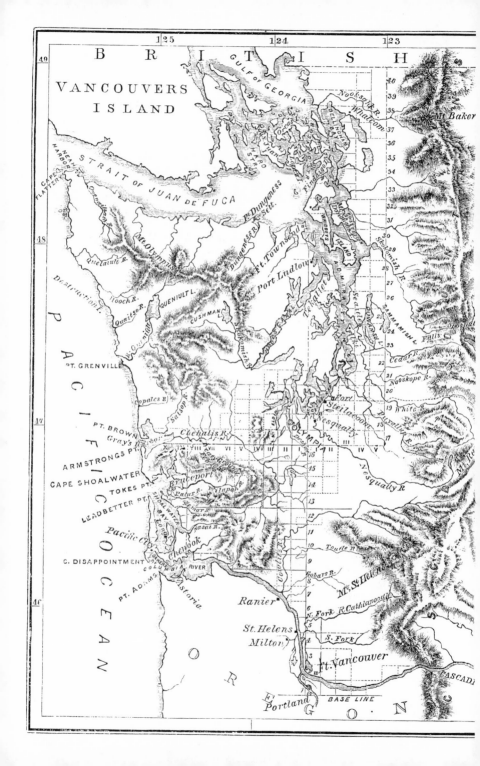

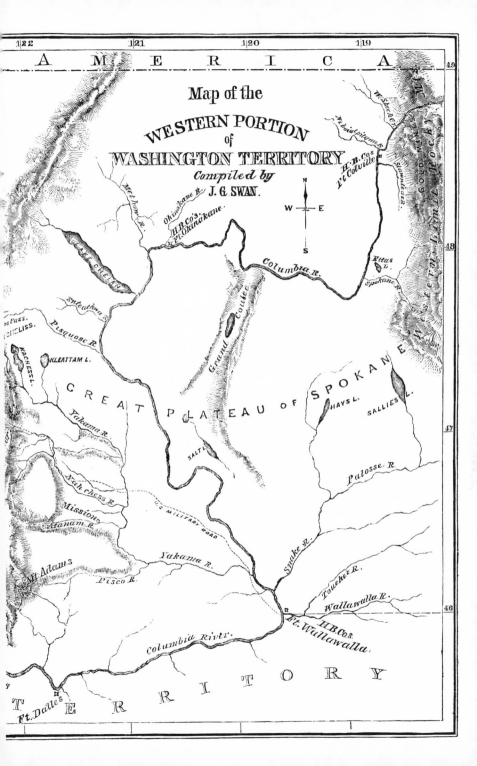

THE NORTHWEST COAST, &c.

CHAPTER I.

Voyage from San Francisco to Shoal-water Bay.—Brig Oriental.—
Passengers on board the Brig.—Ship a heavy Sea.—Mouth of the
Columbia.—Quantities of Drift-wood.—Cross the Bar at Shoal-water
Bay.—Heavy Sea.

DURING the fall of 1852, having received an invitation
from my friend, Mr. Charles J. W. Russell, of Shoal-
water Bay, to make him a visit, I determined to accept
his kind offer, and accordingly secured a passage on
board the brig Oriental, Captain Hill, which was bound
up the Bay for a cargo of piles and spruce timber. I
had always, from my earliest recollections, a strong desire to see the great River Columbia, and to learn something of the habits and customs of the tribes of the
Northwest. This desire had been increased by the visit
of a chief of the Clalam tribe of Indians from Puget
Sound, who arrived at San Francisco, where I was then
residing, and who received a great deal of attention from
me during his visit of two or three weeks.

This chief, whose name was Chetzamokha, and who
is known by the whites as the Duke of York, was very
urgent to have me visit his people. Subsequently, on
his return home, he sent me a present of a beautiful canoe, and a bag containing a quantity of cornelians, which
are found along the shores of the bays and rivers of
Washington and Oregon Territories.

I found, on joining the brig, that there were several

passengers bound to the Bay, and I concluded, as they were all captains of vessels, we should have a very pleasant time. There was Captain Hill, the master, Captain Pratt, the mate, and Captain Baker, Captain Weldon, Captain Swain, Captain Russell, and myself for passengers. I believe, with the exception of myself and the cook, who was called Doctor, every one on board the brig had held some office. I was the only one addressed as Mister, and, as Captain Baker remarked, it was quite refreshing to have one person on board without a title.

We left the harbor of San Francisco about noon on the 20th of November, and the old brig being very light, we were tumbled about in a lively manner while crossing the bar, where there was a tremendous swell running in from the southwest. However, we suffered no damage, and soon found ourselves on our course with a fair wind. We continued on in this manner for three days, without any thing occurring of interest, and the monotony of the scene only broken by the stories of the company of captains, who, sailor-like, never let slip an opportunity of relating a jest or an anecdote. On the fourth day, being in the latitude of the Columbia River, the wind came out ahead, and blew with violence from the northwest. This soon raised a heavy sea, and the brig could make but little progress. On the evening of the 24th, while standing by the cabin table with the captain, looking over the chart, we shipped a sea which stove in the window of the cabin (which looked out on deck), knocked me clear over the table, drenched the captain, put out the lights, and set the whole cabin afloat.

The other passengers had turned into their berths, where they lay telling stories, and they were most intensely delighted with the adventure. The steward soon came, who lighted the lamp, swabbed up the floor, and set us to rights. The next morning we found ourselves about thirty miles to the westward of the Columbia River, from which a huge volume of water was running, carrying in its course great quantities of drift-logs, boards, chips, and saw-dust, with which the whole water around us was covered. During the freshets in this river, the force of the current of fresh water discharged from it is sufficient to discolor the ocean for sixty miles from the coast.

The wind continuing to blow from the northwest, we beat about till the 28th, when, running in-shore, we made Cape Shoal-water, the northern point at the entrance to Shoal-water Bay. A heavy sea was breaking on the bar, and no opening presented itself to us. Russell, who was acting pilot, felt afraid to venture, and wished to stand off; but, by the time he had made up his mind, we had neared the entrance, so that it was impossible for us to turn to windward, and the only alternative was to go ashore or go into the harbor.

Every man was stationed at his post—Captain Hill and one man at the wheel, Captains Swain and Russell on the fore-yard, looking out, Captain Weldon heaving the lead, the sailors at the braces, and Captain Baker and myself watching to see the fun. The breakers were very high, and foamed, and roared, and dashed around us in the most terrific manner; but the old brig was as light on them as a gull, and, without shipping a drop of water, passed over and through them all; and after running up the channel about two miles, we came to anchor in smooth water, and found ourselves safe and sound in Shoal-water Bay.

CHAPTER II.

Discovery of Shoal-water Bay by Meares in 1788.—His Description of it.—Indians come out of the Bay in a Canoe.—Thick Fog.—Meares's Long-boat Expedition to the Bay.—Attack by Indians.—Vancouver's Description.—Alden's Survey.—First Settlers.—Description of Shoal-water Bay.

SHOAL-WATER BAY lies north of the Columbia River, between Capes Shoal-water and Disappointment. Cape Disappointment is in latitude 46° 16′ north, and longitude 124° 01′ west from Greenwich. And Toke's Point, or the extreme northwest point of Cape Shoal-water, and the northern shore at the entrance of Shoal-water Bay, is in latitude 46° 43′ north, and longitude 124° 02′ west, making the distance from the entrance of the Columbia River to that of Shoal-water Bay twenty-seven miles.

Cape Shoal-water and Shoal-water Bay were discovered by Lieutenant John Meares, commanding the East India Company's Ship Felice, of London, on Saturday, July 5th, 1788. Meares, who had been to Nootka, and other trading-posts north, for the purpose of collecting furs, had left a part of his company to build a small schooner, and was proceeding to the south to explore the great river discovered by the Spanish navigator Heceta on the 15th of August, 1775, and named by him Rio de San Roque, or River of St. Roc, and which was afterward entered by Captain Robert Gray, in the ship Columbia, of Boston, in 1792, and named by him the *Columbia*. Meares writes, "At noon our latitude was 47° 01′ north, and the lofty mountains seen the preceding day bore east-northeast distant seven leagues. Our distance might be four leagues from the shore, which appeared to run in the direction of east-southeast and west-northwest, and there appeared to be a large sound or opening in that direction. By two o'clock we were within two miles of the shore, along which we sailed, which appeared to be a perfect forest, without the vestige of a habitation. The land was low and flat, and our soundings were from fifteen to twenty fathoms, over a hard sand. As we were steering for the low point which formed part of the entrance into the bay or sound, we shoaled our water gradually to six fathoms, when breakers were seen to extend quite across it, so that it appeared to be quite inaccessible to ships. We immediately hauled off the shore till we deepened our water to sixteen fathoms.

"This point obtained the name of Low Point (now Leadbetter Point), and the bay that of Shoal-water Bay, and a headland that was high and bluff, which formed the other entrance, was also named Cape Shoal-water. The latitude of the headland we judged to be 46° 47' north, and the longitude 235° 11' east of Greenwich." (Vancouver makes the latitude of Cape Shoal-water 46° 40' north, and longitude 236° east, while Captain Alden, of the United States Coast Survey, makes the latitude 46° 43' minutes north, a mean which is most probable to be correct.) "The distance from Low Point to Cape Shoal-water was too great to admit of an observation in our present situation. The shoals still appeared to run from shore to shore, but when about midway we bore up near them in order to discover if there be not a channel near the cape. We accordingly steered for the mouth of the bay, when we shoaled our water to eight fathoms. At this time the breakers were not more than three miles from us, when it was thought prudent to again haul off. From the mast-head *it was observed*

that this bay extended a considerable way inland, spread-
ing into several arms or branches to the northward and
eastward.   The back of it was bounded by high and
mountainous land, which was at a great distance from us.

"A narrow entrance appeared to the northwest, but it
was too remote for us to discover, even with our glasses,
whether it was a river or low land.   We had concluded
this wild and desolate shore was uninhabited; but this
opinion proved to be erroneous, for a canoe now came
off to us from the point with a man and a boy.   On
their approach to the ship they held up two sea-otter
skins; we therefore hove to, when they came alongside
and took hold of a rope, but could not be persuaded to
come on board.   We then fastened several trifling articles to a cord, and threw them over the side of the ship,
when they were instantly seized by the boy and delivered by him to the man, who did not hesitate a moment to
tie the otter skins to the cord, and waved his hand as a
sign for us to take them on board, which was accordingly done, and an additional present conveyed to him in
the same manner as the former.

"These strangers appeared to be highly delighted
with their unexpected treasure, and seemed at first to be
wholly absorbed in their attention to the articles which
composed it.   But then their curiosity was in a short
time entirely transferred to the ship, and their eyes ran
over every part of it with a most rapid transition, while
their actions expressed such extreme delight as gave us
every reason to conclude that this was the first time they
had ever been gratified with the sight of such an object.   *   *   *   *   During the time we had been lying
to for these natives, the ship had drifted bodily down to
the shoals, which obliged us to make sail, when the canoe paddled into the Bay.

"It was our wish to have sent the long-boat to sound

near the shoals, in order to discover if there was any channel, but the weather was so cloudy, and altogether had so unsettled an appearance, that we were discouraged from executing such a design. Nothing, therefore, was left to us but to coast it along the shore and endeavor to find some place where the ship might be brought to a secure anchorage.

" On the morning of the sixth, the wind blew from the north, with a strong, heavy sea. At half past ten, being within three leagues of Cape Shoal-water, we had a perfect view of it, and with the glasses we traced the line of coast to the southward, which presented no opening that promised any thing like a harbor. A high, bluff promontory bore off us southeast at the distance of only four leagues, for which we steered to double, with the hope that between it and Cape Shoal-water we should find some sort of a harbor.

" We gave the name of Cape Disappointment to the promontory."

Meares having failed to discover the Columbia, or, as it was then called by Heceta, the San Roque, steered for the north, and entered Fuca Straits, and being anxious to procure some farther information and knowledge of the people of Shoal-water Bay, he fitted out his long-boat, and manned her with thirteen of his men, with provisions for one month, intending to send her down to the Bay ; but the boat was attacked while in the strait by the Indians, and the project abandoned.

Vancouver writes that in 1792, "after leaving Cape Disappointment, we made Cape Shoal-water, and endeavored to enter Shoal-water Bay ; but considering, from the appearance of the breakers, that the harbor was inaccessible to the ship, and having a fair wind, we sailed on to the northward."

Although Shoal-water Bay is laid down on the charts

of Captain Cook and Captain Meares, in a publication
November 18, 1790, by J. Walter, No. 169 Piccadilly,
London, on which the mouth of the Columbia is laid
down as Deception Bay, yet it is not laid down on any
subsequent publication till since the survey of Captain
Alden in 1852. The probable reason is that Meares,
having failed to discover the great river San Roque, or
Oregon, concluded that it found its passage to the Pacific
Ocean through Fuca Straits, and has so laid it down
on his map; and the subsequent discovery by Captain
Gray proving the inaccuracy of Meares's chart, it was
thrown aside altogether, and his account of Shoal-water
Bay considered fabulous.

In 1852, Lieutenant Commanding James Alden, in
the United States surveying steamer Active, made a reconnaissance of Shoal-water Bay, and on October 4th of
the same year, in a letter to the superintendent of the
coast survey, he writes: "We have made a reconnaissance of the entrance to Shoal-water Bay, and all the
northern portion of it, comprising an area of about one
hundred square miles. The remainder, which we were
prevented from examining for want of time, is a broad
sheet of water, from four to five miles wide, extending in
a southerly direction to within four miles of Baker's Bay,
Columbia River, and is shut out from the sea by a narrow peninsula, which commences just behind Cape Disappointment, and runs due north some twenty-five miles,
forming at its terminus the south point of the entrance.
It is full of shoals, as its name implies, but there is plenty of water among them, and they are generally bare at
low water. They are easily found, and quite accessible.
The land is well timbered, and I suppose there is plenty
of it sufficiently good for agricultural purposes. At
present there are no whites in the Bay, except a few
who are employed in collecting oysters for the California market."

The next morning after our arrival I went ashore with the rest of the passengers to the house of Mr. Russell, with whom I intended to remain for a short time. I found a few other settlers in the Bay, who were located there (as was also Mr. Russell) for the purpose of procuring oysters for the market of San Francisco. It was during the year 1851 that the first oysters were introduced into the San Francisco market by Mr. Russell, who was then engaged in trade at Pacific City, at the mouth of the Columbia River, and who carried them down in the steamer from Astoria. Sometime in the fall of the same year Captain Fieldsted entered the Bay in a schooner and obtained the first load of oysters ever taken to San Francisco.

A few settlers then came at intervals to locate themselves; and on my arrival there were the following individuals, who constituted the only white inhabitants of the region, viz., Charles J. W. Russell, Mark Winant, John Morgan, Alexander Hanson, Richard J. Milward, Thos. Foster, George G. Bartlett, Richard Hillyer, John W. Champ, Samuel Sweeney, Stephen Marshall, Charles W. Denter, A. E. St. John, and Walter Lynde.

There were also a few persons engaged in cutting timber on the banks of one of the streams emptying into the northeast part of the Bay, and who had engaged to load the brig with piles for the San Francisco market. Their names were Brown, Dousett, Simonds, Chatwick, and Tothill, but they all left in a few months.

While the brig was taking in her cargo, I went with Mr. Russell to examine the Bay. I found it to be, as Captain Alden has described it, a broad sheet of water, full of shoals, through which the different rivers running into it have worn deep channels, where, at all times of tide, there is a good anchorage and plenty of water. The principal river is the Whil-a-pah, a fine stream empty-

B

ing into the Bay at its northeast corner. This river, together with the Necomanchee or Nickomin, and two or three small creeks running into the north end of the Bay, have formed a fine beaten channel, which is known as the North Channel, and is the principal entrance to the Bay at present used by the vessels trading there. Farther to the south, the Palux or Copalux River runs through the shoals, and joins the North Channel near the entrance to the harbor. About fifteen miles south of the Palux the Marhoo or Nemar, and Achaitlin or Big River, join their waters with those of the Nasal, a noble stream, and these, together with the Bear River, Tarlilt, and sundry small creeks and brooks, have worn the deep and excellent passage known as the South Channel. At low tide the flats and shoals are all bare, and the water rushes through the channels with great velocity, making an attempt to stem the current, either in boat or canoe, a very laborious, and, at times, dangerous experiment.

The shoals are covered with shell-fish, among which the oyster is the most abundant, and constitutes the principal article of export. Several varieties of clams, crabs of the largest size, and of a most delicious flavor, shrimps, mussels, and a small species of sand-lobster, are in the greatest abundance, and furnish nutritious food, not only to the different tribes of Indians who resort to the Bay at different seasons to procure supplies, but also to the white settler, who is thus enabled to greatly reduce the expenses of living when compared with those settlements on the Columbia River and interior where provisions of all kinds are usually scarce and high.

The waters of the Bay, and all the streams that enter into it, are well stocked with fish. Salmon of several varieties abound, and are taken in great numbers by the Indians for their own food or for trading with the whites. Sturgeon of a very superior quality are plenty, and form

a principal item in the stock of provisions the Indians lay
by for their winter use.

The rivers and mountain streams abound in trout.
Flatfish, such as turbot, soles, and flounders, are plenty, and in the spring, innumerable shoals of herring visit
the Bay, and are readily caught by the Indians, either
with nets, or in weirs and traps, rudely constructed of
twigs and brush.

The shores of the Bay, with the exception of the west
or peninsular side, are mostly composed of high banks
of a sandy clay, intermingled with strata of shells and
remains of ancient forest-trees that for ages have been
buried. The faces of these cliffs are generally perpendicular, particularly when washed by the waves of the
Bay; but in some places they gradually descend to the
water, having a level space, covered either with grass or
bushes, close to the water's edge. The peninsula is a
flat, marshy, and sandy plain, elevated but a few feet from
the water level, and covered, as is also the whole region
around the Bay, with a dense growth of gigantic forest-
trees, principally spruce, fir, and cedar, with a few specimens of maple and ash, and black alder, which here
grows to a tree.

There are three islands in Shoal-water Bay; one, at
the North Bay, called Pine Island, is a small sand-islet
of some four or five acres in extent, covered with low,
stunted pine-trees and beach-grass. Some of the oystermen reside on it, as it is near the channel and the oyster-
beds.

That portion of the Bay from its northern extremity
to the southern point at the mouth of the River Palux
(called Goose Point) is termed the North Bay, and all
to the south of Goose Point, South Bay. About seventeen miles south of Goose Point is another island, called
Long Island, some six or eight miles long, but narrow,

and not over a mile and a half wide at its greatest width. This island is covered with a thick forest, except in a few places, where there are small prairie patches, very rich, and easily cultivated. The timber, however, is of little account, and would scarcely pay the labor of clearing.

South of Long Island is another small islet, called Round Island, from its shape. It is small, not over two acres in extent, and covered with spruce-trees and bushes.

The various rivers running into the Bay are not of any great length. The Whil-a-pah, which is the longest, is navigable for vessels drawing from twelve to fifteen feet of water twenty miles from its mouth, and for boats to within a short distance of the Cowlitz River. The Palux and Nasal are only navigable for large vessels for a few miles from their mouths; but all the rivers, large and small, run through fine prairie-land, exceedingly rich. That portion nearest the Bay is liable to be overflowed once or twice during the highest tides of winter, and are termed tide lands. This overflowing is, however, of no detriment, although the water is salt, as, wherever the lands have been properly cultivated, they have yielded heavy crops.

These prairies are all covered with grass of an excellent quality, making good grazing for stock, or a nutritious fodder when cut and made into hay.

Elk, deer, and antelope are very plenty, and find ample sustenance at all seasons of the year. The other wild animals which abound are black bears, wolves, lynx, panthers, and in the streams are otter and beaver. There are also raccoons, foxes, rabbits, skunks and squirrels, minks, martens, and a singular species of rat, called the bush-tailed rat (*Neotoma Drummondii*). This animal is of a very mischievous nature, seeming to take delight in collecting all sorts of things, and conveying them to its nest; instances are known of great confusion being occasioned among settlers at the sudden disappearance of articles which were afterward found hidden away by these rats. I have found in an old boot, that had been laid away during the summer, coffee, beans, dried apples, nails, ends of cigars, old pipes, and a variety of other loose trash, which were not fit for food, and could only have been collected for mischief.

The feathered tribe are numerous, and during the season flock hither in clouds: white and black swans, white geese, Canada geese, brant, sheldrake, cormorants, loon, mallard ducks, red-head, gray, and canvas-back ducks, teal, curlew, snipe, plover, pheasant, quail, pigeons, and robins. During the summer months pelican are plenty, and go sailing round in their heavy, lazy flight, occasionally dashing down into the water in the most clumsy manner to catch a fish, and at all times an easy prey and an acceptable banquet to the Indians, who swallow their coarse, fishy, oily flesh with the greatest avidity. Innumerable flocks of gulls of various species are constantly to be seen, and at times, when attracted by any quantities of food, appear like clouds. These birds, also, are readily eaten by the Indians, who never are at a loss to find means to appease their appetite.

Porpoises and seals are plenty in the Bay, and the latter are very easily killed either with spears or by shooting. Their flesh, particularly the young ones, is very palatable, and their blubber makes excellent oil, which is eaten by the Indians. Whales are frequently thrown ashore on the beach bordering the Pacific during the winter and spring months, and their blubber forms an important article of diet with the natives. The salmon, seal, and whale oils form the same important part of the domestic economy of the coast Indians as lard, butter, or olive oil do with the whites; and the Indian who has

not at all times in his lodge a good supply of oil or blubber not only feels very poor, but is so considered by all
his acquaintance and friends.

Shoal-water Bay, as a harbor, will be of great importance to Washington Territory as soon as its advantages
are known and the country becomes settled. The entrance to the Bay from the ocean is very direct and easily found, and the excellent chart by Captain Alden enables vessels of a light draft of water to run in at all
times of tide. There is always, at the lowest stages of
tide, from three to three and a half fathoms of water on
the bar; and as the volume of water discharged from the
Bay is never so great as from the Columbia, there is not
so heavy a swell or so dangerous breakers as may be
found occasionally at the Columbia's mouth; while the
distance between the entrances of the river and bay, being only twenty-seven miles, makes it a ready and safe
harbor of refuge for vessels that, from storms and heavy
breakers, dare not risk crossing the bar of the Columbia;
and I have known of several instances where vessels
have availed themselves of the opportunity.

As a fishing-station, this bay presents many advantages. It is directly and immediately on the whaling-
ground, and small vessels can be fitted out for a cruise
and placed in the right position as readily as the former
whalers of Nantucket, who performed their voyages of a
few weeks or months in sloops or small schooners. By
establishing a trading-post where vessels could obtain
supplies, which can always be speedily replenished at
San Francisco, a fleet of five or six schooners, of a hundred tons each, could be fitted and maintained for less
than the cost of a three years' voyage for one ship from
New Bedford; while the ease with which the oil could
find a market would enable the capital employed to make
many returns before a ship having to make a voyage
round Cape Horn could possibly be heard from.

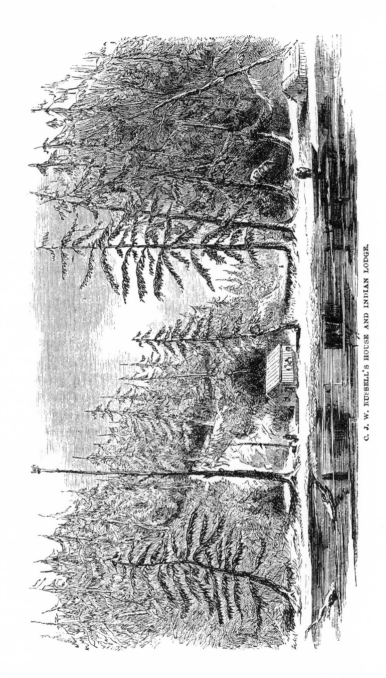

C. J. W. RUSSELL'S HOUSE AND INDIAN LODGE.

Codfish and halibut abound on this part of the coast, and an important and lucrative business in that branch of industry might be readily established. The ease with which communication can be had with San Francisco by means of the mail steamers at Astoria renders the Bay a more desirable locality than points farther north, while the dangers of the entrance are far less than at the Columbia.

CHAPTER III.

Russell's House.—Description of Toke and Suis.—Russell tells the Indians I am a Doctor.—Style of Medicine.—Salmon Fishing on the Palux.—Old Cartumhays.—Our Reception at his Lodge.—Camp on the Palux.—Duck Shooting.—Great Quantities of Salmon.—Falls of the Palux.—The Devil's Walking-stick.—Singular Superstition of the Indians.

RUSSELL'S house was the only frame building at that time in the Bay, and was used by him as a trading-post as well as a dwelling. His business was collecting and shipping oysters to San Francisco, and he consequently employed a great number of Indians to work for him. Near the house was a large lodge, owned by an old chief named Toke, who, with his family and slaves, had taken up their abode, although his own place was across the Bay, at its south side, near Cape Shoal-water, at a point known as Toke's Point, a name still retained by Captain Alden on his chart. Toke had been a man of a great deal of importance among the Indians, but advancing years and an inordinate love of whisky had reduced him to being regarded as an object of contempt and aversion by the whites, and a butt for the jests and ridicule of the Indians. But, when the old fellow was sober, he was full of traditionary tales of prowess, and legends of the days of old. He was also one of the best men in the

B 2

Bay to handle a canoe, or to show the various channels
and streams ; and often afterward I have called his services into requisition, and always found him faithful and
efficient.

His wife, Suis, was a most remarkable woman, possessing a fund of information in all matters relative to
incidents and traditions relating to the Bay, with a
shrewdness and tact in managing her own affairs uncommon among the Indian women.   The other Indians, who
were working for Russell, and who belonged at some distance, either among the Chenooks at the south, or the
Chehalis and Queniult tribes at the north, were camped
around the house in little tents made of mats or their
canoe-sails.

Russell, who had a good deal of the romancing spirit
of the Baron Munchausen in his composition, and who
wished not only to appear great in the eyes of the Indians, but to make them believe all his friends were of
importance, introduced me to these savages as a celebrated doctor, a fable which my utter ignorance of their
language prevented my denying.   However, by the aid
of a medicine-chest of his, containing a few simple drugs,
I went to work, and soon effected some wonderful cures.
The most celebrated and potent medicine was a mixture
of aqua ammoniæ and whale oil, prepared in the form of
a liniment.   This was effectual in curing headaches and
rheumatic affections of various kinds.   The patient was
first required to smell the medicine, which was afterward
rubbed on the affected part, and then faith was expected
to finish the cure.   This was a very popular medicine,
and was considered, from its pungency, to be very potent.
The rest of my stock of medicine consisted of nearly a
pound of dried boneset herb, a couple of pounds of flowers of sulphur, and a pound or so of salts.   My stock in
trade was on a par with my stock of information ; but

great faith on the part of the Indians, with their most excellent constitutions, enabled me to perform my duties to the great satisfaction of all parties.

It was not long, however, before what was at first a mere jest on Russell's part turned out more real than either of us anticipated; for the small-pox breaking out among the whites and Indians, I was obliged to render my services in a far more important and trying manner than I ever expected. A full account will be given of that sad time in another chapter.

As we had brought up barrels and salt from San Francisco for salmon, it was proposed by Russell that we should go out on a fishing expedition, although the season was very far advanced, and the fish had nearly done running for that year. Accordingly, he procured five Indians, and, taking two canoes with us well stocked with provisions, we started for the Palux River, about four miles to the south. We went up the river about ten miles, where we found there were three forks or branches—one running to the southeast, another, or the middle fork, to the east, and called Tomhays River, from an Indian who lived at its junction with the other branches, or north fork. This Indian, whose name is Cartumhays, and certainly one of the greatest liars and thieves I ever saw, continually talks about his great honesty. "No lie, Tomhays," "great chief," "good man," are about the only English words he knows, and which, parrot-like, he constantly repeats when addressing the whites. Tomhays had long been among the whites, both with the Hudson Bay Company people at Chenook, or with the settlers at Astoria, and is pretty generally known to every person around the mouth of the Columbia River; and being, withal, a shrewd fellow, had picked up quite a number of ideas of the white men's style of living.

It was to the lodge of this worthy that Russell directed our Indians to proceed, "for," said he, "we shall have to pass over a big snag up the river, and we may as well wait till near high water, when we can haul over the canoes much easier; and, besides, old Tomhays will give us a good cup of coffee and some nice broiled salmon." We soon landed, and were received by a yelping pack of dogs, who were repaid for their civilities by sundry blows from sticks and stones, indiscriminately bestowed by our copper-colored attendants as a sort of largesse, as the heralds of the knights of old threw purses and handfuls of coin among the retainers of the nobles whom they were about to visit.

The noise made by the dogs and Indians called out old Cartumhays, who, after giving vent to his disgust and indignation at the treatment his hounds and curs had received, invited us into his lodge, which was situated up the hill a short distance from the landing.

He soon prepared a meal, and gave us a nice cup of coffee, which he ground in a hand-mill that he had undoubtedly stolen from some white person.

We remained an hour with him, when, finding the tide to be about right, we started off, and proceeded up the north fork about a mile, where we came to the snag, which was an immense spruce tree fallen directly across the river. We soon hauled the canoes over, and proceeded up three quarters of a mile farther, where we went ashore and camped. The river at this place runs through a deep mountain gorge, and at that time, at low tide, was but a shallow stream, very narrow, and easily forded. The winter rains had not fairly set in, or we could not have camped where we did, for in the rainy season, and in times of freshets, the water comes tumbling, and foaming, and roaring down that narrow pass in a fearful manner. Our camp was easily made. The bushes were cut down, and a couple of forked poles stuck into the ground, hav-

CAMP ON THE PALUX.

ing another pole laid parallel across their tops. From
this ridge-pole a boat-sail we had with us was hung, so
as to form a sort of roof to keep off the dew or rain, and
in front of this was kindled a fire.

While we were getting the camp ready, two of the Indians went to catch some salmon for supper, while I took
my gun to try some of the ducks that were flying through
the gorge in myriads. The great spruce and fir trees
on either side of the river threw their long branches so
as to interlace with each other quite across the stream,
forming not only a dense shade, but obliging the wild
fowl to fly within such circumscribed limits as to be
easily shot. It was nearly dark when we had finished
the camp, but before night the Indians had caught a
dozen fine salmon, and Russell and myself had killed as
many ducks. Our supper was soon prepared, Russell
and myself eating duck, which we cooked to suit our
taste, and the Indians confining their attention to the
salmon, of which they ate inordinate quantities.

After we had smoked our pipes and built an enormous fire, we rolled ourselves in our blankets and went to sleep, from which we were awakened before daylight by the rush of wings of the ducks and other wild fowl getting ready for their morning meal, and the splashing of the salmon in the river.   I was thoroughly roused up by the report of a gun, fired off, as I thought, close to my ear. It proved that one of the Indians, who had waked before the rest, discovered a couple of sheldrake in our camp, feasting on the remains of our last night's supper.   He stealthily reached over to where I was lying, and took my gun, which was beside me, loaded, and shot both the sheldrake at one discharge.   The noise, of course, roused us all up, and we at once commenced preparations for the day.

The implements used by the Indians for catching salmon were a hook and a spear.   The former is in size as large as a shark-hook, having a socket at one end formed of wood.   These hooks are made by the Indians from files and rasps, which they purchase of the traders, and are forged into shape with ingenuity and skill.   The socket is made from the wild raspberry bush (Rubus spectablis), which, having a pith in its centre, is easily worked, and is very strong.   This socket is formed of two parts, which are firmly secured to the hook by means of twine, and the whole covered with a coat of pitch. Attached to this hook is a strong cord about three feet long.   A staff or pole from eighteen to twenty feet long, made of fir, is used, one end of which is fitted to the socket in the hook, into which it is thrust, and the cord firmly tied to the pole.   When the hook is fastened into a salmon it slips off the pole, and the fish is held by the cord, which enables it to perform its antics without breaking the staff, which it would be sure to do if the hook was firmly fastened.   The spear is a flat piece of iron

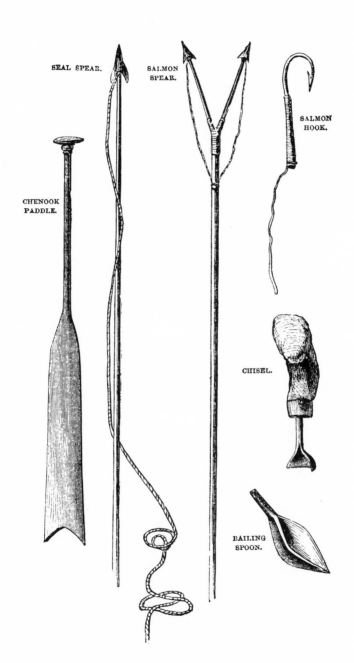

SEAL SPEAR.

SALMON
SPEAR.

SALMON
HOOK.

CHENOOK
PADDLE.

CHISEL.

BAILING
SPOON.

with barbs made of elk horn, and fastened in the same manner as the socket to the hook.   This spear-head has also a line attached to it, which is fastened to the staff in a similar manner as the hook is.   The spear is generally used in shallow water, and the hook in deep water at the mouth of rivers, before the fish run up the streams.

Although the river was filled with salmon, and the banks literally piled with the dead fish killed in attempting to go over the falls, yet, the season being so far advanced, there were comparatively few really prime ones. The salmon, after casting its spawn, grows thin, and the flesh loses its bright pink color.   The fish then is of little value either to the whites or Indians.   Our Indians, who were well skilled, started up stream to commence, as their custom always is to go up the stream, and then, letting the canoe float down, catch the fish as they pass. As the tide fell, the Indians left their canoes and waded in the stream.   We joined them, and such a splashing and dashing I never before witnessed.   I caught seven and Russell about as many, when, getting tired and thoroughly wet, we went back to the camp, and amused ourselves shooting ducks.   When the Indians were tired, they came in, having been about four hours at work, and during that time succeeded in killing over a hundred fine salmon.   After we had eaten our dinners we started up the stream to see the falls, which were a few miles distant.   We found this rather a rough job, as the bed of the river was full of fallen trees, old logs, and rocks.   As we approached the falls, we had to clamber up the steep sides of the banks, which were covered with a growth of shrubbery similar in appearance to sumach, and having its stems covered with sharp thorns, which readily pierce the flesh, and sting like nettles.   The name given to this most villainous shrub is the Devil's walking-stick.   Before we got into a position to see the falls, we had both received several tumbles and got our hands full of the prickles. However, we felt repaid for our trouble. The falls are a succession of cataracts from ten to twenty feet high, and the whole fall of the river is some two hundred feet. Although there was not much water, the scene was fine, and, could it be viewed when the river was full, must be magnificent. We did not remain long, but scrambled back to camp, where we arrived just in time for supper. It was our intention to have remained several days, but the Indians, from some superstitious ideas, refused to fish any more.

One of their superstitions is that the spirits of the dead are always hovering about the homes they left on earth, and when they are displeased with any of the doings of their relatives or friends, they make known their presence in various ways; and when the Indian thinks there are any of the " dead people" about, he will, if away from his home, leave the place he may be at, or, if in his own house, will take measures to drive off the spirit, either by firing a gun or getting the medicine-man to work spells. Our Indians, it appeared, had heard the whistling of a plover the previous night, which I had also heard. They said it was a dead person. Russell told them it was a bird. No, said they, birds don't talk in the night; they talk in the daytime. But, asked Russell, how can you tell that it is the "memelose tillicums," or dead people? They can't talk. No, replied the savage, it is true, they can't talk as we do, but they whistle through their teeth. You are a white man, and don't understand what they say; but Indians know, and they told us not to catch any more salmon, and we are afraid, and must go back to-morrow.

And, sure enough, they did get ready in the morning, and no promises of reward that Russell offered them would induce them to stop one minute after we had done eating breakfast.

As we proceeded down the river on our homeward course, we startled myriads of wild fowl, and had some fine shooting. The Palux River, from the junction of its three forks to its mouth, some eight or ten miles, runs through fine prairie land and marshes covered with luxuriant grass, furnishing excellent grazing for stock. Vessels of four or five hundred tons burden, and drawing eighteen feet of water, can proceed up the river two or three miles, and find every facility for loading timber, which is very easily and readily procured on the banks or up the various creeks and small streams emptying into the main river.

We reached Russell's house about noon, and, after having had our fish cleaned, we salted and packed them in barrels.

CHAPTER IV.

Wreck of the Willemantic.—Joe the Steward and his curry Stews.—Climate of the Pacific.—Causes of the Mildness of Temperature.—Quantities of Rain.—Early Spring.—Method of learning the Indian Language.—Captain Purrington clearing Land.—Immense Trees.—Indians' Small-pox.—Indians die.—Russell sick.—Tomhays sick.—Queaquim dies.—Solemn Scene.

THE brig sailed for San Francisco shortly after this, and Russell being obliged to leave for Astoria on business, I remained alone in charge of the house and store, with no companion but the family of Indians.

I did not remain so long, for the schooner Willemantic having been wrecked in Gray's Harbor, eighteen miles north of us, we received her crew, who were divided round among the settlers. Captain Vail, her owner, with the mate and crew, went down the beach with the different residents ; Joe, the steward, came and stopped with me. Joe was a Dane, but had lived some years at

Sumatra, where he had learned to be an excellent cook, and was particularly fond of curry, which he could prepare to perfection; and when he left the wreck, he managed to save his bottle of curry, which enabled us to have many a savory mess: curried ducks or geese, venison, bear meat, oysters, or fish; and when these failed, he would get up a dish of curried beans; every thing but our coffee or bread was sure to be seasoned with curry. However, Joe was a capital fellow, full of his sea yarns, and, what with his curries and stories, we managed to pass off the short days and long nights very pleasantly.

There had been a fall of snow, although the weather was not very cold, and we amused ourselves in making paths. The climate is very mild, and never so cold as in the same parallel of latitude on the Atlantic coast. This is a fact noticed by all the writers on the Pacific and Northwest Coasts that I have seen. Ross Cox, who was employed by the Fur Company at Astoria, writes that "the climate on the Columbia River, from its mouth to the rapids, is mild. The mercury seldom falls below the freezing point, and never rises above 80°. Westerly winds prevail during the spring and summer months, and are succeeded by northwesters, which blow pretty freshly during the autumn; October ushers in the south wind and the rain, both of which continue without intermission till January, when the wind begins to bear to the westward; but the rain seldom ceases till the termination of April."

In Greenhow's "History of Oregon and California," he remarks, "The countries on the Pacific side of North America differ materially in climate from those east of the great dividing range of mountains situated in the same latitudes, and at equal distances from and elevations above the ocean. These differences are less within the torrid zone, and beyond the 60th parallel; but in the intermediate space, every part of the Pacific section is much warmer and drier than places in the Atlantic or Arctic sections under the same conditions as above expressed. Thus the northwesternmost regions of America appear to be as cold, and to receive as much rain and snow from the heavens, as those surrounding Baffin's Bay, or those in their own immediate vicinity in Asia. But in the countries on the Pacific side, corresponding in latitude and other respects with Wisconsin, Canada, Nova Scotia, and Newfoundland, the ground is rarely covered with snow for more than three or four weeks in each year, and it often remains unfrozen throughout the winter."

Mr. Lorin Blodget, in a letter to the National Intelligencer, published about the first of January, 1857, says of the climate on the Pacific coast:

"Not only the extreme limit at the 49th parallel is warmer than Washington for the winter, but a distance like that from Paris to Aberdeen must be passed over, *beyond the extreme limit at the north of Puget's Sound*, to find a winter as cold as that of this city, Washington. The winter at Puget's Sound is *warmer* than at Paris, the mean being 69½° at the first, and 38° at Paris; and the winter at Sitka is *warmer* than that at Washington (30½° and 36° respectively), notwithstanding they differ 18 degrees of latitude, or nearly 1250 miles, in position on the meridians. Aberdeen, in Scotland, is somewhat warmer, having a winter temperature of 39°, though at the 57th parallel."

Again: "At Washington we were taught by the experience of last winter—and the opening of the present winter repeated the lesson—that the rivers and navigable waters here may be closed by ice for months in succession. Vegetation is dormant for several months, and in this respect the condition is practically similar from

New York to the north of Georgia. This city is near the 30th parallel, and San Francisco is nearly at the 38th; yet, at this last-named city, it was remarked as singular that roses and flowers were cut off temporarily, as they were in the early part of the last winter, though they subsequently recovered their freshness; and through February and March the temperature was as soft as that of the south shores of the Mediterranean. At Puget's Sound, in Washington Territory, ten degrees of latitude farther north, the winter was still mild and open, and the grass in constant growth. Continuing along this course to Sitka, ten degrees of latitude still farther north, it was yet, doubtless, much warmer than at Washington, since the average for the winter is warmer, and the changes in extreme years are there very far less."

My own experience goes to prove the truth of the foregoing remarks, and the cause of this mildness is to be attributed to the fact mentioned by Cox, that the wind blows almost invariably from the ocean. During the winter months the wind is generally from the south to the southeast, veering at times to the southwest. These winds, blowing from the tropics, bring with them warm rains, and it is only during the winter season that thunder and lightning accompany the rain, and these only during the most violent storms. The only severe cold is felt when the wind blows from the northeast, and whenever it gets in that quarter the effects are precisely the same as the northwest winds in the Atlantic states; but I have never known excessive cold weather to continue longer than twelve or fourteen days, when the wind will return to the south, and a warm rain brings on a general thaw.

It is these facts with respect to the climate that make a residence in either Oregon or Washington Territories so desirable; and the remarkable fact should not be lost sight of, that, although Washington Territory is in the same latitude as Nova Scotia, yet the climate is as mild in winter as Pennsylvania, nor is the heat of summer so oppressive as in the same parallel east of the Rocky Mountains. I have seen the thermometer, during the hottest day I ever felt at Shoal-water Bay, reach 95°, but it was but for a few hours, and, as Cox remarks, it rarely exceeds 80°. During the winter the rain falls in the most incredible quantities, but it does not, as has been asserted, rain without intermission. A storm will commence which will last a week, some days raining violently, and accompanied with heavy gales of wind. These blows will last perhaps twenty-four or forty-

SALMON-BERRY, OR WILD RASPBERRY (*Rubus spectablis*).

eight hours, when it will lull, and the rain subside into
a gentle shower, or mere mist and fog ; then perhaps it
will clear off, with eight or ten days of fine, clear weather.
The spring commences much earlier also ; and I may
mention at this time, in evidence, that on the 10th day
of March, 1853, while making a botanical collection, I
gathered the blossoms of the wild raspberry (Rubus
spectablis), the fruit of which is ripe in June, the wild
strawberry, the Trillium (Dikentra formosa), and various
other small flowers ; while in the month of my arrival,
December, 1852, I collected and preserved the blossoms
of the Sallal (Gaultheria Shallon).

SALLAL (*Gaultheria Shallon*).

What part of the country east of the Rocky Mountains, in the latitude of 46° north, can be shown where flowers bloom from March to December? But to return from this digression. As I had not much to amuse myself with, and being desirous of learning the Indian language, I went frequently to the lodge to learn to talk. There were several young men and boys who aided me, and, in particular, one named Cherquel Sha, and by the whites called George, who had been employed for a long time in a small steamer on the Columbia, and could talk English pretty well. George was very sick, and had often come to me for medicines, and had formed a great friendship for me. He would sit by the hour, either in the lodge or at the house, repeating words which I would write down to enable me to remember them. I found at first the Indians were inclined to tell me wrong, but I adopted a plan which proved effectual to enable me to get correct information, which was this: I would repeat the word slowly until I had a correct idea of the sound, then would write the word so that when any other white man saw it he could pronounce it and produce the same sound. Thus I knew that I had correctly spelled the word. Then I would at some other time pronounce the word to a different Indian, and ask him what it meant, when, if he explained it as the first one had, I knew my spelling and explanation were correct. By this method I soon obtained a vocabulary which enabled me to converse readily with them. These Indians were of the Chenook tribe, although some of them belonged to the Chehalis tribe, on Gray's Harbor; consequently they talked either language fluently. I shall refer in another chapter more fully to the tribes of Shoal-water Bay.

Russell, after an absence of a few weeks, returned, bringing with him Captain James S. Purrington, formerly master of a whale-ship, and who, for forty years,

C

had been engaged in the whaling business. Captain Purrington had been at work on the Columbia, and had lost all his labor by two successive freshets, and he concluded to try his hand in Shoal-water Bay. Russell was desirous of making a garden, and we all went to work clearing up a spot near the house. This was not so easy a task as might be imagined. The proposed garden was occupied by some thirty or more immense spruce-trees, from six to eight feet in diameter, and over a hundred feet high.

These immense trees, falling from time to time, make a walk through the forest very difficult, and at times dangerous. I was out one day with Captain Purrington, a few months afterward, to examine a piece of land on our claim, when we came to an open space apparently quite level, and covered with dead wood, moss, and a fine growth of raspberry bushes laden with fruit. While we were engaged picking and eating the berries, all at once the captain disappeared. I called out for him, and directly heard a faint halloo, as I thought, under ground. Directly after, down I went, and then found that the place was a small ravine about thirty feet deep, over which the trees had fallen in every direction so as to completely cover it over, and these, in their turn, had been covered over by an accumulation of limbs, branches, moss, and at last by the bushes. The falling of the trees had been evidently caused by some whirlwind years previous. I asked the captain if he was hurt. "No," said he, "I came down as easy as if I had lit on a feather bed; but if you have a match about you, pass it to me, and I will soon let daylight into this heap. I don't like the idea of burning up all those nice berries, but I have a great curiosity to see how this place will look when it is cleared up." The old man soon kindled a blaze, which very materially altered the appearance of

FORESTS IN OREGON.

the face of the country before it was put out by the rain. We were fortunate in escaping without injury; but the experience was useful, for, in our future explorations, we were more careful where we went.

The enormous growth of the timber trees on the Pacific coast, from California to Hudson's Bay, has often been written about. Ross Cox writes: "The general size of the different species of fir far exceeds any thing east of the Rocky Mountains, and prime sound pine (spruce) from two hundred to two hundred and eighty feet in height, and from twenty to forty feet in circumference, are by no means uncommon. A pine tree discovered in Umpqua county, to the southeast of the Columbia, measured two hundred and sixteen feet to its lowest branch, and in circumference fifty-seven feet."

Ross Cox speaks of these trees as pine, but he is mistaken; for, with the exception of a scrubby growth of the Pinus palustris, found directly on the sea-coast, I have never seen a specimen of pine from the Columbia to Fuca Strait. The timber is white and yellow spruce, red, white, and yellow fir, hemlock, cedar, and yew. Oak is not found on the immediate range of the coast, but is plentiful on the Columbia, and in the region of Puget Sound. A fine quality of ash is also found in those localities. Lewis and Clarke, speaking of the immense size of the trees near Astoria, mention a fir two hundred and thirty feet high, and one hundred and twenty feet of that height without a limb, and its circumference twenty-seven feet. These trees are not to be confounded with the great trees of California: *they* are a distinct species, and are known as red-wood trees, and the wood bears a resemblance to Spanish cedar. But the growth of Oregon and Washington is like the spruce, fir, and hemlock of the State of Maine.

We soon, with the aid of some of the settlers, made a

havoc among the trees, and in a few days most of them were cut down. News now came that several vessels had been wrecked on the coast, north of Cape Disappointment, and Russell and the captain, with several others, started off to render assistance, leaving Joe and myself once more to make and eat curry stews. It is one thing to cut down a big tree, and quite another to clear it away ; but, by the time Russell returned, we, with the help of the Indians, had cleared away all the branches, leaving the trunks of the trees ready for the saw. The wrecking party was absent a week, and brought, on their return, a quantity of boards from the wrecks, which were much needed, as at that time there were no saw-mills in the Bay. They reported that the small-pox had broken out at Clatsop, south of the Columbia. Russell was in great fear lest the Indians should bring the disease over to Shoal-water Bay, and remarked that if he thought it would come, he would at once leave for San Francisco, for he dreaded the small-pox more than any other complaint, although he had been vaccinated.

Joe and the captain now went to work to cut the trees into logs, which we then blew open with powder, and then with beetle and wedges reduced the blocks small enough to handle, and then piled them round the stumps and set fire to them. We usually kept these fires going all night, and the light these tremendous bonfires made could be seen for miles. The Indians enjoyed the fun of piling on logs and making a blaze, and every evening were sure to gather round and have a frolic. We had two young Indians, brothers, working for us, *He-yal-ma* and *Que-a-quim*, funny, lively fellows, always in good nature, and the smartest and best Indians I ever saw. Que-a-quim, the younger, was a great favorite with us all, and, when we had a gang of Indians at work, could always, by his pranks and fun, keep them pleasant.

This young fellow took delight in perching himself on a log every night near the fire, and, pointing out the different constellations in the starry heavens, would tell me the legendary tales of their mythological belief. At such times his demeanor was entirely changed, and, gazing upward with a wild and excited look, would impart his information in an earnest and solemn manner, that showed how deeply he was interested in his subject.

The winter was now wearing away, and the snow had all disappeared, although January had not quite gone, and every pleasant day the sun shone out warm and bright, giving token of an early spring. While we were thus engaged in clearing up land and burning trees, a party of Indians from Chenook arrived, consisting of old Carcumcum (sister of the celebrated Comcomly, the Chenook chief mentioned in Irving's Astoria, and also by Ross Cox), and her son Ellewa, the present chief of the Chenooks, with his wife and two or three slaves. They made a camp on the beach near the house, where they lived under a little old tent. They had been to the wrecks, and among other things found was an India-rubber pillow, which Ellewa had filled with some kind of spirits he had also procured at the same place. He and his squaw, Winchestoh, managed to keep drunk for three or four days, when, their liquor giving out, they were obliged to get sober. As it commenced to rain, they were very miserable, and Ellewa requested Russell to allow the squaw to lie down by the fire in the house, which he did, and the same day Ellewa, with old Carcumcum, returned to Chenook. At supper-time I gave the squaw some tea and toast, and remarked that her face and neck were covered with little spots like flea-bites. I said to Russell, "This woman has either got the small-pox or measles." "Oh!" said he, "don't say that, for I would never have had her in the house if I suspected any such thing." "Well," said I, "we shall see."

Soon after supper I went to bed, as did Joe and the captain, leaving Russell writing. About nine o'clock he called me to come down, for he thought the woman was dying; and, sure enough, when I got down stairs she was entirely dead. We laid her in the store, and the next morning the captain and Joe made her a coffin, and after we had put her in we carried her about five hundred rods from the house, and, having dug a grave, buried her in a Christian manner.

Some ten or twelve days after this Russell was taken with a violent pain in his head and back, and had to take to his bed. Joe and the captain also were attacked, but very slightly, however. They all attributed their sickness to severe colds, but I knew that in Russell's case it was something more serious. I did not dare tell him, as I knew it would only frighten him; nor did I dare tell my fears either to the captain or Joe, or any of the other settlers; there was such a panic in the minds of all, that I knew the bare mention of small-pox would drive them all away from the house, if not from the Bay. I could not leave, as there was no vessel in the Bay at the time, nor would I leave during his illness, although I could easily have gone to Astoria; so I made up my mind to do what I could and keep my own counsel, which I did so effectually that Russell did not know what was the matter till the fever had passed and he was nearly blind, and the captain and Joe did not know what ailed him till he was nearly well and all danger had passed. Joe was so scared that he ran off the same day, but the old man complimented me on my caution, and said that he could then account for the violent attack he had experienced, and which he thought was a severe cold.

As soon as Russell was able, he went to San Francisco, leaving me in charge of his affairs.   His cousin, Walter Lynde, had insisted on seeing him while he was sick, and he was taken next, and I nursed him through, but his attack was very slight.

Several cases occurred among the other settlers, but mostly Indians in their employ, and several of the Indians died.   I thought my hospital duties were at an end, but the hardest case was yet to come off.   Poor Que-a-quim was taken with the unmistakable symptoms, and, rather than have him in the lodge with the other Indians, where I was afraid the infection would spread, I had him brought over and placed in a comfortable position in the chamber near my bed, where the captain and myself did all we could to make him easy.   During his sickness, old Cartumhays, whose wife had just died of the small-pox, sent for me to go to his house on the Palux, as he had the same complaint.   I accordingly went, and found the old fellow in his bed making great lamentations.   After a little time he pulled out from a chest a package of about a dozen different kinds of medicine, that he had either begged, borrowed, or, more probably, stolen.   He said he was very sick, and wished me to help him.

Judging, however, from the presence of five or six empty whisky bottles that his complaint was not a very dangerous one, I recommended him a dose of salts, to be followed up with half a cupful of sulphur and molasses, to be taken instead of preserves or sweetmeats.   The prescription in his case was happily effective, and in two days he was well.

Poor Que-a-quim, however, grew worse.   He had, besides the small-pox, an affection of his liver, which had troubled him a long time.   He knew he should die, and told me so.   His brother, to whom I told this, remarked, " Well, if he wants to die, he will die."   He then

C 2

brought into the house, from the lodge, all the little property of his brother, consisting of a few shirts, a blanket or two, and some few trinkets, with a request that they might be buried with him. The day Que-a-quim died, we felt satisfied, from appearances, that such must be the case, and the captain remarked, " He will die this evening at high water;" and at nine o'clock, just as the tide began to ebb, he died.

Now, then, was a job before us. The Indians would not have any thing to do with the body, nor would we let them, for fear of their taking the infection, neither did we feel disposed to remain all night with the corpse; so the captain procured a piece of old canvas, and, wrapping the body up in several blankets, taking care to inclose all the things which had been brought in from the lodge, the whole was then sewed up in the canvas, and the corpse lashed on to a board, and launched out of the chamber window by the captain, while I received the body from below, and laid it on a barrel till the captain came with a lantern and two shovels, when we took up the corpse, resting the board on our shoulders. Poor Que-a-quim! he was not very heavy, and we soon reached the spot where but a few weeks before we had buried the squaw. It did not take us long to dig a grave in the soft sand, and we soon laid him beside the wife of Ellewa.

"We buried him darkly at dead of night."

The little clock in Russell's house struck twelve as we closed the door on our return.

The time, the place, and the occasion gave rise to the most solemn feelings; neither of us could speak a word. But the old captain, who had seen many a scene of death, and assisted often in launching the bodies of his shipmates into the blue waters of the ocean, could not refrain from shedding a tear to the memory of the poor Indian lad, a tribute of sympathy in which I most heartily joined. This was the last case of small-pox I was called on to attend, and I trust I may not be obliged to pass through such another trial, feeling perfectly satisfied with my acquaintance with that most disgusting and contagious disease.

CHAPTER V.

Arrival of Indians from the North.—Description of the Oysters and Oyster-fishers of Shoal-water Bay.—Hospitality of early Settlers.—Joel L. Brown.—Captain Weldon.—Winter in Oregon.

THE weather was now propitious for prosecuting the oyster-fishery, and hundreds of Indians came to the Bay from Chenook and the tribes at the north. Some of the Indians came as far as the region round Puget Sound. These wandering beings begin to grow restless when the winter approaches its termination, and, as soon as the wild geese make their appearance, the Indians are ready to start on a tramp. I do not know, nor do I assert, that the flight of the wild-fowl and other migratory birds is any sign by which the Indian governs his movements ; but I have noticed that they generally commence operations about the same time.

These Indians, during the summer months, resort to Shoal-water Bay to procure clams and crabs for their own eating, and oysters to sell to the whites. The Shoal-water Bay oysters are different from the oysters on the Atlantic coast, and very much resemble, in taste and appearance, the English Channel oysters, having the same strong, coppery taste. This is acquired, not from any presence of copper, but because they grow in beds on the mud flats, instead of growing, as the Atlantic oysters, in clusters on rocks or on a hard bottom ; and what is called a coppery taste is simply a strong, fishy, salt-water flavor, which, however, is driven off by cook-ing.

These oysters are found on the flats and in shoal wa-ter, in different parts of the Bay, and are readily pro-cured, either by collecting them by hand at low tide, when the flats are bare, or, in the deeper water, by oys-ter-tongs, rakes, or dredges. The best method is by using the tongs. When the tide is nearly out, the boats and canoes start for the oyster-beds, where they wait till the water is gone, when they go to work picking up by hand into baskets, which are emptied into the canoes. These hand-picked oysters are the best, as they are all good; those taken by the tongs, being half shells, have to be carried ashore and culled over, and then put on the beds. Each oysterman has a bed, which is marked by stakes driven into the flats, and can be reached at any time, either by foot at low water, or in boats at high tide.

As the tide rises and covers the flats, the boats and canoes begin to creep ashore; and as soon as they arrive at the beach a lively time ensues, trading, measuring, and shoveling the oysters, and for an hour or two all is bus-tle. This over, the day's work is done, and the Indian goes off to eat and lounge away the rest of the time till the next tide, and the white settler to work in his garden, or do what work is necessary to be done round his house. The arrival of a schooner from San Francisco is a time of general excitement, and particularly at that early time when I first arrived, for, as we had no opportunity to replenish our supplies except by the schooners, the ar-rival of one was a matter of moment.

After each one had procured what few stores he had sent for, the day of loading would be designated, and then each man exerts himself to the utmost to get as many on board as he can. The scows, boats, and canoes are load-

OYSTERMEN WAITING FOR THE TIDE.

ed at low tide, and, as soon as they float, they start off for the vessel. First come, first served, is the motto, and a bustling scene ensues.*

The schooners carry from twelve hundred to two thousand baskets of oysters, and some have even taken four thousand baskets; but it is not considered safe to take so many at once, as the bottom ones are apt to die on the passage. These vessels are loaded with great dispatch; and often I have known a schooner to receive a load of twelve hundred baskets, the cargo all paid for, and the schooner under weigh in four hours from the time she begins to load. These oysters bring, on an average, a dollar a basket alongside the vessel, and, as the exports from the Bay are about fifty thousand baskets per annum, which are paid for in gold on the spot, it can be seen that there is quite a circulation of specie among the hardy oystermen of Shoal-water Bay. They are not, however, exempt from losses, for the year of which I write proved very disastrous to several who had shipped oysters to San Francisco on their own account. The Bruce Company, consisting of Messrs. Winant, Morgan, Hanson, Milward, and Foster, lost several cargoes, the oysters dying on the passage; and Russell, and a company who reside in San Francisco, lost between them some eight or ten thousand baskets of oysters, which were destroyed by the skates and drum-fish. While in Shoal-water Bay, during the winter of 1853-4, every one of us lost our oysters during a heavy frost that lasted three or four days.

The early settlers, whose names I have already men-

---

* In 1855 there were employed in the oyster trade in the Bay,

1 schooner of 20 tons, capable of carrying	600 baskets oysters;
28 boats,	"	"	2200	" "
21 scows,	"	"	1980	" "
13 canoes,	"	"	670	" "
			5450.	

tioned, were some of the most hospitable men that could
be found in any part of the world. Their isolated position, far from any other settlement (the nearest being at
Chenook, some forty miles distant), seemed to knit them
together in a common bond of brotherhood, and each
seemed to vie with the other in acts of kindness to every
stranger that might visit the Bay, either from motives of
curiosity or to become permanent settlers. As emigrants
were now coming in very fast, the hospitality of the worthy settlers was often put to a severe test, and it was not
till after so many persons had arrived that it was impossible to provide for them without remuneration that
these hardy pioneers consented to ask for pay from those
seeking for food and lodging.

Among these emigrants arriving was Mr. Joel L.
Brown, who, with a party, arrived in the Bay, and took a
claim on the River Palux, where he intended erecting a
store for trading purposes, and formed a town. Mr.
Brown and his associates had cut a wagon-road on the
portage, crossing from the Bay to the Columbia River,
and quite an interest was excited by him among the
emigrants of Oregon to make Shoal-water Bay their
home. But, before his plans were hardly commenced, he
died at his house on the Palux, lamented by every one
with whom he was acquainted. Mr. Brown was a man
of energy and perseverance, and, had he lived, would
have made a fine settlement, and undoubtedly induced a
large emigration. Some of the persons who came with
Mr. Brown were, Samuel Woodward, Henry Whitcomb,
Joel and Mark Bullard, and Captain Jackson. Mr. James
Wilson and his family settled at the portage, and afforded assistance to the travelers going or coming to the Bay.
The same season Captain Charles Stewart arrived, and
took a claim at the mouth of the Whil-a-pah River.
Captain David K. Weldon, with his lady, also came from

San Francisco. Captain Weldon erected a fine house and store at the mouth of the Necomanchee or North River, and, together with Mr. George Watkins, erected the first saw-mill. Mrs. Weldon was the first lady who came to the Bay to reside. The settlers now began to come in fast; but, as it is only my object to speak of some of the pioneers, a further mention of names will be unnecessary, except as they may be used in the course of the narrative.

Although it has been stated that the winters in Oregon and Washington are milder than in the same parallels east of the Rocky Mountains, still it must not be supposed that a winter's residence in either territory is attended with the delights of a tropical climate.

The rains are very violent, and at times are attended with heavy gales from the southeast. From the high latitude of Shoal-water Bay, the days are very short, and but little out-door work can be done, and the settler finds it a difficult task to pass off the long, stormy nights, unless with the aid of books or some useful in-door employment. At such periods it is very difficult and dangerous to cross the Bay, and communication with the Columbia is very rarely attempted, and it is only the direst necessity that will compel the settlers to procure supplies from Astoria; consequently, every one, at the time I refer to, depended on the oyster schooners to bring them up their supplies of provisions. The winter of 1852–3 was a hard one for the oystermen. They had supplied themselves, as they supposed, with sufficient provisions for the winter, but the unusual calls on their hospitality from new-comers straitened their means so that they were reduced to pretty short allowances; but they did not complain. Those that had not an abundance were cheerfully supplied by those that had, and as there appeared to be a sort of pride that no stranger should suppose them in want, they managed to change and shift their commodities so as to get through the winter without any difficulty. If one man had a little more flour than he needed, he would exchange with a neighbor who had a surplus of pork; and another, who might have an extra barrel of beef, would get a few potatoes or onions from some one else; so with rice, sugar, molasses, coffee, or tea. Nothing mean or niggardly was known among these people. Their hospitality was the theme of remark all over the Territory, and the oyster-boys of Shoal-water Bay were looked upon as a community of generous and noble-hearted men.

This founding of an infant colony on our extreme northwest frontier was no holiday work, neither was it child's play. The emigrant, come which way he would, either by land or by sea, had to endure much toil, privation, and hardship, and when located in his new home had nothing but work, and hard work at that, to make that new home a comfortable abode. When we consider those families who have struggled their way over the great wilderness of the west, where every mile is marked by the grave of some unfortunate and perhaps much-loved one—who have had to endure the perils of the hostile savage, of sickness or starvation, but yet have manfully pushed on, and now have opened out that beautiful and fertile region, which is a common wealth to our whole country, should we not allow that they who are but the wards of Congress have a right to look to that guardian of our country to bestow upon them its assistance with no niggard hand? The wealth of Oregon and Washington has scarce begun to be developed; but when the vast importance of those territories is appreciated, it must be admitted that every dollar expended by the nation for their support or defense is money well applied, and which will make a hundred-fold return.

Early writers speak of the beauty and fertility of Washington Territory. In 1792, Vancouver, in remarking of the country around Port Discovery, Admiralty Inlet, and Puget Sound, writes:

" To describe the beauties of this region will on some future occasion be a very grateful task to the pen of the skillful panegyrist. The serenity of the climate, the innumerable pleasing landscapes, and the abundant fertility that unassisted nature puts forth, require only to be enriched by the industry of man with villages, mansions, cottages, and other buildings, to render it the most lovely country that can be imagined, while the labor of the inhabitants must be rewarded in the bounties which Nature seems ready to bestow on cultivation." Lewis and Clarke, Ross Cox, and others, also remark favorably upon the region. That it is destined ere long to be of vast importance to our interests in the Pacific must be apparent to the most casual observer.

CHAPTER VI.

Stony Point.—Visit of Walter and myself to the *Memelose Tillicums*, or Dead People.—Basaltic Boulders.—Indian Tradition respecting them. —Legend of the Doctor and his Brother.—The Giants build a great Fire to heat Stones.—They boil out the Bay.—The Doctor finds his Brother in a Fish's Belly.—Bear-hunt on Stony Point.—Bartlett kills the Bear.—Method of burying the Dead.—We find a Mummy.—Russell sends the Mummy to San Francisco.—Opinions of scientific Persons respecting the Mummy.—An instance of another Body being preserved.—I get capsized at Stony Point.—Take a Claim on the Querquelin River.—Description of the Claim and our mode of Living.—Method of Canoe-making.—Seal-catching.—Method of catching Fish.—Indian Food.—Description of the Roots and Berries.—Sea Otter.—River Otter.—Beaver.—Furs.

BEFORE Russell returned from San Francisco I had several walks with his cousin, Walter Lynde, who, being very fond of collecting curiosities, was always ready for a tramp. One day we took our hatchets, determined to explore the heights of a promontory called Stony Point, about an eighth of a mile south, on which were said to be a number of old canoes and other Indian remains. The place was considered sacred, and no Indian ever ventured there. Their usual superstitious reverence, and fear of any thing belonging to the " memelose tillicums," or dead people, prevented their ever going near the spot. Stony Point is a narrow strip of land, or rather sandy clay, with a little soil on the top, extending into the Bay some three or four hundred rods. It has been washed away by repeated storms, so that now it is not more than ten rods wide, perfectly precipitous, with an elevation of some sixty feet from the water. It is approached either by a path from the end next the Bay, or from its junction with the main land. At that time it was thickly covered with spruce-trees, and a thick undergrowth of vine maple, sallal bushes, vines, and other obstructions; and as at the time of our visit no white man had ever had occasion to go upon it, we expected to have quite a job. This promontory rests on boulders of basaltic rocks, which have been washed bare as the waves of the Bay have encroached on the clayey soil of the Point. These rocks are remarkable from the fact that they are the only rocks of the kind that are to be found in the Bay. They appear at some period to have been subjected to the action of fire. The Indian tradition relating to them is that, ages ago, a celebrated medicine-man or doctor, accompanied by his brother, came from the north on a visit to the Bay for the purpose of obtaining clams. One day, while wading in the water for crabs, the brother of the doctor fell into a deep channel, where he was seized by some great sea-monster and swallowed. His lengthened absence from home caused much anxiety, and the doctor, by his divination, ascertained what was the cause. At that time giants, or strong men, lived in the mountains near the Bay. These the doctor caused to bring huge stones, while he himself collected great firs, dried spruce, and other trees wherewith to build a great fire. When this was done, the stones were piled on the top of the wood after the present method the Indians have of heating stones for cooking purposes ; and, when the wood was burned down, the red-hot stones were thrown into the Bay, which caused it to boil so violently that the water soon evaporated. The doctor then seeing the great sea-monster, killed it with his club, and, ripping its belly open, released his brother, who very joyfully proceeded with him to Chenook, where, after performing sundry famous cures, they gave offense to some person more potent than themselves, who changed them to stone. Two rocks near Scarborough's Hill, at Chenook Point, are still shown as the doctor and his brother. As every thing about the region denotes volcanic action, there is no doubt that the origin of the tradition was some great convulsion of nature, the account of which has thus been handed down from generation to generation, clothed with the ideal imagery of the Indian's mind.

These rocks were also the scene of a bear-hunt at a later period. Two of the oystermen, George G. Bartlett, or, as we used to call him, Tom Bartlett, and Stephen Marshall, were one day going round the Point at about half tide, when a large portion of the rocks are bare, when they discovered a half-grown cub on the outer rocks, and, hastily hauling their boat ashore, they got between the bear and the land, and attempted to catch him. Steve had a boat-hook, with which he manfully approached the animal, who felt not a little surprised at his position. Tom had an oar. Their object was to drive the bear into the water, and then keep him off shore till he was exhausted, when they hoped to secure him. But Bruin was not to be so easily taken. After wasting about an hour and gaining no advantage, Stephen rushed up to give the animal a punch with the boat-hook, but he slipped when close up, and in a second the bear broke the boat-hook to atoms, and tore the frock off Marshall's back, who roared out most lustily for Bartlett to aid him. The bear, however, did no more damage, but let him go, which he did in a hurry, never stopping till he had reached his house, screaming and roaring all the way, " Turn out, boys! turn out! Tom Bartlett has been killed by a bear at Stony Point!" This roused up the men of the beach, who ran to Bartlett's assistance, and found him coolly tumbling the bear into his boat, having shot him with a revolver. Marshall was often rallied on his running away, when he always replied, " Well, boys, but I *was* scared, that's a fact!"

Walter and myself, after a deal of cutting among the vines and bushes, came to the old canoes, which had evidently been there many years. They had been used as coffins for the dead, according to the usual custom of the Coast Indians, who place their dead in canoes, which are elevated on four posts, and resting on horizontal bars running through holes mortised in the tops of the posts.

While thus engaged, we attempted to clamber over what we supposed to be a small mound, which was covered with wild currant bushes. As we took hold of these to aid us, they gave way, and we discovered the mound to be an old canoe of large dimensions, which, years before, had fallen from its perch in the air, and had been overgrown by moss and bushes. On turning the canoe over, we discovered under it a small canoe containing the body of an Indian in a complete state of

BEAR-FIGHT ON STONY POINT.

preservation. It looked like a dried mummy. In the canoe, also, were the skeletons of two children, and a lot of beads, brass wrist-rings, and other trinkets. We took out some of the ornaments, and covered the whole up as we had found it. This mummy was afterward visited by every man nearly in the Bay, and several months or a year afterward it was boxed up by Russell, who claimed to have discovered it, and shipped by him to San Francisco, where it excited the wonder and admiration of the quidnuncs, and learned opinions and lengthy dissertations were delivered to show that the North American Indians understood the process of embalming bodies; and one writer went so far as to assert that the veins of this specimen had been injected with pitch. Now my own opinion is simply this: the man, at the time of his death, was much emaciated, and being placed in a current of pure air, that is always fresh at Stony Point, had simply dried up; and this opinion is based on the fact that, during the summer months, all along the Pacific coast the air is very pure and dry. Meat, when placed in the open air, where there is a good circulation, does not putrefy, but dries. I have also made diligent inquiry among the Indians, who have invariably assured me that they knew of no preserving process, and they thought as I did, that the body had dried. There is a peculiarly preservative quality in the land round the Bay. It abounds in silex, which is held in solution, forming petrifactions of various kinds. Agates and cornelians of great beauty are common, and many fossil remains are to be met with.

Some time after this, a young Indian died near my residence, and was placed by his relatives in a large camphor-wood chest, and buried in the sand, where the body remained one year, when it was taken up to be reburied across the Bay, and on opening the chest, the corpse was

D

found as perfect as the day it was buried. Now, if I had sent that specimen to San Francisco without comment, the wise men and philosophers would have been as badly puzzled as they were by the mummy.

I had one more incident occur to me at Stony Point shortly after this. I was going through the rocks with a barrel of beef in my canoe during a heavy squall, when a sea struck her, and she capsized, and the barrel and myself were thrown overboard. I managed, fortunately, to get on the rocks, and got hold of the canoe as she came drifting past, righted her, and paddled her round the Point into calm water, where I bailed her out, and went to the house for a dry suit. I found the beef at low tide the next day.

Russell having returned to take charge of his own affairs, the captain and myself concluded to take a claim, and try our luck at the oysters, which were then selling at a good price, two dollars per basket being asked and obtained.

Old Toke, learning my intentions, offered to show me a good place, and taking his canoe, with Peter, a young fellow in his lodge, to assist, he paddled me to a little stream called the Querquelin, or Mouse River. This is a creek emptying into the Bay about two miles south of Russell's house, and half way between it and the Palux. I had frequently passed by this river without supposing there was any thing more than a mere brook. Quite a cove making in at that point, the distance from the usual direct line of boats passing up or down the Bay to the mouth of the creek was so great, that no one, unless they had especial business, ever thought of going in there, and I was astonished to find a fine stream, about two hundred feet wide, which ran close under a precipitous cliff, a hundred feet high, covered thickly with spruce and fir, and at the water's edge with black alder. On

QUEQUELIN RIVER, AND RESIDENCE OF J. G. SWAN.

the other or north side of the stream was a fine level prairie, containing five or six acres of marsh, and as many more of elevated land above the reach of the highest tides. Two acres of this land was clear of trees, and had been formerly the site of an Indian village. Back of this cleared spot, a fine grove of spruce trees sheltered the place from the north wind. The western side was open to the Bay, with a clear view of the Pacific, and of the two entrances to the Bay. The river wound round this point in the form of a horse-shoe, and then threaded its way through a rich prairie for eight or nine miles, when it forked into two small brooks. This place, from its peculiar position, had always been a favorite residence with the Indians; but the chief having died, the village was deserted, the houses burned down, and the whole grown over with rose-bushes, blackberry vines, wild gooseberry, and a most luxuriant crop of nettles and ferns.

Toke told me that the Indians were afraid to go back there to live on account of the dead people; but if a white man went there they would go back too, for the dead people, *memelose tillicums*, were afraid of the whites. I was very much pleased with the locality, and on my return agreed with the captain to move down there. On the first of May we took possession, and I was perfectly delighted with the place. As no saw-mill had then commenced operation (although Captain Weldon was at work on his), we had to do as well as we could for a shelter. The brig Potomac being then in the Bay, I purchased of the captain a spare topsail, with which we made us a famous tent, or sail house, as the Indians called it. It was a very comfortable place, and we soon commenced operations. Although so early in the season as the first of May, the nettles and ferns were three feet high. However, we cut and slashed among them, getting most woefully stung, and in the course of a few days, had a place cleared away large enough to plant some potatoes, squashes, beans, and other vegetables. The soil was the richest kind of loam, but it had a great many shells in it, and there were heaps and mounds of shells containing thousands of bushels, the accumulation of years of the refuse of the Indians. The ground was full of all kinds of insects, bumble-bees, spiders, ants, beetles, cut - worms, and caterpillars, which, however, wanted only a year or two stirring-up to be banished. We soon had a garden planted, and now turned our attention to oysters. As soon as the Indians found the place was inhabited, they flocked there in numbers, and we had our hands full of trade. They preferred coming to us, as the place was easy of access at all times of tide, and, in case of any gale, their canoes were perfectly safe in the smooth water of the river, which was not so down the beach with the other settlers; for at high tides, in storms, the swell of the Pacific would roll into the Bay, making quite a surf on the beach, often smashing up boats and canoes, and creating considerable damage. Among the Indians who came to the Bay to work was a chief of the Queniült Indians, a tribe who live on the banks of a river of the same name, which empties into the Pacific five miles north of Point Grenville, or about sixty miles north of Shoal-water Bay. This tribe is considered a very hostile race by the other Indians, and numerous massacres have been committed by them on the white traders in earlier times. The chief, whose name is Kape, was accompanied by two of his sons and a large party of his people. He came in a large canoe, which he wished to sell me, and as I wanted one of that description, I purchased his. The old fellow remained with me a couple of weeks, and we formed a great friend-ship for each other. His sons were the finest-looking

Indians I have ever seen. The oldest, whose name is Wamalsh, was about twenty-two years old, six feet high, and most perfectly proportioned. The younger, named Wy Yellock, a lad of eighteen, although much shorter, was full as well proportioned, and very handsome. Neither Kape or his sons could understand a word of the Chenook language, and I had to employ an Indian to interpret. He was also a Qŭeniŭlt, and came with Kape. His name was Hait-lilth, and called by the whites John. He had been with some person from Oregon to the California mines, and could talk very good English. They all stopped with us in our tent, sharing our meals, and sleeping on mats. They were very pleasant, quiet, and well behaved. John, who was the spokesman, was quite intelligent and full of anecdotes, which helped to make the time pass very agreeably. This visit was the foundation of a friendship with Kape and his tribe, which lasted unbroken during my residence in the Territory. The canoe which I had purchased was a beauty. She was *forty-six feet long* and *six feet wide*, and had thirty Indians in her when she crossed the bar at the mouth of the Bay. She was the largest canoe that had been brought from up the coast, although the Indians round Vancouver's and Queen Charlotte's Islands have canoes capable of carrying one hundred warriors. These canoes are beautiful specimens of naval architecture. Formed of a single log of cedar, they present a model of which a white mechanic might well be proud.

CHENOOK CANOE BOUGHT FROM KAPE.

VANCOUVER ISLAND AND CLALAM CANOE.

COWLITZ CANOE.

QUENIŬLT PADDLE.

The other canoes are the forms used by the Indians
about Fuca Straits and farther north, as being best adapted for rough water, and the Cowlitz canoe, which is
mostly used on the rivers of the interior. The broad
bow of the latter form is to enable the Indian to have a
firm footing while he uses his pole to force the canoe
over the rapids. The paddle is the shape used by the
Indians in deep water, and is different from the Chenook
paddle, which is notched at the end.

The manufacture of a canoe is a work of great moment
with these Indians. It is not every man among them
that can make a canoe, but some are, like our white mechanics, more expert than their neighbors. A suitable
tree is first selected, which in all cases is the cedar, and
then cut down. This job was formerly a formidable
one, as the tree was chipped around with stone chisels,
after the fashion adopted by beavers, and looks as if
gnawed off. At present, however, they understand the
use of the axe, and many are expert choppers. When

the tree is down, it is first stripped of its bark, then cut off into the desired length, and the upper part split off with little wedges, till it is reduced to about two thirds the original height of the log. The bows and stern are then chopped into a rough shape, and enough cut out of the inside to lighten it so that it can be easily turned. When all is ready, the log is turned bottom up, and the Indian goes to work to fashion it out. This he does with no instrument of measurement but his eye, and so correct is that, that when he has done his hewing no one could detect the least defect. When the outside is formed and rough-hewn, the log is again turned, and the inside cut out with the axe. This operation was formerly done by fire, but the process was slow and tedious. During the chopping the Indian frequently ascertains the thickness of the sides by placing one hand on the outside and the other on the inside. The canoe is now again turned bottom up, and the whole smoothed off with a peculiar-shaped chisel, used something after the manner of a cooper's adze. This is a very tiresome job, and takes a long time. Then the inside is finished, and the canoe now has to be stretched into shape. It is first nearly filled with water, into which hot stones are thrown, and a fire at the same time of bark is built outside. This in a short time renders the wood so supple that the centre can be spread open at the top from six inches to a foot. This is kept in place by sticks or stretchers, similar to the method of a boat's thwarts. The ends of these stretchers are fastened by means of withes made from the taper ends of cedar limbs, twisted and used instead of cords. When all is finished, the water is emptied out, and then the stem and head-pieces are put on. These are carved from separate sticks, and are fastened on by means of withes and wooden pegs or tree-nails. After the inside is finished to the satisfaction of the maker, the canoe is again turned, and the charred part, occasioned by the bark fire, is rubbed with stones to make the bottom as smooth as possible, when the whole outside is painted over with a black mixture made of burned rushes and whale oil. The inside is also painted red with a mixture of red ochre and oil. The edges all round are studded with little shells, which are the valve joint of the common snail, and, when brass-headed nails can be obtained, they are used in profusion. This description I give is of the making of a canoe near my house, and I saw the progress every day, from the time the tree was cut down till the canoe was finished. This was a medium sized canoe, and took three months to finish it.

As old Kape was an excellent shot, we frequently went out for seals, which abound in the Bay. At such times some of the party would stop on the flats to gather crabs, while others were engaged in catching turbot and flounders. This is very good sport for the Indians. These fish are found in the little pools of water on the flats which have been left by the receding tide. The crabs, which are of a large size, very fat, and of delicious flavor, are plentiful in the spring and early part of summer. We would gather them by the bushel, and when boiled I think them superior to any lobster or craw-fish I have ever eaten. When the Indians catch them they break off the shell, saving only the claw part. This method not only reduces the bulk to be carried, but most effectually cures the biting propensities of these crabs, who can give a pretty severe nip. I was with old Toke one day, and, while wading in one of these pools, a large crab seized him by the heel, which it bit so severely as to draw blood. Old Toke was frantic, and, seizing the crab with both hands, threw it far on the flats; then rushing up, he jumped on it till it was smashed to atoms, uttering all the time the most violent expressions of rage.

The turbot and flounders are caught while wading in the water by means of the feet. The Indian wades along slowly, and, as soon as he feels a fish with his feet, he steps quickly on it and holds it firmly till he can reach hold of it with his hand, when he gives it a jerk, and away it flies far into the flats. This process is repeated till enough fish are caught, when they are picked up, put in a basket, and carried to the canoe. The turbot are much like the English turbot, but smaller; the largest I have ever seen weighed twenty pounds. The flounders are similar to those of the Atlantic at New York or Boston. They are easily taken by this method of the Indians, as their rough backs prevent them slipping from under the feet. The catching affords a deal of fun, as usually quite a number are engaged in the sport, and their splashing, slipping, screaming, and laughing make a lively time. These fish, like all the fish in the Bay, are very fine and well flavored.

Whenever Kape would shoot a seal, which was often, the bullet-hole was first stopped up to save the blood, and as soon as the animal was brought ashore, the following process was invariably adopted. A couple of round logs, eight or ten inches in diameter, were laid parallel to each other, a foot or two apart, and between them kindled a brisk fire of dry chips. The seal is then laid across the logs over the blaze, and, commencing at the nose, the whole body is rolled over and over till all the hair is thoroughly singed off. The skin, which is, by this process, pretty well roasted, is scraped clean with a shell or knife. The blubber is next cut off in strips, which are boiled in water, and the oil skimmed off with shells. After it has settled and cooled, it is poured into a bottle (as they call it), made of the paunch of the ani-

mal blown up like a bladder, and dried.   In every lodge
may be seen these bladder-like bottles, and the more
an Indian has the greater his wealth.   The meat, which
is dark, is boiled with the blood, which they are particular to save, and, when cooked, is tender, and not very
unpalatable.   The liver, particularly, of a young seal is
very nice, and, when fried with pork, resembles hog's
liver.   The oil is eaten freely with all their food, and,
when freshly boiled, is as sweet and free from fishy flavor
as lard.

Toke's method of killing seals was by the spear.   This
is the ancient style, and, as old Toke had been famous
for his prowess among these animals, he chose to retain
the style of weapons he had been most accustomed to.
The staff of his spear was about twenty feet long, made
of fir or yew.   The head of the spear, made like a salmon spear, but larger, was attached to a line thirty
fathoms long, and of a size known on shipboard as a
hand lead-line.   With this armament the old savage
would sally forth, and proceed to some sand island to
the leeward of the seals, who are always, at low tide,
seen basking in the sun, particularly in the spring, when
the young ones are about.   Having fastened his canoe
and divested himself of his clothes, with one end of the
line fastened round his body, and the rest coiled up on
his left arm, he goes into the water, with the spear firmly grasped in his right hand, and floating just under the
surface of the water.   No part of his person, except the
face and top of his head, could be seen, and the hair
floating round made him look very much like a seal.
Cautiously and slowly he gets between the seal and the
deep water ; then wading ashore, careful to keep his
body submerged till he is near enough, he suddenly rises
up, and, darting his spear into the body of the animal,
runs back on the sand, and, setting his heels firmly,

braces himself up for the contest.   He lets but little line
out at first, and, if he is the strongest, easily gains the
mastery.   But with a large old male a fierce struggle ensues, and it is sometimes attended with the loss of the
line ; but generally the old fellow comes out victorious.
When the animal is dead, the first thing is to stop up
the spear-hole with a wooden plug, or a bunch of grass
or fern, which is always carried in the canoe for the
purpose.   The prize is then carried home, and the same
process gone through as before mentioned.   Toke, like
all other Indians I have met with, never ate any thing
before he left home on these seal hunts, and sometimes
he would be twenty-four hours without food.   He said
it made him feel lazy, and he would wonder why I always insisted on eating my breakfast before starting off
on these early morning expeditions.

The large clams and quahaugs are more prized by the
Indians than oysters.   The large clam called by them
metár or smetár are found in the sand about a foot deep.
Their long snouts or necks thrust up to the surface in-
dicate their position.   They are then dug up by scrap-
ing away the sand with the hand, a process in which the
squaws are particularly expert.   The quahaug or hard-
shell clam, called by them clolum, is found near the surface, and in some locations perfectly bare.   These clams
are cured for use as follows : the smetár is opened with
a knife, and the clams stuck on skewers holding about
two dozen ; these are then washed clean, drained, and
dried in smoke.   The *clolum* is opened by being heaped
on stones previously heated, then covered with sea-weed
and mats.   The water contained in the clam runs down
on the hot stones, causing steam, which, being confined
by the mats and sea-weed, soon cooks the whole pile,
containing usually from ten to twenty bushels.   From
twenty minutes to three quarters of an hour are gen-

erally occupied in performing the operation, and the coverings are then removed.   The shells, now being open, are easily separated, and the meat stuck on skewers, like the *metár*, and dried in the smoke.   These dried clams are a great article of trade with the Indians of the interior, and quantities are annually carried from Shoal-water Bay up the Columbia.   When these clams are first taken out of the steaming heap they are most delicious, very tender and sweet, but after they are dried they are rather tough chewing.   They are usually cooked by boiling them, when they get a little softer, and taste pretty well, particularly to a hungry person, the smoky flavor being no objection.   My favorite method of cooking these shell-fish was to make a chowder of the quahogs, and, after cleaning the great sea clam, roll them in meal, and fry them with salt pork.   The long sand clam or razor-fish was also cooked by frying.   Another clam, resembling the common clam of Massachusetts in shape, is also found, and usually eaten raw by the Indians. This is called by them aryuk, and, fried in batter, is very nice.   There are several varieties of mussels found, one of which, a white-meated one, grows singly on the flats near the oyster-beds.   Whenever I could obtain these mussels, which are not very plenty, I always found them preferable to oysters.   Some other varieties of mussel grow in immense beds, and, by making shoals, are a nuisance to the oystermen, whose boats frequently get aground on them, and have to wait sometimes six or eight hours for the return tide.   These mussels, although eaten by the Indians, are not very good, and are seldom partaken of by the whites; still, I never heard of any ill effects attending their use as food.

The common barnacle grows very large on the old logs about the Bay and up the coast.   Some of the Indians, particularly the Queniülts, are very fond of them, but I never saw any of the Bay Indians use them. In the creeks that run into the Bay a small crab is taken in great quantities, which are boiled by the Indians and eaten, shells and all. These shell-fish are not taken during the winter months, and then, if the Indian has been improvident or neglectful of his winter supplies, he is at times reduced to great distress. But as soon as the weather begins to get a little warm, which it does in February or March, he is no longer in want. Vegetation starts very early and grows rapidly. A variety of roots and plants are eaten. The stalks of the cow parsnip and the wild celery are eaten raw. The outer skin is first peeled off, and the tender and aromatic vegetable forms a very grateful addition to the dried salmon eggs which are now brought on for food. The leaves of the yellow dock are boiled, then bruised up into a pulp, and eaten with sugar or molasses, if they can be obtained, or else with oil. The root of the common skunk cabbage, after being boiled and partially deprived of its acrid properties, is eaten with avidity, but I was never very partial to the dish. The most pleasant, cooling, and healthy vegetable is the sprout of the wild raspberry (*Rubus spectablis*). This shoots up with great rapidity, seeming to grow as fast as asparagus. These sprouts are collected in bundles and brought into the lodge, where they are denuded of their tough outer skin, and the centre is as crisp and tender as a cucumber, and, being slightly acid, is delicious. They are slightly astringent ; and as the herring begin to make their appearance at the same time, and from their oily nature, and the immoderate manner in which the Indians eat them, are apt to produce disorders of the bowels, the sprouts, being freely eaten at the same time, counteract the effect. So with the berry of this plant, which is ripe in June, when the salmon begin to be taken in the Columbia. This fruit, which is called the salmon-berry, and is found in the greatest abundance, is also beneficial to counteract any ill effects that might be occasioned by inordinate eating of the rich salmon.   There is also another variety of the raspberry (*Rubus odoratus*), but its fruit is inferior, and of but little account.   Its blossoms differ from those east of the Rocky Mountains, being white instead of pink.

Among the different roots eaten by the Indians in the Bay are three varieties of fern, which are cooked by baking.   The root of the common cat-tail flag is eaten raw, and I found it, sliced with vinegar, very palatable.   Small roots resembling snake-root in appearance, but without flavor, when cooked by boiling are dry and mealy, and are eaten with oil.   The root of a species of rush, found on the sea-shore, of the size of a walnut, is eaten either raw or baked ; its taste raw is similar to the Jerusalem artichokes, and baked resembles a mealy potato. There is also a plant of the Mesembryanthemum species, with a root like a yam, which, baked or boiled, is excellent.   This, also, is found on the sea-side, in the sand near the beach.   As the season advances and the fruits ripen, great quantities are used as food, to the exclusion of fish and meats.   The dry, mealy berries of the Arbutus uva ursi, or bear-berry, are bruised and eaten with oil, and the dried leaves, called quer-lo-e-chintl, are smoked like tobacco.   The salmon-berry just mentioned is the first fruit ripe, and is soon followed by strawberries, great quantities of which are found in the plains of the peninsula, and in all the prairie lands on or near the coast.   Then comes the whortleberry, blueberry, and a beautiful coral-red berry like a currant, called red whortleberry, but of a different character.   This fruit tastes like and resembles the common red currant, and I think, by cultivation, it would make not only a beautiful and ornamental shrub, but the quantity and quality of the fruit would be improved. Blackberries, gooseberries, and wild black currants next follow, and then comes the sallal (*Gaultheria Shallon*). This beautiful evergreen shrub may be found varying in height from two feet to ten. The leaf is a dark green, like the laurel; the bark on the smaller limbs and twigs is red, or of a reddish-brown. The flowers are in clusters, like the currant, having from fourteen to twenty-one on one stem. The fruit, when ripe, is a very dark purple, almost black, rough on the outside, very juicy, and of a sweetish, slightly acid taste, and of the size of large buck-shot. It is excellent cooked in any form, and is dried by the Indians, and pressed into cakes containing some five or six pounds, which are covered with leaves and rushes, so as to exclude the air, and then put away in a dry place for winter's use. This plant continues to blossom till late in December in certain localities, although it has but one crop, which is ripe in August. The wild crab-apple also grows in abundance, and is eaten by the Indians after being simply boiled. These apples are very small, of an oval shape, with a long stem, and grow in clusters of from six to ten. The cranberry, which is very plentiful, and forms quite an article of traffic between the whites and Indians, is next in season, and is followed by a species of whortleberry, called by the Indians shot-berries, which last till December, when the rains beat the fruit off the bushes. The berries grow in clusters, and resemble the prim. The leaf is small, of oval shape, with finely-serrated edges. It is also an excellent berry, and, if kept dry and cool, can be preserved fresh for several months. It is, however, usually dried by the Indians, and eaten early in the spring, before the other berries begin to ripen.

On the Columbia River, an excellent root, called the

wappatoo, which is the bulb of the common Saggitafolia, or arrow-head, is found in abundance, and is a favorite food of the wild swans, which are very plentiful. The wappatoo is an article much sought after by the interior Indians, but there is none found on the coast, except in very small quantities. The *Cammasia esculenta* is found all over both territories, and is known by various names. The Indians call it *La Cammass*, which is the name taught them by the early French voyageurs. This is spelled by different writers as Kammæus, Lackamas, Camarus, Camash, and Kamas, but they all mean the same. Every tribe, in its own peculiar language, has a different name for this root; but in conversation with the whites, they use the Jargon, or trade language, which is a barbarous mixture of Chenook, English, and French; and if writers of Indian Jargon words would but consider their origin, they would not be so liable to such wide differences in their method of spelling.

This root, which resembles an onion in appearance, is a species of lily, found in moist places on the prairies. After the plant has done flowering, or when the Indians consider it ripe, which is usually in September and October, the root is dug up by the squaws, who go out in parties for the purpose, and are generally absent several days. After sufficient has been collected, the leaves and loose outhusks are removed, and the whole roasted on hot stones. The method is as follows: A large pile of dry wood is made, on the top of which a quantity of stones are piled; fire is then applied, and kept up till all the wood is burned, leaving nothing but the hot stones and ashes. Fern-leaves are then laid on the stones, and on these mats are placed; the cammass-roots are then placed on the mats, and spread level; water is then thrown over them, and immediately they are covered with mats, blankets, and the whole covered up with sand,

every care being taken to keep in all the steam.   This
heap is allowed to remain till it is cold, which, according
to the size of the fire and the quantity of roots used, va-
ries from twelve to twenty-four hours.   The roots then
are soft and very sweet, much like a baked sweet potato.
The natives preserve them by pressing them into loaves,
which, when eaten, are cut in slices like pudding.   I
never have met with a white person who was not fond
of baked cammass, and I do not know any vegetable, except fried bananas, so delicious.   There are, undoubtedly, many other roots, fruits, and vegetables eaten by the
Indians, but I do not recollect any others except those
mentioned.

Old Kape and his sons were good hunters, and every
season came to the Bay laden with furs, which they carried to the store of the Hudson Bay Company at Chenook, on the Columbia River.   The most valuable skins
they brought were the sea-otter, which they shoot in
considerable quantities at Point Grenville, on the coast,
about sixty miles north of Shoal-water Bay.   The sea-
otter is the most valuable of the fur animals taken on
the Pacific coast, those to the north of the Columbia being considered of more value than those taken south and
along the coast of California.

In Jewett's narrative of a three years' residence among
the savages at Nootka, in 1803–6, he gives the following
description: " The sea-otter is nearly five feet in length,
exclusive of the tail, which is about twelve inches long,
and is very thick and broad where it joins the body, but
gradually tapers to the end, which is tipped with white.
The color of the rest is a shining, silky black, with the
exception of a broad white stripe on the top of the head.
Nothing can be more beautiful than one of these animals
when seen swimming, especially when on the look-out
for any object.   At such times it raises its head quite

above the surface, and the contrast between the shining black and white, together with its sharp ears, and a long tuft of hair rising from the middle of its forehead, which look like three small horns, render it a novel and attractive object.

" The skin is held in great estimation in China, more especially that of the tail, which is finer and closer set than that on the body.

" The value of a skin is determined by its size, that being considered as a prime skin which will reach in length from a man's chin to his feet.

".The food of the sea-otter is fish, which he is very dexterous in taking, being an excellent swimmer, with feet webbed like those of a goose."

At the time Jewett was on the coast, fire-arms had not come into general use, the bow and spear being the weapons. The otters then were not at all shy, and might be seen at any time swimming about. He mentions seeing the old ones with their young, like so many rats, frolicking and sporting about in the most lively manner. They usually have four young ones at a time, born early in the spring. The sea-otter is never found in fresh water, or in any of the rivers of the interior. Like the seal, its home is in the salt water, and its haunts about the rocks and ledges of the coast.

The river-otter, which abounds all over the Territory, may be taken easily either by traps, or by hunting with dogs, or shooting. I have had good sport chasing otters, for, once get them out of the water, although almost as spry as a cat, they are no match for a dog in speed; but they are very savage when at bay, and, unless a dog is well trained, he is very likely to be hurt. These otters breed in holes either under some old stump or in the side of a hill, always being sure to have such ready access to the water that they can take to it on the least alarm.

SEA-OTTER HUNT.

The beaver is also found in incredible numbers, but as a description can be had in any work on natural history, I will merely subjoin the following extract from Lewis and Clarke's description, which may interest some.

" The beaver of this country is large and fat. The flesh is very palatable, and at our table was a real luxury. On the 7th of January, 1806, our hunter found a beaver in his traps, of which he made a bait for taking others. This bait will entice a beaver to the trap as far as he can smell it, and this may fairly be stated to be at the distance of a mile, as their sense of smelling is very acute. To prepare beaver-bait, the castor or bark-stone is first gently pressed from the bladder-like bag which contains it into a vial of four ounces with a wide mouth. Five or six of these stones are taken, to which must be added a nutmeg, a dozen or fifteen cloves, and thirty grains of cinnamon, finely pulverized and stirred together, and as much ardent spirits added as will make the whole to the consistency of mustard. This must be carefully corked, as it soon loses its efficacy on exposure to the air. The scent becomes much stronger in four or five days after its preparation, and, with proper caution, will retain its efficacy for months. Any strong aromatic spices will answer, their sole virtue being to give variety and pungency to the scent of the bark-stone.

" The male beaver has six stones, two of which contain a substance like finely pulverized bark, of a pale yellow color, and are called bark-stones or castor. Two others, which, like the bark-stones, resemble small bladders, contain pure strong oil, and are called oil-stones. The other two are the testicles."

Formerly the Americans had a very extensive trade for furs on the Northwest Coast, and this was carried on principally by the merchants of Boston. The Indians, hearing the name of Boston so often repeated, supposed that to be the name of the country these people and ships came from; consequently, all Americans are to this day called by the Northwest Coast Indians *Boston tillicums*, or Boston people. English, Scotch, and Irish are called King George people, and the French, Passaieux. The derivation of this last term I do not understand, but it is undoubtedly an Indian corruption of some Canadian French patois word. This Northwest fur trade has been gradually taken from the Americans by that grasping monopoly and incubus on all attempts at American enterprise in the Territory, the Hudson Bay Company, who will be noticed more at length in another chapter.

Whenever Kape or any of the Queniŭlt people came down with their furs, they usually called at my place, as it was convenient for them to stop at to rest themselves before they proceeded to the Columbia River, some forty miles distant. Kape generally, on such occasions, would remain all night. After supper he would open his sacks of skins and display the rich furs, with the expectation of inducing me to trade; for, if he could make a sale in the Bay, it saved him the trouble of a long journey to Chenook and back. However, not desiring to purchase, I contented myself with looking over his assortment, with the desire to gain information, and to see the variety of furs found along the coast. He seldom brought any others than the sea and river otter and beaver, but occasionally he had a few mink, sable, silver and red fox, and black bear skins.

The whole coast region is full of fur animals, which have wonderfully increased during the last twelve or fifteen years, from the fact that the Hudson Bay Company, having turned their attention to agricultural and mill purposes in their possessions around the Columbia, have not held out inducements to the Indians to procure furs, being more inclined to require their services in catching salmon, or working among the lumber or on the farms, trusting to the other portions of their vast territories for their supplies of fur; hence there has been but little trapping or hunting in the whole Territory from the Columbia to Fuca Straits, and wild animals have increased very fast as a consequence.

CHAPTER VII.

Visit to the Columbia River.—Our Troubles while crossing the Portage.—Description of the Beach around Baker's Bay to Chenook.—Scarborough's Hill.—Captain Scarborough.—The Priest's House at Chenook.—Bill M'Carty or Brandywine.—Salmon-fishing at Chenook.—Splendid View of Mount Saint Helen's.—Description of the Salmon and of the Fishery.—Indian Customs on the first Appearance of Salmon.—The present Remnant of the Chenook Tribe.—Description of Chenook Village.—Its favorable Location.—Washington Hall, Esq., the Postmaster.—Indian Lodges.—A Description of the method of building them.—Our Return home, and the funny Scenes we passed through.—Old Champ and his Fish.

ALTHOUGH I had been for several months a resident of Shoal-water Bay, I had not seen the Columbia, and, having an opportunity, I started in a sail-boat on Friday, June 3d, in company with Mr. F. Rotan (the owner of a schooner then loading in the Bay, and who was going to Astoria to take the steamer for San Francisco), John W. Champ, and a young man named Baldt. It was nearly high tide, and the wind was blowing a fine breeze from the west, when the boat with the three individuals came up the little river, and requested me to go with them. I was not long getting ready, and we were soon under weigh, going along at a fine rate. Champ remarked that, with the breeze we then had, we would reach Wilson's house at the portage before sundown, and then, crossing over to M'Carty's house, on the other side of the portage, could take a canoe, which would carry us

E

down the Wappalooche, or Chenook River, to its mouth, where we would land and walk to Chenook Beach. As we could not expect to perform this feat that night, we proposed stopping at M'Carty's, and start early in the morning.

We had a very pleasant sail for seventeen miles till we reached Long Island, when the wind began to die away, and by the time we reached Round Island, at the mouth of Bear River, it fell dead calm, and we were obliged to take the oars, and pull up the river against the tide, which was now running strong ebb. We had about three miles to go before reaching Wilson's house; but it was now past sundown, and the wind, which had been from the west and northwest all day, now blew from the southeast in short puffs, with every indication of rain. As night closed in, it grew intensely dark, and it was with difficulty we reached the landing at Wilson's, and not till ten o'clock.

Before we were all ashore it began to rain, and, to crown all, we found the house closed, the family having gone to Chenook to attend the fishery for salmon, which had just commenced. Rotan, who had been over the portage before and had stopped at the house, knew how to open the door, and we all went in; but there was neither wood cut, nor axe to cut with; so we were obliged to go out and feel round under the trees for some dry branches and chips. While engaged in this occupation, old Champ slipped on a clay bank, and slid, otter fashion, plump into the spring, from whence he emerged wet, muddy, and angry. However, we managed to get some wood and make a roaring blaze, and, while old Champ was drying his clothes, the rest of us, having found some salt salmon and potatoes, and an iron pot, made out to boil a mess for supper, which we ate with a good appetite, and then lay down to sleep, Rotan and Baldt sleep-

ing in a bed which was in the front room, and Champ
and myself rolled up in blankets before the fire, the old
man having taken the precaution to hang his clothes up
in the fireplace to dry, where also the others had set their
boots and placed their hats for the same purpose. I was
tired, and slept very soundly till toward morning, when I
was waked up by a stream of water running through a
hole in the roof directly into my ear. I found that it
was storming violently, and the rain pouring down in
torrents. Champ declared he had been kept awake all
night by a bush-tailed rat, who was performing a waltz
in an old tin baker which was on a table near by. The
old fellow, however, was pretty comfortable, as his head
was out of the wet. Thinking it time to get up, he reached his hand into the fireplace for his pants, and was disgusted and enraged to find that a stream of water had
been running directly through them and into his boots,
which were full. The fireplace was a bed of mud. The
pot of fish and potatoes left from our supper of last
night was spoiled, and the boots and hats of Rotan and
Baldt were drenched. I had slept with my clothes on,
so the rain had not troubled me, and I came out perfectly dry. Although we were far from a merry mood, we
could not help laughing at the intense indignation of
Champ, who squeezed the water from his pantaloons
with any thing but expressions of pleasure. As it was
impossible to build a fire, we started off for a tramp over
the portage to M'Carty's house, where we hoped to get
some breakfast. The road was the one made by Mr. J.
L. Brown, and was a mere cart-path, full of stumps and
logs, over high hills and down deep valleys, soft from the
rain, and nearly knee-deep with mud and water. Over
this trail we climbed, and slipped, and splashed, and
jumped, till finally we emerged from the woods at M'Carty's house, covered with mud, and wet to the skin from

rain and the wet bushes we had passed through. M'Car-ty and his people were also absent at Chenook, catching salmon; but an old hump-backed squaw in a lodge near by, who had remained to take care of the pigs and chickens, gave us a breakfast of broiled fish, cold water, and hard bread, while we dried our clothes at the lodge fire. While waiting for the tide, which was out, the rain ceased, and the wind, changing to the west, gave assurance of a pleasant day; and by the time the tide was up enough to float the canoe, the sun shone out bright and warm, serving to cheer our spirits and dry our clothes, which were still somewhat damp, notwithstanding the smoke and heat of the fire in the lodge. The squaw carried us down to the mouth of the river, where we landed at the house of Mr. George Dawson, who had, like the rest of the settlers, gone to Chenook to fish. We had now to walk nine miles to reach the village, and our road lay for the whole distance over the beach; but the tide rising very fast, and with a heavy surf from the effects of the storm the previous evening, we were obliged to keep high up among the drift logs and loose sand, which impeded our progress, so that we did not reach the village till late in the afternoon.

The beach from the Wappalooche River to Chenook Point forms the eastern side of Baker's Bay, at the mouth of the Columbia River. The view from this beach, looking westward, is directly out to sea. On the right, in the distance, Cape Disappointment, a bluff, rocky promontory, rears its weather-beaten and forbidding-looking front, and to the left the low sand-spit, called Point Adams, stretches far out into the river, while midway between the two capes lies a sand-island covered with drift logs, timber, and the *debris* of the saw-mills up the river. All along the beach we were walking, the drift stuff of the river formed a continued row at high-water mark, where it had been thrown by the waves, and left by the receding tide.

Huge trees that had been torn up by the roots, timber that had been prepared for the mill, logs of spruce, fir, cedar, and ash, sycamore and cottonwood, with boards, and joist, and scantling, were mixed in most inextricable confusion, and in a manner that nothing but the waves of ocean could have effected. As we approached Chenook Point, the tide had fallen enough to enable us to walk on firmer sand, and far enough down to clear all the drift stuff. As we turned the Point, the beautiful green hill known as Scarborough's Hill presented itself to our view. This hill, which is one of the most prominent objects seen while entering the Columbia, and which has the appearance of a green field, is a clearing which has been made either by accident or design, and is thickly covered with fern. Captain James Scarborough, the owner of the claim, had for many years been in the employ of the Hudson Bay Company as master of one of their vessels trading on the coast, and, having left their service and taken a claim at Chenook, was officiating as river pilot to the mail steamers from California. The captain had a fine farm, with excellent fruit-trees, and a large herd of cattle. Like all old sea-captains, he was fond of his own opinion, and was looked upon as a sort of oracle by the neighbors, and particularly by those who, like himself, had formerly been in the Company's employ. Although he claimed to be an American citizen, as did also all these former employés of the Company, yet they never could forget the time when the Hudson Bay people held undisputed sway, and they looked upon the advent of the trading, swapping Yankees from across the plains with peculiar aversion, and lost no occasion to prejudice the minds of the Indians against the Boston tillicums, as all Americans are designated. Still the old captain was a good man. He had received a good education, and always knew when he met a gentleman, and to any such he was at all times most courteous. He had good cause for his antipathy against the American population, having been swindled by some sharpers out of large sums of money at different times.

Passing by Captain Scarborough's house, we next came to the dwelling of the Catholic priest, called by the Indians Le Plate, being as near as they can pronounce the French Le Pretre. This priest, who was a Frenchman, had resided at Chenook for several years, devoting his time to the conversion of the Indians, but with indifferent success, the whole known fruits of his labors consisting in the various names he had baptized them with. This fact he afterward acknowledged in a letter written by him, on his return to France, to the postmaster of Chenook.

We now drew near the village proper, which consisted of some twelve or fourteen houses, occupied by whites, and nearly the same number of Indian lodges. It was in the beginning of the salmon season, and every one, from the priest to the Indians, was engaged in the fishery. Champ, who was our pilot, took us directly to M'Carty's quarters, who had a nice zinc house, and was driving a smart business in the fishery. M'Carty soon had an excellent meal of fresh salmon set before us, which, with hard bread, and coffee with milk—a luxury I had not seen for months—enabled us to suppress our feelings of hunger which our walk on the beach had produced.

Old Bill M'Carty, or, as he was called, old Brandywine, from having formerly sailed in the Brandywine frigate, had lived for several years on the Columbia River, and having married an Indian girl, a daughter of old Carcowan, chief of the Chehalis Indians, he had taken a claim at the portage we had just crossed, where he had a fine farm cleared and planted. M'Carty was a very hospitable man, and no one was ever refused by him either a night's lodging or a hearty meal. He was, however, shortly after this time, drowned by the upsetting of a canoe, leaving a little daughter some ten or twelve years old.

After we had eaten our supper and smoked our pipes, M'Carty advised us to go to bed, so as to be up in the morning to witness the salmon fishing. We readily complied with his suggestion, as we were both tired and sleepy.

The next morning, at early dawn, we were aroused by Mac, who was hallooing to his Indians to get ready for work. I went out and perched myself on a log that overlooked the busy scene. Looking up the river, almost in a line due east, Mount St. Helen's reared its snowy head high in the region of the clouds. The rapidly increasing morning rendered it distinctly visible, although a hundred miles in the interior.

And now the whole population of the village was astir—white men and Indians, squaws, children, and dogs—all were awake and eager to enter upon the labors of the morning, and long before the sun was up all were intently engaged.

The Chenook salmon commences to enter the river the last of May, and is most plentiful about the 20th of June. It is, without doubt, the finest salmon in the world, and, being taken so near the ocean, has its fine flavor in perfection. The salmon, when entering a river to spawn, do not at once proceed to the head-waters, but linger round the mouth for several weeks before they are prepared to go farther up. It has been supposed that they can not go immediately from the ocean to the cold fresh water, but remain for a time where the water is brackish before they venture on so great a change. Be that as it may, one thing is certain, that the early salmon taken at Chenook are far superior in flavor to any that are subsequently taken farther up the river, and this excellence is so generally acknowledged that Chenook salmon command a higher price than any other.

These salmon resemble those of the Kennebec and Penobscot Rivers in Maine, but are much larger and fatter. I have seen those that weighed eighty pounds; and one gentleman informed me that twelve salmon he had in his smoke-house averaged sixty-five pounds each, the largest weighing seventy-eight pounds. The Chenook fishery is carried on by means of nets. These are made by the whites of the twine prepared for the purpose, and sold as salmon-twine, and rigged with floats and sinkers in the usual style. The nets of the Indians are made of a twine spun by themselves from the fibres of spruce roots prepared for the purpose, or from a species of grass brought from the north by the Indians. It is very strong, and answers the purpose admirably. Peculiar-shaped sticks of dry cedar are used for floats, and the weights at the bottom are round beach pebbles, about a pound each, notched to keep them from slipping from their fastenings, and securely held by withes of cedar firmly twisted and woven into the foot-rope of the net.

The nets vary in size from a hundred feet long to a hundred fathoms, or six hundred feet, and from seven to sixteen feet deep.

Three persons are required to work a net, except the very large ones, which require more help to land them. The time the fishing is commenced is at the top of high-water, just as the tide begins to ebb. A short distance from the shore the current is very swift, and with its aid these nets are hauled. Two persons get into the canoe, on the stern of which is coiled the net on a frame made

SALMON FISHING AT CHENOOK.

for the purpose, resting on the canoe's gunwale. She is then paddled up the stream, close in to the beach, where the current is not so strong.   A tow-line, with a wooden float attached to it, is then thrown to the third person, who remains on the beach, and immediately the two in the canoe paddle her into the rapid stream as quickly as they can, throwing out the net all the time.   When this is all out, they paddle ashore, having the end of the other tow-line made fast to the canoe.   Before all this is accomplished, the net is carried down the stream, by the force of the ebb, about the eighth of a mile, the man on the shore walking along slowly, holding on to the line till the others are ready, when all haul in together.   As it gradually closes on the fish, great caution must be used to prevent them from jumping over; and as every salmon has to be knocked on the head with a club for the purpose, which every canoe carries, it requires some skill and practice to perform this feat so as not to bruise or disfigure the fish.

The fishermen are not always lucky.   Sometimes the net is hauled repeatedly without success; but in seasons of plenty, great hauls are often made, and frequently a hundred fine fish of various sizes are taken at one cast of the seine.   It happened to be a good day while we were there, and M'Carty caught about forty, which was considered good fishing for so early in the season.   The others did quite as well, some even getting more than he did.

It was formerly the custom among the Chenook Indians, on the appearance of the first salmon, to have a grand feast, with dancing and other performances suited to the occasion; but the tribe has now dwindled down to a mere handful, and they content themselves simply with taking out the salmon's heart as soon as caught— a ceremony they religiously observe, fearful lest by any means a dog should eat one, in which case they think they can catch no more fish that season. The fish taken by the whites are served in the same manner by the Indians in their employ.

As soon as the tide has done running ebb, the fishing for the day is over, and the Indians, after selecting what they wish for themselves, take the rest to the whites to trade off for different articles, whisky in all cases holding the pre-eminence; but, as the United States law is very stringent, and attended with a severe penalty, it is very difficult for them to get liquor at Chenook, although they can readily get it across the river at Astoria. They will manage some way or other to get it, even if they have to go a hundred miles for a supply. During the fishing season a good deal of drunkenness may be seen among them, and for the most part they are a miserable, whisky-drinking set of vagabonds. However, the race of the Chenooks is nearly run. From a large and powerful tribe in the days of Comcomly, the one-eyed chief, they have dwindled down to about a hundred individuals, men, women, and children.

We did not wait till the fishing was over for our breakfast, but, when the sun got up high enough to shine clear above the peak of Mount St. Helen's, old Brandywine called us up from the beach, and gave us a glorious repast of salmon, just out of the water, cooked in real Indian style by his Indian wife.

The choice part of a salmon with the Indians is the head, which is stuck on a stick, and slowly roasted by the fire. The other part is cut into large, flat slices, with skewers stuck through to keep them spread; then, placed in a split stick, as a palm-leaf fan is placed in its handle, with the ends of this stick or handle projecting far enough beyond the fish to be tied with a wisp of beach grass to secure the whole, this stick is thrust in the sand firmly and at the right distance from the fire, so that the fish can roast without scorching. Clamshells are placed underneath to catch the oil, which will run from these rich, fat salmon almost in a stream. Neither pepper, salt, nor butter were allowed during this culinary operation, nor did I find they were needed; the delicate and delicious flavor would have been spoiled by the addition of either.

I was so much pleased with this style of cooking salmon that I never wish to have it cooked in any other form, either boiled and served with melted butter, or fried with salt pork, or baked with spices. The simpler a fat salmon can be cooked, the better; it retains its flavor with perfection, and is more easily digested; and the only style is to roast it before an open fire.

After breakfast we went to the Hudson Bay Company trading store, kept by their very polite and hospitable agent, Mr. Roc Ducheney. Mr. Rotan here purchased a new outfit to replace his damaged garments, which were about spoiled during our adventures on the portage, and, together with Champ, went across the River to Astoria, where he was to take the steamer for San Francisco.

Baldt and myself had nothing else to do but to stroll around and see the place.

Chenook is situated on the north bank of the Columbia, near its mouth, where the river widens out into Baker's Bay. From Point Ellice to Chenook Point, a distance of about two miles, the land is little more than a sand-beach, from half a mile to a mile wide in its widest, and from twenty to fifty rods at its narrowest place, running all the way under the bluff of a range of hills terminating at Chenook Point with the high green hill known as Scarborough's Hill or Head.

This is the head-quarters of the once powerful tribe of Chenook Indians, and it was here that their chief,

Comcomly, celebrated in the annals of Astoria, and mentioned by Ross Cox, Lewis and Clarke, and Irving, held his sway. The tribe then was numerous; but those scourges to the human race, measles and small-pox, have swept them off in such numbers that at present they number but little over a hundred persons, and these are a depraved, licentious, drunken set, of but little use to themselves, and of no account to any one else. Chenook has always been celebrated for its salmon fishery, and it was to prosecute this business that induced the whites to first settle there. It is, however, so favorably situated as a place of landing or debarkation for persons having business either at Astoria or up the river, that it is most generally the point resorted to by the settlers of Shoalwater Bay, and has grown to be a little village of considerable importance; and no one seems to take a greater interest in its welfare than the worthy postmaster, Washington Hall, Esq., who was one of the first to settle there.

The little soil that has gathered on the sands is very rich, and yields good crops of garden vegetables, and, except in these cleared patches, is covered with bushes and young trees, thriftily growing to the edge of high-water mark.

The Indian lodges, like all that I have seen on the Northwest Coast, are made of boards split from the cedar. The Indians perform this operation by means of little wedges, and manifest a good deal of dexterity and skill; for, if the wedges are not placed properly, the board will be full of twists and creeps. The lodges are strongly and comfortably made by first setting posts firmly into the ground four or five feet high, one at each corner. The tops of these posts are notched, and poles laid along to form the eaves. The ridge-pole is supported at its ends by the boards of the outside, which are placed upright, and in the centre by posts elevated for the purpose. From the eaves to the ridge-pole rafters are laid, and on these the boards of the roof are laid, with feather-edges overlapping each other to shed the rain, and secured by withes to the rafters to keep from blowing off in gales of wind. The sides and ends are formed of upright boards driven into the soil, with overlapping edges, and with chinks and crevices stopped up with moss. The top boards of the roof next the ridge-pole are movable, so as to be easily opened from the inside to admit a free passage for the smoke. All round the interior of the lodge, next the side, are arranged sleeping-berths, similar to those on board vessels, and in front of these berths is a raised platform, five or six inches high, on which mats are spread to sit or lie upon. All the rest of the centre of the lodge floor is used for fire and for cooking purposes. Overhead, poles are laid, on which salmon, berries, or any thing else they wish to preserve is placed to be dried by the smoke. At one end is the door, which is usually a round or oval hole, just big enough to creep through, and secured by a door made of a single piece of board, which hangs loose by a string, like a sort of pendulum, and is sure to close of itself after any ingress or egress. Some of these lodges are very large, and can contain several families. They are very comfortable habitations, and are often used by the white settlers while building their own houses.

Baldt and myself went into several of these, to see the method the Indians adopted to cure their salmon. In all cases the women perform this duty. The salmon is split down the back, so as to separate the head, backbone, ribs, and tail from the rest of the body. The backbone, which has a large portion of the fish adhering to it, is generally eaten first, and is cooked either by boiling or roasting; the heads and tails are strung together and dried. The rest of the fish is sliced in thin wafers, and is also dried in the smoke without salt. When perfectly cured, it is packed in baskets for winter's use or for trading, and stored in a dry place. For trading with the interior Indians, the salmon is frequently pounded up fine, and firmly pressed into baskets of ten or twelve pounds each. While the Indians are engaged in curing salmon, or when they are boiling the blubber of a whale or seal, they are as necessarily dirty as the crew of a whale-ship or butchers in a slaughter-house; and at such times, casual visitors form an opinion that they are a filthy, greasy set, and we find many writers willing to assert that they regularly anoint their bodies with fish-oil and red ochre. Such, however, is not the fact. As soon as their work is done, they wash themselves, and generally bathe two or three times a day. All the painting or oiling I have ever seen them do is to rub a little grease and vermilion, or red ochre, between their hands, and then smear it over their faces. The women will also paint the head, in the line of the parting of the hair, with dry vermilion, and give an extra touch to their eyebrows; but I never have seen either men or women put oil or grease of any kind on their bodies. The women tattoo their legs and arms with dotted lines, but without any particular figure or design; they are also fond, during the blackberry season, of dotting their limbs with blackberry juice. The tattooing is done with charcoal and water, and pricked into the skin with needles. I very seldom saw a man with tattoo-marks on him, and it appears more as a sort of pastime—like sailors on board ship—than any sort of system or religious ceremony. Whatever may have been the former practice among the Chenook Indians relative to personal decoration, they certainly have relinquished the custom, and are only anxious at present to get white people's garments to clothe themselves with, wearing, as their only ornament, a sort of band of black ostrich feathers round their caps, which they purchase of the Hudson Bay Company.

As Champ did not return from Astoria till the afternoon, too late to start for our return to Shoal-water Bay, it was agreed to be ready early in the morning. We had all made purchases, and as to our own loads Champ wished to add two or three hundred pounds of salt salmon, we hired two Indians to take us in a canoe to M'Carty's portage, where old Mac had told us we might find his horse and pack-saddle, both of which we could use to transport our things over to Wilson's landing.

The next morning, after an early breakfast, we launched the canoe, and, having made room for an old gentleman who was waiting to go to the Bay (Mr. Samuel Woodward, Sen.), and getting all our things stowed, we began to look up our Indians, and found those worthies quite drunk; but Champ, who officiated as master of ceremonies, soon got them into the canoe, one at the head and the other at the stern. One of these savages was old Toke, who, with his people, had been some time at Chenook, and the other a powerful fellow named Yancumux, who lived in Baker's Bay, and who owned the canoe. We paddled out into the stream, and were rapidly carried by the swiftly-ebbing tide to Chenook Point, and from thence slowly made our way to the mouth of the Wappalooche River, which we entered; and as the tide by that time was too low for us to go up, we went ashore at the lodge of an Indian named Sal-leel, who had been catching sturgeon, from which he prepared us a very palatable meal.

As the tide rose we proceeded up the stream. There were two creeks, which joined near M'Carty's house, forming one, and, at certain stages of the tide, either of them could be used. Champ insisted on going up the

first one we came to, but the Indians objected on account
of a log which lay directly across, a short distance up.
But Champ was determined; so on we went till we
came to the snag, which lay in such a manner that we
could neither go under or over it.   The Indians refused
to go back, saying that they would remain till the tide
rose, or, if we would help, they would put the canoe over
the log.   This was a feat we all considered impossible,
for the canoe, with all our things, weighed over a ton;
so we decided to go ashore and walk to M'Carty's house,
where we would wait for the canoe.

As we were going ashore, Yancumux asked me if I
was afraid.   I told him I was not, but I had no desire
to sit in the canoe with old Toke and himself waiting
for the tide.   He said I would not have to wait long, as
he was going to put the canoe over the log himself.   I
was curious to see the operation, and consented to wait.
Both the Indians stripped themselves and jumped into
the water, which was only a few inches deep, but the
mud was soft, and they sank nearly to their waists in it.
They placed themselves at the bow and stern; and, as
the bottom of the canoe, like all those of Chenook, was
flat and smooth, they worked her gradually on the soft,
greasy mud, up the side of the bank, till she was nearly
as high as the log.   The mud here was a little firmer,
and I took hold and helped them, when, with a powerful
jerk, we started her, and away she launched over the
log, and down the other side into the water, the Indians
yelling and laughing all the time.   The uproar caused
Champ and Baldt to come and see what was the matter,
and they were perfectly astonished at the wonderful feat
of strength performed by those two half-drunken Indians.

While the tide was rising enough to enable us to get
to the landing-place, we left the Indians and canoe to

hunt up the old squaw who had the key of the house where the pack-saddle was.

After a long search, we found her, with two other squaws, picking berries, and soon had her back to the house and the saddle ready; but, while we were hunting for her, a couple of Indians had come from Shoal-water Bay, bringing some whisky with them, which they had given to our Indians, whom we found quite drunk again. They, however, started out for the horse, who was quietly feeding in the meadow. They could not catch him, after chasing him round for an hour. I told Champ I would wait no longer, but, with Baldt and old Mr. Woodward, would take what we could pack on our backs, and go over the portage to Wilson's house, where we would clean out the boat and get supper ready.

The road had dried up since we had passed over it, and we found no difficulty in reaching Wilson's. As it was still daylight, we had time to clean the boat and get our supper ready. We waited till long after dark for Champ, who had not yet made his appearance, when, getting tired, we ate our supper, and, while smoking our pipes preparatory to going to bed, heard the voices of Indians singing. Baldt remarked that Champ must have pressed some new recruits into his service, for Toke and Yancumux were not in a condition, when we left them, to be very tuneful. The singers soon came in, and proved to be a couple of squaws that Champ had hired to help him pack his fish. He came in a few minutes afterward, and, as soon as he could get breath, related that he had loaded the two Indians with the fish, but, after they had proceeded a quarter of a mile, they threw down their loads, and using them as pillows, were soon sound asleep. The old fellow's outcries and frantic attempts to wake them had attracted the attention of the squaws, who were in the woods picking berries, and they went to find out the cause of the uproar, when Champ hired them, and left the two men fast asleep.

We did not have a very pleasant night, for no sooner had we lain down than the house was filled with swarms of gnats and sand-flies, that filled our hair, nose, ears, and eyes, and stung us so that sleep was impossible, and we were glad at early dawn to get into the boat and start down the river for Shoal-water Bay.

It was a glorious morning, rendered doubly delightful by the songs of myriads of birds, who filled the air with their sweet notes. As we proceeded down the stream, we roused great flocks of water-fowl—swans, geese, and ducks of various kinds—which whirled away with a mighty rushing sound, alighting a short distance in advance, to be again and again startled as we proceeded on our course. Every where the paths of elk and deer could be seen, where they had broke through and beat down the sedge on the river banks as they had crossed the stream. Turning a sharp angle in the river, we came suddenly on a big black bear, who was seated on an old spruce stump that overhung the stream. In his hurry and fright he slipped, and fell some ten feet, with a great splash, into the water, out of which he scrambled with some trouble, and disappeared in the forest. We had no fire-arms with us, or we could have shot plenty of game.

We ran down the river and bay with the ebb tide in fine style, with every prospect of a quick trip, till we were nearly half way across, when Champ, who was pilot, ran us high and dry on a sand-bank, where we had to remain six hours for the returning flood. While waiting here, we amused ourselves by gathering oysters and clams, and in tracing out the course of the channel, which at low tide is distinctly visible and easily marked. I was not sorry for the opportunity of learning the right way to navigate up and down the Bay, and I never afterward got aground, although almost constantly cruising about the Bay and creeks.

There is no difficulty at present for persons wishing to visit Shoal-water Bay, as usually boats can be had at the portage, or Indians can be hired at Chenook who will go through. This is the best method of traveling in any Indian country; that is to say, always, whatever may be the party, have some Indians in the company, who are useful as guides or servants, and in a new country are far better pilots than most of the white men that can be obtained.

As soon as the tide had risen enough to float our boat, we made sail, and with a fair wind reached our quarters, not a little pleased to be at the termination of our cruise.

CHAPTER VIII.

The Country of the Columbia.—Discovery of the Columbia.—Gray's Harbor.—The Coast north of the Columbia.—Fuca Strait.—Puget Sound.—Geographical Errors in naming Places.—Excellent Harbors. —Mount Olympus.—Separation of Washington from Oregon.—The Columbia and its Tributaries.—The Dalles.—Wappatoo Island.— Heceta's Voyage.—Attack by Savages.—Point Grenville and Destruction Island.—River St. Roc.—Vancouver.—Sloop Washington and Ship Columbia.—Captain Gray.—Lieutenant Broughton and the Brig Chatham.—Account of the Outfit of the Ship Columbia in 1787. —Captain John Kendrick.—Gray discovers the Columbia.—Building of the Adventure at Clyoquot.

THE region west of the Rocky Mountains drained by the Columbia and its tributaries, and which may properly be termed the Columbia country, is contained in the space between the forty-second and forty-ninth parallels, and is about four hundred thousand square miles in superficial extent. Its southernmost points are in the same latitude with Boston and with Florence, while its northernmost correspond with the northern extremities of New-foundland and with the northern shores of the Baltic Sea.

The Pacific coast of this territory extends in a line nearly due north from the boundary between California and Oregon to Cape Flattery. The shores south of the Columbia are perilous to navigators, from the steep and rocky shores, and the presence of reefs and sand-bars. There are no large harbors on this line of the coast, but small vessels find safe anchorage at Port Orford, and can also enter the River Umpqua, a short distance north, and also a small inlet named Coose Bay.

North of the Columbia the coast is less beset with dangers, and offers the excellent harbor of Shoal-water Bay, where at high water vessels drawing eighteen feet can safely enter. Immediately north of Shoal-water Bay, and directly under the forty-seventh parallel, is Gray's Harbor, a small port, safe and good for vessels of light draft. This bay was discovered in May, 1792, by Captain Robert Gray, of the ship Columbia, of Boston, and named by him Bulfinch Harbor, after one of the owners of his ship, though it is commonly called Gray's Harbor, and is frequently represented on the old English maps as Whidbey's Bay.

North of Gray's Harbor there is no other bay or river that can be entered from the ocean, although several fine streams flow directly into the Pacific; but their mouths are so choked up by the waves beating directly into them that they have openings scarce large enough to admit canoes. There are several rocks and islets lying between Gray's Harbor and Fuca Straits, but none of them are worthy of particular notice except Destruction Island, in latitude 47½ degrees, named by the captain of an Austrian ship in 1787, in consequence of the murder of some of his men by the natives of the adjacent country.

The Strait of Juan de Fuca is an arm of the sea separating the great island of Quadra and Vancouver, or, as it is now called, Vancouver's Island, from the continent on the south and east. It extends from the ocean eastward about one hundred miles, varying in breadth from ten to thirty miles, between the 48th and 49th parallels of latitude; thence it turns to the northwest, in which direction it runs, first expanding into a long, wide bay, and then contracting into narrow and intricate passages among islands, three hundred miles farther, to its reunion with the Pacific under the 51st parallel.

From its southeastern extremity, a great gulf, called Admiralty Inlet, stretches southward into the continent more than one hundred miles, dividing into many branches, of which the principal are, Hood's Canal on the west, and Puget Sound, the southernmost, extending nearly to the 47th parallel. This inlet possesses many excellent harbors, and the adjacent country being delightful and productive, make it one of the most valuable portions of the territory, agriculturally as well as commercially. A strange geographical error has gained credence in the commercial world of calling all the waters on the north of Washington Territory Puget Sound.

This error has been principally caused by ignorant newspaper reporters, particularly those of San Francisco, who always report vessels arriving from any of the different harbors in Fuca Strait as from Puget Sound.

There are many excellent harbors in the Strait of Fuca, of which the principal are Port Townsend, near the entrance to Admiralty Inlet, said by Vancouver to be one of the best in the Pacific; Neah Bay, called by Vancouver Poverty Cove, and by the Spaniards Port Nuñez Gaona, situated a few miles east of Cape Flattery; New Dungeness, False Dungeness, and Bellingham's Bay, an arm of the Gulf of Georgia; while in Admiralty Inlet are several bays on Whidbey's Island, Seattle, Alki, and Tekalet, on Hood's Canal. Cape Flattery was named by Captain Cook. It is a conspicuous promontory, in the latitude of 48° 27′, near which is a large rock called Tatooche Island, united to the promontory by a rocky ledge, at times partially covered with water.

The shore between the Cape and Admiralty Inlet is composed of sandy cliffs, overhanging a beach of sand and stones. From it the land gradually rises to a chain of mountains stretching southwardly along the Pacific to the vicinity of the Columbia, the highest point of which received, in 1788, the name of Mount Olympus.

The whole of this region was organized as the Territory of Oregon, by which name it was known till 1853, when it was separated into two territories, that lying north of the Columbia being called Washington. The Columbia is the dividing line between the two territories from its mouth to near Fort Walla Walla, where the 49th parallel is the boundary the rest of the distance. "This magnificent river," says Greenhow, "enters the Pacific Ocean between two points of land seven miles apart—Cape Disappointment on the north, and Cape Adams on the south, of which the former is in the latitude of 46° 16′ (corresponding nearly with Quebec, in Canada, and Geneva, in Switzerland), and in longitude 47° west from Washington, or 124° west from Greenwich. The main river is formed at the distance of two hundred and fifty miles from its mouth by the union of two large streams, one from the north, which is usually considered as the principal branch, and the other, called Snake River, from the southeast. These two great confluents receive in their course many other streams, and thus they collect together all the waters flowing from the western sides of the Rocky Mountains, between the 42d and the 54th parallels of latitude.

" The northern branch of the Columbia rises in the Rocky Mountains, near the 53d degree of latitude. One of its head-waters, the Canoe River, runs from a small lake situated in a remarkable cleft of the great chain called the Punch Bowl, at the distance of only a few feet from another lake, whence flows the westernmost stream of the Athabasca River, a tributary to the Mackenzie, emptying into the Arctic Sea. This cleft is described by those who have visited it as presenting scenes of the most terrific grandeur, being overhung by the highest peaks in the dividing range, of which one, called Mount Brown, is not less than sixteen thousand feet, and another, Mount Hooker, exceeds fifteen thousand feet above the ocean level.

" At a place called Boat Encampment, near the 52d degree of latitude, Canoe River joins two other streams, the one at the north, the other, the largest of the three, running along the base of the Rocky Mountains from the south. The river thus formed, considered as the main Columbia, takes its course nearly due south through defiles between lofty mountains, being generally a third of a mile in width, but in some places spreading out into broad lakes, for about three hundred miles, to the latitude of 48½ degrees, where it receives the Flatbow or M'Gillivray's River, a large branch, flowing also from the Rocky Mountains on the east.

" A little farther south, the northern branch unites with the Clarke or Flathead River, scarcely inferior, in the quantity of water supplied, to the other. The sources of the Clarke are situated in the dividing range, near those of the Missouri and Yellow Stone, whence it runs northward along the base of the mountains, and then westward, forming, under the 48th parallel, an extensive sheet of water called the Kullerspelm Lake, surrounded by rich tracts of land, and lofty mountains covered with noble

F

trees. From this lake the river issues in a large and rapid stream, and, after running about seventy miles westward, it falls into the north branch of the Columbia over a ledge of rocks. From the point of union of these two rivers the Columbia turns toward the west, and rushes through a ridge of mountains, where it forms a cataract called the Chaudiere or Kettle Falls. Continuing in the same direction eighty miles, between the 48th and 49th parallels, it receives, in succession, the Spokan from the south, and the Okinagan from the north, and from the mouth of the latter it pursues a southwardly course for one hundred and sixty miles to its junction with the great southern branch, near the 47th degree of latitude."

Of the great southern branch of the Columbia, the Snake River, the farthermost sources are situated in deep valleys or *holes* of the Rocky Mountains, near the 42d degree of latitude, within short distances of those of the Yellow Stone, the Platte, and the Colorado. The most eastern of these head-waters, considered as the main river, issues from Pierre's Hole, between the Rocky Mountains and a parallel range called the Tetons, from three remarkable peaks resembling teats, which rise to a great height above the others. Running westward, this stream unites successively with Henry's Fork from the north, and the Portneuf from the south. Some distance below its junction with the latter, the Snake enters the defile between the Blue Mountains on the west and another rocky chain, called the Salmon River Mountain, on the east, and takes its course northwestward for about six hundred miles to its union with the northern branch, receiving many large streams from each side. The principal of these influent streams are the Malade, or Sickly River, the Boisé, or Reed's River, the Salmon River, and the Kooskooske, from the east, and the Malheur and Powder River from the Blue Mountains on the west.

Of these two great branches of the Columbia and the streams that fall into them, scarcely any portion is navigable by the smallest vessels for more than thirty or forty miles continuously. The northern branch is much used by the British traders for the conveyance of their furs and merchandise, by means of light canoes, which, as well as their cargoes, are carried by the boatmen around the falls and rapids so frequently interrupting their voyage. The Snake River and its streams offer few advantages in that way, as they nearly all rush, in their whole course, through deep and narrow chasms between perpendicular rocks, against which a boat would be momentarily in danger of being dashed by the current.

From the point of junction of these two branches, the course of the Columbia is generally westward to the ocean. A little below that point it receives the Walla Walla, and then, in succession, the Umatilla, John Day's River, and the Chutes, or Falls River, all flowing from the south, and some others of less size from the north. Near the mouth of the Falls River, eighty miles below the Walla Walla, are situated the *Chutes*, or Falls of the Columbia, where the great stream enters a gap in the Cascade range of mountains. Four miles farther down are the Dalles (a corruption of the French D'Aller, a term, as I was informed, applied by the Canadian French to the raceway of a mill, which this part of the river resembles). The Dalles are rapids formed by the passage of the water between vast masses of rock; and thirty miles below these are the Cascades, a series of falls and rapids extending more than half a mile, at the foot of which the tides are observable, at the distance of a hundred and twenty miles from the Pacific.

A few miles below the Cascades, a large river, called the Willamet (the Multnomah of Lewis and Clarke), enters the Columbia from the south by two mouths, between which is an extensive island named Wappatoo Island, from an edible root (*Saggitafolia*) so called, found growing upon it in abundance. Twenty-five miles from the mouth of this river are its falls, where its waters are precipitated over a ledge of rocks more than forty feet in height. Beyond this point the Willamet has been traced about two hundred miles, in a tortuous course, through a narrow but fertile valley, to its sources in the Coast Range mountains, near the 43d degree of latitude. In this valley were formed the earliest agricultural settlements by citizens of the United States west of the Rocky Mountains.

Descending the Columbia forty miles from the lower mouth of the Willamet, we find a small stream, called the Cowlitz, entering it from the north; and thirty miles lower down, the great river, which is nowhere above more than a mile wide, expands to the breadth of four, and in some places of seven miles, before mingling its waters with those of the Pacific. It, however, preserves its character as a river, being rapid in its current, and perfectly fresh and potable to within a league of the ocean, except during the very dry seasons and the prevalence of violent westerly winds.

The discovery of the Columbia, which has been the cause of so much controversy between England and America, is now universally awarded to Captain Robert Gray, of the ship Columbia, of Boston. But Gray was, in fact, the rediscoverer, as the river was first seen by Captain Bruno Heceta, commanding the Spanish ship Santiago, on the 15th of August, 1775. The ship was accompanied by a small schooner called the Sonora, commanded by Lieutenant Juan Francisco de la Bodega y

Quadra. These two vessels sailed together from San Blas on the 15th of March, 1775, and, after stopping at various places on the coast, came to anchor on the 10th of June in a small roadstead, where they landed, and took possession of the country in the name of their sovereign with religious ceremonies, bestowing upon the harbor the name of Port Trinidad. After having erected a cross near the shore with an inscription, setting forth the fact of their having visited the place and taken possession of it, they sailed for the north on the 19th of June, and were obliged to keep out of sight of land for three weeks, at the end of which time they again came in sight of it, in the latitude of 48° 27'. Here they expected to find the Straits of Fuca, but, being disappointed, they came to anchor near the land, though at some distance from each other, to procure wood and water, and to trade with the natives.

Here a severe misfortune befell the schooner Sonora on the 14th of July. Seven of her men, who had been sent ashore in her *only boat*, although well armed, were attacked and murdered by the natives immediately they had landed, and it was with difficulty the savages were prevented from boarding the schooner, which was surrounded during the whole day by the Indians, in great numbers, in their canoes.

In commemoration of this melancholy event, the place was called Punta de Martires — Martyrs' Point. It is in the latitude of 47° 20', and on English maps is called Point Grenville. A small island, situated a few miles farther north, was also named Isla de Dolores—Isle of Sorrows. Twelve years afterward, this same island was named by the captain of the ship Imperial Eagle, of Ostend, *Destruction Island*, in consequence of a similar massacre of some of his crew by the Indians on the main land opposite. These Indians are known as the Quaitso tribe, and those at Point Grenville as the Queniūlt, and were formerly very savage and dangerous.

This disaster, together with the appearance of the scurvy among the crew, decided Heceta to return to Monterey ; but he was opposed by Bodega, and finally gave his unwilling consent to proceed north, which they did on the 20th of July. They were, however, shortly afterward separated in a storm, whereupon Heceta determined to go back to Monterey, while Bodega persevered in his endeavors to accomplish as far as possible the object of his expedition.

After Heceta parted company with the schooner he steered south, and on the 15th of August arrived opposite an opening, in the latitude of 46° 17', from which rushed a current so strong as to prevent his entering it. This circumstance convinced him that it was the mouth of some great river. He, in consequence, remained in its vicinity another day, in the hope of ascertaining the true character of the place ; but still being unable to enter the opening, he continued his voyage toward the south.

This opening in the coast thus discovered Heceta named *Enseñada de Asuncion*—Assumption Inlet ; calling the north point Cape San Roque, and that on the south *Cape Frondoso*—Leafy Cape. In the chart published at Mexico soon after the conclusion of the voyage, the entrance is, however, called *Enseñada de Heceta* —Heceta's Inlet, and *Rio de San Roque*—River of St. Roc. Greenhow remarks that it was undoubtedly the mouth of the greatest river on the western side of America, the same which in 1792 was first entered by the ship Columbia, and the evidence of its first discovery by Heceta is unquestionable.

Thirteen years afterward, Meares, as has already been stated, attempted to find this River of St. Roc, but without success. After changing the name of Cape San Roque to Cape Disappointment, in token of his failure, he writes, " *We can now with safety assert that there is no such river as that of St. Roc exists* as laid down on Spanish charts."

In 1792 Vancouver sailed up the coast, and when in the latitude of· 46° 19′ he came up with Cape Disappointment, and, considering the opening of the Columbia to be what Meares had previously named Deception Bay, he writes, "*Not considering this opening worthy of more attention,* I continued our pursuit to the northwest," being satisfied " that all· the rivers or inlets that had been described as discharging their contents into the Pacific between the 40th and the 48th degrees of north latitude were reduced to *brooks insufficient for our vessels to navigate,* or to bays inaccessible as harbors for refitting."

On the 29th of April, 1792, Vancouver spoke the Columbia, of Boston, commanded by Robert Gray, who informed him that he had lain off the mouth of a river in the latitude of 46° 10′, where the outset or reflux was so strong that for nine days he was prevented from entering it; but as Vancouver had passed the same place on the forenoon of the 27th, he gave no credit to Captain Gray's statement, and writes " that if any inlet or river should be found, it must be a very intricate one, and *inaccessible to vessels* of our burden, owing to the reefs and broken water."

Satisfied with his conclusions, Vancouver continued on to the north, while Captain Gray, determined to ascertain the truth of his belief that he had seen the mouth of a river, proceeded on his course south. It was while in command of the sloop Washington, in August, 1788, that Gray discovered and attempted to enter the opening near the 46th degree of latitude; but the sloop grounded on the bar and came near being lost, and was also attacked by the Indians, who killed one man and wounded the mate; but she escaped without farther injury, and reached Nootka on the 17th of September.

Gray was shortly afterward transferred to the command of the Columbia, and returned to Boston, and was now on another cruise, 1792.

After parting with the English commander, Gray sailed along the coast south, and on the 7th of May he discovered, in latitude 46° 58′, the entrance to a bay, which he passed through, and found himself in a good harbor, "well sheltered from the sea by long sand-bars and spits," where he remained three days trading with the natives.

He named this place Bulfinch Harbor, but it is now known as Gray's Harbor.

At daybreak on the 11th he resumed his voyage, and shortly afterward discovered "the entrance of his desired port bearing east-southeast distant six leagues;" and unlike Meares and Vancouver, who had pronounced the breakers impassable, he boldly steered between them, with all sail set, and at one o'clock anchored "*in a large river of fresh water*," ten miles above its mouth, where he remained three days engaged in trading with the natives and filling his casks with water, and then sailed up some ten or twelve miles farther along the northern shore, where he came to anchor, being unable to proceed any farther from having, as he writes, "taken the wrong channel." During the following week several attempts were made to go to sea, but they were unable to cross the bar till the 20th, when, a fresh breeze springing up from the west, they beat the ship out, and at five P.M. were clear of all the bars and in twenty fathoms of water.

On leaving the river, Captain Gray gave it the name of his ship, the *Columbia*, a name it has ever since retained, and also named the sand-bank which makes out from the southern side of the entrance Point Adams, and the bluff, rocky promontory on the northern side he called Cape Hancock, but afterward changed it to Cape Disappointment, on learning that Meares had previously bestowed that name upon it.

After leaving the Columbia Gray proceeded to Nootka, where he met the Spanish commander Quadra, to whom he gave a rough chart of the river. Vancouver, who had been prosecuting his discoveries in the Straits of Fuca, returned to Nootka, where he was furnished by Quadra with copies of the charts given him by Gray.

On the 13th of October, 1792, he sailed from Nootka with his three vessels, the Discovery, Dædalus, and Chatham, and on the 17th, being opposite the entrance to Gray's Harbor, he detached Lieutenant Whidbey, in the Dædalus, to examine the bay, while he himself proceeded with the other vessels to the Columbia. Being still convinced of the impossibility of his ship passing the bar, he continued his course south for the Bay of San Francisco, leaving Lieutenant Broughton, in the brig Chatham, to enter the river, which he did without difficulty on the 20th of October, and to his surprise found the brig Jenny, of Bristol, Captain Baker, lying there at anchor, having arrived from Nootka a few days previous. Lieutenant Broughton then proceeded up the river in his boat eighty miles, when, finding the current too strong for them to proceed without great labor, they abandoned the survey and returned to the brig.

The point of land where they were obliged to relinquish their design was named Point Vancouver, and an inlet on the north shore of the river, where Gray had anchored, was named Gray's Bay, and another inlet, immediately inside Cape Disappointment, was named Baker's Bay, in compliment to the captain of the brig

Jenny. Both the Chatham and Jenny sailed from the Columbia on the 10th of November, and arrived at San Francisco before the end of the month. Greenhow remarks " that, had Gray, after parting with the English ships, not returned to the river and ascended it as he did, there is every reason to believe that it would have long remained unknown ; for the assertions of Vancouver that *no opening, harbor, or place of refuge for vessels was to be found between Cape Mendocino and the Strait of Fuca*, and that *this part of the coast formed one compact, solid, and nearly straight barrier against the sea*, would have served completely to overthrow the evidence of the American fur-trader, and to prevent any further attempts to examine those shores, or even to approach them."

As the names of Robert Gray and his ship will always be remembered in connection with the Columbia River, Gray's Bay, and Gray's Harbor, a brief statement of the original outfitting from Boston will be of interest.

In 1787, some merchants of Boston, who were engaged in the China trade, finding that, from the inferiority of the articles of American manufacture, they were unable to cope with the English or other foreign nations in the Canton market, formed an association for the purpose of combining the fur-trade with the traffic in teas and silks. The names of these copartners were Messrs. Barrell, Brown, Bulfinch, Darby, Hatch, and Pintard.

During the summer of 1787 they fitted out the ship Columbia, of two hundred and twenty tons, and the sloop Washington, of ninety tons, and loaded them with blankets, knives, iron bars, copper pans, and other articles proper for the trade with the Northwest Indians.

The Columbia was commanded by John Kendrick, who had also the command of the expedition. The name of the mate was Joseph Ingraham.

The Washington was commanded by Robert Gray. They also carried with them, for distribution among the natives, a number of halfpence recently coined by the State of Massachusetts, and also medals of copper struck expressly for the purpose, having a representation of the ship and sloop, with their names and that of Captain

Kendrick on one side, and the names of the owners, with the date and object of the enterprise, on the reverse. These medals are but rarely met with at the present time. The two vessels sailed from Boston on the 30th of September, 1787, and, after touching at the Cape Verde and Falkland Islands, they proceeded on their voyage, and in January, 1788, doubled Cape Horn, where they were separated during a violent gale. Nootka having been appointed as the place of rendezvous, both vessels steered for it. They did not reach the Northwest Coast till the following August, when, as has before been mentioned, Gray first saw the mouth of the Columbia, where he came near losing the sloop Washington, and it was not till the 17th of September that he reached Nootka, having been nearly a year out from Boston.

The Columbia arrived a few days after, and the two

vessels remained in Nootka Sound all winter, the Washington occasionally making short trading excursions north and south for furs, which were placed on board the Columbia, who remained at anchor. After the ship was loaded, it was agreed between the two captains that Gray should take command of the Columbia and proceed to Canton, while Kendrick should remain on the coast and take charge of the sloop. Gray accordingly proceeded to Canton, where he arrived on the 6th of December, 1789, and, having sold his furs and taken in a cargo of tea, he sailed for Boston, where he arrived on the 10th of August, 1790, having carried the flag of the United States for the first time round the world. Gray, having speedily refitted his ship, again sailed from Boston on the 28th of September (1790), and arrived at Clyoquot, near the entrance to the Straits of Fuca, on the 5th of June, 1791. While trading and exploring the islands and coast in the vicinity of Queen Charlotte's Island, he met with a melancholy accident at a place called by him Massacre Cove. His second mate, named Caswell, and two men, were murdered there on the 22d of August.

The Columbia wintered at Clyoquot, where her crew built a small vessel called the Adventure. This was the second vessel built on the Northwest, Meares having constructed one at Nootka during the year 1788, which was named the Northwest America.

The following spring of 1792, as has already been related, Gray sailed south for the purpose of exploring the Columbia, which purpose he effected; and, after leaving the mouth of the river, sailed to the east coast of Queen Charlotte's Island, where his ship struck on a rock, and was so much injured that she was with difficulty kept afloat till she reached Nootka, where she was repaired; and as soon as Gray had completed his business, he sailed for Canton in September, and thence to the United States.

Gray continued to command trading vessels from Boston till 1809, about which time he died.

CHAPTER IX.

The Oystermen celebrate the 4th of July.—A Speech and a great Bonfire.—Arrival of Emigrants.—Colonel H. K. Stevens.—Fishing-party on the Nasal River.—We go up the River to an Indian Camp.—Method of catching Salmon.—We catch rotten Logs.—The Colonel falls overboard. —A Chase after a Salmon. —Indian Style of catching Trout.—Their Medicine to allure Fish.—Immense Quantities of Salmon in Shoal-water Bay.—Wreck of Brig Palos.—Description of my House.—High Tides.—Quantities of Wild-fowl.—A Gale of Wind. —Heavy Rain.—The Gale increases, and blows down our Chimney. —Damage done by the Storm.—Narrow Escape from being killed by a falling Precipice.—Arrival of Indians.—Pepper Coffee.—Ludicrous Plight of the Natives.—Their Superstition.—They try to shoot a Ghost.—They are scared by a Pumpkin Lantern.—Poisoning Crows. —Method of preserving Cabbages from the Indians.

AFTER my return from Chenook, nothing of any particular interest transpired till toward the first of July, when it was announced to me that the boys, as the oystermen were termed, intended celebrating the 4th of July at my tent; and accordingly, as the time drew near, all hands were engaged in making preparations; for it was not intended that I should be at the expense of the celebration, but only bear my proportionate part. The day was ushered in by a tremendous bonfire, which Baldt and myself kindled on Pine Island, which was answered by every one who had a gun and powder blazing away. Toward two o'clock they began to assemble, some coming in boats, others in canoes, and a few by walking round the beach, which they could easily do at any time after the tide was quarter ebb.

Each one brought something: one had a great oyster pie, baked in a milk-pan; another had a boiled ham; a third brought a cold pudding; others had pies, doughnuts, or loaves of bread; and my neighbor Russell came, bringing with him a long oration of his own composing, and half a dozen boxes of sardines. When all were assembled, the performances were commenced by the reading of the Declaration of Independence by Mr. St. John, extracts from Webster's oration at Boston on Adams and Jefferson, then Russell's oration, which was followed by the banquet, and after that a feu-de-joie by the guns and rifles of the whole company.

These ceremonies over, it was proposed to close the performances for the day by going on top of the cliff opposite, and make a tremendous big blaze. This was acceded to, and some six or eight immediately crossed the creek and soon scrambled to the top of the hill, where we found an old hollow cedar stump about twenty feet high. We could enter this on one side, and found it a mere shell of what had once been a monster tree.

I had with me a little rifle, which measured, stock and all, but three feet long. With this I measured across the space, and found it was just six lengths of my rifle, or eighteen feet, and the tree undoubtedly, when sound, must have measured, with the bark on, at least sixty feet in circumference.

We went to work with a will, and soon had the old stump filled full of dry spruce limbs, which were lying about in great quantities, and then set fire to the whole. It made the best bonfire I ever saw; and after burning all night and part of the next day, finally set fire to the forest, which continued to burn for several months, till the winter rains finally extinguished it. The party broke up at an early hour, and all declared that, with the exception of the absence of a cannon, they never had a pleasanter " fourth."

The emigrants now began to come into the Bay, and "claims" of land were taken up on all sides. Among others who came to settle was an old friend, Colonel H. K. Stevens, who, with a friend named Hinckley, had taken a claim on the Nasal River, which he had named the Kennebec. The colonel was not a colonel then; he had not been elected to that high office at that early day. He was simply Harry Stevens, and remained as such until the ensuing year, when the residents, feeling a dread of the aborigines, chose him as their leader.

He had brought some goods over from the Columbia to trade with, and intended to build a store on the Point, where he had located himself. Although I had been repeatedly urged by him to make a visit to the Nasal, I never found any fitting opportunity till toward the last of August, when the salmon first begin to run up the rivers of Shoal-water Bay.

One day old Toke came to me with the information that there were plenty of salmon in the Nasal, and he wished to borrow my large canoe, as his was not large enough to carry all his people. I consented, provided I could go with them; to this he gladly assented, and we soon got our things ready for a week's sport. After we had safely stowed our blankets, guns, hooks, spears, and provisions, we started off, with my little canoe in tow to act as a tender. The Nasal was distant about eighteen or twenty miles, and as the Indians did not feel in any hurry, we did not reach the mouth of the river till after dark; when, not seeing any light or signs of Stevens's house, we went ashore on the opposite side of the river, where there was a fine spring, near which we made our camp, and remained all night.

A person traveling with Indians, particularly in canoes, should make up his mind not to be in a hurry; they move just as it suits them. If the wind is fair, they make sail if they have one, or, in lieu of that, will hoist a blanket, and go as the wind blows. But if it is ahead or is calm, they paddle along in a very lazy sort of manner. If night is likely to overtake them before getting to their destination, they always try to go ashore before dark, where they can find fresh water and make a good camp; and when their fire is made and their supper cooked, they feel as much at home as if in their own lodge. There is no hurrying with them to reach the next tavern, or, like the youth tied to his mother's apron-strings, feeling obliged to be at home when the bell rings for nine o'clock in the evening. Wherever night finds them, there they rest, and sleep secure. Our party slept so well that it was sunrise before we awoke the next morning. After we had washed our eyes open, we discovered the smoke of Stevens's fire nearly opposite, and shortly paddled across the river, where I met with a most cordial welcome from the colonel and his friend Hinckley, and another person who had joined him, Mr. Van Cleave. After we had finished breakfast, we all started up the river for a camp ten miles distant, where a party of Indians were engaged catching salmon, and where our Indians proposed stopping. Stevens got into the big canoe with me, Van took the small canoe we had been towing, and Hinckley took a small boat or batteau he owned. In this style we proceeded, sometimes with sail and then with paddle, and at length reached the camp about three P.M. As far as we went we found the Nasal a fine deep stream, flowing through rich prairie-lands, some of which were free from timber, and covered with a heavy crop of grass, and the rest covered with a growth of fine spruce and fir trees, very readily accessible to the stream, presenting great inducements for settlers to locate on them.

On arriving at camp, we found the Indians who were

already there had plenty of salmon, which they were drying for winter's use. They gave us a hearty meal, and then it was proposed that, while the Indians were preparing our camp, we should try our luck at the fishery. I got into my small canoe with two Indians who came with me, George and Peter, while Van Cleave and Stevens took the batteau. We proceeded up the stream about a mile, where we commenced floating down with the ebb. The water was from ten to twenty feet deep, and the process of catching the salmon was as follows:

The hooks, which have been described, after being properly adjusted to the poles, which were about twenty feet long, are put over the side and held in a vertical position, keeping the hook just clear of the bottom. It is usual to have but two persons in a canoe, one to steer, and the other, who sits at the bow, to fish. As the boat drifts down with the tide, the pole, with the hook attached to it, comes in contact with the salmon, who, when not in active motion, usually lie near the bottom, and are generally quiet as soon as the tide begins to ebb.

As soon as the Indian feels the fish, he jerks up the pole, and rarely fails to fasten the hook into the salmon, who is then pulled on board and knocked on the head. The whole operation requires a great deal of dexterity and practice, not only to distinguish the difference between a salmon and old logs, with which the bottoms of the rivers are usually covered, but also to get the fish into the canoe; for the salmon is a very powerful fish, and a large one makes a great commotion when hauled to the surface of the water, splashing and thrashing about in a fearful manner.

We had drifted down a short distance, when I found that it was useless for me to attempt fishing. I had hauled up no less than five respectable-sized logs of wood, each time sure I had a salmon, while George, who sat in the bow of the canoe, was pulling in the real Simon Pure ones as fast as he could. The colonel, who, with Van, was drifting along close to us, was quite sure that he could catch salmon as well as an Indian, and having hooked into what he supposed a very large one, gave a vigorous jerk, which served to bury the hook into an old rotten log, and at the same time losing his balance, he fell splash into the water, from whence he was rescued by Van, and conveyed ashore to get dry. Of course the exploit caused shouts of laughter from all who witnessed it, in which Harry joined, and seemed to enjoy the fun as much as any one. Meanwhile we had drifted down to where the water was very deep, and George, having fastened to a large salmon, lost his pole by the fish suddenly diving and pulling the stick out of his hands. Now, then, for a chase. The fish kept in the deep water, swimming rapidly from side to side, but, as the pole was buoyant, the end of it always kept above water. So we paddled first up and then down stream, then to the right and then to the left, Peter and myself paddling, while George tried to catch hold of the pole; but it seemed as if the fish knew when we were near; for, every time we approached, he would suddenly dive, and the next we would see of the end of the pole would be some rods distant. We chased that fish over half an hour before we got him, but he repaid our trouble, as he was very large and fat. By this time it had become dark, and, as I had become tired, the Indians set me ashore, while they proceeded on to continue their fishing. I found the colonel with his tent pitched, himself rolled in his blankets, and his clothes drying at a roaring fire, which the Indians were attending to. I was soon with him, and shortly both of us were asleep.

The Indians did not get through till near midnight, and had caught, during the time they were employed, twenty-three fine fish.

The next morning Stevens and his friends went down
the river, and I went up stream to catch trout.   About
four miles above our camp the stream was quite shallow,
with occasional deep holes, where overhanging roots made
just the shade the trout like for their hiding-places.   I
had some of the nicest sort of flies, of various patterns
and styles, and I anticipated rare sport, but after trying
half an hour without the least semblance of a bite, I returned to the canoe, from whence I had strolled a short
distance, and there found the two Indians who were with
me very leisurely and lazily engaged in pulling in the
trout as fast as they saw fit to throw their hooks overboard.   I call it lazy kind of trout-fishing to be engaged
as they were, for one lay flat on his back in the bow of
the canoe, with a line in his hand about three fathoms
long, having a hook attached to it baited with a roe of
the salmon.   No sooner would this touch the water than
the trout would dart at it from all quarters, and the Indian, with a sleight-of-hand jerk, would send the captive
fish spinning up in the air, from whence he was sure to
fall into the canoe.   The other Indian was half reclin-
ing across the stern, with one foot in the canoe and the
other in the water, amusing himself by dividing his time
between baiting his hook and starting off chips on voyages of discovery.

I found that flies were of no account among these wild
fish.   They had not learned the ways of a civilized state
of society ; so, putting up my patent apparatus, I adopted the Indian plan, and between us three we caught
a barrelful in about three hours' fishing.   There is no
doubt but that fresh salmon roe is the best bait in the
world for a trout, and, in fact, all fish that can get to it
devour it greedily.   I remained three days at the camp,
either catching trout or shooting ducks during the day,
and the Indians catching the salmon during the evening

and night. When the fish were shy or the Indians were unsuccessful, they would rub their hooks with the root of the wild celery, which has a very aromatic smell, and is believed by the Indians to be very grateful to the salmon and sure to attract them. I have also seen the Indians rub the celery root into their nets at Chenook for the same purpose, though I never have tried its effect, and have some doubt about its value.

After we had filled our canoe with dry salmon and a couple of barrels which we salted, we started down the river, and reached Stevens's tent just as the tide was beginning to run flood. Here we remained all that day and night, and by daylight the next morning started down the Bay with the ebb, and reached home at twelve o'clock.

The salmon in Shoal-water Bay, although excellent, are not equal to the early spring salmon at Chenook; in fact, they are a different species—although having the same form, they differ in color. The Chenook fish is of a dark brown or black on the back, with the sides and belly of a glistening silvery white. The fall salmon of Shoal-water Bay has dark, speckled sides, and a dull, whitish belly, nor is it so fat as the Chenook salmon. There are several varieties of fall salmon, the most plentiful of which is the hawk-nosed, or hook-billed, or dog-tooth salmon (for it has all those names). From the last of August to the first of December these salmon come into the Bay in myriads, and every river, brook, creek, or little stream is completely crammed with them, and late in the fall the banks of the rivers are literally piled up in rows with the dead fish killed in attempting to go over the falls. After they have cast their spawn their flesh loses its pink color, and is as white as a codfish. At this period they are not considered of any value either by whites or Indians, who term them *musachee*, or bad. I, however, have salted these fish, and have found them fully equal to salt cod, which they greatly resemble in taste.

During the early part of September, the brig Palos, which had taken a cargo of timber out of the Bay for San Francisco, on returning for another load, was wrecked at the mouth of the harbor on Leadbetter Point. The weather was very fine, and the wind quite light, so much so that the captain thought he could not stem the current of the ebb tide, and came to anchor just inside the breakers, when, not having sufficient scope to his cable, she dragged during the night, and went on to the beach. She had several passengers, who, with her crew, were safely landed, but the captain, in attempting to go on board during the night alone, was either capsized in the surf or fell overboard, and was drowned. His body was found the next day, and was buried by the settlers. It was found impracticable to get the brig off, from want of men; so she was stripped, and when the winter storms set in, she was dashed into a thousand fragments.

Captain Purrington and myself had been living all this time in our tent, and although we had a house framed and nearly ready for raising, we concluded it was our wisest plan to put up a temporary cottage, provided we could find boards. The tent was comfortable enough for summer, but an occasional rainy day gave us warning to prepare for winter. I soon heard of an old deserted lodge, which I bought of the Indians for a trifle, and taking the best boards, which I brought down the Bay in my big canoe, we made a very comfortable and respectable little cottage, consisting of one room fifteen by twenty feet square. At one end were two bed-places or bunks, screened from observation by red cotton curtains, and at the other end were the door and fireplace, which was of large dimensions, built, as was also the chimney, of the sandy clay of which the cliffs around the Bay are composed. This clay, which appears to be undergoing the slow process of transformation into sand-stone, falls from the cliffs in huge blocks, which can be easily cut with a hatchet, and split with as clean a frac-ture as slate-stone. Out of this material I fashioned a famous chimney. It was the pride of the Bay, although some of the knowing ones thought it was too handsome to last long; but I told them they were envious; and certainly, when the fireplace was filled with great logs of wood, blazing, and roaring, and sending showers of sparks and clouds of smoke up that famous chimney, they did acknowledge that it was the best chimney in the county. Tom Bartlett had given me some iron hatch-bars and chain-plates to make a crane, and hooks, and trammels, and when we had our tea-kettle singing in one corner, and the big iron pot bubbling and boiling, full of something good, with a loaf of hot bread in the Dutch oven, and a pot of strong coffee beside it, we felt, with our tight roof, that we would be as comfortable as any one else in the settlement.

The Indians now brought us in plenty of salmon, and we had our hands full, salting and packing away for winter's use. We turned our tent into a smoke-house, and soon had that filled with salmon, which we had first slightly salted. Our garden had yielded well, and we had plenty of vegetables, so we felt pretty safe for the winter.

The tides, which are always the highest during the winter months, now began to increase, and we found that they were getting rather close upon our old tent; but we did not feel any apprehension, so did not move any thing. The location of the mouth of the river was an excellent one for wild-fowl; and whenever there was a blow from the south, the water would be full of ducks, brant, and geese, with thousands of curlew, plover, and snipe, not to mention clouds of gulls, crows, and eagles that were flying round, filling the air with their harsh notes.   At such times we had no difficulty in keeping our larder well supplied, and never felt sorry when the weather gave indications of a southeaster. We soon had enough to satisfy us.   On the 30th of November it began to blow, and at high water, which was at two P.M., the tide came up so high and so rapidly that it washed away our tent and all our salmon, and set our house-frame, weather-boarding, and some ten or twelve thousand shingles drifting up stream.

I soon got the Indians out, and, with their help, managed to save nearly all the lumber and fish ; but the latter was in a very indifferent state, as the heads of the barrels were mostly out, and the salt water spoiled them all.   We had not got them all secure when it began to rain.   There had been a smart shower all the time for the last twenty-four hours, but now it began to rain, and, as the sun went down, the wind increased into a gale, and at times great gusts would come sweeping over the cliff, and, descending on us with a whirl, seemed as if they would tear every thing before them.

We had taken the precaution, before dark, to bring in a good pile of wood, and having heaped on as much as our fireplace would hold, which was about half a cord, we ate our supper, smoked our pipes, and went to bed, but not to sleep.   Now the storm raged fiercer, and was accompanied with thunder, and lightning, and hail. This music of the elements increased from forte to fortissimo —accompanied with the crashing of the trees, which had been partially burned, on the cliff opposite, and were falling with a tremendous noise—till near midnight, when, the constant torrent of rain having loosened the chimney, it fell down with a crash ; and at the instant a squall of wind whirled into the fireplace, blowing about a couple of bushels of coals and ashes into the middle of the room. The captain and myself were out of our beds nearly at the same time, and had to work pretty lively to keep the floor from taking fire. We scraped up the coals at last, though not without scorching our feet by treading on the hot cinders. One of the Indians now came in with the information that our canoes were adrift. We did not stop to dress, but hastily lighting a lantern, and launching a small canoe that had fortunately been hauled up out of reach of the tide, jumped into her, and, after a long search, recovered all the canoes but one, which went out to sea, and was afterward picked up on the beach nearly up to Gray's Harbor. Toward morning the wind lulled and the rain ceased, when we succeeded in putting up a wooden substitute for my beautiful chimney; then cleared out the bed of wet ashes, and got some breakfast.

While we were engaged in eating we were called on by a young man who was living with Mr. Russell. He said that the storm had done them a deal of damage; the tide had washed away Russell's garden and fences, and almost set his house adrift, and he wished me to go down and see the wreck. I did as he requested, and was astonished to see the damage done. Not only was Russell's nice garden washed away, but a bulkhead that he had been all summer building was torn to fragments, and his house badly shattered. Farther down the beach the damage was not so great, and the people were glad to get off with the loss of their boats and scows. But every one had been kept awake, and all considered it a very severe tempest.

I came very near losing my life on my return. I had waited till afternoon, and as it was impossible to get back in a canoe, I was obliged to return by the beach;

and the tide being up, I had to keep close in to the cliffs. As night closed in the wind began to rise, and before I had reached half way home it blew violently, accompanied with a drizzling rain that served to nearly blind me, and it was with difficulty I stumbled along over the trees and avalanches of earth that the storm had hurled down from the cliffs above. I had now to pass round a precipitous point which projected into the Bay, and around which the water was about two feet deep, although the tide was rapidly ebbing. The wind dashed the waves against this cliff so that the spray flew higher than my head, and wet me through. I had reached the outer point, and could only creep along by keeping as close as possible to the bank, which rose perpendicularly over my head a hundred feet, while the waters of the Bay prevented my going out on the flats, which is usually done at low tide, for fear of the falling trees and clay. Suddenly I heard an uproar overhead, and felt a trembling of the earth, which plainly indicated a landslide. There I was, pinned up between the cliff and the water, with no alternative but to wade along. At length down came a portion of the cliff directly behind me, bringing in its descent three or four enormous spruce trees, and with a noise that nearly stunned me, and with a splash that completely covered me with the muddy water. I did not know where it was coming next, but had every reason to believe that the whole face of the cliff was falling. I, however, succeeded in getting round the point, and past all danger, and shortly reached the house, covered with yellow mud. The captain, who had been expecting me, had heard the noise of the falling mass, and, apprehending some accident, was about starting out with the dogs and lantern, when my appearance satisfied him that at least I was alive. I did not realize the danger, from the excitement consequent upon such a

G

situation, till I had fairly calmed down, and began to reflect on the narrow escape I had.

The next morning we visited the place, and judged that the quantity of clay that had fallen exceeded a thousand tons. The trees, one of which measured six feet through at the butt, were splintered into fragments by the concussion of the fall, and their limbs lay strewed along the beach under the foot of the cliff. I learned enough by that adventure never to attempt the feat again, and would rather have stopped a week with some of the neighbors down the beach than to have endeavored reaching home by walking around the cliffs after dark, in a gale of wind, and nearly high tide.

Shortly after this occurrence, a Chenook chief, named To-mán-a-wos, came over from the Columbia, and stopped in the lodge with Toke's people. I did not fancy this arrangement at all, as we had no work to set them about, and I knew we should be continually annoyed by their begging, for they had come to pass the winter. They got one dose, however, that warmed them up finely. We always bought the whole pepper, preferring it to the mixture of dirt, cinders, corn-meal, and store sweepings usually sold as ground pepper, and, when we wished any ground or pulverized, were accustomed to use our coffee-mill, and, after finishing the pepper, would clean the mill by grinding a handful or two of coffee, which afterward was thrown away.

One morning, the captain, having ground some pepper and cleaned the mill in the usual manner, left the mixture of coffee and pepper in a tea-cup on the table, and both of us went out to chop some wood.

Old Suis, being desirous to treat her friends to a cup of coffee (a beverage all the Coast Indians are fond of), sent over to our house to borrow some. The little girl who came, not finding either of us in, and seeing a cup full of freshly-ground coffee, took it without saying any thing, and carried it to old Suis, who poured it into a tea-kettle and gave it a good boiling, after which the decoction was served round with plenty of sugar, and drunk as hot as they could bear it.   The first we learned of the matter was seeing the whole of the Indians, old and young, running toward us with their mouths open, tongues out, and all blowing like so many locomotive engines.   "Holloa!" said the captain to me, "what's the matter now, do you suppose?   What jugglery can they be up to, puffing away at that rate?"   I was as much at a loss as he was, and watched them till they all came up and sat down around us.   At last old Suis, who had a quart pot of water with her to cool her tongue in, made out to tell me what was the matter, and to charge me with having put some bad medicine in the coffee to kill them.

When we understood what was the trouble, we laughed so that I could not explain to them the state of affairs ; but, finding they did not consider the matter as a joke—certainly not a cool one—I told them the reason the pepper was with the coffee, and took occasion to read them a lecture on taking things without asking.   They were careful after that to find out what were the ingredients of coffee before they ventured to drink.   The dose did not harm them, although they went blowing round all day, to the intense delight of the captain, who was always glad to have them " served out," as he called it, whenever they went round pilfering.

I have before mentioned their superstitious belief in the spirits of the dead, or *memelose*, as they term them, and we soon had another sample.   One night we heard three reports of gunshots in the lodge.   " Now they are having sport," said the old man ; " well, let them fight it out, I sha'n't go near them."   He had scarcely spoken, when one of the Indians, looking half scared to death, burst open the door, and begged me to take my lantern and go over to the lodge. I asked him what was the matter. He said that they had heard a canoe with many paddles come up the river, and supposing it to contain some friends, went out to meet them; but, although they called several times, they received no reply, when they became alarmed, and Tománawos fired off his rifle; but the *memelose* chased them into the lodge, and then Tománawos fired his double-barreled gun. But the *memelose* was there still, and they were all afraid, and wished me to go over, as the *memelose* were afraid of a white man and would leave. I accordingly lit my lantern and followed the Indian over. I found them all hudded into their bunks, afraid to stir. Tománawos then handed me his gun, which he had again loaded, with the request that I would fire it off. I did so, sending both charges directly through the roof, when they pronounced the *memelose* to be driven off, and all came out of their hiding-places highly gratified. It was of no use for me to attempt to reason with them on the folly of their superstition; they would not reason or talk on the subject; but to any attempt to convince them of the absurdity of their fears they had but one reply, " You are a white man, and can't see or hear our *memelose;* but we Indians can, and we understand their talk, and you do not."

The captain made all sorts of fun of the nonsense, as he called it, and was always laughing at them; but I, on the contrary, endeavored to get them to explain their views to me, and always tried to respect their feelings. When I returned and related the circumstances to the old man, he was very much delighted, and promised to fix up a *memelose* for them the next night, provided I would not say any thing to the Indians. He then selected a

pumpkin with a green rind, and hollowed it out, scrap-
ing the inside down to the thin skin for nose, eyes, and
mouth, so that, by placing a candle inside, a green and
ghastly-looking spectre was produced. This was kept
out of sight till the next night, when he carried it over,
and placed it directly in front of the lodge door, among
some bushes. He then went in and sat down by the
lodge fire. After a few minutes one of the slaves step-
ped out for some wood, but directly came back and whispered to old Suis, who, in turn, whispered to the rest,
and then they huddled round the door to see what was
there.

Tománawos and Peter got down their guns, and gave
the object a couple of shots without effect; but, while
they were loading again, old Toke, who had just returned in his canoe, came up without seeing the light, and
stumbled over a log, and fell directly on the object of
their terror. Then they discovered what it was, and were
highly pleased when they found it to be a joke.

But it did not have the effect the captain intended,
and I advised him not to attempt any more experiments
on their credulity.

I turned their belief in my medical knowledge to good
account on several occasions, and was able, by a very
simple experiment, to save all of our cabbages, of which
the Indians were very fond. We had been annoyed,
while packing our salmon, by thousands of crows, who
would light down in flocks on our salmon, and eat them
up before our eyes; but the cunning rascals knew what
a gun was, and, although they were so bold that they
would walk about like poultry, yet the moment they saw
us take a gun from the house they were off. I had shot
several, but it was of no use; it seemed that for every
one I killed there was an increase of a hundred. At
length one day, while overhauling my trunk, I found a

paper of strychnine.   I immediately put some on three or four salmon, which I laid out for the crows.   Down they came and gobbled up the fish, and then, with a squawk, would roll over on their backs and die.   In this manner I slew a great number, and it had the effect of frightening the rest so bad that they did not trouble us any more.

The Indians saw the whole affair, and at first were very much pleased to see me kill those "bad birds," as they call the crows; but old Suis told them she was afraid, if I got vexed, that I might put some of that white medicine where they themselves would be poisoned.   I assured her such would not be the case except with the cabbages, for I had found some of her people had been helping themselves; so I selected out a dozen heads, which I told her she might have, and then asked her to go round with me and see me put the white medicine on the rest.   She did so, and I sprinkled every cabbage-head with flour, which I had previously put into a blue paper similar to that the strychnine was in.   The effect was excellent, and we never lost another cabbage.

CHAPTER X.

Old Suis relates about the Indians of the Bay.—A Description of the
Coast Indians.—Writers apt to confuse the Reader in Accounts of
Indians.—General Appearance.—Dress of Women.—Dress of Men.
—Smoking.—Fondness for Ardent Spirits.—Whom they received the
first from.—Gambling.—A Description of gambling Games.—Orna-
ments.—Description of the Hɑwqua or Wampum.—Method of ob-
taining the Shells.—Evidences of Wealth.—Great Weight of Ear Or-
naments.—Position of Females among the Coast Tribes.—Duties of
Women. — Various Manufactures. — Lodge Furniture. — Ancient
Method of Cooking. — Bread-making. — Peter's Method of making
Bread.—Time of Eating.— Slaves.—Fondness of Indians for their
Children.—Method of flattening the Head.—Flat Head a mark of
Aristocracy.—Reception of Strangers.—Reception of Friends.—Singular Custom.—Great Newsmongers.—Polygamy.—Customs toward
young Girls.—Singular Superstition.—Fasts.—Religion.—Heathen-
ism.

Old Suis had formerly lived on the same spot where
we were now residing, and it was there her first husband
was killed.   It was many years ago, she said, that a
party of warriors from Chehalis, called the *Que-nái-nar*,
or the Strong Men, came to her lodge, and, having got
into a wrangle with her husband, chased him across the
creek and killed him.   They then went up the Palux
to near where old Tomhays had built his lodge, where
they had a fight, and killed a great number of Palux Indians ; and the place was ever after called A-wil-ka-túm-
ar, or the Bloody Ground.   The chief who headed the
expedition was named Kaith-lah-wil'-nu, a very savage
fellow, who was soon afterward killed by the Queniūlt
Indians.

As I became more familiar with the language, and the
Indians became better acquainted with me, they gradually threw off their reserve, and were much more ready

to communicate information on any subject I wished to speak about than they at first had been.

We are too apt to consider the Indian as the being he is represented in those fictitious tales and poems of imaginary Indian life which have been in use from the first days of the settlement of the American continent. "It was supposed," says Schoolcraft, "that the Indian was at all times and in all places 'a stoic of the woods,' always statuesque, always formal, always passionless, always on stilts, always speaking in metaphors, a cold imbodiment of bravery, endurance, and savage heroism. Writers depicted him as a man who uttered nothing but principles of natural right, who always harangued eloquently, and was ready, with unmoved philosophy, on all occasions, to sing his death-song at the stake, to show the world how a warrior should die." The Indian is naturally reserved before strangers, and very suspicious. He is full of superstitious beliefs, and distrustful, deeming every man his enemy till he has proved to the contrary. At all times and places he is under influences of hopes and fears, and it is his fear that makes him suspicious, and his ignorance that makes him superstitious; and those persons who have only met the Indian under such circumstances can only view him as the individual represented above. But let the Indian once get acquainted, and feel that he is in the presence of a friend and one who feels an interest in his welfare, and he then throws off this reserve, and then it is seen that he can talk and laugh like the rest of the human family. His reserve is most completely thrown off when at home in the midst of his lodge circle, or in seasons of leisure and retirement in the depths of the forest. Then the stranger who may have gained his confidence not only has the opportunity to learn his method of domestic economy, but can hear the relation of those tales and legends which have been handed down from generation to generation, and which the casual visitor or stranger is never permitted to listen to.

As it was not till after I had become well acquainted with the people and their language that I was enabled to get their ideas of their origin, I shall leave that subject for a future consideration, and commence with a description of these Indians just as I found them ; and as I only intend giving an account of what I actually saw, I trust that my descriptions of the Indians may be understood to refer to those tribes on the coast from the Columbia to Fuca's Straits, and not to Indians of the interior, whose habits and customs are necessarily different ; for, although the whole Pacific region, and, in fact, the whole American continent, from the Esquimaux at the north to the Patagonians at the south, appears to be peopled with one and the same race, differing but slightly, considering the varieties of soil, climate, and situation, and the consequent varieties in the mode of life, yet writers are too apt, in speaking of the American Indians, to confound the customs of tribes whose manners, in fact, are entirely different. This only serves to confuse the reader, without answering any good end. Thus one writer on the Indians of California and Oregon asserts that it is the universal custom of the Indians to burn the bodies of their dead. Another, with equal earnestness, states that they always bury their dead in canoes ; while another, quite as certain, states that they are buried in rude boxes deposited in the earth. These writers were all right so far as what they had personally witnessed. The Digger Indians of California *do* burn their dead, but the Chenook and other Coast Indians bury their dead in canoes, and the Indians of the interior, who have no canoes, perform their interments in the earth.

Of the Coast Indians that I have seen there seems to

be so little difference in their style of living that a description of one family will answer for the whole.

The Indians north of the Columbia are, for the most part, good-looking, robust men, some of them having fine, symmetrical forms. They have been represented as diminutive, with crooked legs and uncouth features. This is not correct; but, as a general rule, the direct reverse is the truth. Their complexion is that of the usual copper color of the North American Indians, but their color is much lighter than the Indians of California, or those of Missouri, Alabama, or Florida. The hair of both sexes is long and very black, that of the men hanging loose over the shoulders, while the women, as a usual thing, tie theirs up behind in a sort of cue, and the young girls braid theirs into two tails, with the ends tied with ribbons or twine. Both sexes part the hair on the top of the head, and take great pains to keep it well combed, although their combs have usually very coarse teeth, not well adapted to remove either dirt or insects. They are very fond of dress, and are apt and excellent imitators. The women are expert with the needle, and fashion and make their dresses with great rapidity, imitating as near as they can the dresses of the white women they may have seen. They prefer calicoes with small figures on them; and a blue ground, with little white dots or sprigs, seems to be the most in demand. White blankets are usually preferred, but some will wear blue or green, and a few buy red ones; but white, with a very narrow black stripe across the ends, is the favorite.

They are excellent judges of such articles as they want and are accustomed to. The women try the calicoes, to ascertain if the colors are fast, by chewing the cloth in their mouths. The men are fond of getting boots or shoes, and stockings, though, as a general thing, neither men or women wear any thing on their feet, the mildness of the climate, and their being so much in the water, making them too much of an incumbrance; and I have frequently seen persons of both sexes, who had been sitting in the house for some time with shoes and stockings on, take them off as soon as they were ready to get into their canoes.   Before the introduction of blankets and calicoes among them, they used the dressed skins of the deer, bear, and sea-otter.   The women wore a sort of skirt or tunic, made from the inner bark of the young cedar, prepared by beating till it was soft, and then spun into a yarn-like thread, which was woven thickly on a string that passed around the body, the ends hanging down like a thick fringe reaching to the knees.   This garment is still used by old women, and by all the females when they are at work in the water, and is called by them their *siwash coat*, or Indian gown.

The young men dress in clothes procured from the whites, and some of them, when dressed up, look well enough to appear in almost any company.   The old men, like old Toke and his old brother Colote, seldom wear any clothing but a shirt and a blanket.

Some of them are very fond of smoking tobacco, but the practice is not common.   They mix the dried leaves of the bearberry (*Arbutus uva ursi*) with their tobacco, which they then call *kinuse* or *kinutl*.   The plant is called quer-lo-e-chintl.   Tobacco, when thus mixed, is much improved, and I prefer it, for smoking, to the common coarse, cheap trash usually found for sale on the frontiers.   Some of these Indians will stupefy themselves for a short time by swallowing quantities of smoke, which, after being retained in the stomach and lungs a while, is poured out in volumes from the mouth and nostrils.   They are all extravagantly fond of ardent spirits, and are not particular what kind they have, provided it is strong, and gets them drunk quickly.   This habit they have acquired since the visit of Lewis and Clarke in 1805, for they state that they had not observed any liquors of an intoxicating kind used among any of the Indians west of the Rocky Mountains; and old Carcumcum has related to me the fact of her remembering the first time that any liquor was given to the Chenook Indians, and, from her description, I should think it was when Broughton went into the Columbia in the brig Chatham, for she said the *tyee*, or chief of the vessel, had *gold dollar* things, meaning epaulets, on his shoulders, and was in a man-of-war. They drank some rum out of a wine-glass—how much she did not recollect; but she *did* recollect that they got drunk, and were so scared at the strange feeling that they ran into the woods and hid till they were sober. The rest, who did not get any rum, thought they had gone crazy or had turned foolish, and applied to them the word *pilton* or *pelton*, meaning a crazy or foolish man, a term which is still applied to a drunken person. *Partlelum* is another term for drunkenness—*partle*, full; *lum*, rum; or, full of rum. They have been apt learners since that time, and now will do any thing for the sake of whisky. Old Carcumcum said they had but a very little rum from the traders till the settlement of Astoria, when they began to get a little more used to it; and as the country has become settled, they can get it readily from all quarters.

Another, and the more natural vice, these Indians possess is an attachment to gambling, which they will pursue at all hazards, and with a most fearful earnestness. Not only will they stake all their property, even to stripping themselves of their shirts and blankets, but I have known them sell themselves as slaves for a term of years, or till another lucky chance enables them to pay up their bets.

Frequent wrangles, fights, and deadly strife are caused during these gambling scenes, and whenever any whisky can be obtained, serious results often ensue.   The principal and favorite game is called La-hull.   This, though apparently a word of French origin, is, I believe, an Indian word, for I know of no French word sounding any thing like it which is at all applicable to the game, which is thus played : A mat is first placed on the floor, with the centre raised up so as to form a small ridge, which is kept in its place by four wooden pins stuck through the mat into the ground.   Two persons play at this game, who are seated at each end of the mat.   Each player has ten discs of wood, two inches in diameter, and a little over an eighth of an inch thick, resembling the men used in playing backgammon, but much larger. The only distinguishing feature about these men, or wheels, is the different manner the edges are colored. There are but two pieces of value; one has the edge blackened entirely round, and the other is perfectly plain, while the others have different quantities of color on them, varying from the black to the white.   These discs are then inclosed in a quantity of the inner bark of the cedar, pounded very fine, and called *tupsoe.*   The player, after twisting and shuffling them up in all sorts of forms, separates them into two equal parts, both being enveloped in the tupsoe.   These are then rapidly moved about on the mat from side to side, the other player keeping his eyes most intently fixed upon them all the time. He has bet either on the black or the white one, and now, to win, has to point out which of the two parcels contains it.   As soon as he makes his selection, which is done by a gesture of his hand, the parcel is opened, and each piece is rolled down the mat to the ridge in the centre.   He can thus see the edges of all, and knows whether he has lost or won.   They will play at this game sometimes for weeks, particularly during the winter season, only leaving off to sleep a little, or eat.

Another game is played by little sticks or stones, which are rapidly thrown from hand to hand with the skill of experienced jugglers, accompanied all the while by some song adapted to the occasion, the winning or losing the game depending on being able to guess correctly which hand the stick is in. This game can be played by any number of persons, and is usually resorted to when the members of two different tribes meet, and is a sort of trial of superiority. Before commencing the game the betting begins, and each article staked is put before the owner, and whoever wins takes the whole pile.

Another game, which is usually played by the women, consists in a sort of dice made of beaver's teeth, with hieroglyphics on them. These are shaken in the hand, and thrown down, the game being according to the mark on the teeth, as the spots are counted on dice.

The ornaments worn by these Indians are not very various, the men being contented with a black ostrich plume tied like a band round their caps, though some will occasionally stick an eagle's feather in their hair, or add a few of the tail-feathers of the blue jay to their cap ornament.

The women are fond of dark blue cut glass beads, which are highly prized. Light blue ones are only worn by the slaves. But the most valued ornament is the howqua or wampum. This is a species of small shell, of a cylindrical shape, pointed at one end, slightly curved, and resembling a nearly straight horn. It is a species of the Denticularium, and is found by the northern Indians somewhere north of Vancouver's Island. It passes as money among them, and is called *Siwash* dollars.

The method by which this shell is obtained is said by Jewett to be thus : A piece of wood a foot square is filled full of little pegs, which are sharpened to a fine point. This block is fastened to a long pole, and thrust down into the water till it reaches the shell-fish, and the sharp points enter the hollow shells, breaking them from their hold on the bottom, and bringing them to the surface. Another method described to me by the Indians is to tie a large piece of seal or whale meat to a pole, and press that down firmly on the shells, which, becoming imbedded in the meat, are easily broken off, and thus secured. I, however, have never seen the operation, therefore can not speak positively on the subject.   These shells are pure white, and, when made up into bands for the forehead or for ear ornaments, are very pretty, and form a striking contrast with the jet black hair of the females. As these shells are evidences of wealth, the women are anxious to display as many as they can on great occasions.   Some of these girls I have seen with the whole rim of their ears bored full of holes, into each of which would be inserted a string of these shells that reached to the floor, and the whole weighing so heavy that, to save their ears from being pulled off, they were obliged to wear a band across the top of the head.   In addition to these shell ornaments, which are seldom worn, they have, for common wear, brass rings around their wrists and arms, and gold, silver, or brass finger-rings.   Silver rings are preferred, and these are usually made by the brothers or lovers for the young girls out of the silver coin they get from the whites.

The rest of their ornaments are, like those of the white women, made up from shawls, or ribbons, or some showy pattern for a dress.

They are very eager to get the camphor-wood trunks that come from China, covered with bright red or green paint, and studded with brass nails. Into these they will stow every thing they can get.

Articles of crockery are very desirable; and although they seldom use knives and forks, or dishes, still they like to have them, and feel proud, when a white person eats with them, to have a chance to show out their table furniture.

With these Indians the position of the women is not so degraded as with the tribes of the Plains. Lewis and Clarke, who noticed the fact from its marked difference from those tribes they had journeyed among, remark:

"The treatment of women is often considered as the standard by which the moral qualities of savages are to be estimated. Our own observation, however, induces us to think that the importance of the female in savage life has no necessary relation to the virtues of the men, but is regulated wholly by their capacity to be useful. Where the women can aid in procuring sustenance for the tribe, they are treated with more equality, and their importance is proportioned to the share which they take in that labor, while in countries where the sustenance is chiefly procured by the exertions of the men, the women are considered and treated as burdens. Thus among the Clatsops and Chenooks, who live chiefly upon fish and roots, which the women are equally expert with the men in procuring, the former have a rank and influence very rarely found among the Indians. The females are permitted to speak freely before the men, to whom, indeed, they sometimes address themselves in a tone of authority. On many subjects their judgments and opinions are respected, and in matters of trade their advice is generally asked and pursued. The labors of the family, too, are shared almost equally. The men collect the wood and make fires, assist in cleaning fish, make the houses, canoes, and wooden utensils, and, whenever a stranger is entertained or a feast is to be prepared, the meats are cooked and served up by the men."

The peculiar province of the women is to prepare and take care of the fish and berries for the winter's use ; to collect roots, make the mats, which are made from rushes, and to manufacture the various articles which are made of rushes, flags, cedar bark, and bear grass. But the management of the canoes, and many of the occupations which elsewhere devolve on the female, are here common to both sexes.

The manufacture of mats is a very important one, as the mat serves many useful purposes. It is used to sit upon during the day ; it forms the bed at night ; it lines the inside of the lodge, to keep out both wind and rain, and forms the tent when traveling about. The common bulrush, or cat-tail flag, is used for the purpose, and is called *lisquis tupsoe*, or mat-grass. This is cut during the months of July and August, and carefully dried in the sun, and, when in a proper state, is stowed away in some dry place till the fall and winter, when the rains keep them at work within doors. When mats are to be made, the head woman of the family sorts out the rushes or flags, and cuts them of the desired length, which is usually three feet. These are then taken, two at a time, placing the top or small end of one with the bottom or large end of the other. These are fastened by a cord twisted round the ends, and the process continued till enough are secured to make a mat of the length required. Those for sleeping on are six or seven feet long. The lining mats may vary with the size of the lodge, and are from ten to twenty, and sometimes thirty feet in length. After each length has been determined on, it is rolled up till wanted for manufacturing. Each female, whether slave or free, then has her mat assigned her to make. The rushes are laid down on the lodge floor, or, if the weather is pleasant, are carried out of doors. Two pegs or stakes driven into the ground, one at each end of the mat, and to which the string which binds the ends is made fast, secure the whole. The operator then takes a needle, made from the small bone in the second joint of the wing of the common blue crane, which is straight, long, and slender, and which has a hole drilled in one end for an eye, and the other sharpened similar to cutting off a quill when about making a pen. Into this needle is fastened a piece of twine, made of the rushes twisted by hand, and of a length in accordance with the size of the mat. The needle is then passed through every one of the rushes, and the string drawn firm and smooth. A creased bone is then rubbed over the whole length of the twine, which serves to set the work and mark the thread distinctly. The operation is then repeated, the threads being inserted parallel to each other, about four inches apart. When the stitching is done, the whole is bound around with a flat, three-ply braid of rushes, and the mat is finished.

Some are very prettily ornamented round the edges with colored grasses, neatly worked and woven in. These mats are so well made that they shed water like a duck's back, and, when set on their edge, as effectually exclude rain as the best shingle roof. They are very light, and are excellent, while traveling, to wrap around blankets or clothes. The newly-made ones have a very fragrant smell, which makes them pleasant and healthy to sleep upon. When the mats are all made, the next work is basket-making. These are woven from spruce roots, bear-grass, and willow bark. They are exceedingly strong, and so compact and tight as to hold water. These are woven with figures of horses, dogs, and birds depicted on them by means of different colored grasses. Black, red, and yellow are the extent of their dyes. The black is produced by burying the willow bark or grass in the black mud of the Bay for a few weeks; the red, by the bark of the black alder; and the yellow, by a mixture of nettle roots with some shrub they procure from the Northern Indians. Occasionally they make baskets and hats of the pure white grass, and they are very handsome. The hats of the Queniūlt and other Northern Indians are made of precisely the same conical form as the Chinese hats, and are only worn in wet weather to shed rain. This peculiar form has either been handed down to them by tradition, or was introduced among them by the Chinese who were carried to Nootka by Meares from Canton in 1788, to assist in building the schooner Northwest America, and who, he writes, remained with the Indians, and took wives among them.

The usual articles in a lodge for domestic use are their iron pots or kettles, or brass kettles, tin pots, cups, and pans, an axe or two, three or four knives and a few spoons, all of which are procured from the Hudson Bay Company. They manufacture for themselves bowls, platters, and spoons of wood, usually of maple or black alder, which grows here very large, some that I have seen being sixty or seventy feet high, and from two to four feet in diameter. They also make spoons of the horn of the musk-ox, which they procure in trade of the Indians from the North. These spoons, which are curiously shaped, and are often elaborately carved, are formed by first boiling or steaming the horn, and then, while it is soft, moulding it in the desired shape.

The women confine their operations to cooking, making mats and baskets, and their own dresses, and also spin the thread and twine for making nets. This operation is performed in a very simple and primitive manner by twisting the strands between the palm of the hand and the bare leg, similar to the method a shoemaker uses to make his "waxed ends" for sewing leather. These cords, when spun, are tied up in hanks of thirty or forty fathoms each, and carefully stowed away for future use. The men make the nets, spears, fish-hooks, daggers, and carve out the spoons, bowls, and dishes.

These are the usual occupations of the winter during rainy weather, when they prefer being in the house; and although they will generally stop work when a stranger enters their lodge, and by many such are deemed perfectly idle and worthless, yet they manage, during the course of the winter, to make a great many articles which are disposed of to the whites.

Their method of cooking is by simply roasting or boiling. This latter process was formerly done in baskets by means of hot stones. The article, whether fish or flesh, was put in the basket, then covered with water, and a supply of hot stones kept up till the whole was cooked. I have seen them perform this process, as they fancy their salmon tastes better when cooked this way. The stones, when taken from the fire red hot, were first dipped in water to remove any dirt or ashes, then thrown into the basket, and soon the water would boil violently. I never perceived that any improvement to the flavor of either fish or meat was gained by this style, and much prefer our own custom of boiling victuals in an iron vessel over the fire. The roasting process is the same as that described at Chenook. Bread is made of flour and water without salt, baked in thin cakes in the ashes. When hot it is very good, but rather tough when cold. Most of them can make good bread when they feel like it, and some are able to make good cake and pies. These accomplishments have been learned from the white women they have occasionally met with.

Peter, the young Indian in Toke's lodge, had a method of making most excellent bread, which I will describe for the benefit of persons going to the frontiers, and who think that without brewer's yeast, or soda, or saleratus, no bread can be made fit to eat.   Peter had lived some time with Cale Weeks, of Astoria, who had imparted to him this chemical secret.   The process was simply this : Half a teaspoonful of fine salt is added to a teacupful of flour, and water enough added to make a stiff batter ; this is usually mixed in a tin pint pot, which is then set into a pan of blood-warm water, and placed near enough to the fire to keep up about the same temperature.   In ten or fifteen minutes it begins to ferment, and when the mass has swelled so as nearly to fill the pot, it is mixed up with flour and warm water into dough, which must be well kneaded.   The Dutch oven or tin baker is being warmed during this process, and the dough is immediately put into it and set by the fire, but not too near, and shortly it will begin to rise.   When the bake-kettle is nearly full, bake the whole over a bed of hot coals, and the bread, when done, is most excellent.   The only trouble with this method is that it wants more watching than the ordinary way of bread-making.   However, the method is one that is useful to miners, and should be known.   There is many a poor fellow who has lost his health by living on " flippers" fried in pork fat because he could not get any saleratus, that might have saved the troubles consequent upon sickness in the mines, had he but known this simple recipe.

When meat or fish is boiled, it is taken on to a large wooden platter or tin pan, and, after being cut up, is divided round by the matron of the establishment, each one receiving an equal share.   The water which the food has been boiled in is considered a luxury, and each one has a clam shell, which is dipped into the kettle as often as they desire to drink of the broth.

They usually have three regular meals a day : early

in the morning, at noon, and at sundown. They, however, do not confine their appetites to these set times, but eat whenever and as often as they take a fancy, even getting up during the night to cook. But these outside meals are not from the family supply of provisions: that, the matron looks after with a jealous eye; but any one who may bring in game, fish, or oysters usually distributes them to those who wish.

Their property consists in movable or personal property. They never considered land of any value till they were taught so by the whites. If I or any of the settlers had been allowed to have purchased the Indian titles to the land when we first went there, the whole tract from the Columbia to Fuca Straits could have been bought for a few trifling presents. All the value they set upon their grounds is for hunting and fishing, and the only bounds are such as they set between themselves and neighboring tribes. All such property is common stock, each member of the tribe owning as much interest in it as the chiefs, although, when dealing with the whites, the chiefs assume to own the whole.

They were glad to have us settle on and improve their lands. They knew they could not do so themselves, and they were content to be paid for the land so used by what the settlers saw fit to give them of the potatoes or wheat raised.

What they consider as property is any thing they can exchange or barter away for articles they desire to possess. This consists of Chinese chests, blue beads, blankets, calico, brass kettles, and other culinary articles, guns, fishing apparatus, canoes, and slaves or horses.

Their slaves are purchased from the Northern Indians, and are either stolen or captives of war, and were regularly brought down and sold to the southern tribes. The price is from one to five hundred dollars, or from twenty to one hundred blankets, valued at five dollars each. Some are even higher than that, and not unfrequently a valuable canoe is added to the bargain.

In their domestic relations they seem very fond of each other, and the parents seem devotedly affectionate to their children. I have never known of an instance, during their wildest drunken freaks of fury or rage, where one of their own children was hurt or badly treated, although at such times they are very apt to treat their slaves with barbarity.

The most singular custom among these people is that of flattening or compressing the head of the infant. Where this custom originated is hard to tell. Lewis and Clarke state that it is not peculiar to that part of the continent, since it was among the first objects that struck the attention of Columbus. " But," they add, " wherever it began, or what was its origin, the practice is now universal among the tribes west of the Rocky Mountains, in the region of the Columbia, and it is confined to them, for, with the exception of the Snake Indians, who are called Flat-heads, the fashion is not known to the east of that barrier."

The method adopted to produce this deformity is as follows : A cradle, like a bread trough, is hollowed out from a piece of cedar, and, according to the taste of the parent, is either fancifully carved, or is as simple in its artistic appearance as a pig's trough. This cradle, or *canim*, or canoe, as they term it, is lined inside with the softest of cedar bark, well pounded and cleaned so as to be as soft as wool. On this the infant is placed as soon as it is born, and covered with the softest cloth or skins they can find. A little pillow at one end slightly elevates the head. The child is placed flat on its back, and a cushion of wool or feathers laid on its forehead. An oblong square piece of wood or bark, having one end

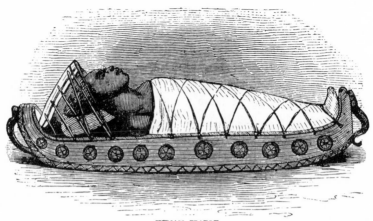

INDIAN CRADLE.

fastened by strings to the head of the canoe, is now brought down on the cushion, and firmly secured by strings tied to the sides of the cradle, and causing the cushion to press upon the child's forehead. The infant is then so bound into the cradle that it can not stir hand or foot, and in this position it remains a year or more, only being taken out to be washed and for exercise.

This pressure on the forehead causes the head to expand laterally, giving an expression of great broadness to the face; but I never perceived that it affected the mind at all, although it disfigures them very much in appearance. I have seen several whose heads had not been thus pressed, and they were smart, intelligent, and quite good-looking; but they were laughed at by the others, who asserted that their mothers were too lazy to shape their heads properly. This flattening of the head appears to be a sort of mark of royalty or badge of aristocracy, for their slaves are not permitted to treat their children thus; but, although I have seen persons with and others without this deformity, I never could discover any superiority of intellect of one over the other.

When a stranger, either a white man or an Indian, of

rank visits them, the head of the house, or tyee, always cooks the meal which he serves up. This mark of attention is always given to those they respect; and any person who has had his food prepared by the women in a chief's lodge on his first arrival, may rest assured that he was considered as a *kultus tillicum*, or common person. Their method of reception and salutation, even of their own relatives, is singular, and I have often been amused to witness it. I have seen instances where they were expecting friends they had not seen for a long time. As the time approached, they would be careful to collect as much food as they could, to give their friends a kind reception, and some one or other was kept constantly on the watch for the expected canoe. The weather, the wind, the state of the tide, all were discussed, as to the probable effect each would have to hasten or retard the coming of their friends. At length a canoe is seen in the distance. Can it be they? No, that is not like their sail; but perhaps they have got another. Yes, it must be; it is they. All now is glee, and the canoe comes up the creek, and nears the shore. Instead of rushing into each other's arms with congratulations and embraces, not a soul advances to greet them. All have gone into the lodge, and each one, at his accustomed place, appears as calm, and is pursuing his avocations as if they never dreamed of any one approaching them. The party in the canoe then come ashore, leaving all their traveling equipage in charge of a slave or two, apparently for the purpose of first ascertaining if their visit is welcome.

They all then enter the lodge, and seat themselves around the fire and near the door. No one takes the slightest notice of them, nor is a word spoken. I have thus seen them sit for ten minutes. At last a few guttural words from the visitors are answered by a grunt

H

from the others.   Other clucking sounds are then heard,
and gradually they begin to talk, but not much.   Food
is now set before them, and, while they eat, they begin
to grow social, and at length they throw off all restraint,
and gabble like so many geese.

What newspapers are to us, these traveling Indians
are with each other, and it is astonishing with what dispatch and correctness information is transmitted from
one part of the country to another.   I have frequently,
by this means, obtained correct intelligence of matters
transpiring in other portions of the territory weeks before the regular mail communication.   Old Suis was an
excellent person to spread news, and no sooner did any
of her people come with any information, but, woman-
like, she would run over and inform the captain and myself.   It was not customary to place much dependence
on information derived from such sources, but I often
found their tales were entirely to be relied on.

The marriage ceremony is very simple, and consists in
merely paying the parent or friends of the girl such articles as may be agreed upon, either slaves, canoes,
guns, blankets, or any thing else they may happen to
possess.   Polygamy is allowed among them, but is not
very common; only those who have plenty of means to
buy wives care to trouble themselves with more than
one.   I have noticed, as a general thing, that the young
men marry women much older than themselves, while
the young girls are married to men much their seniors.
The reason for this is, as I was told by them, that if the
young men marry young girls, both are so foolish they
do not know how to take care of each other; so the
young man takes a wife who has the experience requisite
to take her proper place in the lodge, and the young girl
is assisted and taught her duties by her more mature
husband.

When a young girl reaches womanhood, she has to go through a process of purification, which lasts a *moon*, or month. This is simply by bathing several times a day, and rubbing the body with rotten wood procured from the hemlock-tree. They are not allowed, during this period, to eat of any thing that is in season, either salmon, sturgeon, shell-fish, or berries, as it is believed that, in such cases, the fish would disappear, the shell-fish would make them sick, and the berries would fall off the bushes without ripening. And should there be a southeast wind, with signs of rain, they must, on no pretense, go out of the house, for *Toö-lux*, the south wind, is so offended if one of these young girls go out of doors, that he sends *Hah-ness'*, the thunder-bird, who shakes his wings, and causes the roaring thunder, his eyes, the mean while, sending forth sharp flashes of lightning. I never knew a thunder-storm occur while I resided in the Territory but what was attributed to some girl going out during her season of purification. It is at this period of life that both young men and women go through a ceremony which is to determine their future course in life, and is termed by them seeing their Tomáhnawos or Tománawos. Those who pass through this ordeal safely are generally the doctors, strong men, or skilled in all the Indian ways. Schoolcraft's remarks on the fasts of the Algonquins, though not precisely adapted to the Coast Indians, are so near to my own views that I quote the article entire:

" The rite of fasting is one of the most deep-seated and universal in the Indian ritual. It is practiced among all the American tribes, and is deemed by them essential to their success in life in every situation. No young man is fitted and prepared to begin the career of life until he has accomplished his great fast. Seven days appear to have been the ancient maximum limit of endurance, and the success of the devotee is inferred from the length of continued abstinence to which he is known to have attained. These fasts are anticipated by youth as one of the most important events of life. They are awaited with interest, prepared for with solemnity, and endured with a self-devotion bordering upon the heroic. Character is thought to be fixed from this period, and the primary fast thus prepared for and successfully established seems to hold that relative importance to subsequent years that is attached to a public profession of religious faith in civilized communities. It is at this period that the young men and young women 'see visions and dream dreams,' and fortune or misfortune is predicted from the guardian spirit chosen during this, to them, religious ordeal. The hallucinations of the mind are taken for divine inspiration. The effect is deeply felt and strongly impressed on the mind; too deeply, indeed, to be ever obliterated in after life. The father in the circle of his lodge, the hunter in the pursuit of the chase, and the warrior in the field of battle, think of the guardian genius which they fancy to accompany them, and trust to his power and benign influence under every circumstance. This genius is the absorbing theme of their silent meditations, and stands to them in all respects in place of the Christian's hope, with the single difference that, however deeply mused upon, the *name* is never uttered, and every circumstance connected with its selection, and the devotion paid to it, is most studiously and professedly concealed even from their nearest friends. Fasts in subsequent life appear to have for their object a renewal of the powers and virtues which they attribute to the rite; and they are observed more frequently by those who strive to preserve unaltered the ancient state of society among them, or by men who assume austere habits for the purpose of acquiring influence in the tribe, or as preparatives for war or some extraordinary feat. It is not known that there is any fixed day to be observed as a general fast. So far as the rule is followed, a general fast seems to have been observed in the spring, and to have *preceded* the general and customary feasts at that season.

" It will be inferred from these facts that the Indians believe fasts to be very meritorious. They are deemed most acceptable to the manitoes, or spirits, whose influence and protection they wish to engage or preserve. And it is thus clearly deducible that a very large portion of the time devoted by the Indians to secret worship, so to say, is devoted to these guardians or intermediate spirits, and not to the Great Spirit, or Creator."

These guardian spirits, or manitoes, of the Algonquin, are the Tománawos of the Coast Indian. It is his Tománawos that he seeks in early life, and, whatever it may be, he never will utter its name even to his nearest or dearest friend. This name, *Tománawos*, is also applied to works of magic performed by doctors, as, for instance, *mamoke Tománawos*, working medicine or spells; and a doctor or doctress is termed *Tománawos man* or *Tománawos woman;* but when spoken of as *nika, mika,* or *yaka Tománawos*, it refers to and means my, your, or their guardian spirit. The common people either have not passed through the ordeal of the long fast, or, having attempted, have failed. Those that have are considered as having *seen* their Tománawos, or having had supernatural revelations, which enable them to perform cures, and drive away the evil spirits who molest the sick. But all have their own private guardian spirit, to whom they make known their wants and troubles, either to ask for help, or to bewail and lament the loss of a friend. They do not, as is generally supposed, address a Great Spirit, neither do they believe in one overruling almighty maker of the world and all things contained therein; consequently, they do not address themselves except to their own private Tománawos, or Fetish, or Joss; and, as this worship or petition is always done in private, it is the reason why persons, not seeing any outward ceremonies among them, assert that they have no belief either in God or a future state.

They do not believe in the Christian revelation of a divine Creator, although many of them have been taught the precepts of Christianity by the Catholic priest who formerly resided at Chenook, and can give a very general account of all the prominent historical parts of the Bible from Genesis to our Savior's time; but that, they say, is about the white man's God, and has nothing to do with them. Their heaven is in the centre of the earth, which they believe to be hollow, and there all is happiness. No one reigns supreme there, but those who were chiefs on the earth retain their rank in a future state. They do not fight, but have a very pleasant time; and every night, if they feel disposed, they can go about revisiting the places they lived at while on earth.

The only evidence I have met with among them respecting a belief in future punishments appears to be in a species of transmigration of souls, which are supposed to be turned into birds, beasts, fishes, or even into inanimate subjects.

The creaking of trees in the forest is to them the wailing of some *memelose* or dead person, who has been transformed into the tree as a punishment for some offense committed during life.

Crows, eagles, owls, blue jays, and various beasts and reptiles, are the representations of bad spirits or devils, and are called *skookums*. Even the stones around the Bay have their peculiar legend. There are two large rocks near the south head of Long Island, in the Bay,

called *Mis'chin*, or Louse Rocks, and the legend is that
they were formerly a chief and his wife, who were very
bad people, and by their magic first introduced lice
among Indians; and one day, while bathing, they were,
by a superior medicine-man, turned into stones as a punishment.

Their ideas of sins which are to be punished are, however, very limited, and apply only to those who commit
some great crime, as the introduction of disease, or the
mischin, or other calamities among the tribe.

When a young person wishes to go through the ordeal of the fast, he is usually some time preparing his
mind for the event, and gradually accustoms himself to
a reduction of diet preparatory to fasting.   When he is
fully ready, he goes alone in his canoe to the nearest
landing-place, at the foot of some high mountain, taking
nothing with him but his axe and a bowl for water.
After hauling up the canoe and securing it, he fills his
bowl with water, first having washed himself in the river.   Then he proceeds to the top of the hill or mountain, and, having selected a suitable spot, builds a fire.
His duty now is to keep that fire burning constantly
during the period of his fast, which lasts from three to
seven days.   During this time he neither sleeps nor
eats.   He may drink a little water, but he must frequently wash himself, and on no account let the fire go out.
This continued fast, together with keeping awake, and
jumping about over and through the fire and smoke,
singing, and calling on his Tománawos to appear, gradually weakens his nerves so that he sees strange visions.

A young Indian who had been out for three days, and
then went to sleep, and did not succeed in his attempt to
become a doctor, told me that he saw what appeared to
be the ocean, and out of it all sorts of animals and fish
were projecting their heads—whales, salmon, bears, seals,

lizards, and skookums, or devils. But he had not strength to continue his fast any longer, which he should have done so that the medicine Tománawos would have appeared to him. It is only the strong men or women who see the medicine Tománawos; all others see Tománawos of inferior grade. His, instead of being a medicine, taught him to make canoes and catch salmon and sturgeon.

What he had seen was the fog rising from the river, and the tops of the spruce and fir trees reaching above it had appeared to his disordered fancy to be the beasts, fishes, and devils he had supposed them.

CHAPTER XI.

Doctors, or Medicine-men.—Simples used as Medicine.—Polypodium. —Wild-cat Hair.—An excellent Salve.—Disinclination of Indians to impart Information in regard to their Medicines.—Necromancy of the Doctors.—Sickness of Suis.—Sacodlye, the Doctor, and his Magic. — Old John, the Doctor, and his Method.— John removes the Devil and Suis recovers.—Old Sal-tsi-mar's Sickness and Death.— Description of the Burial.—Funeral Ceremonies.—Death Songs.— Change of Names on the Death of a Friend.—Meaning of Indian Names.—Superstitions and Ceremonies.—Effects of Christianity.— Missionaries.—The Indian Idea of the Christian Religion.

THE doctors, or medicine-men, are supposed to possess the power of exorcising or driving away the memelose, or spirits of the dead, and the skookums, or evil spirits, that are supposed to prey on the vitals of a sick person, causing death.

In all instances where I have seen the doctors performing cures, it has been by the agency of mesmeric influence; and the stronger that power is possessed by the doctor, the more famous does he become as a practitioner.

The young men, after passing through the fast, and being found qualified, are farther instructed by some of the old doctors, but particularly as to the nature of the skookums, and whether cures can not be effected by simples, without resort to mesmerism. As the doctors always require high pay for their services, they are not called except in extreme cases, that will not yield to common treatment.

The doctors are sometimes subjected to pretty rough treatment, and occasionally lose their lives from the assaults of relatives of persons of consequence who may have died under their operations.

Sometimes these doctors make threats against the life of persons, and, whenever such a person may subsequently die, the doctor is considered as being the means of causing the death, and he is then in danger of his own life.

It has been asserted that it is a universal custom among the Indians of Oregon to kill the doctors whenever they happen to lose a patient; but this is not the fact, as the numerous old doctors to be found all over the Territories will testify. It is only in isolated cases; and although I have heard of several instances from persons of undoubted veracity, I never had one come under my own observation, but, on the contrary, have known many doctors who have lost patients of high rank among the tribes, and who are still living, and considered as persons of great importance.

Among the medicines I have seen used by the Indians is a species of diminutive cress, found in the dark ravines of the forest, which, when pounded up and applied to the skin, will produce a blister as quick as Spanish flies. Another method I have seen adopted for the cure of the headache, or inflamed eyes, is to apply a coal of fire to the back of the neck, shoulders, or temples. This is pretty certain to raise a blister, and is a species

H 2

of pharmacy that is usually on hand, without having to resort either to the forest or the apothecary's shop.

A simple diarrhœa is cured by a tea made from the bark of the young hemlock. This is drunk during the winter season. In the spring, the sprouts of the raspberry, eaten, or a tea made of the leaves, is excellent. Soreness of the joints or ankles from cold is alleviated by nettles pounded up with grease, or nettle-roots boiled, and tied on the afflicted part. The Polypodium Falcatum, or sickle-leaf polypod, or sweet licorice fern, a parasite found on old logs and trees, is a most excellent alterative. This plant, which was sent by me to San Francisco to be classified by the Academy of Natural Sciences, received its name from Doctor Kellogg, the botanist of the society. This plant is found in almost all the Western States, where it is called wild licorice, and is used by some persons to flavor tobacco. It has a sweetish bitter taste, and a decoction is not unpleasant. I think its properties are equal to those of sarsaparilla. It is also of ancient renown, the polypods of the oak being formerly used as a cure for madness. I believe this plant grows in many, if not all the states of the Union. I have seen it in Massachusetts, Alabama, and California, although I never knew its medicinal virtues till I met with it in Washington Territory.

Ulcers, or open sores, are cured by a plaster or salve made from the ashes of the hairs of a wild-cat mixed with grease. I am not aware what particular virtue there is in wild-cat hair over any other; but they have a belief to that effect, and consider a wild-cat or a lynx skin to possess remarkable medicinal properties.

The white bryony (*Bryonia alba*) is found, and its intensely bitter root is used by the whites in cases of fever and ague; but I have never seen the Indians use it. The common herbs, like yarrow, mint, marsh rosemary, and chamomile, are used for colds, and cases where simple remedies only are wanted; but the Indians are not much given to dosing; they usually try the effects of fasting before they attempt any thing else, and that is, in the generality of cases, all that is required.   All these simples are used by the sick before sending for a doctor. He does not give medicine, but works charms or mesmerisms.

There are, undoubtedly, various and numerous kinds of plants and shrubs not enumerated, possessing medicinal virtues, which the Indians know of and use, but none others have come under my own observation.

There is a shrub, bearing a leaf similar to the low whortleberry in appearance, which makes a most excellent tea.   Many white persons prefer it to the teas that are imported.   The Indians collect these leaves, and sell them occasionally to the whites, and often use them themselves.

I found out some simple remedies, which, in a wild country, are well enough to know.   Persons tráveling for a long time on a sand-beach or over snow, and facing a strong wind, are liable to inflamed eyes, and these can be relieved, and usually readily cured, by taking the tea-leaves, after the tea has been drawn, and binding them over the eyes on going to bed at night.   A wash, made by boiling the leaves of the Sallal in water, and frequently bathing the eyes, is also excellent.

Persons working in the salt water in the Bay during the winter and spring were very liable to get scratched or cut with oyster-shells, which frequently caused bad ulcer sores.   These were cured by applying a poultice of raw potato, grated or scraped fine, and renewed often. The potato is a very powerful remedial agent in all cases of scurvy, and is one of those ready remedies that are usually within the reach of every one.   One of the best salves I ever met with was made by these Indians from the pure white gum of the spruce, melted with equal parts of bears' grease or hogs' lard. In the spring, when the sap begins to start, they cut a gash in the side of the tree, and the gum runs out as clear as water. In a short time it hardens, and then looks precisely like camphor. It is then scraped off, and melted in large clam-shells set on hot ashes. It makes an excellent, clean, healthy, and healing salve, and is in much repute. They very seldom bind up any wound, but simply rub on this salve, and leave the rest to nature.

I remarked a general disinclination to impart any information respecting their medicines, and only found out by seeing them prepare the different kinds at various times, when, on my asking what the use of them was, they would tell me. The reason of this is that they are at all times ready to beg of the whites all the medicines they can; and they think, if the white folks know they have remedies of their own, they would be unwilling to give away the drugs that have cost money. Then, again, it is some trouble for them to hunt up medicines when they are sick; for, till they are sick, they never think of collecting a stock to be kept on hand, and it is far easier to get relief from the stock of some white person's medicine-chest than to hunt all over the woods and marshes for simples. Bathing in cold water is a remedy they use for rheumatism. On the Columbia the Indians use sweat-houses, but I never have met with any on the Coast. They there cause a perspiration by drinking hot herb tea, and rolling themselves up in blankets near the fire.

The doctors have various kinds of necromancy or jugglery which they perform for the cure of their patients. Nor do they all possess the same gifts. One is celebrated for his power in driving away the *memelose*, or spirits of the dead, and another for exorcising the skookums or evil spirits.   A description of the method practiced by two doctors to cure a woman who recovered and another who died, will serve to show the general method adopted by all the doctors of the Coast tribes, it being borne in mind that each doctor has his own peculiar songs and methods of manipulation.

Old Suis had been attacked with liver complaint, and was very sick.   Both the captain and myself were perfectly aware of the nature of her sickness, but we had no suitable medicine to give her.   She at last grew so ill that her death was expected at any moment.   She had deferred sending for a doctor, as she knew they would expect her to pay a round price, and she did not feel inclined to part with her property.   However, at last she consented, and sent for a doctor named Sa-ço-dlye, who had married a relative of hers.   When he came he brought his family with him, consisting of his wife and a little girl.   Sa-co-dlye was famous for driving away the memelose.   The superstition relative to these departed spirits is that they enjoy themselves so much in their new state of existence that they wish all their friends to join them, and, whenever they find any one slightly ill, they try all in their power to induce the invalid to go with them to the *memelose illihe*, or the land of the dead. They even believe that we think as they do in some respects.   They have heard the priest speak of angels, and, on one occasion, having showed some of them a print whereon was depicted a sleeping saint surrounded by angels beckoning her to go to heaven, they exclaimed, " There! that is like our memelose, only ours have not got birds' wings like yours."   The idea conveyed to us was precisely the same as their own, of spirits hovering in the air, but *they* were puzzled to know where our memelose got their wings from.

Now Sa-co-dlye was famous for inducing these spirits to go home to their own quarters, and let his friends and patients alone. Supposing, therefore, the illness of old Suis to proceed from the visits of her dead friends—possibly some of her departed husbands; for, like the woman of Samaria, she had had seven—he went to work to send them away.

After he had eaten, and the lodge was all cleaned out and fresh sand strewed over the floor, Suis was laid on some nice new mats, and covered with new white blankets. A large fire was made in the centre of the lodge, and a great blaze kept up by one whose business it was to occasionally pour oil into the flames. The occupants of the lodge seated themselves around the fire, each having a pole long enough to reach the roof overhead, which they kept thumping all the while, to keep time to a plaintive chant they all sung.

Sa-co-dlye knelt at the feet of the patient, and commenced by singing a refrain, when the rest would join and sing in the chorus, the burden of the song being an address to the spirits of the dead, with a request for them to leave their mother with them a little longer, closing with a request that the memelose would *clattawah kee-quilly*, or go down to their abode. The singing was accompanied with violent gestures by Sa-co-dlye, who would roll up his eyes in a fearful manner, and then pass his hands over the face and person of the patient, precisely the same that I have frequently seen performed by professors of mesmerism. The result was that Suis went to sleep, and when she awoke, some hours after, she was much refreshed, not having had any sleep before for several days. Sa-co-dlye performed these ceremonies several times, both night and day, and the plaintive chorus, in which the men, women, and children joined, sounded melancholy and solemn as it fell on the ear during the stillness of the night.

However, Sa-co-dlye found that his charms did not produce the desired effect. Suis had a skookum or evil spirit in her which he could not remove, and which was devouring her vitals. He was certainly right in his conjecture, as any one who has ever had the liver complaint can attest. They, therefore, sent across the Bay for another celebrated doctor, who always went by the name of Old John. He was a powerful magnetizer and clairvoyant, and could read the internal structure of a patient as easily as a white man could a newspaper. This fact they took great pains to tell me when I suggested that one doctor was enough. He, they said, *kumtux hiyu ickters*, knows many things. So Old John came, bringing with him his family, consisting of some half a dozen persons. These, added to the others, who all remained, made a very formidable battery with which to attack the poor old roof while the doctor should *mamoke Tománawos*, or work charms. The style of operations was now materially changed. Old John sat down at the patient's feet, with his head covered up under his blanket, and there he remained a long time, nearly half or three quarters of an hour. A large fire which had previously been built was now reduced to a bed of coals, which were kept alive by additions of rotten wood, which did not blaze, but made a smoke. All at once he threw off his blanket, and commenced singing in a loud voice a most barbarous song, and throwing himself about in a most excited manner. In his hands he had large scallop-shells, which he rattled like castanets, the chorus in the mean time keeping up their pounding, with the addition, over the other performance, of a couple of tin pans and a brass kettle, which served very perceptibly to increase the din.

John then, throwing down his castanets, went through the mesmeric passes till Suis was asleep. Then he bore his whole weight, pressing his clenched fists on to the patient's chest till I thought he would kill the woman.   Then he would scoop his hands together as if he had caught something, which he would then try and blow through his hands into the coals.   These ceremonies continued for an hour, or till the old fellow was so exhausted with his exertions he could do no more.

When Suis waked up she did not feel particularly refreshed, but complained of severe pain.   John said it was right, for he had seen the skookum, and, no doubt, should remove it.   I inquired why they in one case cast oil on the fire, and in the other had no blaze, but only smoke.   They said that the memelose wished Suis to go with them, so she might be happier and have more comforts; but they wished to show the memelose that she had plenty of both friends and property; so they built a big blaze, that the memelose could see the nice clean lodge she had, and the plenty with which she was surrounded.

But in the other case, all they wanted of the fire was to burn the skookum as soon as Old John should catch it.   He had nearly caught it, but it had slipped out of his hand; but they were certain he would get it in a day or two.   John continued his operations through the night at intervals of three or four hours, and the next day Suis was taken with vomiting, and, to the utter astonishment of the captain and myself, recovered, and was well in less than a week.

Whether the cure was effected by the severe manipulation she had undergone, or by the effects of mesmerism, or from her own strong constitution receiving reaction by her fasting, I am not prepared to say, but simply state the fact that she got perfectly well.

The other case to which I alluded was that of an old woman named Sal-tsi-mar, who lived with her people on a little creek about an eighth of a mile from us. She was quite old, and had been for a long time troubled with the liver complaint, similar to Suis. This sort of sickness appears to be quite common among them, and may be caused by their living on such rank, oily food as whale's blubber, seals, and stale salmon-eggs. Be that as it may, I have noticed the complaint frequently in both old and young. Sometimes, on its first appearance, they will blister their sides with a poultice of the cress I before mentioned, and commonly this relieves them. Old Sal-tsi-mar was too old and too far gone for either blisters or doctors to do her any good, and, consequently, she died. She had considerable property in blankets and Chinese chests, and also had hoarded up a large quantity of silver money. Consequently, when it was announced that she was about to die, she found herself surrounded (as many an old white woman of property has been) by a host of disconsolate friends, weeping and lamenting at her approaching end, ready, when the last breath is drawn, to dry their eyes and go to fighting for the spoils.

In this instance old Cartumhays, and old Mahar, a celebrated doctor, were the chief mourners, probably from being the smartest scamps among the relatives. Their duty was to prepare the canoe for the reception of the body. One of the largest and best the deceased had owned was then hauled into the woods, at some distance back of the lodge, after having been first thoroughly washed and scrubbed. Two large square holes were then cut in the bottom, at the bow and stern, for the twofold purpose of rendering the canoe unfit for further use, and therefore less likely to excite the cupidity of the whites (who are but too apt to help themselves to these depositories for the dead), and also to allow any rain to pass off readily.

When the canoe was ready, the corpse, wrapped in blankets, was brought out, and laid in it on mats previously spread. All the wearing apparel was next put in beside the body, together with her trinkets, beads, little baskets, and various trifles she had prized. More blankets were then covered over the body, and mats smoothed over all. Next, a small canoe, which fitted into the large one, was placed, bottom up, over the corpse, and the whole then covered with mats. The canoe was then raised up and placed on two parallel bars, elevated four or five feet from the ground, and supported by being inserted through holes mortised at the top of four stout posts previously firmly planted in the earth. Around these poles were then hung blankets, and all the cooking utensils of the deceased, pots, kettles, and pans, each with a hole punched through it, and all her crockery-ware, every piece of which was first cracked or broken, to render it useless; and then, when all was done, they left her to remain for one year, when the bones would be buried in a box in the earth directly under the canoe; but that, with all its appendages, would never be molested, but left to go to gradual decay.

They regard these canoes precisely as we regard coffins, and would no more think of using one than we should of using our own grave-yard relics; and it is, in their view, as much of a desecration for a white man to meddle or interfere with these, to them, sacred mementoes, as it would be to us to have an Indian break open the graves of our relatives. Many thoughtless white men have done this, and animosities have been thus occasioned.

While the corpse remained in the house, not a word was spoken except in a whisper, nor did they commence their lamentations till the whole funeral ceremonies were over; then, the signal being given, they began to sing a

METHOD OF BURIAL.

death-song, and thump the roof with their long poles, Tomhays and Mahar alternately leading off the recitative, while the rest joined in the chorus.   The burden of the song, as it was afterward related to me in Jargon, may be translated as follows.   It is simply an address to the dead, stating their love for her, the many years she had lived with and taught them, that she was not poor, and had no occasion to go to a better country, and they saw no reason why she should go to the land of the dead, and was something like this:

"Oh, our mother! why did you go and leave us so sad? We can scarcely see by reason of the water that falls from our eyes.

"Many years have you lived with us, and taught us the words of wisdom.

"You were not poor, neither are we poor; neither were you weak, but your heart and limbs were strong.

"You should have lived with us many years, and told us more of the deeds of ancient times."

Every day, at sunrise and sunset, this chant is repeated by the relatives for thirty days — when the days of mourning are ended—but never, on any pretense, must the name of the deceased be spoken till after the bones are finally deposited in their last resting-place; and frequently years will elapse before they dare call the name again.

On these occasions they always change their own names, as they think the spirits of the dead will come back if they hear the same name called that they were accustomed to hear before death.   Toke, who had lost a daughter just previous to my going to the Bay, called himself Chehait.   Heyalma, whose brother died at Russell's, called himself Cletheas.   Tomhays changed his to Senequa, and Tománawos his to Winasie.   Yancumux, a brother of Tománawos, changed his to Yakowilk.

I always supposed that Indian names had some direct

reference to objects of nature, as "The White Flower of the Prairie," "The War-eagle," &c., and the hundred other poetical names made familiar to us by skillful pens of ready poets.

But in the case of these Indians it was not so. Undoubtedly, could their names be traced up to their origin, they, like our own, would be found to refer to some incident long ago forgotten. I frequently asked the meaning of different persons' names, and was told that they did not mean any thing. Those that I have mentioned were names of some of their ancestors, but what those names meant they did not know. One day, while being more than usually inquisitive, old Suis, to whom I was talking, after trying to make me understand that the names I was asking about had no meaning, at last said, "Why, you white people have names like ours; some mean something, and others mean nothing. I know your name, Swan, is like our word Cocumb, and means a big bird; and Mr. Lake's name is for water, like Shoalwater Bay. But what does Mr. Russell's, or Baldt's, or Champ's, or Hillyer's, or Sweeney's, or Weldon's name mean?"

I told her I did not know. "Well," she replied, "so it is with us. We don't know what those names *you* have asked mean; all we know is that they were the names of our ancestors—*elip tillicums*, or first people."

Those names that she knew she explained to me; for instance, Carcowan's son was named *Tleyuk*, meaning a spark of fire; another was named *Yelloh*, or the whale; another chief's name is *Cocumb*, or the swan; another, from his ingenuity, was called *Squintum*, or the white man; and a young squaw, named *Spaärk*, or the rose; and another, named *Wheeark*, or the eagle. Others are named for some deformity, as *Dusheerhutch*, the long back; or *Keer-ukso*, crooked nose.

This system of names they apply to the whites. One who had a large beard was called *Chepoochucks;* another one, marked by the small-pox, was named *Pekose;* a freckled man was called *Tsum Bill;* and old M'Carty, whose hair was short and bristly, was named *Cushu* Bill, or Hog Bill. This propensity to change names and adopt new ones appears to have been common with the tribes on the northeastern coast as well as the northwest. In Douglas's summary of the History of the British Possessions in North America, published in 1747, he says of the Indians of New England:

" There is not the same reason for preserving the names of the countries, nations, tribes, mountains, and rivers as there is for preserving the Greek, Roman, and other more modern names of such things in Europe. The Indians have no civil or classical history to require it. The Indians change their own personal names, and the names of other things, upon the most trifling occasions. Our Indians affect to have English names ; thus Massasoit's two sons desired of the court of Plymouth to give them names. They were accordingly named Alexander and Philip."

Although the Indians mentioned had changed their names, they were called by the whites usually after the old style, particularly Tomhays, and Toke, and Yancumux. We knew them by those cognomens, and it was difficult, under the name of Chehait, to recognize drunken old Toke, or, under that of Senequa, to call to mind the cunning, thieving, lying Cartumhays, or to address the jolly, good-natured Yancumux as Yakowilk; but we managed very well with the others, and called them by whichever name we happened to think of.

At the expiration of one year from the time a person dies, the friends assemble, and after collecting the bones, wrap them up in a new cotton cloth, and either bury them directly under the canoe, as before stated, or, in some instances, collect them, and have them buried in one family cemetery. Toke's ancestors and his own family had been buried at Toke's Point, but several of the connections of the family had been buried at different parts of the Bay. It was at length decided to collect all these remains together, and transport them to Toke's Point. This was performed during the ensuing summer; but, although they allowed me to cross the Bay with them, they left me sitting in the lodge we had stopped at eating sturgeon, and slipped off with their relics, which they buried at another place. I asked them, when they returned, what they meant by treating me so. They replied that at first they were willing I should witness their ceremonies; but when they reflected that the spirits of all those dead persons, and hosts of others, were standing round, watching to see that every thing was rightly performed, they felt afraid to have me with them, lest the *memelose* should be angry.

All the fasts or observances I had witnessed bore no resemblance to any form which we denominate worship; and, as has before been remarked, they have each a private Tománawos, or guardian spirit, to whom they make all their wants known, and that in the most private manner. It must not be supposed, however, that they have no religious sentiment. In fact, the Indian is at all times impressed with the sense of the actual presence of his Tománawos; and whatever he does, whether it be good or bad, stealing or helping, murdering or giving aid, he always looks for assistance from his Tománawos. The only outward demonstration of address to the spiritual world that I saw was during cases of sickness, or when bewailing the dead.

All of them had a general idea of the Christian religion, but not one believed it, although several had been considered, during the residence of the priest at Chenook, as exemplary members of the Church. But when the restrictions of the Church were taken away by the absence of the priest, they all returned to their old heathenism again. They can not strictly be termed idolators, for they do not worship the outward symbols of any thing; that is directly opposed to their system of studiously concealing the *name* of their Tománawos; and if that Tománawos should chance to have been a bear or a salmon, by making an image of either, and addressing it in terms of adoration or supplication, they would at once reveal the name and object of their secret worship.

The only way, in my opinion, in which an Indian can be thoroughly changed and Christianized is by either taking the child from its parents and bringing it up under Christian instruction, and away from tribal influences and prejudices, or to gradually civilize a tribe, and let the rising generation make the change. In all the accounts we have that are to be relied upon, it will be seen that any and all Christian Indians are those of a generation succeeding that to whom the missionaries first addressed themselves; and all the missionaries who have really and truly succeeded, have done so by *first* teaching the Indian the manners of a civilized life, and gradually, as he became accustomed to a change of life, they could teach him a change of heart. All other converts, or seeming converts, who have been suffered to live in their primitive style, are sure at heart to retain their ancient religion. Nor is this strange. From their earliest infancy they have heard the legends and mythological tales told them daily, and on every occasion, by the ancient people, by their own parents, and repeated by their playfellows. These early impressions can not be easily eradicated.

The same difficulties in approaching the Indian tribes

I

was experienced in the early settlement of the country. The missionaries are not always chosen from the right class of people; zealous themselves, they press their zeal without knowledge, and attempt to make the Indians understand the mysterious doctrines of our religion, when, in fact, the Indian is like an infant scarce able to either talk or understand.

Douglass, in his Summary* (vol. ii., p. 161), writing on the religion of the Indians of New England, gives his ideas of the method practiced by the missionaries at that time, which is very applicable to the present. He remarks: " Some Indians of sagacity, a little civilized and instructed toward the Christian religion, can give no distinct account of any Indian religion, and stumble much at the mysteries of our Christian religion, being indiscreetly crowded upon them at once, and with too much impetuosity, without previous instruction. 'If you do not believe immediately you will be damned,' is the expression of our zealots; whereas they ought to be first tamed by familiarity and fair dealing. * * * Our missionaries, void of common prudence, in a reverse preposterous manner, begin with the abstruse articles of the Christian religion, and thence proceed to instruct them in the plain, easy dictates of nature.

" In a silly, low, cant way, some of our preachers tell the Indians that the Christians' God is a better God than the Indians' God, whereas they ought to inform them that there is but one supreme God, and that our manner of worshipping this God is more agreeable to the Godhead, as being more natural and decent.

" If some of our traders were instructed, and, at a public charge, capacitated to sell cheap among the In-

* See "A Summary, Historical and Political, of the first Planting, Progressive Improvements, and Present State of the British Settlements in North America, by William Douglass, M.D. 2 vols. 8vo. J. Dodsley, London. 1760."

dians, they would gain their affections in this trading familiar manner, and lay a good foundation for their conversion toward Christianity.   An abrupt Christian mission among them seems absurd.   If the Emperor of China, or the Grand Turk, should send such missionaries into Great Britain to convert the people there to the doctrines of Confucius or Mohammed, instead of gaining proselytes he would avert them."

Dr. Douglass then states, " I do not find that Christianity is like to have any footing among the Indians.   We are not exemplary enough in our dealings or in common life.   The Indians say that they can not perceive mankind the better for being Christians ; Christians cheat them out of their lands and other effects, and sometimes deprive them of their lives.   The Indians are in all respects wild, and know nothing of the rudiments of religion ; and the missionaries, instead of first taming and civilizing them, and next instructing them in the principles of natural religion and morality, begin with the sublime mysteries of our religion, such as, How many persons are there in the Godhead ? and the like.   Thus from the beginning they are bewildered and lost forever. Some practice *piæ fraudes*, which at first may amuse, but afterward, when discovered, leave a permanent prejudice against the Christian religion.   Thus it is said that some French missionaries, in relating to the Indians the history of our Savior's birth and suffering, tell them that the Virgin Mary was a French woman, and that the English crucified our Savior."

I do not know that the missionaries of the present enlightened age go quite so far as those mentioned by Douglass, but the results are little better.   Greenhow remarks of the results of the Jesuits in California, " That their efforts are attended with good can not be denied ; for those who were the objects of their immediate care were certainly rendered happier, more comfortable, and more free from vice than they would otherwise have been; but, although they did introduce a certain degree of civilization, or apparent civilization, among these people, yet there is no reason to believe that, by any means as yet employed for the purpose, a single Californian Indian has been rendered a useful or even an innocuous member of society."

The present state of the Indian population in Oregon and Washington does not reflect much credit on their Christian acquirements; and although, in times of peace, they are willing to flock round the missions, and receive spiritual as well as temporal food, yet no sooner does an opportunity occur when they can raise the war-whoop, than we find these Christian converts among the most ruthless of the savages in their horrid deeds of blood.

The Indians can see but little or no difference between their system of Tománawos and our own views as taught them. For instance, the talipus, or fox, is their emblem of the creative power; the smispee, or duck, that of wisdom. And they say that the Boston people, or Americans, have for their Tománawos the *wheark*, or eagle, and that the King George, or English people, have a lion for their Tománawos.

In matters of religion, as taught them by the priest, they have no idea of their spiritual signification. The emblem of the Holy Spirit is to them a simple pigeon, and the Agnus Dei but a sheep, *la mouton* being the only word which can be used to express the meaning of the emblem. Nor can they be made to understand or believe the miraculous history of our Savior's birth. The difficulty with these, as with all other savage tribes, is the want of suitable words to convey our ideas. The Indian must first be taught the English language, and then they can understand what the English or Americans wish to

teach them; for it is impossible, in their barbarous jargon, to convey any but the most commonplace ideas, and
the above instances cited are but a few of the difficulties
to be contended with in an attempt to establish a free
and perfect interchange of thought.

As the country becomes more thickly settled, and they
are brought more in contact with civilization, their condition may improve, and they become able to understand
what, to them, now are but words of foolishness.

CHAPTER XII.

Amusements.—Games.—Children's Amusements.—Imitate the Priest.
—Readily learn Needle-work.—Fond of Singing.—Songs.—History
of the Chenooks and Chehalis.—Difficulty of understanding the Legends.—Creation of Man.—Origin of Coast Tribes.—Evidences of
Emigration.—Tradition of a Junk wrecked at Clatsop Beach.—Bees-
wax found on the Beach.—Remarks on the various Theories respect-
ing the Origin of the Indians.—Lewis and Clarke's Names of Tribes.
—The correct Names of the Tribes.—Former Tribes of Shoal-water
Bay.—Evidences of great Mortality among the Coast Tribes.—The
Feeling of the Indians respecting the Dead.—Meares's Account of
the Nootkans being Cannibals.—Vancouver doubts the Truth of
Meares.—Indian Dread of Skulls.—Anecdote respecting their Fears.

DURING the whole of my residence among the Coast
Indians, I never witnessed among the adults any disposition to play athletic games, such as wrestling, running
races, or playing ball.   Young fellows will occasionally,
when half drunk, have a rough-and-tumble scuffle with
each other, but without any system that would dignify
it with the name of game, as applied to gymnastic or
other feats of strength.   All they seem to care for in the
way of amusement is gambling.   The children, however,
are full of play, and are in all respects like little white
folks, differing only in being a little more wild and shy
of strangers.   I can only compare the two to the chicks

of the partridge on the one hand and the chickens of the domestic hen on the other. The little Indian children, when disturbed in their play, will run, like young partridges, not to their mother, but into the nearest bush or tall grass, from whence their little, black, shining eyes can be seen peeping out to catch a glimpse of the intruder.

There were a number of children in the vicinity of my house, and as I always noticed them when they came with their parents, and gave them plenty of sugar to eat, or boiled rice, of which they are very fond, I gradually won their confidence, and occasionally old Suis would have a lot of these little boys and girls to visit her, when they would throw off all restraint, and perform their little plays as if no stranger was among them. Like all children, they are very fond of a swing; and to amuse them, Peter, who, though a young man, felt like a child for play, made a swing by putting up a couple of spars like the shears used on board ship, and from the top of these spars, which were joined together at their upper end, hung a single rope, with a loop at its lower extremity. Into this loop they would get, one or two at a time, and swing away for hours, taking turns in causing the momentum by means of pulling a line attached to the bottom of the swing.

The boys were fond of making canoes either from flags, which were twisted so as to form a sort of boat, or from chips, on which they would hoist a leaf for a sail, and start them off on voyages down the creek. Sometimes a lad with more ingenuity than the rest would carve out a pretty model of a canoe from a cedar stick; and I have seen boys, with little canoes which they had made, scarce three feet long, fearlessly paddle about the water in these little cockles, which seemed ready at any moment to sink.

Sometimes the boys would catch a lot of minnows, and then the girls would join them, and, having made a little fire and a miniature rack for smoking fish, would imitate the manner of curing salmon, which, when done, were served up as a repast. The girls were very fond of making rag babies and dressing up clam-shells like children. One of these girls, a sister of Peter and a niece of old Suis, had a small trunk full of these rag dolls dressed in all sorts of style, which she used to parade out whenever her little friends came to see her. One day, when a number of these children were there on a visit, I noticed they were very busy on the beach, where they seemed intently engaged in some very quiet games. I went where they were seated, and found they were playing church, and were imitating the Catholic service that they had seen at Chenook. One smart little fellow, about fifteen years old, named Quel-láh-ho, was officiating as priest, and had proceeded so far as the baptism, which at that time he was engaged in, bestowing names on all the dolls belonging to the party. He would rattle over the Latin, or what to him seemed as such, giving the priest's intonations in a most astonishing manner, and so nearly right that a person at a short distance might readily suppose he was actually performing the Catholic service. As the girls objected to his putting water on their babies, he was using dry sand instead, and when it came the time to chant, they all joined in as near an imitation as they could.

When I came up they did not observe me till I had watched them some time, when they all got into the greatest glee, thinking the whole subject a capital joke. "*Ensika mamoke heehee La Plate*," or, "We are playing priest," said they, in answer to my inquiry what they were doing. I told them it was not right for them to make fun of the priest, and they must not play priest any more. They promised that they would not, but insisted that their dolls should retain the names their priest had given them.

I afterward found that this was one of the favorite plays with the children, and showed how much value the ritual of the Church had either in their eyes or in their parents', who used to encourage them to mimic the ceremonies that they had seen at Chenook.

The girls all learn the use of the needle early, and, although their style of sewing is not what would show well on fine muslin, yet, like that kind of tailoring said to have been performed by a celebrated personage, who mended his garments by sewing them with a rope, if it is not neat, it is strong.

I have seen one of these little girls, Anwillik, Peter's sister, who was not over twelve years old, take a piece of calico, cut out dresses for herself and two other little girls who were her slaves, and have the gowns made up and be wearing them in less than half a day.

They are all very fond of singing, and some of their tunes are plaintive and sweet.

The following are some of those that I can recollect. They generally improvise as they sing; but, when they have no particular object to sing about, they use certain words which have about the same meaning as our fa, sol, la.

BOAT SONG.

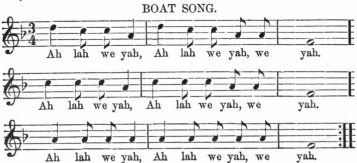

Ah lah we yah, Ah lah we yah, we yah.

Ah lah we yah, Ah lah we yah, we yah.

Ah lah we yah, Ah lah we yah, we yah.

The preceding song is repeated over and over till the singer is tired.

FISHING SONG.

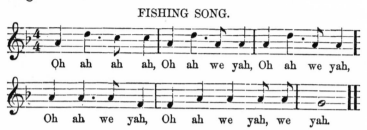

Oh ah ah ah, Oh ah we yah, Oh ah we yah,

Oh ah we yah, Oh ah we yah, we yah.

INDIAN WOMAN'S SONG TO HER HUSBAND WHO ABSENTS HIMSELF.

Cah mi - ka Klat - te-wah, Cah mi - ka Klat - te-wah.

Kor - na - way sun, Hiu - - kly An-na - wil - lee.

Oh nika tenas, hias cla hai am, hiu kly, kornaway sun, nika tenas,
Kornaway halo, ensika muck a muck, wake siah memelose, nika tenas.

"Where do you go to every day, and cause me to cry all the time? My little child is poor and hungry, but has nothing to eat, as our food is all gone, and before long my little one will be dead."

There does not appear to be any regular form of words used like songs with us, but almost always the incidents of the moment form themes for their tunes, as with us they are subjects for conversation.

SUIS'S SONG TO HER TOMÁNAWOS.

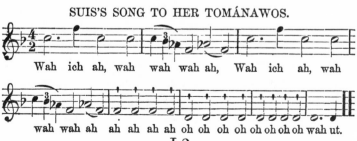

Wah ich ah, wah wah wah ah, Wah ich ah, wah

wah wah ah ah ah ah ah oh oh oh oh oh oh oh oh wah ut.

I 2

SA-CO-DLYE'S TOMÁNAWOS SONG.

Ah ah ah   ah we yah, Ah ah ah   ah we yah.

GAMBLING SONG.

Wa - - - - ich e - - e,   Wa - - - - -

ich e - - e,   Wa - ich   Wa - ich   ah ah ah ah.

MEDICINE SONG.

`hi tu   e   oo ha ha hi tu   e   oo ha   ha

ha ha ha ha ha ha ha ha hi tu   e - -

yah oh - o - o - o - o - o - o - o - o - o - - oh.

While these songs are sung, time is kept by beating
with sticks, or thumping the roof of the lodge with a
pole.

Of the early history of the Chenook or Chehalis tribes
nothing possibly can be known with certainty. Like all
the rest of the North American Indians, they have no
written legends; neither have these tribes any monuments, or any other relics of antiquity. A few hieroglyphics, rudely painted on cedar slabs, are the only records that I have met with, and these were only the To-

mánawos or Totem of individual chiefs or doctors, and
served rather, like the inscriptions on our grave-stones,
to perpetuate the memory of the deceased, than to give,
or attempt to give, any historical information.

All that we learn of the early history of these aborigines comes to us in the shadowy form of myths, and al-
legories, and traditions related by the old.   This is but
poor authority for events that have transpired centuries
ago, and we are only left to speculative theories to help
us form what, from its very uncertainty, must be but a
faint glimmering of the truth.

The great difficulty of rightly comprehending the pre-
cise meaning of these legends, and the want of system
in translating, are also obstacles which every writer on
Indian history finds in his way, no two translators being
found who will render the same legend in the same manner.   The tale of the origin of mankind, or, rather, of
their tribe, for the Chenook and Chehalis appear to have
the same account, was related to me several times by
different Indians, but they did not agree together in detail.   The substance of the tradition is this:

Ages ago, an old man named Toölux (or the South
Wind), while traveling to the north, met an old woman,
named Quoots-hooi, who was an ogress and a giantess.
He asked her for food, when she gave him a net, telling
him that she had nothing to eat, and he must go and try
to catch some fish.   He accordingly dragged the net,
and succeeded in catching a grampus, or, as the Indians
called it, " a little whale."   This he was about to cut
with his knife, when the old woman cried out to him to
take a sharp shell, and not to cut the fish crossways, but
split it down the back.   He, without giving heed to what
she said, cut the fish across the side, and was about to
take off a piece of blubber, but the fish immediately
changed into an immense bird, that when flying com-

pletely obscured the sun, and the noise made by its wings shook the earth. This bird, which they called Hahness, then flew away to the north, and lit on the top of the Saddleback Mountain, near the Columbia River. Toölux and the old woman then journeyed north in search of Hahness, and one day, while Quoots-hooi was engaged in picking berries on the side of the mountain, she found the nest of the thunder-bird, full of eggs, which she commenced breaking and eating, and from these mankind were produced.

The thunder-bird came back, and, finding its nest destroyed, returned to Toölux for redress; but neither of them ever after could find the ogress, although they regularly returned to the north every year.

It is probably this tradition which has caused their present superstitious belief that the first salmon caught must not be cut across, but must be split down the back, and then split in thin flakes. If it should be cut contrary to their practice, then all the salmon will leave, and no more be taken that season. The same result would ensue if a salmon's heart should be lost or eaten by a dog.

This allegorical tale, if it means any thing, would seem to refer to the coming of their ancestors from the south, either California or Mexico. But the Mexican traditions, on the contrary, according to Prescott, continually refer to the fact of *their* ancestors coming from the north.

Some writers have asserted that the Indians are the lost tribes of Israel; others that they came over from the Asiatic shores and from China. Some that they found their way around by the northwest, either by crossing Behring's Straits, and proceeding gradually down the main land, or coming directly across from the northeastern shores of Asia in canoes or ancient vessels similar to the Japanese and Chinese junks.

Other and more modern writers consider that these Indians came from the east of the Rocky Mountains, being forced away from the buffalo region by their more formidable neighbors.   Of this latter class is General George Gibbs, who for many years has devoted himself to ethnological researches among the North American Indians, and who for the past six years has resided in Oregon and Washington Territories, and whose opinion is entitled to consideration.   General Gibbs, in a letter to me, dated Fort Steilacoom, Washington Territory, July 31, 1856, writes: "In reading Longfellow's Hiawatha, that much-abused, praised, laughed at, and admired poem, I find some startling resemblances to the Nisqually and Klikatat tales, so much so as to confirm the belief I already entertained of all these tribes having originated east of the Rocky Mountains, in the buffalo country, and emigrated by the northern passes to the great Western basin, and thence down Frazer's River and the Columbia to their present homes, forced away by more powerful neighbors."

That General Gibbs's theory is correct, so far as relates to the tribes of Oregon and Washington, I can not dispute, having no evidence to the contrary.   One thing is certain, that all the tribes are a wandering, restless race, and are as likely to have come from the east of the Rocky Mountains as any where else.   There is, however, no disputing the fact that they have occasionally received additions from the Asiatic side, although to what extent is not known.   The prevailing northwest trade-wind of the summer season renders it very easy for canoes to come over from the northeast Russian coast; and in evidence of that fact, I can state that, during my residence in the Territory, a canoe, with three sailors in her, who ran away from a vessel at Kodiak, arrived safe at Shoal-water Bay, after coming a distance of nearly eight hundred miles.

There is also a tradition among the Indians that a Chinese or Japanese junk was wrecked years ago on Clatsop Beach, south of the Columbia. Part of her cargo was bees'-wax. And, to prove the correctness of this tradition, there are to this day occasionally, after great storms, lumps and pieces of this wax found on the beach. There are no wild honey-bees west of the Rocky Mountains, consequently the wax was not the product of that part of the continent, but must have been brought as the Indians state. I have had some of this wax given me by an old Indian doctor, who had picked it up on the beach. The crevices were still full of sand, and the action of salt water and sun had bleached it nearly white. The specimen was sent by me to the California Academy of Natural Sciences. Wilkes also mentions the fact of a Chinese junk having been wrecked at Point Grenville in 1833, and three of the Japanese were rescued from the Indians by the Hudson Bay Company.

These instances simply prove that communication between the two shores of the North Pacific could be, and has been made, but show nothing farther. My own belief is that, whatever was the origin of different tribes or families, the whole race of American Indians are native and indigenous to the soil. There is no proof that they are either the lost tribes of Israel or emigrants from any part of the Old World. They are a separate and as distinct a race as either the Ethiopian, Caucasian, or Mongolian; and because they are not particularly described in the Mosaic account of the creation is no more an evidence that they are not as ancient a race as the Jews, than it is that the American continent was not formed at the same time the Garden of Eden was, simply because Moses did not know about it.

In the absence of all proof to the contrary, it seems to me to be both rational and consistent to assume that the

Creator placed the Red race on the American continent as early as he created the beasts and reptiles that inhabit it. In Nott and Gliddon's Types of Mankind, chapter ix., on the Aboriginal Races of America, may be found the following extracts, illustrative of the position taken of the Red man of America having originated on this continent instead of having migrated.

" The continent of America is often designated by the appellation of the *New World;* but the researches of modern geologists and archæologists have shown that the evidences in favor of a high antiquity, during *our* geological epoch, as well as for fauna and flora, are, to say the least, quite as great on this as on the Eastern hemisphere. Professor Agassiz, whose authority will hardly be questioned in matters of this kind, tells us that geology finds the oldest landmarks here; and Sir Charles Lyell, from a mass of well-digested facts, and from the corroborating testimony of other good authorities, concludes that the Mississippi River has been running in its present bed for more than one hundred thousand years.

" Dr. Dowler, of New-Orleans, supplies some extraordinary facts in confirmation of the great age of the Delta of the Mississippi, assumed by Lyell, Carpenter, Forshey, and others. From an investigation of the successive growths of cypress forests around that city, the stumps of which are still found at different depths directly overlying each other; from the great size and age of these trees, and from the remains of Indian bones and pottery found below the roots of some of these stumps, he arrives at the following conclusion : ' From these data it appears that the human race existed in the Delta more than 57,000 years ago, and that ten subterranean forests, and the one now growing, will show that an exuberant flora existed in Louisiana more than 100,000 years anterior to these evidences of man's existence.'

"These authorities in support of the extreme age of the geological era to which man belongs, though startling to the unscientific, are not simply the opinions of the few, but such conclusions are substantially adopted by the leading geologists every where; and though antiquity so extreme for man's existence on earth may shock some preconceived opinions, it is none the less certain that the rapid accumulation of new facts is fast familiarizing the minds of the scientific world to this conviction.

"The monuments of Egypt have already carried us far beyond all chronologies heretofore adopted; and when these barriers are once overleaped, it is in vain for us to attempt to approximate even to the epoch of man's creation.

"Now the question naturally springs up whether the aborigines of America were not contemporary with the earliest races known to us of the Eastern Continent.

"If, as is conceded, Caucasian, Negro, Mongol, and other races existed in the Old World already distinct, what reason can be assigned to show that the aborigines of America did not also exist 5000 years ago? The naturalist must infer that the fauna and flora of the two continents were contemporary. All facts, all analogy war against the supposition that America should have been left by the Creator a dreary waste for thousands of years, while the other half of the world was teeming with organized beings. This view is also strengthened by the acknowledged fact that not a single animal, bird, reptile, fish, or plant was common to the Old and New Worlds. No naturalist of our day doubts that the animal and vegetable kingdoms of America were created where they are found, and not in Asia.

"The races of men alone have been made an exception to this general law; but this exception can not be maintained by any course of scientific reasoning.

"America, it will be remembered, was not only unknown to the early Greeks and Romans, but to the Egyptians; and when discovered, less than four centuries ago, it was found to be inhabited from the Arctic to Cape Horn, and from ocean to ocean, by a population displaying peculiar physical traits, unlike any races in the Old World, speaking languages bearing no resemblance in structure to other languages, and living every where among animals and plants specifically distinct from those of Europe, Asia, Africa, and Oceanica.

"Morton and Agassiz assume that all mankind did not spring from one pair, or even each race from distinct pairs, but that men were created in *nations* in the different zoological provinces where history first finds them. Niebuhr also expresses the same views in one of his letters. (See Bunsen, Life and Letters of B. S. Niebuhr. New York, ed. 1852.) He writes: ' I believe, further, that the origin of the human race is not connected with any given place, but is to be sought every where over the face of the earth ; and that it is an idea more worthy of the power and wisdom of the Creator to assume that he gave to each zone and climate its proper inhabitants, to whom that climate and zone would be most suitable, than to assume that the human species has degenerated in such innumerable instances.'"

The limits of this work, however, will not permit me to pursue this subject further; but those who feel a curiosity and a desire to pursue the investigation, can find great assistance in the works quoted above. Future explorers among the ruins of Central America may find among the hieroglyphic writings of the ancient inhabitants some record or some token which may aid to unveil what is to us now an unfathomable mystery.

The only accounts we have of the tribes around the mouth of the Columbia are those of Ross Cox, who does not appear to have devoted much time to the investigation of the subject, but treats it in rather a flippant style, and Lewis and Clarke's account.   This last is the one usually quoted, but is most singularly incorrect.   Lewis and Clarke, however, have the good sense to state that the short time they remained at the mouth of the Columbia did not enable them to obtain any very reliable facts or information.   They write, "A particular detail of the character, manners, and habits of the tribes must be left to some future adventurer, who may have more leisure and a better opportunity than we had to accomplish this object.   Those who first visit the ground can only be expected to furnish sketches rude and imperfect."

In May, 1855, General Gibbs, who was connected with Governor Stevens's commission for treating with the Indians of Washington Territory, wrote me for the purpose of ascertaining the names of the Coast tribes, and, after quoting Lewis and Clarke's account, adds, "If you can puzzle out these names with the assistance of the Indians, I shall be very glad."

The list, as made out by Lewis and Clarke, are the Chenooks, Chilts, Killaxthokle, Clamoitomish, Potoashees, Pailsk, Quinults, Chillates, Calasthorle, Quinnechaut.

The names given me by the Indians, and by which the tribes from the Columbia to Fuca Strait are known, are,

Chenooks, on the Columbia.

Kar-wee′wee, or Arts′milsh, the name of the Shoalwater Bay tribes, which are now nearly extinct, and are usually considered as Chenooks.

Che-ha′lis, on Gray's Harbor and Chehalis River.

Co-pa′lis, on the Copalis River, eighteen miles north of Gray's Harbor.

Que′ni-ūlt, at Point Grenville.

This name is incorrectly spelled by General Gibbs as *Quinaiutl.* The Indians pronounce the word as if spelled *Que'ni-ūlt*, accenting the first syllable strongly, and pronouncing the last so soft that many persons consider they call themselves simply *Que'nai.* The ending *tl* does not appear at all in the manner the Indians pronounce the word. Next north of the Queniūlt tribe are the Quai'tso, then the Hooch or Hooh, Que-lai'ūlt, and Que-nait'sath.

It is a custom among these tribes to name families and villages from the river they may be located on. In this way it is probable Lewis and Clarke may have mistaken the names of some of the tribes which they have mentioned. The Indians of Shoal-water Bay had no distinct language of their own, but used the Chenook or Chehalis promiscuously, with the exception of the tribe on the Whil'a-pah River, who spoke a language somewhat resembling the Cowlitz. There are two or three of the Whil'a-pah Indians still living at Shoal-water Bay, but the rest of their tribe is all extinct. The other names of the Shoal-water Bay Indians were the Necoman'chee or Nick'omin, who resided on a river of that name flowing into the north side of the Bay.

The Que-lap'ton-lilt, whose village was at the mouth of the Whil'a-pah River, on the banks of a creek whose name they took, and where at present the house and claim of Captain Charles Stewart are.

The Whar'hoots village occupied the present site of the town of Bruceport, and the Quer'quelin village at the mouth of the creek where my house was.

The Palux Indians, on the Copa'lux or Palux River, the Mar'hoo, the Nasal, and several other villages on the peninsula of little account.

The relics of old lodges, canoes, heaps of shells, and other remains, give evidence that at some period there must have been a large body of Indians around Shoal-water Bay. These deserted villages are to be met with all over the coast portion of the Territory, and have attracted the attention of the early discoverers. Vancouver, alluding to this fact, attributes it either to the wandering disposition of the natives or to sickness, but adds " that it is impossible to draw any just conclusions of the true cause of this havoc among the human race, and it may not be improbable to conjecture that the depopulation may have arisen in some measure from the disposition of the Indians to move from place to place for the purpose of trade."

My opinion about the cause of these deserted villages is this. It is the universal custom with these Indians never to live in a lodge where a person has died. If a person of importance dies, the lodge is usually burned down, or taken down and removed to some other part of the Bay; and it can readily be seen that in the case of the Palux Indians, who had been attacked by the Chehalis people, as before stated, their relatives chose at once to leave for some other place. This objection to living in a lodge where a person has died is the reason why their sick slaves are invariably carried out into the woods, where they remain either to recover or die. There is, however, no disputing the fact that an immense mortality has occurred among these people, and they are now reduced to a mere handful. The tribes of the interior, whether originally more numerous than the Coast tribes, are vastly superior in point of numbers, and are the ones who have been engaged in the late hostilities.

The great superstitious dread these Indians have for a dead person, and their horror of touching a corpse, oftentimes gives rise to difficulty as to who shall perform the funeral ceremonies; for any person who handles a dead body must not eat of salmon or sturgeon for thirty days. Sometimes, in cases of small-pox, I have known them leave the corpse in the lodge, and all remove elsewhere; and in two instances that came to my knowledge, the whites had to burn the lodges, with the bodies in them, to prevent infection.

So, in the instances I have before mentioned, where we had buried Indians, not one of their friends or relatives could be seen. All kept in their lodges, singing and drumming to keep away the spirits of the dead.

Meares, writing of the Nootka Indians, June, 1788, allowed himself to be so far imposed upon as to assert that the Nootkans were cannibals, and states that a chief named Callicum " reposed his head every night on a bag filled with human skulls ;" and that the two chiefs, Maquilla and Callicum, regularly killed a slave once a month; nor did they hesitate to confess that they had eaten human flesh, and to express their delight in banqueting on their fellow-creatures. Vancouver, however, in alluding to Meares's statements, entirely discredits any such tale, and states that " in May, 1792, while in Admiralty Inlet, he offered some venison pie to the natives, who, conceiving it to be human flesh, threw it from them with the greatest aversion and displeasure; and it was only by showing the rest of a haunch that remained in the boat that they were undeceived, and were willing to eat of the pie."*

Then, referring to Meares's statements, he remarks, " Were such barbarities practiced once a month as stated, it is but natural to suppose that these natives would not have shown the least aversion to eating flesh

* It is very possible that the aversion of the Indians to Vancouver's venison pie arose partly from the pepper or other condiments contained in it; for an Indian can not bear the least particle of pepper or mustard in his mouth, and it is pretty certain that the old navigator would probably have his game pie well seasoned.

of any kind ; but, on the contrary, it is not possible to conceive a greater degree of abhorrence than was manifested by these people, till their minds were made easy that it was not human flesh they were eating."

The Indians have a great aversion to seeing a skull, and a great dread of having one in the house ; and it can not be possible that one among them could be found with the hardihood to sleep nightly on a bag filled with skulls.

One of their superstitions relating to skulls is that, if a lodge near the waters of the Bay contains one, the water will gradually wash away the bank till it reaches the skull, which is then carried off by the waves. I witnessed a singular incident relative to this superstition. Dr. Cooper, who had been connected with Governor Stevens's expedition across the Rocky Mountains, and who was residing at Shoal-water Bay with Mr. Russell, making collections of natural curiosities, had collected several specimens of skulls, which were placed in a box under Russell's house. The Indians predicted that the house would be washed away, and, sure enough, the ensuing winter the tide came up so high that it nearly capsized Russell's house, and confirmed the Indians in the belief of the correctness of their predictions.

From what I have seen of the great and very universal superstitious dread they have of a dead body, I can not believe they ever could have been cannibals, although the early accounts of their ferocity might give some ground to believe such an assertion. Still, those early records of voyages do not always convey the whole truth ; and while we are led to believe the Indians were at all times of a hostile disposition, we are carefully kept in the dark as to whether imprudence or ignorance on the part of the whites did not occasion all the ill feeling. One thing is certain : these Indians at the present time have lost a great deal of that alleged fierceness, and I have always found them, when treated well, to be kind and hospitable.

CHAPTER XIII.

Trip to San Francisco.—Captain Smith and his Goggles.—We get nearly wrecked by reason of the Fog on Captain Smith's "Specks."—Arrive safe at last.—Return to the Columbia in Steamer Peytona.—Port Orford.—Captain Tichenor.—Cedar of Port Orford.—Mouth of the Columbia.—Not so terrible as generally represented.—Arrival at Astoria.—History of Astoria.—Captain Smith, of the Ship Albatross.—John Jacob Astor.—Ship Tonquin, Captain Thorne.—Ship Beaver, Captain Sowles.—Ross Cox's Description of Astoria.—Loss of the Tonquin.—Ship Lark.—Astoria sold to the Northwest Company.—The Raccoon Sloop-of-war.—Brig Peddler.—Ship Isaac Todd and her Passengers.—First white Woman.—Death of Mr. M'Tavish.—Restoration of Astoria to the Americans.—H. B. M. Frigate Blossom salutes the Flag.—Various Expeditions, &c.—First Emigration.—Jesuits.—Present Appearance of Astoria.—Military Road, &c.

As it was impossible to collect oysters during the winter season, I concluded to go to San Francisco for a few months, and, taking passage in the schooner Maryland, then ready to sail, we left our anchorage on the first day of January, 1854, and, with a fair wind from the northeast, put out to sea. The captain of the schooner, whose name was Smith, was a regular trading, swapping, Down-East Yankee, a very good navigator when he had plenty of sea-room, but in close work or running by land-marks he was at fault. The cause of this was partly owing to the fact of his eyesight being dim, and rendered still dimmer by wearing green goggles, which, when covered, as they often were, with fog, almost totally extinguished Captain Smith's powers of sight.

We ran down the coast with a fair wind and fine weather till we had passed Cape Mendocino, the wind having hauled in the mean time into the west. The weather now began to grow thick and foggy, but, as Captain Smith had what he called a fair start, we drove ahead with all sail set, sure of running into San Francisco before dark.

There is an indentation in the coast a few miles north of the entrance to San Francisco, called False San Francisco, where several vessels and steamers have been lost. In foggy weather this opening is mistaken for the true entrance to the harbor, which gives rise to the accidents.

Into this place we were driving right before the wind, although the captain was assured we were going into the wrong place. At length the watch forward assured the captain we were going ashore, but he knew better. Finally he acknowledged that the fog had settled on his spectacles so that objects had quite a vague and indistinct appearance to him, and he requested me to take a look, which I did, and assured him we were going head on to a reef not more than half a dozen lengths of the schooner ahead. The helm was put down, and the vessel put sharp on the wind, which had now lulled down almost to a calm, but there was a heavy rolling sea that set us in toward the shore. I saw we were nearing a point, and if we kept on that tack would go ashore, as every sea threw us bodily to leeward. Finally the captain ordered the schooner to be put on the other tack. She had just headway enough to come about, although it was with the merest accident that the jib filled on the other tack; but she did get round, and as we gathered way, I could have tossed a biscuit on the reef astern, and had she missed stays we would have been inevitably dashed to atoms, for in ten minutes afterward the wind came out of the southwest and blew a gale. However, we made one tack inside the Farallones, and stood

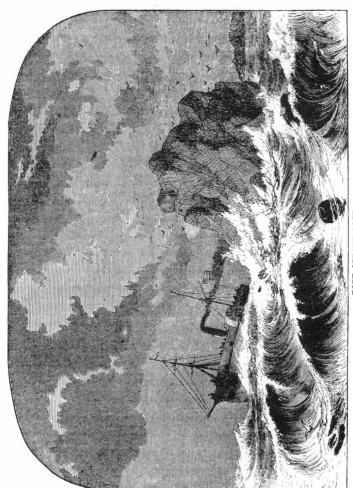

PORT ORFORD ROCK.

in by Point Bonita, and ran into the harbor of San Francisco safe and sound.

I remained in San Francisco a few months, and on the last of May again started up the coast in the steamer Peytona, Captain Sampson.   We stopped at Crescent City, Trinidad, and Port Orford, where the celebrated Captain Tichenor, formerly of the steamer Sea-Gull, had landed a party some fourteen months previous, while he proceeded on his voyage to the Columbia.   On his return, Captain Tichenor found that his party had fought a severe conflict on a cliff called Battle Rock, from whence they had been driven by the Indians.   Tichenor took on board a small six-pounder which he had left, and proceeded to San Francisco, where he obtained another party, and effected a lodgment, and finally settled the present flourishing town of Port Orford.   The first party had made their way through the forest and wilderness to some of the towns in Oregon, where they published a statement of their toils and privations.

The settlement of Port Orford was attended with as much, if not more difficulty with the Indians of that section than any other settlement on the coast.   There is a variety of cedar found at Port Orford, as white as white pine, and of a peculiar fragrant smell, almost equal to sandal-wood.   Messrs. Neefus and Tichenor, of San Francisco, have a saw-mill there for the purpose of cutting this cedar into boards, which are then sent to San Francisco, where they meet with a ready sale at high prices.   Even the saw-dust from this cedar is in demand, and is used to strew the floors of saloons and grocery stores in San Francisco, where it is prized for its perfume.

A pleasant run of three days brought us to the mouth of the Columbia, where, having obtained a pilot, we crossed the bar, and found the water as smooth as a millpond, where, from all accounts, I had expected to have seen the most fearful breakers.   The Columbia River is not such an awful place for mariners as many writers would make it appear.   The terrors of its bar are a good deal like the terrors of a Cape Horn passage, which, till it was found to the contrary, was considered one of the most appalling voyages a mariner could make.

The early navigators to the Northwest Coast were looked upon when they returned as great curiosities, and any fables they might relate were eagerly swallowed by the gaping crowd.   So, to prevent others from attempting to interfere with their trade, and also to magnify the dangers themselves had passed, those ancient mariners were wont to tell of tales that, if true, were enough to deter the stoutest-hearted from going the dread voyage around Cape Horn, and over the horrid breakers at the Columbia's mouth.

But when the gold discoveries of California induced men to send to sea old rotten hulks, that were ready to be condemned at New York or Boston, and when it was seen that those old vessels all doubled the Cape in safety, people found that the actual danger had been greatly exaggerated.

And so with the Columbia; when people began to get acquainted with the navigation, they no longer feared. There are many captains who have always been accustomed to sail to and from ports where there was no bar or dangerous breakers, and such would always cry out about the dangers of the Columbia; but I have never seen a man accustomed to the coasting-trade of the Atlantic who considered the entrance to the Columbia any more dangerous, if as much so, as some of the harbors on the Atlantic.

I do not mean to be understood as stating that there are no dangers on the Columbia bar.   On the contrary,

FIGHT ON BATTLE ROCK.

there are times when there is a very heavy sea breaking there; but I mean that the *real* danger is not so great as has been represented.

It was about sundown when we arrived off the.wharf where the steamer was to stop to send such passengers ashore as intended stopping, and, with two or three others, I clambered into the boat, and in a few minutes was landed on the shores of the town of Astoria.

The account of the settlement of Astoria given by Greenhow being the most concise, I shall quote from that work, and give a short history of that famous little town, which is familiarly known by name to almost every one in the United States, and certainly deserves to be a much larger settlement than it is at present. It is most admirably located for business, being directly at the mouth of the largest river running into the Pacific, and is sure, when the country increases in population, and consequently in trade, to be a place of great importance to the Territory of Oregon.

During the year 1810, Captain Smith, commander of the ship Albatross, attempted to found a post for trade with the Indians at a place called Oak Point, on the south bank of the Columbia, about forty miles from its mouth. For this purpose a house was built, and a garden laid out and planted there; but the site was badly chosen in all respects, and the scheme was abandoned before the close of the year.

In the same year an association was formed at New York for the prosecution of the fur trade in the central and northwestern parts of the continent in connection with the China trade. This association was called the *Pacific Fur Company*, and at its head was John Jacob Astor, a German merchant of New York, who had been for many years extensively engaged in the commerce of the Pacific and China.

His object was to concentrate in the hands of the company the fur trade of every part of the unsettled territory of America claimed by the United States.

Posts were to be established on the Missouri, the Columbia, and the coasts of the Pacific contiguous to the latter river. For the purposes of this expedition, one party was to proceed across the land, while another detachment was to proceed by sea around Cape Horn. Mr. Astor had already, in 1809, dispatched the ship Enterprise, under Captain Ebbetts, to make observations at various places on the Northwest Coasts of America, and to prepare the way for the new establishments.

The preparations for commencing the enterprise having been completed, four of the partners, M'Kay, M'Dougal, David Stuart, Robert Stuart, with eleven clerks, thirteen Canadian *voyageurs*, and five mechanics, all British subjects, took their departure from New York for the mouth of the Columbia River in September, 1810, in the ship Tonquin, commanded by Captain Jonathan Thorne. In January following, the second detachment, commanded by Mr. Hunt, the chief agent, and Messrs. M'Lellan, M'Kenzie, and Crooks, set out for the same point by way of the Missouri River; and in October, 1811, the ship Beaver, under Captain Sowles, carried out from New York to the North Pacific Mr. Clark, with six clerks and a number of other persons.

On the 24th of March the Tonquin arrived at the Columbia, which she entered with difficulty, after losing three of her men, whom Captain Thorne foolishly sent out in a boat to sound the channel. The ship came to anchor in Baker's Bay, just within Cape Disappointment, where the passengers were landed, and sheds were built for their temporary accommodation. A few days afterward the partners set off in search of a place suitable for the establishment of a factory, and they soon selected for that object a spot on the south bank of the river, distant about ten miles from the ocean, which had received from Broughton, in 1792, the name of *Point George.*

To this place the Tonquin was removed, and having landed her passengers and such part of the cargo as was intended for the establishment, sailed on the 5th of June for the Northern Coast, taking Mr. M'Kay, who was to conduct the trade, Mr. Lewis, one of the clerks, and an Indian as an interpreter.

During the ensuing summer much progress was made in the building of the factory, which, in honor of its founder, was named ASTORIA.

On the 5th of May, 1812, the ship Beaver, commanded by Captain Sowles, arrived in the Columbia from New York, bringing a third detachment of persons in the service of the Pacific Company, under the direction of Mr. Clarke, and twenty-six natives of the Sandwich Islands. Ross Cox, who arrived in the Beaver, gives the following account of Astoria as it then appeared:

" The spot selected for the fort (Astoria) was a handsome eminence, called Point George, which commanded an extensive view of the majestic Columbia in front, bounded by the bold and thickly-wooded northern shore.

" On the right, about three miles distant, a long, high, and rocky peninsula, covered with timber, called Tongue Point, extended a considerable distance into the river from the southern side, with which it was connected by a narrow neck of land, while on the extreme left, Cape Disappointment, with the bar and its terrific chain of breakers, were distinctly visible. The buildings consisted of apartments for the proprietors and clerks, with a capacious dining-hall for both; extensive warehouses for the trading goods and furs, a provision store, a trading-shop, smith's forge, carpenter's shop, &c., the whole sur-

K 2

rounded by stockades, forming a square, and reaching about fifteen feet above the ground. A gallery ran around the stockades, in which loop-holes were placed sufficiently large for musketry. Two strong bastions, built of logs, commanded the four sides of the square; each bastion had two stories, in which a number of chosen men slept every night; a six-pounder was placed in the lower story of each, and they were both well provided with small-arms. Immediately in front of the fort was a gentle declivity, sloping down to the river's side, which had been turned into an excellent kitchen garden; and a few hundred rods to the left, a tolerable wharf had been run out, by which boats and batteaux were enabled to land their cargoes at low water without sustaining any damage.

"An impenetrable forest of gigantic pines rose in the rear, and the ground was covered with a thick underwood of brier and whortleberry, intermingled with fern and honeysuckle."

The Beaver also brought a letter from Owyhee that had been left there by Captain Ebbetts, of the ship Enterprise, containing positive information of the destruction of the Tonquin and her crew by the savages on the Coast, near the Straits of Fuca. The particulars of this melancholy affair were afterward brought by the Indian who had gone in the Tonquin as interpreter, and who was the only survivor of those who had gone in the ill-fated ship.

The Tonquin, it appears, anchored in the middle of June, 1811, opposite a village on the Bay of Clyoquot, near the Straits of Fuca. Captain Thorne, who is represented to have been totally unfitted to trade with the Indians, had given a mortal affront to one of the chiefs by slapping him in the face with an otter-skin he was offering for sale. The Indians seized the opportunity when the men were busily engaged about their duties on board the ship to get possession of her, and put to death every one of the crew and passengers except the interpreter, the clerk, Mr. Lewis, and five or six sailors. The interpreter was saved by leaping into a canoe where there were some women, who concealed him. Four of the men managed to leave in the boat during the night, but were taken by the savages, and murdered in the most cruel manner. The following day, while the ship was crowded with Indians, she was blown up by Mr. Lewis, as was supposed, killing by the explosion a great number of the savages.

The loss of the Tonquin was a severe blow to the Pacific Company; and it was determined that Mr. Hunt should embark in the Beaver, and proceed north to trade and visit the Russian establishments, as Mr. M'Kay would have done but for the destruction of the Tonquin. He accordingly sailed in the Beaver in August, 1812, leaving the superintendence of the factory in the hands of Mr. M'Dougal.

It was not till January, 1813, that they learned of the war between the United States and Great Britain; and the gloom caused by this information was increased by the report that the Beaver was lying in Canton blockaded by a British ship of war. And soon after, Messrs. M'Tavish and Laroque, partners in the Northwest Company, arrived near Astoria, bringing accounts of the success of the British arms on the northern frontiers of the United States.

With these facts before them, it was decided by M'Dougal and M'Kenzie that the company should be dissolved on the first of July.

From the United States no assistance came. The ship Lark was dispatched from New York in March, 1813, with men and goods for the Columbia, but she was wrecked the October following near one of the Sandwich Islands.

The American government also had determined, in consequence of the representations of Mr. Astor, to send the sloop-of-war John Adams for the protection of the infant colony; but, just as the vessel was about to sail from New York, it became necessary to transfer her crew to Lake Ontario.

In the mean time, Mr. Hunt, who had sailed from the Columbia in the Beaver, as already mentioned, had proceeded to the Russian settlements at the North, where he had procured a large quantity of furs, and then had proceeded direct to the Sandwich Islands instead of returning to the Columbia, and, having directed Captain Sowles to proceed to Canton, chartered the ship Albatross, of Boston, which had just arrived at Woahoo from Canton, and proceeded in her to the Columbia, where he arrived on the fourth of August; but, finding the condition of affairs, he immediately sailed in the Albatross for the Sandwich Islands in search of some vessel to take off the property of the Pacific Company from the Columbia. On his arrival he chartered a small brig, called the Peddler, and sailed in her for Astoria, where he arrived in February, 1814; but before the Peddler arrived the fate of Astoria had been decided.

A few days after Hunt had sailed in the Albatross, Mr. M'Tavish and his followers of the Northwest Company again appeared at Astoria, and gave information that a ship, called the Isaac Todd, had sailed from London with a full cargo for the Columbia, and was daily expected under convoy of a British squadron, who had orders to take and destroy every thing American on the Northwest Coast. M'Dougal and M'Kenzie then concluded to sell out the whole establishment to the Northwest Company, and an agreement was made on October

16th, 1813, between M'Tavish and Stuart on one part, and M'Dougal, M'Kenzie, and Clarke on the other, for the conveyance of the property, which was signed and conveyed that day for the sum of about fifty-eight thousand dollars.

Just after this transfer had been made, the sloop-of-war Raccoon, commanded by Captain Black, arrived in the river, having been sent there by Commodore Hillyer from the South Pacific to take possession of all the American forts and property on the Columbia.

Captain Black was intensely disgusted at finding the state of affairs, and had to content himself by hauling down the American colors and hoisting the English colors instead, and then, with all solemnity and proper formality, changed the name of the establishment to *Fort George.*

The brig Peddler arrived at the Columbia, as before said, on the 28th of February, 1814, and Mr. Hunt found M'Dougal superintending the factory, not as chief agent of the Pacific Company, but as partner of the Northwest Company, into which he had been admitted. Hunt had, therefore, merely to close the concerns of the American Association in that quarter, and take bills on Montreal given in payment for its effects, after which he embarked in the Peddler with two of the clerks, and proceeded, by way of Canton and the Cape of Good Hope, to New York. Such was the termination of the Astoria enterprise.

The Isaac Todd reached Fort George on the 17th of April, 1814, thirteen months after her departure from England, bringing a large stock of supplies, by the aid of which the partners of the Northwest Company were enabled to establish themselves more firmly in the country.

The Isaac Todd brought out as passengers John

M'Tavish and John M'Donald, proprietors; Alexander and James M'Tavish, Alexander Frazer and Alexander M'Kenzie, clerks, with Dr. Swan, a medical gentleman, engaged as a resident physician at the fort.

" She also brought out," says Ross Cox, "the first white woman who ever entered the Columbia River, Miss Jane Barnes, a flaxen-haired, blue-eyed daughter of Albion, who, in a fit of erratic enthusiasm, had consented to accompany one of the Macs as *compagnon du voyage.* She was very fond of displaying herself to the savages arrayed in all the latest English styles of fashion, and had attracted the admiration of a son of Comcomly, the principal chief of the Chenooks, who fell in love with her and wanted to marry her.   He offered to give her friends one hundred sea-otter skins, which was a very high price; but Miss Jane could not forget her old ideas and predilections respecting mankind, among which she did not include a flat head, a half-naked body, or a copper-colored skin besmeared with whale oil."

" Early in June, 1813," writes Cox, " Mr. Donald M'Tavish, one of the oldest and earliest proprietors of the Northwest Fur Company, was drowned while attempting to cross the Columbia in a boat.   His remains, with those of four men who were drowned at the same time, were interred behind the northeast bastion of Fort George."

The capture of Astoria by the British, and the transfer of the Pacific Company's establishments on the Columbia to the Northwest Company, were not known to the plenipotentiaries of the United States at Ghent on the 24th of December, 1814, when they signed the treaty of peace between their country and Great Britain.

It was nevertheless agreed, in the first article of the treaty of Ghent, that " *all territory, places, and possessions whatsoever, taken by either party during the war, or which may be taken after the signing of this treaty, excepting only the islands hereinafter mentioned* (in the Bay of Fundy), *shall be restored without delay.*"

In virtue of this article, Mr. Monroe, then Secretary of State of the United States, on the 18th of May, 1815, announced to Mr. Baker, the *chargé d'affaires* of Great Britain at Washington, that the President intended immediately to reoccupy the post at the mouth of the Columbia; but no measures were adopted for the purpose till September, 1817, when Captain J. Biddle, commanding the sloop-of-war Ontario, and Mr. J. B. Prevost, were jointly commissioned to proceed in that ship to the mouth of the Columbia, and then to assert the claim of the United States to the sovereignty of the adjacent country in a friendly and peaceable manner, and without the employment of force. After a little demur on the part of the British government, Lord Castlereagh, the British Secretary for Foreign Affairs, finally, on the claim being urged by Mr. Rush, the American minister at London, admitted the right of the Americans to be reinstated, and it was finally agreed that the post should be restored to them; and accordingly, orders were issued by Lord Bathurst, the British Colonial Secretary, to the agents of the Northwest Company at the mouth of the Columbia, directing them to afford due facilities for the reoccupation of the post by the Americans. An order was at the same time issued from the Admiralty to the same effect, to the commander of the British naval forces in the Pacific.

The Ontario arrived at Valparaiso in February, 1818, where, Mr. Prevost having to transact some business for his government, it was agreed between the commissioners that he should remain, while Captain Biddle should proceed to the Columbia in the Ontario, which he did, and on the 9th of August took temporary possession of the country on that river in the name of the United States, after which he returned to the South Pacific.

In the mean time, Captain Sheriff, the senior officer of the British ships in the Pacific, having received instructions from Commodore Bowles, the British naval commander of the forces in the South Seas, informed Mr. Prevost, and offered him a passage to the Columbia for the purpose of completing the business.   He accordingly accepted the offer, and proceeded to the Columbia in the British frigate Blossom, where he arrived in the beginning of October, 1818.

On the 6th of the month, Captain Hickey, commander of the Blossom, and Mr. Keith, the superintending partner of the Northwest Company, as joint commissioners on the part of Great Britain, exchanged with Mr. Prevost documents setting forth the facts of the restoration of the territory on the one part, and the acceptance of the settlement for his government on the other.   The British flag was then formally lowered, and that of the United States, having been hoisted in its stead over the fort, was saluted by the Blossom.   Thus was Fort Astoria once more under the American flag.   But the British traders continued to occupy the post, and carry on their operations the same as previous to the change of flags.

A good deal of enmity had subsisted between the Northwest and Hudson's Bay Companies, which was only displayed in words, or in the commission of petty acts of injury or annoyance to each other till 1814, when a regular war broke out between them, and on the 19th of June, 1816, a battle was fought between the Northwest people and some Scotch settlers on Red River at a place called *Ossinobia*, when the latter were routed, having seventeen of their number, including their governor, Mr. Semple, killed.

These troubles were brought before the British Parliament in June, 1819, and, after a long debate, in which the merits of both companies were discussed, an act was passed effecting a union between the two rival companies, and in 1824, the Northwest Company having surrendered its rights, and possessions, and interests to the Hudson's Bay Company, all the operations were thenceforward conducted in the name of that company alone.

Great efforts were now made and vast expenses incurred by this company to found settlements on the Columbia River, and to acquire influence over the natives of the surrounding country; and so successful were those efforts, that the citizens of the United States not only renounced all ideas of renewing their establishments in that part of America, but even withdrew their vessels from its coasts; and for more than ten years after the capture of Astoria by the British, scarcely an American citizen was to be seen in those countries. Trading expeditions were indeed made from the Missouri to the head-waters of the Platte and Colorado, but the Americans had no settlement of any kind, and their government exercised no jurisdiction whatever west of the Rocky Mountains.

The first attempt to re-establish commercial communication between the United States and the territories west of the Rocky Mountains was made by General W. H. Ashley, of St. Louis, Missouri, in the spring of 1823. His explorations and expeditions, however, were confined to Southern Oregon and California; but, unfortunately, they made no astronomical observations; and, being unacquainted with any branch of physical science, very little information has been derived through their means.

In 1827, Mr. Pilcher went from Council Bluffs, on the Missouri, with forty-five men and more than one hundred horses, and spent the winter on the Colorado. The following year he proceeded to Louis's River, and thence northward, along the foot of the Rocky Mountains, to the Flat Head Lake, near the 47th parallel of latitude. Here he remained till the spring of 1829, when he descended the Clarke River to Fort Colville, on the Columbia, and from thence he returned to the United States through the long and circuitous route of the Upper Columbia, the Athabasca, the Assinaboin, Red River, and the Upper Missouri.

In 1832, Captain Bonneville, of the army of the United States, while on a furlough, led a band of more than a hundred men, with twenty wagons, and many horses and mules carrying merchandise, from Missouri to the countries of the Colorado and the Columbia, in which he passed more than two years, engaged in hunting, trapping, and trading. About the same time (1832), Captain Nathaniel Wyeth, of Massachusetts, endeavored to establish a system of commercial intercourse between the Union and the countries of the Columbia, to which the general name of *Oregon* now began to be universally applied by the Americans. Captain Wyeth's plan of operation was like that of Mr. Astor in 1810, which was to send manufactured goods to the Pacific countries by means of overland expeditions, and also by the way of Cape Horn, and to transport in exchange furs, and even salmon, which abound in all the waters of Northwest America, and to extend his trade to China.

With these objects in view, he made two expeditions overland to the Columbia, in the latter of which he founded a trading-post, called Fort Hall, on the south side of the Snake River, or the Lewis branch of that river, at the entrance of the Port Neuf, about a hundred miles north of the Utah Lake; and he then established another post, principally for fishing purposes, on Wap-

patoo Island, near the confluence of the Willamet River
with the Columbia, a hundred miles above the mouth of
the latter.

Wyeth's plans, however, were not successful; for the
Hudson Bay Company agents, taking the alarm, founded
a counter trading-post, called Fort Boisé, at the entrance
of the Boisé, or Read's River, into the Lewis, some distance below Fort Hall, where they offered goods to the
Indians at prices so much lower than the Americans
could afford, that Wyeth was driven out of the market,
and was forced to compromise with his opponents by
selling his fort and engaging to desist from the fur trade.

Meanwhile a brig, which he had dispatched from Boston, arrived in the Columbia, and proceeded to Wappatoo
Island, where, after making some further arrangements
with the Hudson Bay Company, she returned to the
United States, taking a cargo of salmon.   But, the result of the voyage not being very profitable, a further
prosecution of the enterprise was abandoned.

The prices of articles of trade were nominally high, as
every thing was exchanged in barter for furs, there being
no money among the hunters, trappers, or traders; and
in a price-current at a rendezvous on the Green River
in the summer of 1838, we find whisky at three dollars
per pint, gunpowder at six dollars per pint, tobacco at
five dollars per pound, dogs (for food) at fifteen dollars
each, &c.

About the time of Wyeth's expedition also took place
the earliest emigration to the territories of the Columbia
for the purpose of settlement, without any commercial
objects.   The first of these colonies were founded in
1834, in the valley of the Willamet River, in which a
few retired servants of the Hudson Bay Company had
established themselves by permission of that body, and
were engaged in herding cattle.   "The Americans," says

Greenhow, "who first settled there, were mostly Methodists, under direction of ministers of their own sect; and colonies of Presbyterians or Congregationalists were afterward planted in the Walla Walla and Spokan countries.

"In these places schools for the education of the natives were opened, and in 1839 a printing-press was first set up at Walla Walla, on which were struck off the first sheets ever printed on the Pacific side of America, north of Mexico." The Jesuits of St. Louis then engaged in the labor of converting the Indians, in which they appear, according to their own accounts, to have met with extraordinary success; but, if the following extracts from *De Smet's Letters* (published at Philadelphia in 1843, and which I copy from Greenhow, page 361) are any evidence, certainly that evidence is very poor. The quotation states "that the Jesuits, De Smet, Mengarini, Point, and others, have, since 1840, made several missionary tours through the Indian countries, in the course of which they baptized some thousands of Indians;" they also erected a church at a place called the Kullerspelm Lake, on Clarke's River, where the Blessed Virgin appeared in person to a little Indian boy, "whose youth, piety, and sincerity," say the good fathers, "joined to the nature of facts which he related, forbade us to doubt of the truth of his statement."

If the Catholics base their calculations of the number and fervor of their converts among the Indians on such trash as the idea of a little Indian boy having seen the Virgin Mary, a just estimate can be formed of their actual worth by those persons who, knowing the Indian nature, place but very little reliance on such idle and apocryphal tales.

From this period, 1836, the emigration began to increase until 1843, when, a promise of protection from the federal government to emigrants having been held out by the passage through the Senate of a bill for the immediate occupation of Oregon, a thousand persons assembled at Westport, near the Missouri River, on the frontier of the State of Missouri, from which they began their march to Oregon, with a large number of wagons, horses, and cattle, in June, 1843.

They arrived in the Willamet Valley in October, after having undergone a laborious and fatiguing journey of more than two thousand miles. They were subjected to sickness and privation, and seven of the party died by the way; but the difficulties, upon the whole, were much less than had been anticipated even by the most sanguine, and their success encouraged a much greater emigration in 1844, before the end of which year the population of Oregon exceeded three thousand. This expedition utterly refuted and overthrew an article which appeared in the Edinburgh Review of 1843, "and which, though generally correct," says Greenhow, yet affirmed, *ex cathedra*, that, "however the political questions between England and America as to the ownership of Oregon may be decided, Oregon will never be colonized *overland* from the United States. The world must assume a new face before the American wagons make plain the road to the Columbia as they have done to the Ohio." Yet, in face of this assertion of what was supposed to be superior wisdom, the American emigrants *did* reach Oregon by a road that Nature has made as plain as that from the Atlantic to the Ohio.

From this time the emigration gradually increased till the discovery of gold in California in 1849, when not only was a large portion of the emigration diverted to the California trade, but many of the actual settlers of Oregon left for the country of gold.

The reaction is slowly taking place, and at the time

of my landing at Astoria I found it to be quite a thriving town, with some six hundred inhabitants, a custom-house, general distributing post-office for the two Territories of Oregon and Washington, ten or twelve saw and grist mills, and a general bustle and stirring business appearance. Astoria is divided into two villages: Upper Astoria, where the custom-house and two or three saw-mills are, is near Tongue Point; and Lower Astoria, consisting of the old settlement of Fort George, contains the post-office, several saw and grist mills, and the principal portion of the business community, among which latter should always be named with honorable mention the trading-house of Leonard & Green, and the tavern-house of Mr. Bolin, where the tired traveler may at all times find repose and all necessary refreshments at reasonable charges.

A military road from Astoria to Salem, the seat of government of Oregon, was provided for by an act of the thirty-third Congress, appropriating $25,000 to be expended under the direction of the Secretary of War. Early in 1855, Lieutenant Derby, well known as a facetious writer over the signature of "Phœnix," *alias* "Squibob," *alias* "Butterfield," and sundry other *nommes de plume*, was ordered to take charge of the work, and during that spring (1855) he proceeded to Astoria, and commenced operations, and has worked at it at intervals, until recently (1856) it has been placed under the charge of Lieutenant Mendell. The road has been made fit for wagons to pass over from Astoria, in the direction of the Tualiten Plains, a distance of twenty-two miles. This road commences at Astoria, near the custom-house, and about one mile east of the old town.

A farther appropriation of $10,000 has been asked from Congress to complete this road, which will, when finished, be of vast importance to Oregon, both in a military point of view, and also as opening a means of communication with the interior, which will be of incalculable benefit to emigrants and settlers.

When a military road shall have been made from the Columbia opposite Astoria to Olympia, the seat of government of Washington Territory, the two roads can be connected by a ferry, and a line of communication uninterrupted can be kept up throughout the year between the capitals of both Territories—a movement which is very much needed at present, as during the winter months the floods or ice block up the roads and streams in the interior, often preventing mail communication for weeks.

Astoria is the sea-port of the Oregon side of the Columbia, and when the military road now in progress between Astoria and Salem shall be completed, it will be a place of importance, and undoubtedly the largest trading town in Oregon.

CHAPTER XIV.

Cross the Columbia to Chenook.—Meet Fiddler Smith.—We start for Shoal-water Bay with Captain Johnson.—Johnson falls overboard. —John Edmands.—Ox-team Express.—Get stuck in the Swamp.— Captain Nichols and his Whale-boat.—The Fiddler and myself take Passage.—Safe Arrival.—Another Start for Astoria.—Detention by Storm.—General Adair, of Astoria.—Canoe Adventure with Peter.— Sturgeon-fishing. — Salleel and his Sturgeons' Heads. — Johnson's Lake.—A hard Walk.—Toke in the Mud.—Brook Navigation.—Indian Method of making Fire.—Rate of Speed home.—Strawberry Expedition.

AFTER waiting over night at Astoria, I crossed the river to Chenook, where I found a person named Smith, who was waiting an opportunity to go to Shoal-water Bay. We soon made a bargain with Captain Johnson, an old settler at Baker's Bay, and a former pilot on the river, to take us to the portage on the Wallacut River, known at that time as Feister's Portage, Smith (who was named by the whites Fiddler Smith, to designate him from several other members of that remarkably prolific family) having assured me that we could get an ox-team to transport our effects, which he averred could not be had at M'Carty's, on the Wappalooche River. We had a very nice sail till we reached the bar at the entrance of the Wallacut, where Johnson, finding the tide out and the channel intricate, took in sail, and, jumping overboard, with the boat's painter over his shoulder, started out boldly to tow us through the shallow water. He had not made any calculations for two or three deep holes into which he floundered, coming up as wet and as shiny as an otter; but he managed to get us over the bar and into deep water, when he and the fiddler took to the oars, while I steered the boat.

The Wallacut is a small, crooked stream, running through excellent prairie-lands, which are very fertile.

At the mouth of the river we passed the house and farm of Mr. John Edmands, a settler who has resided many years on the Columbia, and has a most excellent farm well stocked.

John Edmands is a celebrated hunter, and yearly slaughters quantities of elk, deer, and bears, all of which are very plentiful around his claim. He is a capital shot as well as a capital fellow, and an animal must make sure to die when John " draws a bead" on him with his fine rifle.

As we proceeded up the river we passed several clearings and claims, occupied by persons who were strangers to me, and finally, about noon, arrived at a raft of drift-logs, which formed the head of navigation, and, on landing, found ourselves at Feister's.

We soon had a team with two yoke of oxen, and, placing our traps into the wagon, started off to walk over the portage, which at this crossing is three miles or more across.   The road was most execrable—much worse than the other or M'Carty's portage; and, after floundering in the mud a while, old Johnson, who was with us, proposed taking a short cut through the woods, to which we agreed, Johnson acting as pilot; but we had better have kept the cart-path, for he led us into a bog, where we got most completely mired, and extricated ourselves with difficulty, and at last reached the house of Mrs. Paulding, situated at the other end of the portage.   Our ox-express shortly arrived; and, after wasting several hours in the fruitless endeavor to procure a boat or canoe, were at length cheered by the sight of a sail; and shortly a whale-boat, owned and commanded by an ancient mariner, called Captain Nichols, and manned by himself and a Dutchman, arrived, and, for a consideration then and there agreed upon, the worthy Nichols agreed to transport us across the Bay.   Bidding good-by to Captain Johnson, we embarked in Captain Nichols's boat, and shortly were under all sail, beating down the Bay.   We reached a settlement some fifteen or twenty miles distant, called Oysterville, where quite a number of oystermen had collected during my absence to San Francisco. As it was dark, and the tide being out, we concluded to sleep on board the boat, Smith and myself not being anxious to try old Johnson's experience on the Wallacut of sounding the depth of sundry holes between us and the shore.

In the morning, as soon as we could see, I went ashore to carry letters and papers (for we had brought the mail). Here I found encamped a lot of Indians, who were very glad to see me; and shortly the whole camp was roused, and came flocking to us to learn the news.   After tak-

L

ing breakfast with my friend Harry Stevens, we again made sail, and stood across the Bay to the mouth of the little Querquelin, where I went ashore, and found Captain Purrington well, and every thing looking as fresh and green as a fertile soil and warm June sun could make it. I found that during my absence there had been quite an emigration to the Bay, and some neighbors were located quite near. Captain William Lake, an old Staten Island oysterman, had put up a house down the beach about half a mile, and just beyond him Baldt and two others had built another residence.

So, as far as neighbors were concerned, our prospects were much better than when I had left the Bay five months previous; but the cold weather, which had commenced on the day I left (January 1st, 1854), and continued ten days, had destroyed not only our bed of oysters, but also those of every person in the Bay. This was a pecuniary matter not particularly pleasant, but could not be helped.

I had been but two or three days in the Bay, when I had occasion to go to Astoria, and took a passage with Toke's family, who were going to visit Tománawos's people, who resided on Baker's Bay. We took the same portage I had recently crossed, and, after passing one night on the road, and sleeping in an old wagon I found at the portage, we arrived at the lodge of the Indians on Baker's Bay, near which was the residence of J. D. Holman, Esq., the postmaster of Pacific City, who, with his family, were always ready to extend their hospitalities to all travelers.

I was received with a cordial and hearty welcome by Mr. Holman, and invited to pass the night at his house, which I did, intending to cross the Columbia the next morning in Johnson's boat to Astoria; but, when morning came, so did a violent southeast storm of wind and rain, which kept me four days unable to get away, and, when we did start, that is to say, old Johnson and myself, there was so much wind and such a sea that we had to run for the mouth of the Wappalooche or Chenook River, which we reached after running through the breakers in fine style, and landed under the lee of the bank near George Dawson's house, and from thence walked round the beach to Chenook.

The next morning (June 9th, 1854) I crossed the river to Astoria, and proceeded to the custom-house, where the collector, General John Adair, appointed me to take charge of the interests of the United States Treasury Department for that portion of the coast north of the Columbia, including Shoal-water Bay and Gray's Harbor, to Cape Flattery; the duties of the office being to report all vessels arriving at or departing from Shoal-water Bay, and to keep a diligent watch on the coast to see that none of the Russian or Hudson Bay Companies' vessels came around either for smuggling or trading with the Indians. After this matter was properly arranged, I returned to the Bay with Peter, the Indian lad, in a small canoe. Toward the first of July I found it necessary to again visit Astoria, and, as Peter wished to take up Toke's large canoe to the portage for the purpose of bringing the family back from Chenook, where they had been fishing, I consented to help him get the canoe across the Bay, which, considering that the wind was fair, seemed an easy job, but we found it a tough one before we got through. The wind, which favored us at the start, died away before we were half way across the Bay, and by the time we had reached the mouth of the Tarlilt Creek, on our way over the portage to Baker's Bay, the tide was all out, and it was past sundown. We wished to proceed up the creek some two miles to where we intended landing, at Mrs. Paulding's, but had to remain at the mouth of the river waiting for the tide. The wind had now hauled into the south, with every indication of rain; but we were tired out, and lay down in the canoe and went to sleep. We were awakened about midnight, and found the canoe half full of water, the wind blowing a gale, and the rain falling in torrents. I had on a suit of India-rubber clothes, but, as I had been lying down in the canoe, the water had run down my neck and up the legs of my pantaloons, and I was as wet as if I had been overboard; however, there was no help but to try and get up the creek. Although the tide was now rising and in our favor, yet the wind blew down stream with such violence that at times I thought it would blow the old canoe into the prairie, and it was not till nearly three o'clock in the morning that we reached Mrs. Paulding's. We found no one at home but two little boys, who got us some breakfast, while we dried our clothes as we best could around the fire. It was still raining violently and blowing hard as we commenced our journey over the portage, which by this time was nearly impassable from fallen limbs and trunks of trees broken by the gale. As we reached Feister's house we met Captain John Vail, who begged us to go in out of the storm, but we declined, as we were then wet, and did not care for the rain, having the whole day before us to travel in; so we pushed on through the wet grass in the prairie, and over the now swollen stream of the Wallacut, which we managed to cross on drift logs, and at last reached the mouth of the river, where we were ferried over by John Edmands' son, and then took up our line of march for the Wappalooche or Chenook River, which we crossed in a canoe we got from old Salleel, and then walked to Chenook, where we arrived about five o'clock P.M., having walked about eighteen miles through a violent rain-storm since breakfast. However, we were very well satisfied, for the rain ceased when we reached Chenook, and the sun set bright and clear, giving token of a pleasant day for the morrow. The next day I crossed the river to Astoria, and on my return, which was late in the afternoon, made arrangements with the Indians to start for the Bay the day following.

As there were a number of Indians going to the mouth of the river, near Cape Disappointment, we all started together as soon as the tide began to ebb the next morning. As we were crossing Baker's Bay, I saw several Indians fishing for sturgeon.

Their·method is to fasten a salmon-hook to a long line similar to a large-sized cod-line. The hook is then placed on the end of a pole, and the Indian goes along slowly in his canoe over the shoals, with the pole down, feeling for the fish in the same manner as described before for taking salmon. When the Indian feels the sturgeon, he sticks the hook into it, and, quickly hauling in the pole, slacks out some of the line, and prepares for a race. As soon as the sturgeon feels the hook, away he starts like an arrow, and the canoe goes whizzing and spinning along at a fearful rate, and requires a good deal of dexterous management to prevent being turned over. As the fish slackens speed, the Indian hauls in the line, and by perseverance at last tires the fish so that it is hauled to the surface of the water, and stunned by a blow on the head or nose with a heavy club carried for the purpose. The trouble now is to get the sturgeon into the canoe, for sometimes these fish weigh from three to four hundred pounds, and are from twelve to fifteen feet long. The Indian contrives to get the sturgeon's head over the gunwale of the canoe, and with a peculiar twist suddenly jerks the fish in without any apparent difficulty. I have thus seen two Indians get a sturgeon into a little canoe that white men never could have accomplished except by lifting the fish bodily, and then gently depositing it into the bottom of the canoe, so as not to capsize it. Sometimes an Indian will catch two or three great sturgeon during one tide, for they generally begin to fish as the tide begins to flood, when the sturgeon follow up in the shoal water to feed.

The fish, after being carried home, is opened, care being taken to save all the blood, which is put into a kettle with some choice cuts, and then boiled. The head, like that of the salmon, is esteemed the best part, and is either boiled, or cut in strips and broiled or roasted before the fire. The pith of the back bone is considered a great luxury, and is eaten raw; and, although not having more flavor than the white of an egg, is not unpalatable.

The rest of the fish is then cut in thin strips and dried in the smoke. The sturgeon taken at the mouth of the Columbia and in Shoal-water Bay are more delicate flavored and tender, finer grained than any sturgeon I have ever seen in any part of the world. The Indians prefer them to salmon, but it is much more difficult to take them. Old Salleel, at the mouth of the Wappalooche or Chenook River, was a great hand at catching sturgeon, and usually had three or four sturgeons' heads, on as many poles, stuck up around his lodge, where they filled the air with their perfume. What his object was no one appeared to know, and as he was the only Indian whom I met with that seemed to fancy such ornaments, I presumed it was to gratify some freak of his own. He was among the fishermen as we passed, and made us a present of as much as we wanted of a fine fat sturgeon he had just caught.

We landed near the lodge of Tománawos; and while I went to Mr. Holman's to get the mail for Shoal-water Bay, the Indians were packing their things across a short portage to a small sheet of water called Johnson's Lake.

I soon joined them, but found that the water was so low at the outlet to the lake we should have to walk.

This was the longest possible way to cross over from the Columbia to Shoal-water Bay, the route being almost diagonally across the peninsula. However, we each took our pack and started. Our road lay over a quaking bog for nearly the whole distance, and was certainly only fit to be traveled by Indians. Part of the time we had to jump over from one bunch of grass to another to clear the soft mud between; but we got along very well, except old Toke, who, having a heavy load on his back, slipped on a bunch of grass, and sank into the mud up to his arm-pits. I asked him if he felt bottom; but he said not, and thought his bundle was the means of preventing his sinking entirely out of sight. I asked why they preferred crossing such a dangerous place, when they could have kept on high land. " Oh," they said, " that was the way they always did." As we came to the outlet to the lake, which was but a mere brook, we found the bushes so thick that it was decided to follow the channel down till we reached the canoe. This was a pretty piece of navigation ; sometimes the water would be two inches deep, and in three steps more it would be four or five feet deep. But we did not care ; the weather was warm and pleasant, the bushes full of berries, and after we had once got drenched it made no difference how deep the water was. But we reached the canoe safely, and in two or three minutes had a fire blazing and some sturgeon cooking. The Indians would always and invariably kindle a fire whenever we would stop for half an hour either to wait for some one to come up or while waiting for the tide. They are the most expert people to build fires in wet weather I ever met with. I was one night obliged to camp out during a heavy rain, being unable to cross the Bay on account of the wind blowing

violently.   I saw no possible means of procuring a fire.
We were at a place where there were no large trees, and
all the drift-wood was saturated with water; but the Indians soon had a blaze, which they kindled in this manner: There was plenty of the dry, dead stalks of the
wild or cow-parsnip lying about.   These stalks are hollow, with a dry substance inside that burns like tinder;
and no matter how much it may rain, the inside of
these dead stalks is always dry.   The Indians had used
this material, and after once starting a blaze, soon managed to have a roaring fire.

As soon as all our party arrived we started for home,
and, having proceeded as far as Long Island, went
ashore some fifteen miles from where we had left, and
made a camp, where we stopped all night.   We could
have reached home easily, but, as there was no occasion
for haste, I preferred to travel just as the Indians were
used to going, without hurrying them up continually,
which only vexes them to no purpose.   Indians can be
hired to go as quick as a person desires, but when they
are traveling with their families, they dislike very much
being obliged to go faster than a very moderate pace.

When in the canoe, all hands will paddle vehemently,
and one would suppose the journey would be speedily
accomplished, the canoe seeming almost to fly.   This
speed will be kept up for a hundred rods, when they
cease paddling, and all begin talking.   Perhaps one has
spied something, which he has to describe while the rest
listen; or another thinks of some funny anecdote or occurrence that has transpired among the Indians they
have been visiting, that has to be related; or they are
passing some remarkable tree, or cliff, or stone, which has
a legend attached to it, and which the old folks never
can pass without relating to the young, who all give the
most respectful attention.   When the tale is over, the

steersman gives the word " *Que-nuk, que-nuk, whid-tuck*" (now, now, hurry), when all again paddle away with a desperate energy for a few minutes, and then the same scene is again enacted.   But if the wind happens to be fair, then they are happy ; the sail is set if they have one, or, if not, some one's blanket serves instead, and down they sit in the bottom of the canoe, and eat dried fish and tell stories.   If the wind is very fresh and squally, they sit to the windward, and whenever a puff strikes the sail strong enough to threaten a capsize, they all dip their paddles deep into the water, bringing the broadside of the blade toward the bottom of the canoe, which serves the purpose of righting her and throwing the sail up into the wind.   They are exceedingly expert in their canoes, and very seldom meet with accidents.

We reached the Querquelin Creek early the next morning, and found the captain as busy as a bee collecting oysters and cultivating cabbages.   The next day being the fourth of July, we concluded to celebrate it by going after berries ; so, taking our tent and large canoe, we went across the Bay to the point of the peninsula, called Leadbetter Point, where we found a number of Indians camped, and any quantity of berries—strawberries, blackberries, raspberries, and blueberries, black currants, and huckleberries.   These berries the Indian women and children picked when the tide was up, but at low water they collected clams for drying, while the men shot seals or caught sturgeon.

It appears to me as if Shoal-water Bay is an Indian's paradise.   There is no time of the year, excepting winter, and only a short time then, but what a plenty of food can be obtained by any one who is not too lazy to go out for it.   The captain and myself amused ourselves by going to the weather beach, or the Pacific coast beach, to collect spikes, bolts, or any useful matters we could find among the drift-stuff which had been thrown ashore during the winter storms. Whenever we returned to our tent, we were sure to find a basket or two of nice fresh berries covered over with green leaves. We remained at the camp a couple of days, and then returned, leaving the Indians, who intended stopping longer, to lay in a stock of dried clams.

CHAPTER XV.

Visit to the Queniült Indians with Winant and Roberts.—Cross the Bay and camp with the Indians.—Carcowan and Tleyuk.—Trouble on starting.—Arrival at Gray's Harbor.—Armstrong's Point.—Difficulty with Caslahhan.—Sam fires at Caslahhan.—A Settlement.—Swarms of Fleas.—Our Camp.—We proceed up the Beach.—Adventure with a Bear.—Reach the Copalis River.—Wreck of the Steamer General Warren.—The Current north of the Columbia.—Appearance of the Coast.—Point Grenville.—Arrive at Queniült.—Peculiar Variety of Salmon.—Indian Tricks.—I am taken sick.—Old Carcowan wishes to have me killed.—Description of the Queniülts.—Start for Shoal-water Bay.—Indian Hospitality.—Bird Feast at Point Grenville.—Style of Cooking.—Heavy Surf and a Capsize.—We proceed through the Breakers.—Arrive at Gray's Harbor.—A Feast.—Fine View.—Reach Home.

THERE were a good many Indians in the Bay at this time, who had been collecting oysters for the whites, and I had several invitations to go up the Coast; but the reputation of the Coast tribes was so bad that I did not care to go among them, and particularly as I had just heard of their bad treatment of Colonel Simmons, the Indian agent, who had been robbed by some of the Quaitso Indians only a few weeks previous.

At last they hit upon a plan which was pretty sure to call me up, which was this. They had found out that if any vessel had arrived at any point on the Coast, it was necessary for me to proceed to her. So they came one day with a report that there was a *fire-ship*, or steamer, at anchor near Point Grenville, trading with the Queniūlt Indians. They also produced some fine specimens of coal, which they asserted was to be had in any quantity directly on the Coast; and they still farther asserted that there was plenty of gold in the mountains of the interior. I knew of no steamers on the Coast trading with the Indians, unless it might be either the Hudson Bay steamers or some one of the Russians; however, it was necessary for me to go, and accordingly I at once proceeded to make preparations.

Two of the settlers, Messrs. Samuel Winant and R. Roberts, agreed to accompany me. I had accustomed myself to the use of Indian food, and could get along very well with dried salmon and the new potatoes, which were then ready for use. The others, however, had no idea of stinting themselves to such fare, and, accordingly, we made preparations by boiling a ham, filling a bag with ship-bread, some rice, sugar, and coffee, not to forget salt, pepper, and vinegar. These preparations being completed, I engaged two Indians, Peter and Cletheas, to carry my blankets and assist me; and Sam Winant and Roberts had an Indian, called George, and two or three others of little use. Our plan of proceeding, as agreed on, was to cross the Bay, and then walk by way of the beach to Gray's Harbor, eighteen miles distant, and, after crossing that bay, to again proceed, either on foot or on horseback, over the beach to the place of our destination. We had to pass through the lands of the Chehalis and Copalis tribes to reach the Queniūlt country, and, as there were a number of Indians of each tribe who were going home and intended accompanying us, we at first did not know what course to pursue so as to avoid giving offense, for each insisted on being the party to carry us through. Carcowan and his son Tleyuk, the chiefs of the Chehalis Indians, insisted that, as we would pass through their lands first, they were entitled to let the horses and canoes for the whole distance; but the Copalis said they had better horses than Carcowan, and we must take theirs; while the Queniülts, whom we were going to visit, asserted that we were their guests, and none of the others had a right to interfere.   This anxiety to render us a service, it should be remembered, did not arise from their particular fondness for us, or from any natural love of hospitality, but simply to get what pay they could out of us.

This difficulty seemed likely to be serious, and, after crossing the Bay, it was concluded to make a camp and remain till the next morning, and, in the mean time, have the matter fairly understood.   So the subject was, as Roberts remarked, fully discussed by the natives, and fully cursed by us.

At last old Carcowan, who was the oldest person present, and who was the spokesman, agreed to leave the matter to me to decide, which I did at once by agreeing that we would use his horses while passing through his lands, and when we crossed the bay of Gray's Harbor would take the guidance of the Copalis Indians till we should reach the Copalis River, and then the Queniülts should take us the rest of the way.   This arrangement appeared to please all parties except old Carcowan, who wished to grab all the costs of the expedition; but we did not mind him, and, to show that we did not care to humor him, concluded to walk, and only take one horse to pack our blankets and provisions.

Early the next morning we started, after seeing that the canoe that was to take us across Gray's Harbor had first set out; for she had to be taken round the beach through the surf, and her owner, whose name was Caslah'han—an ugly-looking scamp, with but one eye—had the reputation of being a very tricky fellow, so we were determined to make him start first, which he did, having another Indian with him to assist. After we had packed our horse we started off single file, the horse ahead, led by an Indian, and the rest of the party straggling on to suit their own convenience. Our road at first lay through a thick forest of small trees, which extends in a belt about two miles wide. From this we emerged into a sandy plain, covered with beach-grass, and, passing that, found ourselves on the beautiful beach which extends in a line nearly north for eighteen miles to Gray's Harbor. We remained here a short time for the stragglers to come up, and to make sure that Caslah'han and his canoe were coming, and shortly we perceived them like a speck on the horizon just coming round the point of Shoal-water Bay. It was a splendid morning, and a fresh northwest wind was throwing up a fine surf on the beach, and the white tops of the breakers could be seen as far as the eye could reach either north or south. Myriads of sea-fowl were flying round, and, as each of us had a gun, we amused ourselves by blazing away with pretty good success. Sam and Roberts did not feel in any hurry; they were not much used to walking, and, as the sun got up, we found it pretty warm work. But I noticed the Indian with the pack-horse going on at a pretty good pace, and, as I thought it best to have an eye on our effects, I concluded to keep up with him.

Accordingly, I soon found myself far in advance of the party, and at length arrived at Armstrong's Point, or Point Brown, as the maps have it; but the settlers call it Armstrong's Point, as Mr. Armstrong, owner of a mill on the Chehalis River, had built a house there, a year or so previous, for a Dr. Roundtree, who intended to found a city, and go into the manufacture of salt. The project, however, was abandoned, and I found the house in a very dilapidated condition, but, with the assistance of the Indian, soon had a fire for the purpose of cooking dinner for the others. I was very hot and thirsty, having walked six hours over the sand-beach in a hot sun, and began to look round for some water. The Indian pointed me to the spring, which was at a short distance, but when I reached it I found a dead rat in the water. This the Indian soon cleaned out with the aid of an old tin kettle, and by the time the rest of the party arrived the water had become sufficiently sweet to drink, although strongly impregnated with the unpleasant odor. While we were eating our dinner, Caslah han arrived with the canoe, tired and angry, for it appeared that he had quarreled with the Indian who was helping him bring the canoe round, and the fellow had unceremoniously jumped ashore, leaving Caslah'han to get on the best he could.

The canoe, which was a large one, was the only means we had to cross the Bay, for Carcowan's people, with all their canoes, were off up the river. But Caslah'han, who lived on the north side of the Bay, had determined to go on alone, and had already pushed off with a fair wind, and was some ten or twelve rods off from the shore, when Carcowan came up and asked Sam to run down and hail him, which he did, but, receiving no reply, Carcowan urged him to fire, which Sam, without thinking, did, and the ball from his rifle came near enough to Caslah'han's head to cause him to take in his sail and put back.

As soon as he landed, he came directly to me, and asked why Sam had fired at him. I replied that the surf was making so much noise on the beach that he did not seem to hear when he was hailed, and Sam had merely fired to attract his attention. " Well," said he, " he had no occasion to have fired *at* me, and if he had hit me you would all have been killed." I, however,

pacified him, and Sam made him a present, which settled the matter amicably. He now consented to ferry
us across the Bay, and we reached the other side late in
the afternoon, and were landed at his residence.

The house in which he had resided during the winter
was deserted, and part of the boards were removed, while
the family were living in a mat house at a little distance.
The reason of this was soon made known; for, on walking into the lodge, we were instantly covered with
swarms of fleas, so numerous and large that they seemed
to me like flax-seed, they were so big and shiny. We
had to run into the water to get rid of these unwelcome
intruders, and then found that the Indians had been
fairly driven out of their lodge by these swarms. I suggested that they had better burn up the remainder of the
house, so as to destroy the fleas; but the Indians said,
" Oh! never mind; when the winter comes they will all
go away." But they did not go away from us so readily, for we were tormented with them all night. We
had made for ourselves a rude shelter of boards, under
which we tried to get a little sleep, but we did not succeed very well, and by daylight were all up and ready
for breakfast.

Sam and Roberts now complained of fatigue, and said
they would walk no more, but wait for horses, their experience of the preceding twenty-four hours being of a
nature little calculated to elevate their spirits. The
horses, however, were at Copalis, eighteen miles distant.
They dispatched an Indian for them, and concluded to
wait where they were till the horses came; but I, not
feeling any fatigue, thought that, with George the Indian,
we would start on and walk. George took a heavy pack
on his back and a double-barreled gun, and both of us
set out for a tramp.

We had now to pass over a sand-waste covered with

beach grass and stunted lupin bushes, and marked all over with the footprints of wild animals—bears, panthers, elk, deer, wolves, and foxes. It appeared to be a perfect highway for the brute creation.

This barren tract was about three miles wide, reaching from the ocean to a dense forest of firs, and growing narrower, till at Copalis it was but a few rods wide, the forest growing to the edge of high-water mark. We crossed the desert as soon as we could, and when on the open beach sat down on a log to rest. Looking down the beach toward Gray's Harbor, I saw the rest of the party coming along slowly. They had become tired of waiting, and had gained the beach by a more direct route than we had taken.

As far as the eye could reach might be seen immense flocks of gulls, plover, curlew, snipe, crows, ravens, and eagles. We amused ourselves as we went along shooting these birds, and soon had enough for our dinner. Far in the distance I saw a large black object, which the Indian told me was a bear. Away I started to get between it and the woods, forgetting in my hurry that my gun was only loaded with shot. The Indian, who had more sense, called me back; but, supposing that he merely wished to get the first shot, I kept on, and he started after me on a run, but he could not keep up on account of his pack.

I soon discovered that the object of my pursuit was an old bear, and that she had a half-grown cub with her, which I had not noticed before. The old one had a fish in her mouth, which she had just picked up out of the surf, and the pair were leisurely moving toward the woods. They came up without taking any notice of me, and as soon as the old one was near enough, I fired, and struck her just back of the shoulder.

The surprise and shock caused her to start and roll

over; for, although the gun was only loaded with shot, I was so near that the charge had but little chance to scatter. She recovered in an instant, and, after looking at her cub, started after me. But George had come up by this time, and fired off both barrels of his gun, which had the effect of starting her in another direction; and away she went, bleeding profusely, and, with her cub, was soon out of sight in the bush. While this skirmish was going on, the rest of the party came up, and, having consulted, it was concluded to proceed, and not attempt any farther attack on the bears; and while we were talking, we spied the horses we had so long expected. In a few minutes they came up, bringing a motley-looking crew of savages, whooping, yelling, and screaming, who, after showing us several of their feats of horsemanship, dismounted, and all hands proceeded to take a lunch. When we had our blankets and provisions secured on the pack-horse, Winant and Roberts mounted two other horses and started off ahead; but I preferred to walk, for my bear adventure had induced me to think that possibly I might get another shot. But I saw nothing more except a pine marten, which one of the Indians killed with a stick, and, after taking off the skin, tied it round my cap as a sort of trophy for my bravery in attacking a bear with a shot-gun—an adventure which I had by that time begun to consider as a most reprehensible act of folly.

I reached the mouth of the Copalis River about sundown, and found that Sam and Roberts had a tent pitched, a fine fire made, and a nice supper ready cooked. The tent, by the way, was not much of an affair, being simply a boat's sail spread over a pole, and secured at the edges to keep it from blowing away; but it answered very well, for all we wanted was simply to keep off the dew while we slept.

The Copalis River is a small stream that makes its way through the beach into the Pacific. The waves constantly beating directly into its mouth have made bars which render it impossible for vessels to enter it, and commercially the river is of no value. We did not go up the stream, but it appeared to run for some distance through a prairie, where no doubt good farms could be made. The river, at its mouth and for a mile up, is about four hundred feet wide, with from two to four feet of water at low tide. Like all the streams on the coast, it was a favorite resort for salmon, but at the time we were there they had not commenced running. The natives, however, had been catching great quantities of fish like the sculpin, which they impaled on sticks and roasted by the fire. We tried some, and found them sweet and good. These Indians were very hospitable, and gave us plenty of such food as they had.

A party of Indians now arrived from Queniūlt, consisting of Haitlailth or John, with two of Kape's sons, and a lot of squaws, who were going a short distance farther for the purpose of cutting rushes for making mats. John and his wife, and Kape's boys, immediately concluded to return with us to Queniūlt the next morning.

Sam and Roberts now declared their intention of going no farther, but insisted on dividing the provisions with me, and said they intended to turn back that very night, and, as it was bright and clear, they would reach Gray's Harbor by midnight, as they could easily trot their horses over the beach in three hours. I tried to dissuade them, but to no purpose. But now a new difficulty arose. The Indians had no idea of going back, and to prevent Sam and Bob from going, they drove all the horses across the river, under pretense of putting them to pasture; so we all lay down and went to sleep.

Early next morning I took a pack-horse, and, with a

dozen Indians, started across the river, and commenced our journey along the beach. About a mile from the river I discovered the whole of the stern frame of the propeller *General Warren*, which had been wrecked on Clatsop Spit, at the mouth of the Columbia, two years previous. The strong current which sets north from the Columbia during the winter season had drifted this wreck till it was washed ashore forty miles from the Columbia, up the coast. I have noticed on some charts that the current is represénted as setting south; but I have known of a great many boats and canoes which have broke adrift in Shoal-water Bay, and been carried by the ebb-tide out to sea, and in every instance were thrown ashore *north* of Shoal-water Bay, generally between it and Gray's Harbor, proving, together with the wreck of the General Warren, just mentioned, the fact that the current always sets north from the mouth of the Columbia.

As we proceeded on our course, we found the high land approach much nearer the beach; and I also noticed that the cliffs, which presented the same general appearance as the shores around Shoal-water Bay, were composed of sandstone of various grades, some very coarse, and others as fine as the best quality of Nova Scotia blue grindstone. After passing a ledge of rocks which projected out into the ocean, we stopped under a bluff to cook our breakfast; and while one was making a fire, another climbed up on the cliff, and procured some nice potatoes from a field or patch belonging to a chief of the Copalis named Herkoisk; and a squaw coming along with a back-load of dry salmon, Kape's boy unceremoniously helped himself to half a dozen, and we soon had a very palatable breakfast. While we were eating, I noticed Sam and Bob coming up on horseback. They had changed their minds, they said, and were now going as far as Queniūlt, feeling a little pride about backing out and letting me go on alone. I told them they had better ride on, as I had determined to walk; so they started ahead, and were soon out of sight.

As we walked along, I occasionally went to the top of the ridge of shingle and ballast stones which the storms had piled up in long rows, and through which, at short intervals, water was running in little silver streams. I found invariably these proceeded from some brook, whose mouth was stopped up by the stones, forming dams, behind which little ponds had formed, whose clear waters were well stocked with trout. There were a great many of these brooks on the route, and the Indians assured me they were all well stocked with beaver and otter. The whole distance thus far had been over the hard, smooth beach, with the exception of crossing the Copalis River and Gray's Harbor, and I had walked without any difficulty. We were now approaching Point Grenville, and the path was a little more difficult, being obstructed with stones and ledges of rock. We found Point Grenville to be a bluff, rocky promontory, rising abruptly from the ocean, into which it extended a short distance in a semicircular shape. A few hundred rods from the southeast corner of the Point were two pyramidal rocks, some seventy or eighty feet high, which were covered with innumerable sea-fowl. This point is a good place for sea-otters, and it is where the Queniūlt Indians shoot their supply.

There was a very difficult trail over the Point, and with some little trouble we got ourselves and horse over, though the horse could hardly scramble up the steep sides, and we had to pack our luggage on our own backs. From the top of this cliff was a fine view of the ocean and the shores that we had passed. As it was in the cove at this point where the Indians had represented

QUENIÚLT VILLAGE.

the steamer was lying at anchor, I thought it was time to make some further inquiries; but, on discovering the marks of the coast survey, I concluded that the steamer was the United States surveying vessel, the "Active," Captain James Alden; and upon questioning the Indians, they acknowledged that she was a "Boston man-of-war fire-ship." So far as related to smuggling, I had walked sixty miles up the beach for no purpose, but I did not regret having started, as I had seen a line of coast which few, if any, white men had been over before.

Descending the north side of Point Grenville, I found the shore very bold, and the heavy rollers of the Pacific dashing with tremendous force against the rocks, although there was little or no wind. The cliffs were of fine sandstone; but, from the impossibility of shipping the stone, it can never be put to any useful purpose, except its being occasionally used, as at present, to sharpen the hooks, knives, and axes of the Indians.

Some five miles farther north we came to the mouth of the Queniūlt River, and shortly reached the village, which is pleasantly situated on the south bank of the stream, near its mouth. The entrance to the Queniūlt is so badly blocked up with stones and gravel, piled up by the waves, that it is difficult of entrance except for canoes, and only for these during calm intervals; but, once in the river, and it is found to be a beautiful little stream. The stopping of its mouth has caused the formation of a pretty little bay, whose waters are as pure as crystal. Early in the spring, a species of small salmon enter this river, which are justly celebrated among all the Indians for their superior richness of flavor. This variety is from fourteen to twenty inches in length, rarely exceeding two feet, and weighs from five to ten pounds. Its general appearance is similar to the Columbia River salmon, but it never attains a larger size than that just mentioned, while in the Columbia fish weighing eighty pounds are not uncommon.

The Queniŭlt Indians take these fish principally by means of weirs, which they build with a great deal of skill, and also by spears and hooks.*

I found, on my arrival, that my friends Sam and Roberts had rested themselves, while I began to feel the effects of my three days' promenade. I told them what I had discovered about the smuggling steamer, and we had a hearty laugh about it. I now questioned the Indians about the coal, and they said some Indians from the north brought it to them. I knew better than to believe such a tale, as Indians are not generally in the practice of carrying about lumps of coal or any other geological specimens. So I told them they had procured the coal from the steamer Active, which at first they had denied, but finally acknowledged, and thought the whole affair was a good joke. They had devised the plan for the purpose of getting us to visit them, as they had tried every inducement to prevail on me to go to Queniŭlt for a long time without success.

As we found no chance of any farther discovery in that vicinity, it was proposed to return the next day; but I had taken a severe cold in my face, which was badly swelled, and caused me much pain. Accordingly, my two companions left the next morning, while I preferred to remain till I felt better. I had been invited by Kape to stop in his lodge, and every attention was shown me. A bed was made up of a quantity of new mats, over which I spread my blankets, and contrived to make myself pretty comfortable; but my face continuing to swell,

---

* Whenever I make mention of catching salmon by hooks, it should be understood that these are large hooks, which are used as a *gaff*, and not, as many might suppose, with bait. The Indians never attempt to catch salmon with a baited hook.

I asked the Indians to give me some remedies of their preparing.

One of the squaws then went out and gathered some herbs, which were burned to a cinder and mixed with grease, with which she anointed my face till I was as black as an Ethiopian.

While I lay in this uncomfortable manner, old Carcowan arrived, with a slave named Pohks, who was foolish, and who afforded much fun to the Indians by imitating war-dances and sundry specimens of buffoonery.

Carcowan soon had a crowd around him in the lodge, when they commenced gambling, and kept it up all day and nearly all night.

I noticed that Carcowan was making some proposition to the rest which did not appear to meet with their approbation; and, although I did not understand the language he was using, yet his frequent repetition of the word *squintum*, or white man, made me certain he was talking about me. However, he made no impression on his auditors, and presently he got up in a rage and went off home. I then questioned Peter and Cletheas, who were in the lodge, and they stated that Carcowan was proposing to the Queniülts to kill Sam, Bob, and myself, for the reason that Governor Stevens had hung some acquaintances or friends of theirs at Nesqually, and also because Sam had fired at Caslahhan. But the Queniülts told Carcowan they would have nothing to do with any such business, and redoubled their attentions to me.

I had not seen how my face looked, and on asking for a glass they all began to laugh, and so did I when I saw myself. I at once got some water and washed off the mess, and, having found some cooling leaves, bound them on my face and reduced the swelling.

The third day I felt well enough to start for home,

M

but first, at their request, went up the river ten or fifteen miles, and visited several lodges. I found plenty of white pipe-clay, and the Indians make use of it to paint or whitewash the interior of some of their lodges, and then, with red ochre and charcoal, they make hideous drawings of whales, salmon, bears, or any other animal they wish to illustrate. This whitewashing process is by no means a general one, although it is certainly a great improvement.

Although the Queniŭlt is a very beautiful stream, it does not present any thing very attractive to the white settler, and I doubt if any person locates there for a long time to come. Farther in the interior is a fine sheet of water called Queniŭlt Lake, around which, I have been informed, is some excellent land; but, as I did not go up there, I can not speak from personal experience.

Many, if not all the young Indians on the river never had seen a white person before, and they were as wild and shy as deer. I found that, like all the other Indian children I had met with, they were very fond of boiled rice and sugar, and as I had some of both, I managed in a short time to gain the good-will of the children, and by the aid of some plugs of tobacco made friends with the parents.

In Kape's lodge were four families: his own, John or Haitlilth's, Wahmalsh, Kape's oldest son, and another, whose name I did not learn.

Kape had some ten or twelve children—a most remarkable occurrence, as these Indians are not prolific, rarely having more than three or four.

Kape's wife caused great envy by her numerous progeny, and was called in derision *Squintoo*, or the Hen Partridge. Her eldest son was married, and her youngest son was but three weeks old, and the intermediate children were all ages from two to eighteen. She, how-

ever, did not know their ages, for, like the rest of the
Indians on the Coast, they never keep an account of
any person's age.   John's wife had two children, and
thought herself very well off.   The rest of the families
had no children, but there were quite enough.

Kape's oldest daughter was about sixteen years of
age, and, for an Indian, was quite pretty, but she was as
wild as a fox.   Her mother told her to hand me some
rice one day while I was sick, and just as she reached
me a plate John's wife said something, when she dropped
the rice, breaking the plate, and rushed out of the lodge.
I did not see her again while I remained.   The rest
burst into a regular gale of merriment, and finally John
told me that his wife told the girl I had come to buy
her of her father, which was the cause of the sudden
fright.   I could not blame her much, for my face, painted
over with grease and soot, did not look very attractive.

This village was composed of five lodges, to each of
which was a small inclosure, where they raised most
excellent potatoes.   The lodges were made of cedar
boards, similar in all respects to those lodges of Shoal-
water Bay, and were remarkably well built, and very
clean.   On the bank of the river they had erected a huge
flag-staff, from the top of which a red shirt was flutter-
ing, as a rude imitation of the flags of the white men
they had seen either at Vancouver's Island or at the Columbia River.   Between the lodges and the sea-beach
was a large canoe, in which were the remains of some
dead person, and the different colored blankets and calicoes hung round gave the place an appearance of clothes
hung out to dry on a washing day.

The morning we were to start, Kape went out and
shot a fine fat raccoon, which was cleaned and boiled in a
large iron kettle; John's wife baked some bread in the
ashes; another squaw boiled a mess of salmon and po-

tatoes; Kape's wife dug up a bushel of potatoes, and put them in a new basket; and another squaw brought in a fine salmon trout and roasted it.   I watched all this proceeding without knowing what was to be done with it, but found, on going to the canoe, that it was for me and my two Indians, and was already firmly secured in the canoe, so as not to fall out if she should happen to capsize.

Some of the tribe who were going to Gray's Harbor agreed to keep us company, and accordingly launched two canoes, one of which contained twenty persons, and the other ten—men, women, children, and slaves; and among the latter was Pohks, Carcowan's fool, who had been left when Carcowan returned home.   It was early in the morning when we started, and, as the tide was nearly out, we went over the breakers without any difficulty.   It was a lovely morning.   Not a breath of air was stirring, and the water was as smooth as oil, with the exception of the line of breakers on the beach.   The canoe I was in was quite small, and contained Cletheas, who steered, Peter, who sat in the bow, and myself.   I had nothing to do but sit still, or lie down in the bottom of the canoe as ballast.   She was a mere cockle of a thing, and yet we were about to travel sixty miles down the coast in her; but I had every confidence in the skill of the Indians, and was not afraid to venture where they did.   We soon doubled the bluff of Point Grenville, and I noticed that the Indians were all heading in toward the beach instead of proceeding at once to Gray's Harbor. I asked the Indians why they were going ashore, and received for reply the invariable "*Kló-nas*," or, "I don't know;" a term which is fully as expressive and as often used as the Mexican *Quien sabe*.   After we were all landed, it appeared that the Indians were going to have some birds; so, hauling up the largest canoe on the beach,

POINT GRENVILLE.

they put all the effects into her, and, taking the other two canoes and my gun, started off for the rocks. They were gone nearly an hour, and, when they returned, brought with them thirty half-fledged loons—which were the size of ducks, and very fat—and five pelicans.

During the time they had been absent, the women—who, with the children, remained behind—had built a large fire of dry limbs and drift stuff, and heaped a pile of stones on top of the burning pile, and by the time the birds had been prepared, which was by simply removing the entrails, the fire had burned down, leaving nothing but hot ashes and stones. On to these some fern leaves were laid, and on the ferns the birds were placed. A bucket or two of water was dashed over the whole, and the heap then covered as quick as possible with mats and blankets, and sand heaped over all to keep in the steam.

In about half an hour the pile was opened, and the birds taken out thoroughly cooked. The skin and feathers readily came off, and I thought the flavor of the birds thus cooked was excellent. As it was scarcely noon when we had finished, I supposed we should at once proceed, and get as far as the Copalis River; but the Indians had no such intention, but preferred rolling round on the sand in the hot sun. There was very little wind all that day, and at night we had the full moon and a cloudless sky to enliven the scene. We had done very well for lazy folks, having progressed six miles on our journey.

The next morning we were all up and started on our course just as the day dawned, and as the wind was still calm and the water smooth, I hoped we should go direct to Gray's Harbor, which I could have reached in a whale-boat, with four men to pull her, in a few hours; but as we approached the Copalis River, I saw they again headed in for the beach, at the place where the ledge of rocks make out that I noticed while coming up.

The coast runs off at this place quite suddenly, and the heavy ground swells which were now rolling in from the northwest dashed up on the beach in a manner not at all calculated to inspire any confidence or desire to go among them. This, it appeared, was the only place where they could land, for here the sea broke directly on the beach with one huge breaker; while farther along, both north and south, where the water was shoal, the breakers extended out a great way, making it pretty certain, if the first one was passed in safety, that the canoe would be capsized in some of the others before she could reach the shore. I asked them what they wanted to go ashore there for. I had enough of delay the day before, during the bird expedition, and had no wish to pass another day idle on the beach; but it appeared they were afraid there was going to be a blow. I had been amusing myself by sticking my paddle through the jellyfish, which were very plenty, and that was a bad omen, and a certain sign of wind; go ashore they would, and haul the canoes through the breakers. I was vexed, for I did not see how we were going through that heavy surf with only our little paddles; but I could not help myself, so I sat down and braced myself as firmly as I could, and, having lit my pipe, waited to see the result. The first canoe got ashore in admirable style, but the next one, which was the largest, did not succeed so well. The Indians were too sure; and, while laughing at me for being afraid, they were caught by a huge roller and pitched end over end, sending every thing flying. Men, women, and children were swimming for the shore, and mats, blankets, paddles, and every thing that could float drifting round in great confusion. They were all, however, hauled out safely on the beach, where they were spread round to dry, while the men hauled up the canoe, to bail out the sand and water with which she was filled, and get ready for another start.

It was now our turn; but Peter and Cletheas, feeling a little skittish at the sight of the other canoe, were very cautious, and let several waves pass under us without attempting to go ashore. At last a huge roller coming in, we started on the top of it, and, by paddling with all our might, kept on the crest, and were thrown some twenty feet up on the beach with the bubbling foam. The other Indians who were ashore stood ready to catch us as we struck the sand, and ran us up high and dry out of the reach of the waves.

While we were getting ready for another start, Caslahhan came riding up, bringing the skin of the bear I had shot while going up the beach. He said he had found her lying just on the edge of the brush into which she had run when I shot her. It was a very large and fine skin, jet black, and as big as a bullock's hide. This skin I placed in the bottom of the canoe, and it made a capital seat.

We now were ready to start, and our progress was altogether of a novel character to me. We pushed out into the breakers, and then, keeping between the line of two seas that had broken on the beach, shoved the canoe along through the surf with poles. I was astonished to see how dexterous these Indians were, although at first I could scarcely keep from being pitched out at every time a sea struck us, but soon got used to it; and we pushed on merrily till we reached the Copalis River, where we stopped to take breakfast and to wait for the others, who could not get along so fast as we did, their canoes being large and heavy, and only two men in each, all the others, with the women and children, walking down the beach, carrying their effects on their backs, which they prefer to do, both to lighten the canoes, and to keep their things from getting wet.

We stopped at Copalis an hour or two, and, after getting rested and refreshed, again started for another jaunt through the surf. I asked the boys to go outside the breakers, as the water was smooth and there was no wind, but they would not, for they were afraid of a blow, but there was not the slightest indication of wind from any quarter. So on we went, jolting, and tumbling, and rolling till noon, when we hauled the canoe up and took some dinner. We had kept a long way ahead of the others, and waited for them. During this time a strange Indian and a boy came up, the former dragging a fine salmon, which he had killed in the surf. This he sold me for a couple of charges of powder, and now I had plenty of provision.

As we approached Gray's Harbor we found that the water grew smoother, and at last found ourselves going through a narrow passage, quite inside, and out of the reach of the breakers. The sands at the north entrance to Gray's Harbor extend out a great way, and at low tide it is a long and very tedious passage round the Point; but fortunately there is this narrow passage I mentioned through the sands, which the Indians avail themselves of at low water, and which is an excellent and safe place to pass through with canoes.

The banks of this passage were full of quahaug clams, and we shortly had a bushel of them. When judging that I had enough to make a feast of fat things, we pushed ahead, and arrived in Gray's Harbor just after sundown, and went ashore, where we soon built a fire among the drift-logs on the beach, and, by the light of the moon, brought our things up from the canoe. The others shortly arrived and joined us, when I borrowed a kettle from one of the squaws, and soon had a fine supper cooking for the whole party. There was boiled rice and boiled salmon, boiled and roast potatoes, roast salmon, roasted crabs and clams, cold raccoon, dried salmon, seal oil and whale oil, to say nothing of hard bread, a pudding made from boiled flour, and tea made from a species of huckleberry leaves.

Pepper and salt were of no use to this party, but the tea and the savages were sweetened up by the application of some five or six pounds of sugar, which my friend Sam had kindly bestowed on me when he divided the provisions. After we had eaten, we amused ourselves by setting Pohks dancing till he was tired, when we all went to sleep among the logs on the beach. It was truly a magnificent night; not a cloud was to be seen, and the moon and stars shone out with a peculiarly brilliant light, while the screaming of the gulls and plover made it appear almost like day. I awoke about three o'clock in the morning, just as day began to dawn. The moon was still looking down with her great, broad face; but I had no time for reveries or poetic imaginings, for the tide had now nearly reached our sleeping quarters, having come up unusually high; and in a few minutes more a swash of the sea put out the remains of our watch-fire, and waked up all hands; and by the time it was beginning to ebb, we were all ready for a start. The Indians from Queniült, having only to cross the Bay, where their friends resided, now left us; and soon after we left for the mouth of the Bay. We passed close by the sand island where the schooner Willemantic was wrecked; but she had been got off the preceding summer. The island is nothing more than a bank of sand at the entrance to the harbor, bare at all times of tide, and covered with logs and driftwood.

As we neared Armstrong's Point, we saw Tleyuk, Carcowan's son, coming down the beach on horseback. He advised Cletheas and Peter to go outside of the breakers, as the weather was so calm. This movement I concurred in, for I was tired of pounding along through the breakers; accordingly, we watched an opportunity, and went through the surf clear outside of all.

By this time the sun had risen, and the prospect was very fine. We paddled off a mile from the beach, and had a fine view of Mount Olympus, near Puget Sound, the Cathlapoodle Mountains, Mount St. Helen's, the Saddle-back Mountain, and Cape Disappointment. The summits of the three first were white with snow, and, contrasting with the dark green foliage of the forests of spruce and fir, looked magnificently.

A slight breeze now springing up, we hoisted a blanket for a sail, and then sat down to breakfast on the remains of our last night's supper.

As the sun got up in the heavens, the breeze died away, and at last fell dead calm, leaving us no other alternative but to take to our paddles. We took our time, and went along leisurely, as the sun was very warm, and, reflecting from the glassy surface of the water, made it very uncomfortable.

About noon we crossed the bar. The water was as smooth as oil, with no appearance of any breakers except directly on the beach; and in an hour more we landed safe and sound at my house on the Querquelin.

CHAPTER XVI.

Arrival of Winant and Roberts.—An Election.—Our first Justice,
Squire Champ.—Big Charley.—First Court in the Bay.—Constable
Charley makes an Arrest.—A Trial, and a celebrated Verdict.—
Another Arrest and Trial.—Joe locked up in a Hen-house.—First
Vessel built in the Bay.—Bruce Company.—Uncle Ned.—Captain
John Morgan.—Monument of Oyster Shells to Russell.—Hay-e-mar.
—A Trip up the Whil-a-pah for Salmon.—Walter's Point.—Sam
Woodward's Claim.—Roaring Bill.—Ancient Mariners.—Old Chille-
wit.—Night Fishing.—Lively Time.—Start for Home.—Shoot a
Lynx.—Otter Shooting.—Charley sees the *Memelose* or dead Folks.
—Singular Occurrence.—We get rid of Charley.—First Trail from
the Cowlitz.—Lime-kiln for burning Shells.

I WENT down the beach the next day to see my friends,
Winant and Roberts, and learned from them that they
were in a very indifferent state of health.   It appeared
that, after they left Queniūlt, they got along very well
till they reached the north side of Shoal-water Bay, and
then they had to wait, as there was no canoe.   For two
days did they keep up signal-fires, and at last, just as
they had finished their last meal, they managed to attract the attention of their friends on the opposite side
of the Bay, who went over in a boat and took them off.

They were particularly chagrined to think that, during
the time they were amusing themselves by making bonfires, very much against their will, an election was taking place which they were very anxious to attend.

We had reached that point in the history of the Territory when we were called upon to elect our officers for
the Legislature and the county.   Now, this being looked
upon by the oystermen as a farce (for what did we want
of laws? we were a law unto ourselves), every one
seemed inclined to treat it as such.   So, among other

officers, they had elected John W. Champ as justice of
the peace, and Charles W. Denter as constable.

Now Champ was a perfect *character* to serve as a
justice.   He had originally emigrated from Vermont to
Wisconsin, but when, the memory of the oldest inhab-
itant did not pretend to approach, for the oldest inhab-
itant was none other than Champ himself, and he declared that he was too young to remember much.   He
had lived many years in Wisconsin, and when the emigration had first commenced to cross the Rocky Mountains, he had joined a party bound to Oregon, where he
resided several years, and finally settled in Shoal-water
Bay.   At this period Champ was about sixty-five years
old, tall, wiry, and muscular, with an iron constitution,
that had withstood the rough-and-tumble of a long border life.   Like all the rest of the frontier people, he was
fond of Old Rye, and, when under its influence, was a
noisy and rough customer ; but when sober, was a sensible, common-sense, kind-hearted old fellow, ready at
all times to do a good turn or lend a helping hand.

The constable, or Big Charley, as we used to call him,
was a good-natured, lazy fellow, who, from driving logs
on the Penobscot River, in the State of Maine, had shipped on board a whaler, and, like some old stray spar or
loose kelp, had been washed up into the Bay without
exactly knowing when, where, or how.   Charley was an
excellent woodsman, and could handle an axe or build a
log house with the best man in the Bay.   But Charley
preferred his ease and a bottle of whisky to any thing
else.   We thought the justice and constable would do
very well.   We had been very peaceable, having no lawsuits or bickerings.   If any of the boys got vexed with
each other, they would step out and settle the difficulty
with a fist-fight, and then the trouble was over.   But,
now that we had a 'squire, every one seemed anxious

to bring him some business, and it was not long before the justice held his first court in Shoal-water Bay.

A fellow that Russell had hired to take charge of his affairs while he himself should go to California, had been found to have stolen a small sum of money from Russell. This information was soon known among the settlers, but there was neither proof nor any one to prosecute. At length the sheriff, who was always ready for a joke, partly in sport and partly in earnest, wrote a notice to the thief that he must leave the Bay or he would be lynched. This paper was then taken to Champ (who, although he could sign his name, could not see to read very well, having smashed his spectacles on a frolic), and he was requested to sign the "warrant for arrest." Champ, supposing it made out in due form (for the sheriff was a scholar), signed his name, and, calling up Big Charley, ordered him to proceed at once and arrest the offender, and have him up for examination. Charley accordingly went to where the fellow was residing, some two miles distant, and, being apprehensive that he should meet with resistance, adopted the following unique method of arrest: Walking in where the chap was sitting, he asked him very coolly for something to drink. Bowman (for that was the man's name) replied that he had nothing. Well, says Charley, Old Champ has just got a demijohn of first-rate whisky: s'pose we walk down there and get some. The other, nothing loth, consented, and the pair walked down to the squire's. The boys began to collect, and at last the squire, who had been out feeding his chickens and wetting his whistle, came in and took a seat.

"Order in the court!" said he; then, facing the prisoner, he addressed him thus:

"Well, this is a pretty how-d'ye-do; why, what have you been about, hey?"

"What have I been about?" asked Bowman, with surprise; "nothing in particular, that I know of; where's your whisky, squire?"

"Where's my whisky?" says the squire, now getting into a rage; "where's my whisky? Don't you know you're 'rested? and do you think to throw contempt into my court by asking for whisky?"

"I did not know," replied the other, "that I was arrested; pray what is the charge?"

"Why, you big loafer," said Champ to the constable, "didn't you show that paper to Bowman?"

"Yes," growled Charley, "I did."

"I never saw it," says Bowman: "let me have it now."

Champ then, after expressing his disgust at Charley for not attending to his business in a legal manner, ordered him forthwith to arrest Bowman, and show him the warrant. Charley then produced the paper, and arrested the man in the name of the United States. Bowman read it, and remarked that it was more of a lynch-law notice than a warrant, and then inquired of what he was accused.

"What are you 'cused of?" said Champ, with the greatest contempt for the supposed sham ignorance of the prisoner; "why, you are 'cused of stealing Mr. Russell's money."

"I should like to know who accuses me, and who are the witnesses against me," said Bowman, who now began to think that something serious was to happen.

"See here, Bowman," says the 'squire, "I don't want any witnesses; and as for who accuses you, why, I accuse you, and every body on the beach accuses you, and you know you are guilty as well as I do: there is no use of wasting time over this matter. I am bound to sentence you, and my sentence is that you leave the Bay in twenty-four hours, or receive fifty lashes if you are here after that time. And now, Charley, do you take charge of the prisoner: treat him well, but if you let him escape we will tie you up in his stead."

Some one here remarked that Charley must have a hard show of it; but the 'squire replied, "Well, well, you know what I mean. I want that fellow out of the Bay, and I don't want Charley to let him go, to be prowling about this neighborhood any longer."

The next morning a schooner arrived from San Francisco, bringing Russell, who was soon made acquainted with the affair, and Champ ordered a new trial to take place, adding that, if Russell desired, they would tie up the offender and give him a few dozen by way of remembrance. But Russell had no desire to punish the fellow any more; so the boys, having had their fun, as they called it, collected some money, which they gave to Bowman to pay his expenses to Astoria, and started him off, and he was seen no more.

Thus ended the first court ever held in Shoal-water Bay, Chehalis County, Washington Territory. It was begun in a joke, but the ends of justice were as well or better satisfied than if a dozen lawyers had been about to mystify the 'squire.

The next case of theft that occurred the oystermen tried themselves, not caring to trust to Champ. A miserable loafer that had found his way into the Bay, and who was known by the name of Joe, was caught in the act of stealing a pair of boots from the grocery store; and he was also accused by Captain Hillyer of setting his boat adrift. I happened to be walking down the beach just as the people had Joe into the store to try him, and was invited to join. After the charges were made, Joe acknowledged stealing the boots, but said he knew nothing about the boat. He was urged to confess, but he persisted in his statement.

Dick Hillyer then proposed that Joe be tied up, and his back warmed with a rope's end to freshen up his memory; and we were each requested to give our views on the case.

Now it so happened that the very night previous, old Toke had started off from his lodge in a fit of rage, and Suis supposed he had crossed the Bay to another lodge he had at Toke's Point, recently built; and as I had passed down the beach, I found all the boats and canoes safe except that one of Hillyer's; so I concluded Toke, and not Joe, was the thief. I therefore suggested that we put Joe into Champ's hen-house, and secure him till some one should cross the Bay and see whether Toke had the boat or not.

Now Champ's hen-house was not a slim affair, built of slats, as its name might import, but was a solid log house, as strong as a fort.

Joe begged that he might be put there till he could prove himself innocent of the boat charge. He was accordingly incarcerated among the poultry, and left to his own reflections.

That afternoon Toke returned, bringing back the boat and demanding pay, which he received from Dick in the shape of two dozen lashes, well laid on with a piece of ratlin-stuff, and an injunction for the future to let the white men's property alone.

Dick then went to liberate Joe, and found him very quietly engaged in sucking eggs. This new felony enraged Squire Champ, who was for having Joe immediately flogged; but the people, thinking he had been punished enough, put him on board a boat bound to the portage, and started him out of the Bay, as they had done Bowman. So we freed ourselves of two thieves.

During this year Captain Hillyer built and launched the schooner Elsie, a little craft of twenty tons. She was the first vessel ever built in the Bay, and was launched on the 12th day of September, 1854. She was the second vessel owned in the Bay, the first one, the Mary Taylor, having been purchased several months previous by the Bruce Company, who used her as a regular packet to carry oysters to San Francisco.

This Bruce Company, consisting of Winant, Hanson, Morgan, and Milward, had arrived in the Bay soon after Captain Fieldsted, in 1851, in the schooner Robert Bruce, which was set fire to by the cook and burned to the water's edge. The Bruce boys, as they were then called, went to work, and soon earned enough to buy the schooner Mary Taylor, which was placed under the command of one of their number, Captain Alexander Hanson, familiarly known as Uncle Ned.

Captain Hanson was a North of Europe man, either a Dane or a Swede, a most excellent sailor, and a general favorite with every one in the Bay. Every body liked Uncle Ned, who, with his peculiarities, was really a very worthy man.

The Bruce Company, having been fortunate, found themselves able the following season to purchase another fine schooner, called the Equity, which was commanded by Captain John Morgan, another of the Bruce Company. Morgan was the real representative of that class of our citizens, the American sailor. An excellent navigator and seaman, frank, generous, and brave, he, with the rest of his company, Hanson, Mark and Sam Winant, and Dick Milward, had gained a reputation for generous hospitality that will ever be remembered by the early settlers in the Bay. Russell, who had been largely engaged in the oyster trade, and who had made arrangements to conduct the business still more extensively, had met with reverses which obliged him to relinquish his plans. *His* house, too, like that of the Bruce boys, was always open; his latch-string was never pulled in; and though he had peculiar ways, which rendered him somewhat unpopular, still he was a generous fellow at heart, and always exerted himself for the welfare of those in the Bay. He had a sort of monomania for being called captain, and thinking himself the first discoverer and settler in the Bay. But, as he was actually the first one who introduced oysters into the market of San Francisco, he will be entitled to receive what the California papers proposed to be given to the first who should bring oysters to their state, " a monument of oyster-shells to his memory."

During the summer Captain Purrington and myself had lived alone, as Toke's people had gone to live in their lodge near the house of Mr. Barrows, near Toke's Point. Toward fall, a young Indian from Chenook, named Hay-e-mar, and by the whites called Charley, came and stopped with us. He was smart, active, intelligent, a good carpenter and hunter, and capable of being very useful, but he was generally disliked by both whites and Indians. He had learned all sorts of sleight-of-hand tricks, with which he would astonish the young Indians, and was regarded by the old ones as a sort of a devil. He was continually at his pranks, and had, among other performances, transferred a chest of carpenters' tools, belonging to a man at Point Ellice, on the Columbia, to Astoria, where, on offering them for sale, he was detected, and fled to Shoal-water Bay, and happening to land at my place, concluded to remain, although I told him he was not wanted. But he went to work with an axe, and did great execution among the trees, and soon had so fine a pile of firewood that the captain proposed he should remain and help us. Charley was very well satisfied, and, putting himself on his good behavior, kept us amused with his odd tricks and stories, and soon gave us evidence of his hunting and fishing qualities.

One day he came home with the report that salmon had commenced running up the Whil-a-pah River, and he proposed going with me the next day to get some. I had not been up that river before, and was quite willing to start. It was about the first of October, and, although the days were warm and pleasant, the nights were quite chilly and long. The next morning, after breakfast, we fitted ourselves for the expedition, and started in my small canoe, Charley in the stern to steer, and I with my gun in the bow. We soon reached the mouth of the river, where we found innumerable flocks of curlew and plover, but could not get near enough for a shot, and, having a fair but light wind, kept on our course.

The Whil-a-pah, at its mouth, runs through wide prairies, or tide-lands, as they are called, which are cut up in every direction by creeks and ditches, rendering them difficult of cultivation. A few miles up, the mountains come to the brink of the river, which is here reduced to a narrow pass, called the Narrows, or Walter's Point, from Walter Lynde having taken a claim and built a cottage there. A little farther up we passed the claim and clearing of Captain John Vail, who had erected a house under the shade of some fine large maple-trees, and had a nice farm cleared and planted. The river, although narrower at this place, was quite deep, and was navigable for some miles farther up for large vessels.

The next house and claim was that of Samuel Woodward, some six or eight miles distant from Captain Vail's. Here was another evidence of industry and intelligence well applied. Mr. Woodward had a nice house built, and a most excellent farm, and, with his young wife, was most comfortably settled, and enjoying the respect and confidence of the whole community. On we went, and shortly passed the farm and house of Henry Whitcomb, who, with Sam Woodward, were the first settlers on the

river.   Next was the claim of William Cushing, or, as
he was called, "Roaring Bill;" for, as he was somewhat deaf, he spoke in an unusually loud tone of voice.
The next claims above were those of two old salts, Captains Crocker and Gardiner.   Captain Gardiner, however, had gone to San Francisco, again preferring " a life
on the ocean wave" to a " way across the mountains,"
which it certainly was, to get to his claim by any means
except the river.

Above the residence of the ancient mariners was still
another farm, that of Mark and Joe Bullard, but we did
not go so far.

It was nearly night when we hauled up our canoe at
an Indian lodge, near Captain Crocker's landing.   This
was occupied by old Chillewit, a famous Indian doctor,
and his brother Whilmarlan, who had with him two children, a little boy and girl, whose mother was dead, and
the father was taking care of them with all the affectionate tenderness which these Indians always show toward
their children.   There was no one in the lodge but Chillewit and the two children, and a slave girl named Mary.
The old doctor did not seem at all gratified at seeing
Charley, although he was a relative, for he was evidently afraid of some of his pranks.   However, he told Mary
to give us some supper of boiled salmon, and soon after
we lay down to sleep.

I was quite tired with my trip, and expected, of course,
to sleep all night and get rested, but Mr. Charley had no
such idea.   Whether he felt angry with old Chillewit or
not I did not know, but he evidently intended to leave
at once, and not remain for three or four days, as we had
intended.   About midnight, as near as I could determine, he roused me up, and said it was time to go fishing.
It was intensely dark, as the sky was overcast with
clouds, and the river being narrow at this place, the

great fir-trees cast a still deeper gloom upon the water. In fact, I could not discern my hand before my face; I was entirely blind, to all intents and purposes.   Still, Charley insisted that he could see well enough, and guided me into the canoe, with instructions to keep in the stream, while he sat in the bow to hook the fish.   This was all very well to talk about, provided I could see; but as, to my blindness, he added the injunction not to speak a word for fear of scaring the fish, I could not ask which way to go.   So we floated along with the current at a pretty rapid pace and in a very uncertain manner.

All at once I received a blow in the face that nearly knocked me overboard, and caused a most brilliant display of pyrotechnics to appear before my disordered vision.

"Look out!" says Charley.   "Look out!" said I; "why, I am nearly knocked out.   Why did you not speak before?   What was that hit me just now?"   "Only the limb of a tree we just went under," said he.   He then promised to speak when we were about to run afoul of any more snags, and we kept on, till, coming to some deep water, he began to find and catch the fish.   But sitting still in the canoe had chilled me through, and the fish, splashing and thrashing about, had covered me with blood, and water, and slime, and I told Charley I would not remain any longer for all the salmon in the river. He had by that time caught six splendid ones; and, being quite as much chilled as I was, he consented to paddle back to the lodge, where I hoped to get a nap.   But he had no idea of such a move.   He merely brought our blankets and things down, and, having stowed them, shoved off.   His excuse was that we should save the tide at the mouth of the river; but I think the real truth was his being vexed with old Chillewit, for I never knew an Indian before make quite so much dispatch.

So down the river we started, Charley in the bow with the gun to look out for game and to fend off from snags, for it was still dark.

At last the daylight appeared, and I could make out the course, although I was nearly asleep all the time. Directly I was roused by the report of the gun and a splash in the water. I then found that, while I had been dozing, Charley had spied out a lynx sitting on a log, and, cautiously shoving the canoe within range, had shot the creature directly between the eyes. This was quite a prize, as the Indians consider the lynx skin valuable for its medical properties.

I was now wide awake, and, as the sun got up over the tops of the trees, we felt quite comfortable. In a short time we spied some otters, and made out to get two of them, and considered ourselves quite lucky, having secured six salmon, one lynx, and two otters for our night's work. After washing ourselves, and making a breakfast on some bread and cold salt pork we had brought with us the day before, we took to our paddles, and plied them so effectually that we were soon at the mouth of the river, when, taking a fine wind, we made sail, and arrived home at noon, having been absent but a little over twenty-four hours.

We were very well satisfied with this specimen of Charley's services, and allowed him to loaf round a little—a privilege he took such advantage of that he soon became a nuisance.

We tried every method to get rid of him, but to no purpose, for we could not drive him out of doors, he was such a comical chap. But his own superstition at last induced him to leave. He was possessed of the power of seeing the spirits of the dead, and, if he had not been so full of mischief, would have been considered a great doctor. One night, after we had gone to bed, as Char-

ley was lying before the fire, which was burning brightly, I noticed our two dogs, which had hid themselves
under the captain's bed, come out into the floor, jumping
and wagging their tails as if they were rejoiced at meeting some one.   I was up in an instant and drove them
out of the house, as their services in keeping watch outside were of more importance than their gambols inside.
As I closed the door, Charley said, with a sigh, "What
did you speak for and drive out those dogs?   Did you
not see the *memelose?*"   "No," said I; "who were
they?"   "They were," he said, "Que-a-quim, who had
died at Russell's of small-pox, and George, who had died
at our house during my absence in the spring to California, and who had been buried, a short distance from the
house, in a camphor trunk."   "What does he say?"
asked the captain.   I explained what Charley said.
"Ha! ha! ha!" roared the old man; "memelose, hey?
Well, Charley, what did they tell you?"   He replied,
they had asked him what he was doing there; that it
was not his land, and they did not want him to stop
there.

This information so pleased the captain that he nearly choked himself laughing; for he had no faith in any
of these superstitions, and thought to laugh them out of
the belief.   Charley began to get vexed, and asked me
if I had not seen the dogs jumping up.   I told him I
had.   "Well," said he, "the dogs can see the *memelose*,
and they were jumping round because they were so glad
to see their old friends again."   I asked the old man not
to laugh any more, as it would do no good to make fun
of Charley, but I would use this visitation of the memelose as a means to get rid of him in a quiet manner,
and without giving him offense.

Fortunately, the next day two Indians came from
Chenook, to whom I related my desires, and they made

N

Charley believe that it was necessary for him to leave, which he did that very day.

During the month of July a party came down the River Whil-a-pah, consisting of Messrs. Warbous, Shaffer, Geizey, Roundtree, Pearsall, and Knight. They had come through from the Cowlitz trail to examine the land, and discover if it was of such a nature as to induce emigration, as Mr. Geizey was looking round as agent for a company of farmers, who had emigrated from Pennsylvania to Wisconsin, and, becoming dissatisfied, had sent him to look out a suitable place for them to settle either in Washington or Oregon Territories, and, having visited all the most favorable localities, had at last come through with this party. He reported that he was so well pleased with the land on the Whil-a-pah that he should send for his friends and settle on the prairie-lands, near Messrs. Bullard and Captain Crocker.*

After remaining in the Bay a few days, they returned on the 17th, and were accompanied by some of the settlers, Seth Bullard, Henry Woodward, Roaring Bill, Doctor Cooper, and Mr. Russell. This was the first trail ever opened by the whites between the Bay and the Cowlitz trail. Dr. Cooper and Mr. Russell proceeded on to Olympia, while the others returned by the same trail to finish blazing it out. It is a rough and crooked path at best, but will answer till a better road is made, which will probably be done before long, as the government are aware of the necessity of making a military road from Olympia, the seat of government, to Shoal-

* Mr. Geizey shortly afterward introduced the whole of his party of emigrants, numbering, as I was informed, some forty families, who have now one of the most flourishing settlements in Washington Territory, situated on or near the Beaufort, or, as it is pronounced, Buffaw Prairie, in the valley of the Whil-a-pah River, and can be reached either from Shoal-water Bay by the river, or from the Columbia and interior of the Territory by the Cowlitz trail.

water Bay, and thence to the Columbia, to enable troops to communicate with the military road from Astoria to Salem, the capital of Oregon. When a road is built, so as to open a communication with the interior of Washington Territory, it will show some excellent farming country, which at present lies uncultivated, owing to the difficulty of reaching it by any trails now made.

I had amused myself during the summer by building a kiln out of the clay blocks of the cliffs for burning the shells around our premises into lime, and, after completing it, tried it for the first time just after Charley left, and found that the shells made a very white and strong lime; but there not being any use for lime in the Bay, and the rainy season coming on shortly, I gave up the business till a more favorable time. The shell of the oyster, being thin, did not answer very well, as there was too much sand and mud with them in proportion to the lime they yielded; but the clolum, or hard-shell clam, has a very thick, solid shell, which yields a most excellent quality of pure white lime, and is easily burned. The absence of limestone in the vicinity will eventually make the heaps and mounds of shells around the Bay of value to the settlers.

CHAPTER XVII.

County Line.—Jury Duty.—United States Court at Chenook.—The
Court-house.—Grand Jury.—Trial of Lamley for killing an Indian.
—Grand Jury Room very Fishy.—Witnesses.—Captain Johnson.—
His funny Address to the Court.—He throws himself on the Mercy
of the Court.—Captain Scarborough.—Bill Martindill.—The Cap-
tain's Advice to Bill.—The District Attorney and his Address.—
The Counsel for the Defense quotes from the "Arabian Nights."—
He gains the Case. — Captain Johnson's Vinegar Speculation. —
Johnson's Death.—Death of Captain Scarborough.—Fidelity of an
Indian Squaw.—Return home.—Sharp Work in a Canoe.—Adven-
ture with Caslahhan.

THE place where we had built our house was on what
John Bunyan would call " debatable ground," as it was
claimed by the two counties of Pacific and Chehalis.   I
was satisfied that it was in Chehalis County, but as the
line had not been run, it was a subject of constant debate every time there was any election or any jury duty
to perform; and, as this last business is one that most
people like to get rid of, it was found quite convenient
for our immediate neighborhood to be in either county
we chose.

As the fall term of the United States District Court
approached, the sheriff of Pacific County came over and
notified us all to appear, either as grand or petit jurors.
I was exempt by virtue of holding an office; but, as there
was a great scarcity of people in the county, I concluded
I would go, and accordingly, with Baldt, who had also
been chosen, started in my little canoe for Wilson's
house, at M'Carty's portage.   It was late in the fall,
and the little canoe was hardly the thing to cross the
Bay in, but the weather being fine, we ventured to try,

as we intended keeping close in-shore as far as we could. We were very fortunate, and arrived at the portage early enough to cross over to M'Carty's house by sundown. We found Mac at home, and were most hospitably received; and, after a good supper and a pipe, with a plenty of anecdotes from Mac, we turned in by the fire and had a good sleep. Mac was building a new house, his old one and all his winter provision, with every thing movable he possessed, having been burned down the previous winter, and he was now living in an Indian house he had hastily put up till his new one should be completed. He said he had a pretty hard summer's work to scrape together enough for the coming winter.

The next morning he carried us down to the landing at Dawson's, where, bidding him good morning, we started off to walk over Chenook beach. As the court was to commence the next day, we found the little village crowded, and every one who had any business already there to secure accommodations. The first night Baldt and myself slept in the bowling-alley, and were not very well pleased with our quarters, but we did pretty well considering all things, and, having eaten a hearty breakfast, were prepared to enter on our duty as jurors.

The building selected as a court-house was a small one-story affair, measuring about twelve feet by fifteen, or somewhere near that; at all events, it was so circumscribed in its limits that, when the jury were seated, there was barely room left for the judge, clerk of the court, and counsel, while the sheriff had to keep himself standing in the doorway. The outsiders could neither see nor hear till some one suggested that a few boards be knocked off the other end of the house, which was soon done, and served the purpose admirably.

The grand jury were then called in and sworn, and the usual forms gone through. There was nothing of

294 THE NORTHWEST COAST; OR,

importance on hand except a case of homicide, and the judge charged particularly on that point. It was a charge against a resident of Chenook named Lamley, who was well known to us all, and who had been the former sheriff. It appeared that Lamley, with other white men, had been to the cranberry marshes at Shoal-water Bay to trade with the Indians for cranberries, as was the usual custom every fall. He had taken a house there to trade in, but took his meals at another house a short distance off. One day, while going to his dinner, a drunken Indian came up with a club and insisted on going in. Lamley pushed him away several times, till at last the Indian made at him with his club. This Lamley knocked out of his hand, and, seizing hold of a paddle that was standing beside the door, he again pushed away the Indian, who turned partly round, when Lamley struck him with the paddle. Unfortunately, the edge of the paddle hit the fellow on the neck, just where the spinal column joins the skull, and killed him instantly. Any other person would probably have done as Lamley did—that is, have struck the Indian with the first stick he could have got hold of, though perhaps with no such fatal results.

The counsel for the defense was a former judge of the same court, and considered one of the most able lawyers in the Territory. The prosecuting attorney was a younger brother of his, who was now to make his first attempt to manage a criminal prosecution.

The grand jury, having been duly instructed, were marched into old M'Carty's zinc house near by, as that was the only unoccupied place in town. There were but two rooms in this house, one of which contained several hogsheads of salt salmon, and all of M'Carty's nets and fishing-gear, and had certainly an "ancient and a fish-like" perfume. Although every one of us were well ac-

quainted with the smell of salmon, from partaking of it
every day boiled with potatoes, yet this was too much
of a good thing; but there was no help for it, so we proceeded to business. Now a grand jury are presumed to
do their business in a very quiet manner, and, to further
the ends of justice, a culprit must not know that there is
any bill against him till it is popped in his face by the
sheriff; but old Mac's zinc house was just as sonorous
as a drum, and, for all purposes of secrecy, we had better have held our deliberations on the logs of Chenook
beach than where we were. The outsiders either crawl-
ed under the house or stood outside, where they could
hear perfectly well what was going on; and if any one
was a little deaf, all he had to do was to get a nail and
a stone and punch some holes through the zinc, then
clap his ear to the aperture and become perfectly cognizant of all our proceedings. And, in addition to this pub-
licity, when the petit jury were called, the challenge exhausted all the people present, and they were obliged to
take nine of the grand jury to serve as petit jurors.

First we had to examine a lot of Indians, and the district attorney proceeded to explain to them the nature
of an oath, which they pretended to understand, except
Yancumux, who stated that they neither knew or cared
any thing about the white man's God, although they had
heard the priest tell about him. At this crisis, one of
the jurors from Pacific City, who was a little merry, asked the counsel if he knew that *we* were the grand jury,
and that *he* was the United States District Attorney.
"Yes," said the squire, looking somewhat astonished;
"what of it?" "Oh, nothing, only this: the judge told
us, when we wanted advice, we must call on you. Now
we don't want any of your advice at present, and I move
that you retire, and when we want you we'll send for
you." This speech made some fun; but we soon set-

tled the affair by choosing one of our number, William
M'Gunnicle, interpreter. We passed all that day examining the Indians, but they did not know so much about
the matter as we did.

That night I slept in the jury-room with Baldt; Captain Johnson, another juror, slept in a little bed-room
adjoining. Johnson was one of those thick-headed, stubborn old fellows that, having once made up their mind,
can never be turned. He had, however, from some
cause or other, got an idea that I was versed in the law,
and informed me that he had some matters on his mind
he wished me to advise him about, and he would do
just as I would think best. He said that old M'Carty,
or, as he called him, Brandywine, and himself were old
friends, and that he had loaned Brandywine some money,
and he could not get it, and he meant "to put him
through all the courts of law." I was aware of this fact,
as M'Carty had told me, when I passed the night at his
house, of Johnson's threats to sue him, which made him
afraid to come with us to Chenook.

"Captain Johnson," said I, "have you ever made a
demand on M'Carty?" "Yes, I have." "Did he refuse to pay you?" "No, he didn't exactly refuse; he
said he couldn't pay, as he had no money." "Well,
captain, do you think he would pay you if he had the
means?" "Oh yes, I know he would; he don't mean
to shirk his debts." "Now, Captain Johnson," I added,
"you know very well that Brandywine has lost every
thing he had by that fire last winter, and he can't pay
you. You are not in want of money. Give Mac one
year to pay the amount, take his note and a mortgage
on the new house, and talk no more about sueing him,
for if you do you will lose your debt." Johnson thanked
me for my advice, and I had the satisfaction of saving
two old friends from a quarrel. But there was another

question that I advised him upon which he would not follow, and was quite vexed afterward that he had not. He had learned that an indictment was against him for giving liquor to an Indian, and said that it was true, and he meant to go into court the next morning, and plead guilty, and throw himself on the mercy of the court, and expected the judge would let him off with a fine.   I advised him to let the matter rest till the court called it up, for it was an offense against a law of Congress, in which the fine was five hundred dollars, and the judge had no discretion in the case; and just so sure as he plead guilty, just so sure he would be fined.   Both Baldt and myself tried to convince the old fellow, but it was no use: he knew better.   So the next morning, when the jury went into court, up steps old Johnson to the judge and remarked, " Please your honor, I understand there is an indictment against me for selling liquor to an Indian.   Well, your honor, I plead guilty, and throw myself on the mercy of the court."   As no one but Baldt and myself had the least intimation of the intention of Johnson, all were intensely edified, and filled with profound admiration.

" Mr. Clerk," says the judge, " read the indictment." Dawson, the clerk, gazed at Johnson a minute or two to see if he was crazy or not ; but, as he saw no signs of mental aberration, he slowly unfolded and read the document.

The judge then remarked : " Before you plead to this indictment, Mr. Johnson, I wish to observe that this court has no desire to take any advantage of your ignorance, but the law is one of Congress, and is imperative. I wish that it was otherwise, and that the amount of the fine was in proportion to the offense ; but I have no discretion in the case, and think, before you make your plea, that you had better take the advice of counsel."

Several of the old captain's friends here advised with him, when he plead not guilty, and was then obliged to find sureties to a bond of five hundred dollars. Johnson was quite crestfallen at this result, and looked forward to the trial with a great deal of interest; and when it did come off eventually, the principal witness against him could not swear whether it was whisky or molasses, so he got clear.

But to return to the manslaughter case. Another of our jury was old Captain Scarborough, of whom mention has been made previously. The captain was very deaf, and talked loud. He was a great advocate for the "majesty of the law," and very bold to speak his mind freely on all occasions, but he was respected very much by the inhabitants, and his remarks were usually listened to with deference.

The principal, and, in fact, the only witness in the case was William Martindill, who had been cabin-boy with Captain Scarborough, and had remained with him in the employ of the Hudson Bay Company till he had risen to the rank of second mate. The old captain was in the habit of addressing Bill in the same tone and manner as when on board ship, and Bill always comported himself with the same feeling toward the captain.

When Bill was called in for examination, he was quite tipsy, and pretended not to know any thing of the occurrence. To every question he would reply, "I don't know nothin' about it." Captain Scarborough, who was leaning forward, with his hand behind his ear, to catch the sound of Bill's voice, no sooner fairly comprehended that he was talking nonsense, than he grew intensely indignant. "Bill!" he roared out, "do you know what you are about?" "Oh yes, captain," says Bill, "I am wide awake." "No you ain't," bawled out the irascible old captain; "you're drunk. Go below and get sober." Then, addressing the jury, he remarked, "Gentlemen, you see the fellow is drunk; send him to bed." So Mr. Bill was marched into the bed-room by the sheriff, and comfortably tucked up.

After the jury adjourned, the captain and myself walked in to see Bill, who had then slept himself sober, but very thirsty.

"Now," says the captain, in his loud tone, "are you fairly awake, Bill, and do you know what you have been about? Do you mean to stand up before my face, and tell me a parcel of your lies?" "Oh, captain," says Bill, "just you let me have a drink; my throat is all parched up."

"It will be worse parched in the next world," replied the indignant old mariner, "if you don't belay those lies of yours, and begin to pay out the truth. Not one drop shall you have to drink."

"Well, but, captain, the squire axes me so many hard questions that I don't know what to say; I'm knocked all aback." "Never you mind the 'squire; do you tell the truth. Your course is laid down straight. Keep her full and by, and mind your helm; keep her steady; for if you go on yawing as you did this morning, first falling off your course, and then luffing sharp up in the wind till you make all shiver and shake, you may depend upon it, my lad, you will find yourself ashore before you can think. And I can tell you that if you. touch bottom among these lawyers you will find it will take all hands to heave you off again. If they catch you foul, they will hang you up without waiting to rig a grating. Now I don't want you to say one word to me; but when you go before the jury again, do you just tell the truth like a man."

This excellent though homely advice of the worthy old captain was not lost on Bill, and the result was that an indictment was found against Lamley, and the case called on for trial.

When the jury was called and the challenges exhausted, it was found that there were no more persons to draw from. So the two counsel agreed on a compromise, which was, that nine jurors should be selected from among the grand jury who had just solemnly rendered a true bill against the prisoner. However, in a new country, old forms can not always be adhered to; but as it is considered that any proposition between conflicting parties "is fair if you only agree to it," the jurors were accordingly selected, and the case proceeded.

This being the first time the district attorney had ever addressed a jury on a criminal case, he proceeded to elucidate the points in a speech of considerable length, commencing from the American Revolution, and continuing his deductions to the time of Washington's death, and closing with a beautiful tribute to the memory of the Father of his Country.

This argument had such a direct bearing on the case on trial that the counsel for the defense was forced to reply to it by quotations from ancient authors, and to prove his position by reciting extracts from the Arabian Nights' Entertainments, which, although not considered so orthodox as Coke and Blackstone, had the effect to mystify the prosecuting attorney, who forgot the "order of his going," and, beginning at both ends of his case, broke down in the middle; and the case being submitted to the jury, they returned a verdict of not guilty.

The argument of the two counsel caused the most intense delight to the court and spectators, and the result was just what we all hoped for, and every body was satisfied.

That day and night it rained as it only can rain at the mouth of the Columbia; it came down in torrents, and the noise it made, rattling and pouring on the roof of M'Carty's zinc house, was equal to a young Niagara.

During the evening Captain Johnson proposed to me another problem for solution. His boys, going to school one morning, discovered a barrel lying near the fence at Mr. Holman's house, and, having a great curiosity to find out the contents, adopted the very original method of knocking in one of the heads with an axe lying near by. The contents, being vinegar, were, of course, speedily swallowed up by the dry sand, over which it poured in a promiscuous manner. The owner, after waiting a reasonable time without obtaining any redress from Johnson, had just confidentially intimated that unless Johnson settled the matter at once, he would bring the case before the court in the morning. Johnson was in a great dilemma; his affair in court that day, in regard to the liquor business, had made him quite nervous; and, as he disliked paying out money very much, he wanted to try and get rid of this vinegar question without being obliged to recompense the owner for its loss. "I don't see," said he, "why I should be made to pay for my boys' mischief; in fact, I won't pay a cent. I'll take it through all the courts before I will. The boys are but mere lads, and they did not mean to do any harm."

I then suggested that, if any boy should throw stones and break his windows, he would be very likely to call on the boy's father to pay damages.

"There ain't any of my neighbors got boys big enough to break windows," said he; "and if there were, I'd break their heads." "Well," I replied, "would you not make their fathers pay for the broken glass?" "Yes, I would." "Very well; your boys, instead of breaking glass, have broke a barrel and spilled the contents, and you are obliged to pay for or replace it." "But the owner wants me to pay him a dollar and a half a gallon, and I can buy the best at Astoria for a dollar."

" Well, you see the owner, and, as he is a reasonable man, I know he will only ask you what is just and right." Johnson did as I advised him, and settled by giving his note on short time for thirty gallons vinegar at a dollar a gallon; but when it came due he declared he had been cheated in the gauge, so had the barrel regauged, when it was found to measure forty gallons, which he was forced to pay, very much against his will.

Poor Johnson! He was afterward drowned while crossing the Columbia in a boat with Mr. John Dawson and another, who shared his fate; and, but a few months previous, M'Carty, while returning home from a visit to Johnson's, was drowned while crossing the Wallacut River, and his body was afterward carried by the current out to sea, and eventually picked up on the beach to the north of the Columbia, almost up to the entrance to Shoal-water Bay. Captain Scarborough likewise died shortly previous to Johnson, but he died in his own house very suddenly. I have before remarked on the hostile feeling evinced toward Americans by the former employés of the Hudson Bay Company, and here was a circumstance to corroborate my assertion. Captain Scarborough was known to keep quite a sum of money in his house at all times. He charged an old Indian servant-woman, who lived with him, in case of his death, on no account to tell a Boston man (American) where his money was, but to deliver it either to the Hudson Bay Company's agent at Chenook, or to some of their people up the river, alleging that the Bostons were very bad people, but the King George people were honest and good. As soon as it was known that Captain Scarborough was dead, the judge of probate, coroner, and other county officers proceeded to the house officially; but all their promises or threats were of no avail to obtain one word from the old squaw. " If you burn me in the fire," said she, "I will not tell you; but I will tell a King George man." And they were actually obliged to send up the river and appoint one of the Company's people administrator before the old woman would tell where the money was.

The next day the court adjourned, and, after settling with the deputy marshal for our jury fees, we started for home. When we had crossed the portage and reached the canoe, we were joined by another person, who asked a passage down the Bay, which, of course, was granted, although Baldt objected on account of the canoe being small, and he being unused to a canoe; but I told him it was all right; so we proceeded down the river, and kept close to the eastern shore of the Bay till we reached the mouth of the Nasal River, when we took a stiff southeast breeze, as much as we could stagger under. There was a sharp, short, chopping sea in the channel, but we did not discover it till we were directly in the worst, and then Baldt was sure we were going to capsize: he was terribly frightened. I told him our only hope was to keep on and get through as quiet as possible, for if I attempted to turn back we would certainly swamp; and he and all of us must sit down in the bottom of the canoe, and keep as still as possible. I was only afraid of breaking the paddle I steered by, when she would be sure to broach to and fill. Our situation did not appear particularly desirable; for, while we were in the worst of the sea, a boat to the leeward of us capsized and drifted into shoal water, where we saw the occupants lift her up and put things to rights; but we did get through without taking in one drop of water; and, when fairly out of the swell, Baldt began to regain his courage, and was loud in his praises of the little canoe, which, he thought, could outlive almost any sea. But the grand secret is to know how to manage these canoes. I had been in mine so much that I could handle her as well as an Indian; but if I had felt afraid, or had broken my paddle while crossing the Nasal, we would have met with as bad, if not worse an accident than those in the boat had. But we arrived home safe, and a few days after I had an adventure with Caslah'han, the one-eyed Indian of Gray's Harbor.

Captain Purrington, having occasion to go to Chenook, took the Indians and started, leaving me alone in the house. This was common with both of us, and neither felt any fear of remaining alone, but always went and came as we saw fit.

The evening after he left, as I was about sitting down to my supper, who should come in but Caslah'han. I gave him a welcome, and told him to sit up and eat some supper with me, for, in fact, I was rather glad to have some one to talk to. After we had finished eating we lit our pipes and sat down by the fire. I then inquired of him what brought him down from Gray's Harbor, and where he was going. He simply said he was going to Chenook to sell his furs, and, hearing I was alone, he called to see me. He was a most repulsive-looking savage, his one eye glaring with a most demoniac expression, and his whole looks bore a very sinister appearance. I had heard of some of his exploits at Fort Vancouver, where he had been flogged several times for theft, and also of his killing two Indians in a canoe not far from my house, and I did not wish any thing to do with him; but he had always treated me well, and I had no reason to complain.

He sat a while smoking in silence, and at last said, "You must have a stout heart; are you not afraid of me?" "No," said I; "why should I be afraid of you? We have always been friends, have we not?" "Yes," said he; "but why did you tell Sam to shoot me?" I was perfectly astonished, and asked him what he meant. He replied that the Indians had told him that I was the cause of Sam Winant's firing at him when we were about crossing Gray's Harbor, and he had come now to settle up the business, and in a manner that can be easily imagined, although he did not say how he wished to settle it. "But," said he, "they have told me lies; you never told Sam to shoot me, or else you would have felt afraid when you saw me coming, and I should have seen that you were afraid, and then I should have known that you were guilty; but now I know better." I assured him that I had no ill will against him, and urged him to remain all night, which he did, and kept me amused till a late hour, telling stories, and, when he left the next morning, had the kindness to steal my hatchet, as a token he was on friendly and intimate terms. But I was glad enough to get off that cheap, for I afterward found that he had started to go direct to Chenook; and he called on me after dark, when, if he had so desired, he could have killed me, and kept on, and no one would have suspected him at all. He still continued to profess himself to be my friend, and I suppose he did feel as friendly toward me as a person of his savage disposition could; but after that time I took good care to have either a loaded gun or a good knife at hand in the house whenever any more of his tribe called on me after dark.

Winter now coming on, I had little else to do except to listen to Indian tales and study into their language; and as the Jargon, or language universally used over the Territory, is curious, as tending to show how a language can be formed, I shall now give some description of it.

CHAPTER XVIII.

Language of the Indians.—The Jargon.—Different Methods of spelling
Words by Writers.—Difficulty of rightly understanding the Jargon.
—How a Language can be formed.—Origin of the Indian Language.
—Remarks of Mr. Squier.—Irish-sounding Words in the Chehalis
Tongue.—An amusing Parable.—Views of Mr. Duponceau.—Re-
marks of Gliddon.—Resemblance between Chehalis and Aztec
Words.—Facts relative of Indian Journeys south.—Mrs. Ducheney's
Narrative.—Difficulty of Indians in pronouncing certain Letters.—
Cause of the chuckling Sound of the Northwest Languages.—Per-
sons apt to misunderstand Indian Words.—Dislike of Indians to
learn English.—Winter Amusements.—Tomhays and the Geese.—
Arrival of Settlers.—Doctor Johnson.—The Doctor and myself act
as Lawyers in Champ's Court.—Strong Medicine.—Kohpoh mistaken
for a 'Coon.—Visit of the Klickatats.—Christmas Dinner on Crow.—
Baked Skunk.—Fisherman's Pudding.

THE language of the tribes north of the Columbia is a
guttural sound which to a stranger seems a compound
of the gruntings of a pig and the clucking of a hen.
All the tribes of the Territory (some twenty-five) speak
a language which, though sounding the same to unprac-
ticed ears, is very different when understood; and even
tribes so nearly connected as the Chenooks, Chehalis,
and Queniūlts, being only a few miles distant from each
other, yet members of the one can not understand the
language of the other. Still, there are individuals of
each who, from a roving, trading disposition, have become
familiar with each other's tongue, and can usually make
themselves understood. The Chehalis language is that
most usually spoken at present, for the ancient Chenook
is such a guttural, difficult tongue, that many of the
young Chenook Indians can not speak it, but have been
taught by their parents the Chehalis language and the
Jargon. The Jargon is the medium with which the In-

dians hold intercourse with each other and with the whites.

This Jargon is composed of Chenook, French, and English languages, and is supposed by many to have been formed by the Hudson Bay Company for trading purposes. Such, however, is not the fact. There have been constant additions to the Jargon since the advent of the Hudson Bay Company, for many of the words now in general use in this language are of French and English origin; but I think that, among the Coast Indians in particular, the Indian part of the language has been in use for years.

The first mention I have seen made of this Jargon is in Meares's voyages in 1788, where, in giving an account of a chief named Callicum, who hurt his leg while climbing on board ship, and then sucked the blood from the wound, Meares states he "licked his lips, and, patting his belly, exclaimed *Cloosh, cloosh,* or good, good." Cloosh, or klose, or close, are all the same, and mean good.

Still later than this, in 1803, Jewett, in his narrative of the ship Boston, at Nootka, gives a vocabulary of the words in common use among the Nootkans, and from which I have selected the following, to compare them with the present Chenook dialect or Jargon.

Nootka.	Chenook.	English.
Kloots'mah,	Klooch'man,	Woman.
Ta-nas-sis,	Ta-nas,	Child, or any thing small.
Sick-a-min-ny,	Chink-a-min,	Iron.
Ma'mook,	Ma-mook,	Work.
Kom-me-tak,	Kum-tux,	Understand.
Klu-shish *or* Cloosh,	Klose *or* Close,	Good.
Ty-ee,	Ty-ee,	Chief.
See-yah'poks,	Sear'por-tle,	Cap or hat.
Klack'ko,	Klar'koon,	Good.
Pow,	Pow *or* Po,	Report of a gun or cannon; a gun.
Klat'tur-wah,	Clat'te-wah,	Go off or go away.

The different manner in which the words are spelled is no evidence of a difference of meaning; for no two writers of Indian words fully agree as to the proper method of spelling. As an instance of this variety, I may cite that in the Commissioner's Report on Indian Affairs, 1854, page 215, the Cammassa esculenta, or La Cammass, as the French call it, is by Governor Stevens called and spelled Camash. On page 229, Mr. Gibbs spells it Kamaäs, and Wilkes has it Lackamus. Now these all mean one and the same thing.

There is a river emptying into Shoal-water Bay called the *Marhoo*. This is called by the Chehalis Marh or Marhoo, by the Chenooks *Nemarh*, and by the whites *Nemar*; while some of the latter have given it the name of Neemy. Now no casual reader would ever suppose that *Marh* or *Marhoo* and *Neemy* were the names of the same river; but it serves to illustrate the different impression the sound of words makes on different individuals.

So, also, in writing words, *k* and *c* are used indiscriminately by writers, and although they make a word look different when written or printed, yet they produce in some situations the same sound. For instance, the words Cowlitz, Carcowan, Cultus, Cumtux, etc., can be and are frequently written Kowlitz, Karkowan, Kultus, Kumtux. I think, however, if a rule was adopted to spell all words of French or English origin as originally spelled, it would be correct; but by using *k* it gives a word a sort of an Indian appearance, which some writers affect. Cammass should not be spelled with a *k* any more than Columbia.

The Indians are very quick to detect any difference in the intonation or method of pronunciation of the whites, and sometimes think we speak different languages. An Indian asked me one day (while pointing to a cow) what

was the name we called that animal. I told him cow.
He said that he had just asked another white man, and
he called it a *caow*.

By this means, different Indians who have been with
the whites acquire a habit of pronouncing such English
words as they pick up in the same style and manner as
the person from whom they learn them. This causes a
certain discrepancy in the Jargon, which at first is difficult to get over. And, again, each tribe will add some
local words of their own language, so that while a person can make himself understood among any of the tribes
for the purposes of trade, it is difficult to hold a lengthened conversation on any subject without the aid of
some one who has become more familiar with the peculiar style.

This fact I saw instanced on an occasion of a treaty
made, or attempted to be made, by Governor Stevens
with five tribes on the Chehalis River in the spring of
1855. There were present the Cowlitz, the Chehalis,
Chenook, Queniūlt, and Satchap Indians. Colonel B.
F. Shaw was the interpreter, and spoke the language
fluently; but, although he was perfectly understood by
the Cowlitz and Satchap Indians, he was but imperfect-
ly understood by the Chenooks, Chehalis, and Queniūlts,
and it was necessary for those present who were conversant with the Coast tribes to repeat to them what he
said before they could fully understand.

I experienced the same difficulty; for, as I had been
accustomed to speak a great deal of the Chehalis language with the Jargon, I found that the Indians from the
interior could not readily understand me when making
use of words in the Chehalis dialect.

The Jargon is interesting as showing how a language
can be formed. The words of three distinct languages
—the French, English, and Indian—are made to form a

separate and distinct tongue. It is a language, however, never used except when the Indians and whites are conversing, or by two distant tribes who do not understand each other, and only as an American and a Russian would be likely to talk French to communicate their ideas with each other. The Indians speaking the same language no more think of using the Jargon while talking together than the Americans do.

It is a language confined wholly, I believe, to our Northwestern possessions west of the Rocky Mountains. It originated in the roving, trading spirit of the tribes, and has been added to and increased since the introduction of the whites among them.

Of the origin of any of the languages of the different tribes it is impossible even to conjecture; but it certainly seems to me that if, as has been alleged, these tribes did come from Asia, there would have been some similarity in the languages by which they could be traced.

Mr. Squier makes the following philosophical remarks:

"The casual resemblance of certain words in the languages of America and those of the Old World can not be taken as evidence of common origin. Such coincidences may be easily accounted for as the result of accident, or, at most, of local infusions. It is not in accidental coincidences of sound or meaning, but in a comparison of the general structure and character of the American languages with those of other countries, that we can expect to find similitudes at all conclusive, or worthy of remark in determining the question of a common origin."

Among the Chehalis Indians, and even among the Chenooks, are found words occasionally strikingly resembling those of some foreign country. *Connath innisku,* an expression of derision, which is something

similar to the remark, You are stupid or half drunk, is
certainly very similar in its appearance and sound to
Irish words, but it must be poor evidence by which to
prove that the Indians were originally Irish.　But I believe that there are more Irish-sounding words in the
Chehalis language than there are Hebrew, and, so far
as any sound of words goes, it is as easy to prove their
descent from the Irish as it is from the lost tribes of
Israel.

The following amusing "parable," from Nott & Gliddon's Notes, may do to insert here: "It is well known
that the earlier colonists of Barbadoes, Montserrat, and
some other West India islands were Irish exiles.　Odd
to relate, while a few of their negro slaves actually speak
Gaelic, many have acquired the 'brogue.'

"An Hibernian, fresh from the green isle, arrived one
day at the port of Bridgetown, and was hailed by two
negro boatmen, who offered to take him ashore.　Observing that their names were Pat and Murphy, and that
their brogue was uncommonly rich, the stranger (taking
them to be Irishmen) asked, 'And how long have ye
been from the ould country?'　Misunderstanding him,
one of the darkies replied, 'Sex months, yer honor.'
'Sex months! sex months! only sex months! and turned as black as me hat!　J——!　what a climate!　Row
me back to the ship.　I'm from Cork last, and I'll soon
be there again.'

"Every one laughs at the verdant simplicity which believed that a Celt could be transmuted by climate into a
negro in six months.　All would smile at the notion of
such a possibility within 6, or even 60 years; most
readers will hesitate over 600 years.　Anatomy, history,
and the monuments prove that 6000 years have never
metamorphosed one type of man into another."

As early as 1819, Mr. Duponceau advanced the following conclusion: " That the American languages in general are rich in words and grammatical form, and that, in their complicated construction, the greatest order, method, and regularity prevail; that these complicated forms, which he calls polysthenic, appear to exist in all the languages from Greenland to Cape Horn, and that these forms differ essentially from those of the ancient and modern languages of the old hemisphere."

Gliddon remarks: " The type of a race would never change if kept from adulterations, as may be seen in the case of the Jews and other people. So with languages: we have no reason to believe that a race would ever lose its language if kept aloof from foreign influences. It is a fact that, in the little island of Great Britain, the Welsh and Erse are still spoken, although for two thousand years pressed upon by the strongest influences tending to exterminate a tongue. So with the Basque in France, which can be traced back at least three thousand years, and is still spoken. Coptic was the language of Egypt for at least five thousand years, and still leaves its trace in the languages around. The Chinese has existed equally as long, and is still undisturbed."

We have seen that wherever the Jews, or the Chinese, or the Gipsies, or Negroes, have wandered from one part of the world to the other, they have, either in general appearance or language, retained a separate and distinct position; and it is but natural to conclude that, if the American Indians had come from Asia, they would certainly have retained something, either in language or appearance, like the tribes of the Old World.

We are assured by writers that this diversity of languages was caused by the confusion of tongues at the Tower of Babel; but Gliddon & Nott state that " it is well known to cuneiform students of the present day that Babylon's tower did not exist before the reign of Nebuchadnezzar, who built it during the seventh century B.C. The antiquities of America show it to have been populated fifty thousand years ago."

Leaving what must, to us, remain always an uncertainty as to the origin of the Indian lauguage, and descending to the practical, or language of the present, as we find it, the most casual observer must be struck with the great similarity in the ending of many of the Chehalis words with the Mexican or Aztec *tl;* as, for instance, a-quail-shiltl, the north wind; quer-lo-e-chintl, bear-berry; par-lam-shiltl, raspberry (Rubus odoratus); nar-whatl, yes; ow-whitl, another; jo-quitl, get up; shooks-quitl, to-day; se-cartl, spruce; sheo-quintl, cedar; skaer-kuttl, woman; sartl, two, &c.

That the northern tribes, or those of Oregon and Washington, have been accustomed to long journeys south, is a fact which is easily shown. When Fremont first commenced hostilities in California, a large body of Walla Walla Indians from the Columbia were creating disturbances in the region of Sacramento. These Indians formerly made regular excursions to the south every year, on horseback, for the purpose of trade or plunder.

The wife of Mr. Ducheney, the agent at Chenook for the Hudson Bay Company, who is a very intelligent woman, informed me that her father was a Frenchman, and her mother a Walla Walla Indian, and that, when she was quite a child, she recollected going with her mother and a party of her tribe to the south for a number of months; that they were three months going and three months returning; that they took horses with them, and Indian trinkets, which they exchanged for vermilion and Mexican blankets; and that on their return her mother died, and was buried where the city of Sacramento now stands. I asked her how she knew where Sacramento

O

was, and she replied that some of her friends had since gone to California, to the gold mines, and that on their return they said that it was at Sacramento where her mother was buried.

She was too young to remember how far into Mexico they went, but I judged that the vermilion she mentioned was obtained from the mountains of Almaden, near San José, California. But I have no reason to doubt the statement, as I have heard similar statements from other sources. These facts, taken into consideration with the allegory of the thunder-bird of the Chenooks and Chehalis, would seem to give weight to the supposition that at some time or other the Mexican Indians had been among the Northern tribes; or it may be considered, on the other hand, by those who believe in the northwest exodus from Asia, as a proof that, as the Mexican ending *tl* is found among the tribes still farther north, the Mexicans themselves originated in that quarter. Be that as it may, my present limits and limited information will not allow me to enter upon what must prove but a very unsatisfactory argument.*

In examining the vocabularies in the Appendix, many words of English origin, in the Jargon, are to be found dressed in an Indian phraseology simply by using the letter L instead of R. The reason is that the Indians can not sound R when used as the commencement of a word. Thus, for instance, rice is pronounced lice; rope, lope; Robert, Lobert; run, lun; or bread, bled; le pretre (the priest), la plate; key, klee, &c. Other letters are quite as difficult for them to pronounce, although they can,

* "It should be remembered," says Prescott (Conquest of Mexico, vol. iii., p. 414), "how treacherous a thing is tradition, and how easily the links of the chain are severed. The builders of the Pyramids had been forgotten before the time of the earliest Greek historians. 'Inter omnes eos non constat a quibus factæ sint, justissimo casu, obliteratis tantæ vanitatis auctoribus.'"—Pliny, Hist. Nat., lib. xxxvi., cap. 17.

with exertion. Thus they call shovel, shuml; vinegar, mingar. F is also sounded like p, as pire for fire, pork for fork. It is easy to see that, if every English or French word should be written as the Indians pronounce them, a very large and curious-looking vocabulary could be produced. I have therefore omitted many words of English and French origin, and only given a few, with their derivation, as specimens of the manner the Jargon is gotten up.

In ordinary conversation many of their words are cut short, and those long words in the Chehalis language can thus be made to convey the desired information in a quicker manner. Tolneuch means west wind; it also means off shore, toward the sea, or to the west. Thus, if an Indian, while getting his canoe through the surf, wishes his companion to push her head off shore, he will call out *Tolneuch;* but if he is in a hurry, or there is danger, and it is necessary to move quick, he calls out *neuch neuch.* *Cla-ath-lum* is the east wind, and also means on shore, and that is abbreviated to *clath clath.* This style of abbreviation I learned while taking my jaunt in the canoe from Queniūlt to Shoal-water Bay. I had been accustomed to the Chenook words, as used in the Jargon, *martquilly* and *martinly,* for off shore or on shore, but we could not speak them quite quick enough when a wave was about breaking; so I noticed the Indians adopted the other expressions, which afterward they explained, and I found that *neuch neuch,* or *clath clath,* was quite as easily spoken as any other method of conveying information I was aware of.

The peculiar clucking sound is produced by the tongue pressing against the roof of the mouth, and pronouncing a word ending with *tl* as if there was the letter *k* at the end of the *tl;* but it is impossible, in any form or method of spelling that I know of, to convey the proper guttural clucking sound. Sometimes they will, as if for amusement, end all their words with *tl ;* and the effect is ludicrous to hear three or four talking at the same time with this singular sound, like so many sitting hens.

The Chehalis language is very rich in words, and every one is so expressive that it is not possible, like the Jargon, to make mistakes; for instance, in the Jargon, which is very limited, the same word represents a great many different things.

Tupsoe means hair, feathers, the finely-pounded bark of the young cedar, grass, blossoms, and leaves, but in the Chehalis and Queniült languages each of these things is represented by a specific word. They have also a separate word for every plant, shrub, and flower, as our own botanists have. I noticed this among even the children, who frequently brought me collections of flowers. They readily told me the name of each, and were certainly more conversant with a difference in plants than many of our own children, and even grown people, who are too ready to class all common plants as weeds.

Many of the Jargon words, though entirely different, yet sound so much alike when quickly spoken, that a stranger is apt to get deceived; and I have known persons who did not well understand the Jargon get angry with an Indian, thinking he said something entirely different from what he actually did.

The words *wake*, no, and *wicht*, directly or after, sound, as pronounced, very similar. "*Chā-ko, hiac, chā-ko*," "Come quick! come," said a settler one day to an Indian who was very busy. "*Wicht nika chā-ko*," "I will come directly," said the Indian. But the white man understood him to say, "*Wake nika chā-ko*," "I will not come," consequently got angry. "You don't understand Indian talk; I did not say I would not come," said the Indian. If he had said *Narwitka*, yes, the white man would have understood.

Ulthl means proud, and *ulticut* long, but they are readily confounded with each other. A friend of mine, who was about leaving the Bay, wished to tell some Indians who were working for him that if, on his return, he found they had behaved well, he should feel very proud of them and glad, used the following : *Ulticut nika tumtum*, or, my heart is long, instead of *ulthl nika tumtum*, or, my heart is proud. "He must have a funny heart," said the Indian who related it to me. "He says his heart is long; perhaps it is like a mouse's tail."

There are many other words that are as readily misunderstood, but the above will be sufficient to show that, however writers may agree about methods of spelling, no person can possibly learn the Indian language on the Coast, so as to speak it fluently, without learning it orally from the Indians, and living among them, so as to become familiarized with the different sounds and modulations of the voice. The difficulty of learning either the Chenook, Chehalis, or Queniūlt language is, that the tribes are so near each other, they frequently use each other's words in conversation. For instance, the shrub *Gaultheria Shallon* is called by the Chenooks *Sallal*, by the Chehalis *taärk*, and by the Queniūlts *squasowich*. The heart, also, is called by the three different names of *tumtum*, *aitsemar*, and *squillims*. And as, in conversation with themselves, they readily use either, it gives rise to confusion in precisely the same manner as if one of us, in attempting to speak English with an Indian, to teach him, should make use of French and Latin words.

They appear to have a great aversion to learning the English language, contenting themselves with the Jargon, which they look upon as a sort of white man's talk. They, however, are not so averse to learning French, probably because they can imitate the sounds of French words easier than they can the English. I have several times endeavored to teach the alphabet to the young Indians, but they objected, and yet some of them have the power of imitation so good that they can copy off writing or printing very readily. Peter, who lived with us, would amuse himself often by printing letters. He showed me at one time a strip of paper on which he had printed, with a little brush I had given him, *New York Herald*, in letters precisely like the heading of that paper, and yet he could not tell the name of a single letter, nor would he learn.

The Coast Indians are by no means deficient in intellect. They are, to all appearance, full as intelligent and smart as those tribes where we hear of so much improvement having been effected by teachers. But the tribes of the Coast are broken up into small bands, continually roving about, and the only aim they appear to have is to become tyee or chief, which with them means to get as much property as they can, either in slaves, canoes, blankets, horses, or guns, and then idle away their time.

It is difficult to account for the great dissimilarity to be found among the Indians in regard to language. Living so near to each other, having so ready and constant communication, living in the same style, with the same natural objects around them, it would appear as if they would be more likely to speak the same dialect. We can readily understand how the Indians of the Plains or in remote parts of the country should, from different association, have different forms of expression, but that these bands between the Columbia and Fuca Straits should differ so, is a subject that I am not ethnologist enough to discover.

During the winter we had, with the exception of the usual in-door work, very little to amuse us. We had occasionally some anecdote told of matters down the beach, and a characteristic one of Cartumhays I will relate.   He had purchased a demijohn of some of the settlers, agreeing to pay ten wild geese for it.   Two he paid at once to close the bargain, and then went to shoot the remainder, when he was to receive the demijohn.   In about a week he returned with a bunch of geese tied together by their heads.

" Count them," said he to the owner of the demijohn. He did so, and found eight heads, which was the number of geese required to make up the amount.   The count was reported correct, and the demijohn delivered to Cartumhays ; but when the geese were to be cooked, it was found there were eight heads sure enough, but only six bodies, Tomhays having taken two for his own use.   It is needless to remark that old Tomhays kept clear of that particular log cabin for a long time afterward.

We had now grown into the dignity of a village, and, at a meeting of the settlers, it was voted to name the town Bruceville (which has since been changed to Bruceport).   We had received during the year several additions to the settlement, among whom were Doctor James R. Johnson, with his lady and child.   This was quite a comfort to us, for the doctor, besides being a jolly, good-natured, and hospitable man, was a gentleman, and quite skillful in his profession, and his arrival made us feel safe on the score of medical advice.   A large grocery store had also been opened by Messrs. Coon and Woodward, who also kept a public house.   This was another good thing, as it relieved the old settlers from the necessity of entertaining all the strangers and new-comers into the Bay.   It, however, was a means of relieving the pockets of the travelers, for Mr. Coon did not arrive in the Bay at that primitive period when hospitalities were gratuitously tendered, but, on the contrary, having, as he said, come to make his pile, he appeared anxious to do so in the shortest possible time.

A blacksmith had also arrived with his family some months previous. He was an excellent workman, but a worthless fellow, and finally ran off.

There were fortunately no lawyers, so Doctor Johnson and myself were appointed to take the place of legal wisdom ; and, having found an old copy of Iowa statutes, we expounded law to the learned and erudite justice, Squire Champ, whose court was pretty well attended, either for fun, frolic, or business, to pass off the time during the winter months. But we had no more criminal trials after the one when Joe was locked up in the hen-coop, although several trials of civil cases came up, which the squire usually disposed of in a very uncivil manner. Neither the arguments of the counsel nor the decisions of the court would probably be looked upon as very learned by the legal profession, but they served a very good purpose, and gave the same results that all lawsuits do—satisfaction to the winner and indignation to the loser.

I had another professional call to perform the part of doctor. During the winter, an old Indian, called George or Squintum, who lived near Russell's house, got into a drunken frolic one night in his lodge, during which he received a blow from a hatchet, thrown by his wife's brother, a perfect young savage, named Kohpoh. He was cut in the cords of his neck in such a manner as to perfectly paralyze all his limbs. Dr. Cooper, who was still residing at Russell's, was called, and dressed the wound.

A few days after I met the doctor, when he remarked, "Pray, what is that powerful medicine you have given to the Indians formerly?" I requested him to explain, for I did not know what he meant. He said that he had found it necessary to use caustic to cauterize old George's back, but that individual, not experiencing immediate relief, had told him that I was a better doctor, and had a *skookum*, or strong medicine, which he knew would cure him.

I told the doctor I expected it was the celebrated liniment I had formerly used. He laughed. "Well," he added, "if you have any more, I wish you would try it. It can't hurt the old fellow, if it don't do him any good, and he seems to have great faith in it."

I then went to Dr. Johnson, and getting from him some of the most powerful aqua ammoniæ, proceeded to the lodge of old George. "How are you, George?" I asked. "I have come to give you some medicine." "Good," he replied; "I can't move; I am all dead but my heart and tongue. My heart is strong, and I can talk."

I told his squaw to raise him up, which she did, and I requested him to smell of the ammonia. "Smell hard, George," said I. He gave a powerful sniff at the bottle, and the result was that he was knocked over immediately. "Ugh!" he grunted, as his wife gathered him up; "that is good—that is medicine. Now I will get well."

I then asked his wife for some whale oil, which she brought me, but it smelled so bad that it would have almost killed flies. However, I poured some into a bottle with the ammonia, producing a compound which had, as one remarked, a "solid stink."

This high-scented liniment was then rubbed all over the old fellow, producing, as he said, a sensation like a thousand needles. He was delighted, and expected to get well in a couple of days; but I assured him that if he recovered in six months he would be fortunate. He did, however, recover during the summer so far as to be able to do a little work, and gradually got well; but he always thought that my skookum medicine was what cured him.

Mr. Kohpoh came very near having his head broke the following summer by the captain and myself, through mistake. Kohpoh, or, as the captain called him, "Coffeepot," was a notoriously bad fellow, and was hated by the whites and feared by the Indians.

We had told him never to come round our house, for his character as a thief was too notorious to have his company desirable. It appeared, however, that he got angry with Peter, our boy (or, rather, young man, for both Kohpoh and himself were nearly of the same age, and both over twenty), and he determined to have his revenge.

One evening, after we had gone to bed, we heard our two dogs barking fiercely on the marsh near the house. The captain said he believed they had a 'coon in one of the ditches, and proposed that we take a lantern and go for him. So, without waiting to dress ourselves, we each seized a club, and, taking a lantern, went out among the grass to find and kill the 'coon. The dogs still kept up their yelping, and, as we approached, seemed very much excited. Each of us held up our club to strike, while the old man directed the rays of the lantern to light us to the game. Directly the captain stumbled over a dark object just as he brought down his club with a hollow thump on the ribs of some live animal. "It's a bear!" roared out the captain; "look out for him!" "No, it is not," said I, for I had caught the glimpse of a blue blanket; "it's an Indian." "Hit him," says the captain; "curse him—who is he?" "I think," said I, "it's old Colote; but let us see." With that I seized hold of the fellow's hair, and pulled his face up so that we could ascertain, and then found it was Kohpoh, who, on his knees and elbows, was curled up like a hedgehog. We were both very much vexed when we found who it was, for we knew he was there for no good purpose. "I am sorry," said the captain, "I didn't know who it was, for if I had he would have been very likely to have got what I should have given to a bear; and I have a good mind now to give him something, to learn him better than to prowl around here." "Let us first find out what he wants," said I. Kohpoh, who was very much frightened, then told me that he had come down to do some mischief to Peter, but would go home directly if we let him off. He was afraid of the dogs, which was the reason he had hid in the grass. He did not feel at all easy about his ribs from the thump he had received from the captain's cudgel, and was ready to do any thing I should propose for the sake of getting off. I told him to go up and give Peter his blanket as a settlement of their difficulty, and then leave. He did so, and in a few minutes was out of sight, running for dear life.

He did not relish the parting with his blanket, but took occasion to steal it back from Peter a few days afterward; but he was very careful never to come round us again at night, and very seldom dared to come in the daytime.

I frequently went up the river with Peter, either to shoot ducks or to help him about his otter and beaver traps. One day we extended our journey much farther than usual, and on the edge of a marsh or prairie discovered the poles of some Indian's temporary lodge. We paddled up to see what it was, when Peter pronounced it to have been put there by some Klickatat Indians, for that was their style. Peter was very much frightened, and insisted on returning. I asked him who the Klickatats were. He said they were from the interior; that sometimes they came through the woods to Shoal-water Bay while hunting for elk; that they were very hostile to the Bay and Coast Indians, and did not hesitate to murder them and steal their effects. As I had neither heard nor cared about the Klickatats, I thought it very doubtful about their coming over the mountains to Shoal-water Bay when they could have come easier by the Columbia; but he would go no farther, and we returned home.   Here we found Cletheas and his wife, with a relative of theirs, a Cowlitz Indian, who corroborated all Peter's surmises.   He said that during the past summer a party of Klickatats, with whom he was acquainted, had invited him to join them on a hunt, as they wished to go to Shoal-water Bay, and he knew the way better than they did, as he was a hunter, and constantly in the woods between the Cowlitz and the Bay.

They did not appear, however, very anxious to kill any more game than what they wished to eat on the way, and finally told him that their object was to find out how many white persons there were about the Bay; and they actually went to the residence of every white person, and had ascertained the number of inhabitants; and that it was the same party who had put up the lodge-poles Peter and myself had found.   His impression was that they had some hostile feelings against the Indians of the Bay, and had merely taken the account of the whites as a blind to him of their real motives; and that, fearing they meant to do harm to the Indians, he had come down to tell his relatives to be on their guard. Now this might all have been true; but subsequent events have proved to my mind that it was a part of the system of general rising that was about to take place among the Indians, and which did take place the following year; and among the most hostile and ruthless were this very tribe of Klickatats.   And I think the visit of the Cowlitz Indian was to apprise those of the Bay of the move; but when he learned that I had found out about the old lodge-poles, he artfully told his story to me so as to conceal the truth.   At all events, I paid no attention to it one way or the other, and for a time forgot all about it.

As Christmas drew near the game seemed to decrease; and, although we had a plenty of salt salmon and potatoes, we thought we could not celebrate the day without having a goose, or duck, or some kind of a bird; but nothing came near us but crows. The captain said crow was good, so was eagle, so was owl; he reasoned in this manner: A crow, said he, is good, because it has a crop like a hen; and eagles, hawks, and owls are good, for, although they have no crops, yet they do not feed upon carrion. So we addressed ourselves to the subject of procuring a Christmas dinner. Fortunately or unfortunately, I shot a couple of crows. They were very ancient, entirely void of fat, and altogether presented to my mind a sorry picture of a feast. But the captain was delighted. "I will make a sea-pie of them," said he, "and then you can judge what crow-meat is." The birds were cleaned and cut up, and a fine sea-pie made with dumplings, salt pork, potatoes, and a couple of onions. And precisely at meridian on Christmas-day (for the old captain liked to keep up sea-hours), the contents of the iron pot were emptied into a tin pan, and set before us smoking hot.

I tried my best to eat crow, but it was too tough for me. "How do you like it?" said the old man, as, with a desperate effort, he wrenched off a mouthful from a leg. "I am like the man," said I, "who was once placed in the same position: 'I ken eat crow, but hang me if I *hanker* arter it.'" "Well," says the captain, "it *is* somewhat hard; but try some of the soup and dumplings, and don't condemn crow-meat from this trial, for you shot the grandfather and grandmother of the flock: no wonder they are tough; shoot a young one next time." "No more crow-meat for me, thank you," said

I.   So I finished my Christmas dinner on dumplings and potatoes.

The captain was famous for cooking every thing that had ever lived.   We had eaten of young eagles, hawks, owls, lynx, beaver, seal, otter, gulls, pelican, and, finally, wound up with crow ; and the crow was the worst of the lot.   The captain once tried to bake a skunk, but, not having properly cleaned it, it smelt so unsavory when the bake-kettle was opened that he was forced to throw skunk and kettle into the river, which he did with a sigh, remarking what a pity it was that it smelled so strong, when it was baked so nice and brown.   However, the captain could get up some nice messes, and a favorite pudding of his is well worth knowing how to make ; he called it a fisherman's pudding, and it is made thus : Cut some salt pork up fine, and fry it slightly in the kettle or pot you wish to make the pudding in ; then add some boiling water, and stir in as much molasses as will make it pretty sweet.   This is then put on the fire, and, while boiling, Indian meal is to be gently sifted in with one hand, and well stirred in at the same time with a spoon till the whole acquires the proper consistency, and then, after a puff or two, it is cooked.   A hungry man can soon tell whether it tastes good or not.   I always found that the fisherman's pudding was well liked by every one who partook of it, whether white men or Indians.

CHAPTER XIX.

Indian Treaties.—Invitation to be present at a Treaty on the Chehalis
River.—Journey to the Chehalis.—Various Adventures.—We reach
the River and encamp.—A lively Scene going up to the Treaty-ground.
—Description of the Encampment.—Governor Stevens.—Whites
present.—Indians.—Uniform of the Governor.—Colonel Simmons.—
Story-telling.—The Governor backs up my Stories.—Judge Ford.—
Commissary Cushman.—The Treaty.—Indians will not agree to it.—
Number of Indians in the Coast Tribes.—Tleyuk.—Governor takes
away Tleyuk's "Paper."—Indians have no Faith in the Americans.—
The Conduct of the Hudson Bay Company contrasted with that of
the Americans.—We start for Home and encounter a Storm.—Che-
halis River.—Adventures on our Journey home.—Colonel Anderson's
Adventures.

DURING the winter I received from Governor Stevens
a letter inviting me to be present at a meeting to be held
early in the spring on the Chehalis River, for the purpose
of making a treaty with some of the Coast tribes relative
to a purchase of their lands.   This meeting was to take
place at the clearing of a settler about ten miles from the
mouth of the river, and the day designated was the 25th
of February, 1855.   On the 6th day of February a letter was brought to me from Colonel H. D. Cocke, who
was at that time at Gray's Harbor, superintending the
arrangements for the forthcoming meeting.   This letter
informed me that the colonel would meet me at Armstrong's Point on the 24th of the month, and convey me
up the river.   As Doctor Cooper was desirous to go to
Olympia, he concluded this was a very good opportunity
to accompany the governor on his return, and decided to
go with me.   While we were making our arrangements
for leaving, the Indian sub-agent for the southwestern
section of the Territory, Mr. William B. Tappan, arrived,

on his way to the camp.   He had several Indians with
him, and could and should have taken all the Chenooks
and Shoal-water Bay Indians; but, as he had misunderstood his instructions, he refused to have any of them
accompany us except the few he had with him and the
few who lived on the north side of the Bay, whom he
classed as Chehalis Indians.   Among these last were Old
Toke and his family, who at that time lived on the north
side of the Bay, near the house of Mr. J. F. Barrows, who
had settled there during the preceding year.   After we
had made all our arrangements, and engaged the Indians
to take our blankets, we crossed the Bay in Toke's canoe,
and remained all night at Mr. Barrows's house, the Indians going to their lodge.

   After a most hospitable reception and a good night's
sleep, we were all ready for a start by sunrise the following morning.   It was clear, bright, and frosty, with just
enough of a northwest breeze to make quick walking
agreeable.   We were all in the best of spirits, and as
Tappan was full of anecdotes, which he related in a
sprightly manner, we soon got over the walk we had to
take to join the canoes, which the Indians had paddled
round the point some distance ahead, for we preferred the
walk to sitting still in a canoe.   We shortly arrived at
a little creek which runs into the Bay directly at the foot
of the bluff of Cape Shoal-water.   Here the Indians
stopped to haul up their canoes and turn them bottom
up.   Each one was then assigned a portion of the camp
luggage.   We did not have any thing with us except
our blankets and one day's provisions, as the governor
had sent word that a tent and rations would be ready on
our arrival.   When the Indians had fixed their last pack
and tied their last knot, they pronounced themselves to
be ready, and we set off.   We walked so briskly that
we were soon through the woods, and over the plain, and

on to the beautiful beach.   Here we felt the full force of
the sharp, frosty morning breeze, which had the effect to
quicken our steps, although it was by no means very
cold.   The doctor had a double-barreled fowling-piece,
for the purpose of obtaining specimens of birds.   Tappan
and myself had no weapons, either pistol or gun; but one
carried a loaf of bread, and the other some boxes of sardines, for our lunch.   The Indians could not keep up
with us, as they had, besides our blankets, all their own
camp equipage and provisions, and consequently moved
slow.   At noon we halted at the side of a little stream
of fresh water that runs across the sands of the beach,
and having found a big clam-shell, which we used instead of a dipper, sat down on an old spar and took our
dinner, consisting of sardines, bread, and water.   This
brook of water, however, is only fit to use in the winter
months, as during the summer it is very brackish and
unfit to drink.   There is a large quantity of water discharged from it during the rainy season, and at high tide
it is impossible to cross without swimming; but during
the summer, and at low tide, it is nothing but a mere
brook a few inches deep.

While we were waiting, a son of old Carcowan's came
up on horseback.   The doctor instantly made the Indian an offer to hire it, for he alleged that he was quite
tired, and proposed that we should adopt the old plan
of ride and tie.   I told him that he and Tappan might
do the riding and tying, for I preferred to walk.   So,
after finishing our dinner, we moved along.   First the
doctor rode a short distance, and then waited for Tappan to take the steed.   But I soon found they both
began to look blue, for the air was quite keen, and the
horse not very swift, and riding made them feel quite
chilly.   At last Tappan declined riding any more, and
left the animal to the doctor, who finally concluded that

the best way to keep warm was to get off and walk; but his horse did not like being led, and it was with difficulty the doctor could get him along. In the mean time Tappan and myself had walked on, and about three o'clock arrived at the lodge of old Carcowan, which had recently been built near Armstrong's house. Here we found Colonel Cocke and a son of Judge Ford's, who, with a retinue of Indians, were waiting our arrival, and had ready, roasting at the fire, great strips of juicy beef, which they had brought down the Chehalis River. While we were warming ourselves, the doctor arrived with his Rosinante, and we were soon ready for our meal, which consisted of the aforesaid beef, roast potatoes, coffee, and hard bread, and to this Carcowan's wife, Aunt Sally, gave us some fresh-baked bread, just out of the ashes, so we made a very hearty meal. The colonel now proposed that we should at once start for the camp; but, as the Indians had not yet arrived with our blankets, the doctor and myself concluded to wait till they came up, and let the others go. The wind was blowing fresh, and it was quite rough, but they all bundled into a canoe and started. I watched them a while, and at last saw them coming back, and then found that their canoe leaked so badly they could not keep her free. On hauling her out and examining her, they discovered that a knot had been knocked out of her bottom, and the water was coming in so fast that in a short time they would have foundered. But the Indians stopped up the hole with a bunch of grass, and again they were off, and this time with better luck. Gray's Harbor is a rough place usually, but in the winter and spring months it is quite dangerous to cross it in canoes. It is much worse than Shoal-water Bay in this respect, for the channels are so much narrower that the tide rushes in and out with great velocity and turbulence; yet these Indians are so ac-

INSIDE OF AN INDIAN LODGE.

customed to it that they will cross at almost any time in loaded canoes.

It was now our turn to start, and, as the doctor had made a bargain with my quondam friend Caslah′han to take us up the river, we embarked in his canoe, with as many Indians as could stow into her. Caslah han had very high ideas of the worth of his services, and asked some two or three blankets from the doctor and a couple of bags of flour from me; but the doctor told him the governor would settle when we got to camp, and he was satisfied with that promise.

Our canoe was so crowded that she was scarcely out of the water, which occasionally swashed into her, threatening to give us a ducking; but the Indian bailed it out; and, as the canoe was strong, and did not leak a drop, I felt comparatively safe. Caslah′han soon hoisted his sail, and we crossed the Bay in a short time, and entered the mouth of the Chehalis River just about sundown. The tide was now running out strongly, and the Indians concluded to camp for the night, and, having found a suitable place, we went ashore, and were soon joined by two or three other canoes full of Indians.

As usual, the first thing was to kindle a fire, and then the Indians went to work to cook their supper, which culinary operation, being simply to warm some dried salmon over the coals, was soon accomplished. The doctor and myself, for the sake of amusement, cooked some slices of bacon for our supper, but we had eaten so recently that we gave the principal part to the Indians, and then hunted round for a sheltered spot to pass the night. Under the gnarled roots of a great spruce-tree which grew near the edge of the bank, and had been undermined by the water during some freshet, seemed to be just the place, and here we made our bed. First an India-rubber sheet belonging to the doctor was spread, to keep off any dampness from the ground; then some Indian mats on top of that, covered with a blanket, formed a nice, warm, dry bed, and our other blankets and coats furnished the covering. Our pillows were our carpet-bags, and on them we laid our heads, and slept as soundly as possible till daylight, when the bustling of the Indians waked us up, and we found them all ready to start. We had been joined during the night by some fifteen or twenty canoes of different sizes, all filled with men, women, and children.

As soon as we were ready we all started, with a whoop and a yell, without waiting for breakfast, and away we went up stream for the camp. The scene was both novel and interesting to me, and I watched it with a good deal of attention.

The camp was about ten miles distant up the river; and as we could not get any breakfast until we reached there, and the morning at that early hour was quite frosty, the doctor and myself found it difficult to keep warm. But the Indians did not seem to mind it at all; for, excited with the desire to outvie each other in their attempts to be first to camp, they paddled, and screamed, and shouted, and laughed, and cut up all sorts of antics, which served to keep them in a glow. As we approached the camp we all stopped at a bend in the river, about three quarters of a mile distant, when all began to wash their faces, comb their hair, and put on their best clothes. The women got out their bright shawls and dresses, and painted their faces with vermilion, or red ochre, and grease, and decked themselves out with their beads and trinkets, and in about ten minutes we were a gay-looking set; and certainly the appearance of the canoes filled with Indians dressed in their brightest colors was very picturesque, but I should have enjoyed it better had the weather been a little warmer.

CAMP ON THE TREATY GROUND.

About 9 o'clock we reached the camp, very cold and
hungry.   Governor Stevens gave us a cordial welcome,
and, after expressing the gratification he felt at the sight
of so many canoes filled with well-dressed Indians, told
us to go to the camp-fire, where he had ordered a breakfast to be ready for us, and we soon had a hearty meal
of beefsteak, hot biscuit, and coffee, and were then shown
the tent which had been assigned to us, where we proceeded to put ourselves to rights, and then took a look
around to see the lay of the land.

The camp-ground was situated on a bluff bank of the
river, on its south side, about ten miles from Gray's
Harbor, on the claim of Mr. James Pilkington. A space
of two or three acres had been cleared from logs and
brushwood, which had been piled up so as to form an
oblong square.   One great tree, which formed the southern side to the camp, served also as an immense back-
log, against which our great camp-fire, and sundry other
smaller ones, were kindled, both to cook by and to warm
us.   In the centre of the square, and next the river, was
the governor's tent, and between it and the south side
of the ground were the commissary's and other tents, all
ranged in proper order.   Rude tables, laid in open air,
and a huge frame-work of poles, from which hung car-
casses of beef, mutton, deer, elk, and salmon, with a
cloud of wild geese, ducks, and other small game, gave
evidence that the austerities of Lent were not to form
any part of our services.

Around the sides of the square were ranged the tents
and wigwams of the Indians, each tribe having a space
allotted to it.   The Coast Indians were placed at the
lower part of the camp; first the Chenooks, then the
Chehalis, Queniült and Quaitso, Satsop or Satchap, Upper Chehalis, and Cowlitz.   These different tribes had
sent representatives to the council, and there were pres-

P

ent about three hundred and fifty of them, and the best feelings prevailed among all.

The white persons present consisted of only fourteen, viz., Governor Stevens, General George Gibbs (who officiated as secretary to the commission), Judge Ford, with his two sons, who were assistant interpreters, Lieutenant-colonel B. F. Shaw, the chief interpreter, Colonel Simmons and Mr. Tappan, Indian agents, Dr. Cooper, Mr. Pilkington, the owner of the claim, Colonel Cocke, myself, and last, though by no means the least, Cushman, our commissary, orderly sergeant, provost marshal, chief story-teller, factotum, and life of the party—" Long may he wave." Nor must I omit Green M'Cafferty, the cook, whose name had become famous for his exploits in an expedition to Queen Charlotte's Island to rescue some sailors from the Indians. He was a good cook, and kept us well supplied with hot biscuit and roasted potatoes.

The chief interpreter, Colonel Shaw, had not arrived, and the governor concluded to defer the treaty till he came, as he was not only the principal means of communication with the Indians, but was to bring some chiefs with him. Colonel Cocke and a party therefore went down the river to Armstrong's Point to meet him, while we passed the day telling stories and preparing for the morrow.

Our table was spread in the open air, and at breakfast and supper was pretty sure to be covered with frost, but the hot dishes soon cleared that off, and we found the clear fresh breeze very conducive to a good appetite.

After supper we all gathered round the fire to smoke our pipes, toast our feet, and tell stories. While thus engaged, we heard a gun fired down the river, and shortly the party arrived, having Colonel Shaw with them. He had brought a few Cowlitz Indians and a couple of

OUTSIDE OF AN INDIAN LODGE.

Chenooks; but, as he was very tired, he had not much to say that evening, so we shortly went to bed, the doctor, Mr. Tappan, and myself occupying one tent.

The next morning the council was commenced. The Indians were all drawn up in a large circle in front of the governor's tent and around a table on which were placed the articles of treaty and other papers. The governor, General Gibbs, and Colonel Shaw sat at the table, and the rest of the whites were honored with camp-stools, to sit around as a sort of guard, or as a small cloud of witnesses.

Although we had no regimentals on, we were dressed pretty uniform. His excellency the governor was dressed in a red flannel shirt, dark frock-coat and pants, and these last tucked in his boots California fashion; a black felt hat, with, I think, a pipe stuck through the band, and a paper of fine-cut tobacco in his coat pocket.

The pipe being from time immemorial an emblem of peace among savages, we all had ours, not, however, in our hat-bands; but, as we were not expected to speak on the occasion, we preferred them in our mouths. We also were dressed, like the governor, not in ball-room or dress-parade uniform, but in good, warm, serviceable clothes.

After Colonel Mike Simmons, the agent, and, as he has been termed, the Daniel Boone of the Territory, had marshaled the savages into order, an Indian interpreter was selected from each tribe to interpret the Jargon of Shaw into such language as their tribes could understand. The governor then made a speech, which was translated by Colonel Shaw into Jargon, and spoken to the Indians, in the same manner the good old elders of ancient times were accustomed to deacon out the hymns to the congregation. First the governor spoke a few words, then the colonel interpreted, then the Indians; so that this threefold repetition made it rather a lengthy operation. After this speech the Indians were dismissed till the following day, when the treaty was to be read. We were then requested by the governor to explain to those Indians we were acquainted with what he had said, and they seemed very well satisfied. The governor had purchased of Mr. Pilkington a large pile of potatoes, about a hundred bushels, and he told the Indians to help themselves. They made the heap grow small in a short time, each one taking what he required for food; but, lest any one should get an undue share, Commissary Cushman and Colonel Simmons were detailed to stand guard on the potato pile, which they did with the utmost good feeling, keeping the savages in a roar of laughter by their humorous ways.

At night we again gathered round the fire, and the governor requested that we should enliven the time by telling anecdotes, himself setting the example. Governor Stevens has a rich fund of interesting and amusing incidents that he has picked up in his camp life, and a very happy way of relating them. We all were called upon in turn, and when it came mine, I related tales that I supposed none of the party ever had heard; and as I was particular about place and date, some were inclined to think I had actually made them up as I went along; but it appeared that the governor knew some of the parties I was speaking of, and, to my great astonishment, told the doubters that he would vouch for the truth of whatever I had related. That served very well for me; for, no matter how improbable a joke I afterward told, the remark was, "That must be true, for the governor will vouch for it."

There were some tales told of a wild and romantic nature at that camp, and Judge Ford and Colonel Mike did their part. Old frontiersmen and early settlers, they had many a legend to relate of toil, privation, fun, and frolic; but the palm was conceded to Cushman, who certainly could vie with Baron Munchausen or Sinbad the Sailor in his wonderful romances. His imitative powers were great, and he would take off some speaker at a political gathering or a camp-meeting in so ludicrous a style, that even the governor could not preserve his gravity, but would be obliged to join the rest in a general laughing chorus. Whenever Cushman began one of his harangues, he was sure to draw up a crowd of Indians, who seemed to enjoy the fun as much as we, although they could not understand a word he said. He usually wound up by stirring up the fire; and this, blazing up brightly and throwing off a shower of sparks, would light the old forest, making the night look blacker in the distance, and showing out in full relief the dusky, grinning faces of the Indians, with their blankets drawn around them, standing up just outside the circle where we were sitting. Cushman was a most capital man for a camp expedition, always ready, always prompt and good-natured. He said he came from Maine; whether he did or not, he was certainly the main man among us.

General Gibbs, Mr. Tappan, and Dr. Cooper also furnished their share in the entertainment, and a report of the anecdotes told in that camp would make as good a book as Joe Miller's.

The second morning after our arrival the terms of the treaty were made known. This was read line by line by General Gibbs, and then interpreted by Colonel Shaw to the Indians.

The features and provisions of the treaty were these: The Indians were to cede all the territory, commencing on the Pacific coast, at the divide of the Quaitso and Hooch Rivers, thence east between the same, along the line of the Quillahyute tribe, to the summit of the coast range; thence south, along the line of the Chemakum and Skokomish tribes, to the forks of the Satsop River; thence southeasterly, along the lands ceded by the Nisqually Indians, to the summit of the Black Hills, and across the same to the banks of the Skookumchuck Creek; thence up said creek to the summit of the Cascade range; south, along the range, to the divide between the waters of the Cowlitz and Cathlapoodl Rivers; thence southwestwardly to the land of the Upper Chenooks, to the Columbia River, and down that river to the sea. The Indians were to be placed on a reservation between Gray's Harbor and Cape Flattery, and were to be paid for this tract of land forty thousand dollars in different installments. Four thousand dollars in addition was also to be paid them, to enable them to clear and fence in land and cultivate. No spirituous liquors were to be allowed on the reservation; and any Indian who should be guilty of drinking liquor would have his or her annuity withheld.

Schools, carpenters' and blacksmiths' shops were to be furnished by the United States; also a saw-mill, agricultural implements, teachers, and a doctor. All their slaves were to be free, and none afterward to be bought or sold. The Indians, however, were not to be restricted to the reservation, but were to be allowed to procure their food as they had always done, and were at liberty at any time to leave the reservation to trade with or work for the whites.

After this had all been interpreted to them, they were dismissed till the next day, in order that they might talk the matter over together, and have any part explained to them which they did not understand. The following morning the treaty was again read to them after a speech from the governor, but, although they seemed satisfied, they did not perfectly comprehend. The difficulty was in having so many different tribes to talk to at the same time, and being obliged to use the Jargon, which at best is but a poor medium of conveying intelligence. The governor requested any one of them that wished to reply to him. Several of the chiefs spoke, some in Jargon and some in their own tribal language, which would be interpreted into Jargon by one of their people who was conversant with it; so that, what with this diversity of tongues, it was difficult to have the subject properly understood by all. But their speeches finally resulted in one and the same thing, which was that they felt proud to have the governor talk with them; they liked his proposition to buy their land, but they did not want to go on to the reservation. The speech of Narkarty, one of the Chenook chiefs, will convey the idea they all had. "When you first began to speak," said he to the governor, "we did not understand you; it was all dark to us as the night; but now our hearts are enlightened, and what you say is clear to us as the sun.

"We are proud that our great father in Washington thinks of us. We are poor, and can see how much better off the white men are than we are. We are willing to sell our land, but we do not want to go away from our homes.

"Our fathers, and mothers, and ancestors are buried there, and by them we wish to bury our dead and be buried ourselves. We wish, therefore, each to have a place on our own land where we can live, and you may have the rest; but we can't go to the north among the other tribes. We are not friends, and if we went together we should fight, and soon we would all be killed."

This same idea was expressed by all, and repeated every day. The Indians from the interior did not want to go on a reservation with the Coast or Canoe Indians.

The governor certainly erred in judgment in attempt-

P 2

ing to place these five different tribes on the same reservation; but his motive was, that as they were so few, being mere remnants of once powerful bands, it would be better to have them concentrated at one point. They, however, did not think so; their ancient prejudices were as strong as ever, and they well knew that they never could agree to live together. They were willing to concentrate at a given place on their own lands, and it is a pity the governor did not see the benefit that would arise to them by so doing. A hundred Indians, all that remained of the Chenook tribe, if located at any one point, would be in nobody's way, and certainly there is plenty of room in their possessions. So of each of the other tribes.

The whole together only numbered 843 all told, as may be seen by the following census, which was taken on the ground:

Lower Chehalis	217
Upper do.	216
Queniülts	158
Chenooks	112
Cowlitz	140
	843

But, though few in numbers, there were men among them possessed of shrewdness, sense, and great influence. They felt that, although they were few, they were as fully entitled to a separate treaty as the more powerful tribes in the interior. We all reasoned with them to show the kind intentions of the governor, and how much better off they would be if they could content themselves to live in one community; and our appeals were not altogether in vain; several of the tribes consented, and were ready to sign the treaty; and of these the Queniülts were the most prompt, evidently, however, from the fact that the proposed reservation included their land, and they would, consequently, remain at home.

I think the governor would have eventually succeeded in inducing them all to sign had it not been for the son of Carcowan, the old Chehalis chief. This young savage, whose name is Tleyuk, and who was the recognized chief of his tribe, had obtained great influence among all the Coast Indians. He was very willing at first to sign the treaty, provided the governor would select *his* land for the reservation, and make him grand *Tyee*, or chief, over the whole five tribes ; but when he found he could not effect his purpose, he changed his behavior, and we soon found his bad influence among the other Indians, and the meeting broke up that day with marked symptoms of dissatisfaction.. This ill feeling was increased by old Carcowan, who smuggled some whisky into the camp, and made his appearance before the governor quite intoxicated. He was handed over to Provost-marshal Cushman, with orders to keep him quiet till he got sober. The governor was very much incensed at this breach of his orders, for he had expressly forbidden either whites or Indians bringing one drop of liquor into the camp.

The following day Tleyuk stated that he had no faith in any thing the governor said, for he had been told that it was the intention of the United States government to put them all on board steamers, and send them away out of the country, and that the Americans were not their friends. He gave the names of several white persons who had been industrious in circulating these reports to thwart the governor in his plans, and most all of them had been in the employ of the Hudson Bay Company. He was assured that there was no truth in the report, and pretended to be satisfied, but, in reality, was doing all in his power to break up the meeting. That evening the governor called the chiefs into his tent, but to no purpose, for Tleyuk made some insolent remarks, and peremptorily refused to sign the treaty, and, with his people, refused to have any thing to do with it. That night, in his camp, they behaved in a very disorderly manner, firing off guns, shouting, and making a great uproar.

We did not care a pin for their braggadocio, but the governor did; and the next morning, when the camp was called, he gave Tleyuk a severe reprimand, and taking from him his paper which had been given to show that the government recognized him as chief, he tore it to pieces before the assemblage. Tleyuk felt this disgrace very keenly, but said nothing. The paper was to him of great importance, for they all look on a printed or written document as possessing some wonderful charm. The governor then informed them that, as all would not sign the treaty, it was of no effect, and the camp was then broke up.

Throughout the whole of the conference Governor Stevens evinced a degree of forbearance, and a desire to do every thing he could for the benefit of the Indians. Nothing was done in a hurry. We remained in the camp a week, and ample time was given them each day to perfectly understand the views of the governor. The utmost good feeling prevailed, and every day they were induced to some games of sport to keep them good-humored. Some would have races on the river in their canoes, others danced, and others gambled; all was friendly till the last day, when Tleyuk's bad conduct spoiled the whole.

But, although the alleged reason of their refusing to sign the treaty was that they did not want to leave their homes and live on one reservation, yet there were other causes which operated badly. Our whole system of treaty-making is wrong with these frontier Indians. They can not be made to understand why the agents sent to them to make treaties are not empowered to close the bargain at once, instead of referring the matter back to Washington, and waiting the tardy action of government. Many of them had been at the treaty-making a few years before at the mouth of the Columbia, where Dr. Dart attempted to make a purchase of their lands; but he was so totally unfitted for the duties of the office that his treaty was instantly repudiated at Washington, and himself removed. But the Indians had acted in good faith. They told me that they did not offer their lands to Dr. Dart, but he told them he would give them a certain price, which they agreed to, and they could not understand why they did not get what they were told they should receive. Consequently, they regarded Dr. Dart and his treaties as humbugs, and placed no more credit on what Governor Stevens told them than they had on Dr. Dart, when they found that the governor was also obliged to refer his treaties back to Washington, and that it might be possibly two years before they would be finally placed on the reservation.

They contrasted this dilatory policy of the American government with the prompt and decided course of the Hudson Bay Company, and, as a natural conclusion, were led to look upon the governors and factors of the Company as of vastly more importance than either the governor of the Territory or their Great Father at Washington, who is regarded by them as a sort of a myth. They knew, in all their dealings with the Hudson Bay Company officers, that whatever was agreed upon was promptly executed in good faith, whether it was the purchase of a pack of beaver-skins, or a tract of country, or a treaty of peace and friendship. And it is this fact, more than any thing else, that the Hudson Bay Company have had the power to make and execute treaties, without having to refer the matter to the home government of England, or even the provincial government of

Canada, that has enabled them to live for so many years among these Indians in peace and harmony, and to acquire so great an influence over them.

This wise policy should be imitated by our own government so far as to empower the governors and Indian agents to make treaties with Indians that *shall take effect at the time of the agreement*, and this can easily be done. Let Congress ascertain what the Territory is worth, and then appropriate a sum of money to be expended in its purchase, and allow the agents to have the same judgment in the expenditure as is now done to commissioners, either for purchasing a site for a light-house, custom-house, or post-office, or for constructing a military road. It is folly to think of treating with those wild Indians of the Northwest with the same formality we are wont to adopt toward a foreign nation. They know nothing of law or law terms: all they want is to have matters as simple as possible. If they agree to take a stated sum for their lands, they consider the trade the same as to sell a horse, or canoe, or peltry; it is to them nothing more or less than a trade, and they want their money, or blankets, or whatever equivalent that may be agreed upon paid, and the trade closed. This referring back treaties for alteration is particularly disgusting to them, for it never has been known that the Home Department ever have proposed to pay them any more than the agent first agreed to; and I have no hesitation in asserting that, had Congress agreed upon a certain sum to have been paid to extinguish the Indian titles in Washington Territory, and had empowered Governor Stevens, when he first went to the Territory, to have closed all the treaties as soon as he should have made them, he would not only have effected a final settlement with the whole body of Indians in that section of our country amicably, but have made a saving of millions to the Treasury, which will have been expended before the present war is brought to a close. I think Governor Stevens's course admirably adapted to conciliate the Indians, and, although I have asserted that he erred in judgment in wishing to place the five tribes on one reservation, yet his whole thought and object was for their good, and there can be no doubt that, had they acceded to his views, they would have been benefited. And I firmly believe, from what I saw of Governor Stevens during the week we remained at that camp, and from his general feeling toward the Indians, that, had he been allowed to have carried out his plans unmolested or thwarted by any one, there would not have been a hostile blow struck in the Territory. It is to be regretted that men of intelligence and influence should have been found in the Territory willing, rather than side with the governor and assist him, to countenance certain "lewd fellows of the baser sort" to defame, detract, and throw every obstacle in his way.

When it was determined to break up the camp, we prepared ourselves for the journey home. As Dr. Cooper concluded to go up the river, Mr. Tappan and myself were the only white persons of the party who intended returning to Shoal-water Bay. The governor directed Mr. T—— to pay Caslah han for bringing us up, and to make a new bargain with him for our return. The one-eyed savage, who had been making his calculations on receiving sundry blankets and sacks of flour, found himself more than paid by two calico shirts that Mr. Tappan gave him; but, as he had agreed to take what the governor thought proper, he could not complain.

The weather, which had been rainy for the last two days, now gave indications, by the quick-flying scud, and sighing, moaning sound of wind in the tops of the lofty firs, that a southeast storm was fast approaching, but there was no help for us except to start for home; so, taking with us the Chenook and Shoal-water Bay Indians, we filled Caslah'han's big canoe, and proceeded on our course down the river.

The Chehalis River is a fine stream, and navigable for vessels of three or four hundred tons as far as where we had camped, which was called ten miles. The water appears to be quite deep, and at a bend of the river near the camp a perpendicular hill rises very abruptly from the stream, and at its base the water, as I was informed by the Indians, is upward of fifty feet deep. The river widens as it approaches Gray's Harbor, with frequent shoals, and is much obstructed by drift-logs, which, I believe, could very easily be cleared away, rendering the navigation quite easy and safe. Some ten or fifteen miles above our camp are the excellent saw-mills of Mr. Armstrong, where timber of all kinds is sawed in the best manner. The cedar and ash plank, and boat-stuff I have seen from Armstrong's, was equal to any I ever met with, while the fir and spruce lumber can not be surpassed by any mill in the Union. Some of our Eastern mill men would be doubtful about attempting to cut a log of spruce measuring six feet through the centre, but Mr. Armstrong informed me that he had saws capable of performing such work, although, he confessed, he preferred operating on three and four feet logs, as he could handle them easier.

The country along the river toward its mouth is covered with a dense forest of spruce and fir, with here and there little prairie patches of fertile and easily-cultivated land. We passed two or three houses of the white settlers, but they were absent from home, and we hurried along, as we were anxious to get across the Bay before dark, so as to remain at Carcowan's lodge over night, for there was no other place of shelter till we reached Shoal-water Bay; but when we reached the mouth of the river we felt the full force of the southeast wind, which was blowing so strong as to render it extremely hazardous to attempt crossing the Bay.   Some of the Indians who came down at the same time we did went to a little island near the mouth of the river, on the north side, where they camped; but it being out of the way, we crept along the shore toward the south, hoping to find some good place of shelter for the night.   But we were not very fortunate, for we were obliged at last to go ashore on a low, sandy beach, where there were a few stunted pines and low bushes.   We built a fire with difficulty, and, having found some fresh water, managed to get something to eat for supper.

Mr. Tappan had fortunately brought from the camp two or three cans of preserved meat, and the Indians had with them some potatoes and a few dried salmon.   We made a sort of shelter with the canoe sail, and tried to get some sleep; but we had scarcely lain down when a violent squall of wind and rain came up, which demolished our tent, and it was with the greatest difficulty we could keep our blankets around us; so we were obliged to remain all night exposed to the fury of the elements, wet, cold, and miserable.

As soon as the day began to dawn the wind abated, and, although it was still raining, we at once bundled into the canoe and paddled across the Bay, and landed at a marsh, through which we waded, and at last, having reached a piece of upland, stopped to get some breakfast. We had then to walk eighteen miles to reach Shoal-water Bay, and, the tide being up, could not take the beach, but had to keep on the plains, with the full blast of the wind and rain, which had now again commenced with fury, directly in our faces.   We here met some Indians who had camped the previous night on the island at the mouth of the Chehalis River, and learned from them that a doctor of the Chehalis tribe had shot a young chief of the Quaitso Indians out of mere bravado, and because the Quaitso and Queniūlts had been in favor of the treaty. This piece of intelligence did not tend to exhilarate the feelings of the Indians in our party, so we all moved on, very ill at ease, through the wet grass and bushes. At noon we reached the little brook where we had stopped when we went up, and near it found a rude hovel, which had been put up by some Indians while they were boiling out the blubber of a whale which had been thrown ashore by the waves. Into this miserable old shanty we crept, and, having built a fire, made a hearty dinner on our preserved meats. We remained here much longer than we should have done, for, when we reached the creek where the Indians had left their canoes, it was nearly dark. Here the Indians were determined to remain all night and sleep under their canoes; for, although it was only a couple of miles farther to the lodge, they were too tired, and preferred to remain till morning, and then take their canoes home with them.

Tappan and myself had no idea of stopping at that place, and as we knew of a path which Mr. Barrows had made from the beach through the woods to his house, we preferred to go on and get into good quarters. But it soon grew very dark, and, although we could discern the white line of the beach, yet we failed to discover the path, and, consequently, kept on till we reached the end of the point, about a mile out of our course. The route to Mr. Barrows's house was now across a marsh, and through a clump of pines, and we went stumbling along, like the babes in the wood, and, after falling into a couple of ditches, at last reached the pines. Here we shouted and hallooed, but received no answer, and concluded that we had best make a night of it under the trees, when we discovered the glimmer of a light, and soon after reached the house, where we were most hospitably received. It was quite evident why our shouting had not been heard, for, with the aid of a violin and trombone, the family were raising their voices in melody, chanting some pious anthems, for it was Sunday night. It is needless to add how, in that hospitable house, we were speedily made comfortable, and how, after we had congratulated each other on our change of fortune in not having to pass the night in our wet clothes under the bushes, we retired early and were soon asleep.

When Colonel Shaw passed through the Bay on his way to the camp, he had hired a whale-boat at Wilson's portage, which he had hauled up on the beach near the mouth of the Bay. It was Mr. Tappan's intention to have taken the boat back, and carried with him the Indians bound for Chenook; so, the next morning, he started out in search for her, and, after having been absent nearly all day, returned with the report that she was stove to atoms by the waves. The gale now seemed to increase in fury, and for three days we were obliged to remain, without daring to venture across the Bay, till at length we managed to get over in one of the canoes, and I reached home entirely satisfied with my experience, and with no further inclination to go out on another treaty-making expedition during the rainy season.

The travelers about that section of the country frequently had as bad or worse times than I had. Colonel Anderson, the United States marshal, while taking the census of Washington Territory in 1853, related to me his adventures to Shoal-water Bay from the Chehalis River. It was during the last of September that he arrived at the house of Judge Sidney Ford, on the Chehalis River, near the Skookum Chuck Creek. The judge, or, as he was more familiarly called, Uncle Sid, kept a public house on the Cowlitz road, which was the regular mail-route from Olympia to the Columbia River. Uncle Sid is well known throughout the whole Territory as one of the most hospitable men that ever received a weary traveler to his fireside; and many a poor, half-starved emigrant can testify to the kind and generous sympathy with which their wants and sufferings were relieved, with the usual parting remark of the good old judge, "Never mind any pay; I know what it is to be hard up on a journey. Good-by; keep a bright look-out, and good luck to you!"

Judge Ford's universal kind treatment of the Indians won for him their entire confidence, and, during the late disturbances, he has been of great service in maintaining quiet among the turbulent vagabonds that live in the region about him.

When Colonel Anderson had reached Uncle Sid's house, he procured an Indian and a canoe to take him down the river to Gray's Harbor, and as neither himself nor the judge knew much about the route, he concluded it was best to take some provisions, although he was informed that there were settlers near the Bay. However, the judge insisted on giving him some bread and a pair of roast chickens, and with this the colonel left and proceeded to the mouth of the river, where he stopped at the house of a settler; but he found the family almost entirely destitute of provisions; so, sharing his chickens among the children, he started on, taking with him, besides the Indian, a white man, who wished to go to Shoal-water Bay to try and purchase some stores. This man informed the colonel that it was but a short walk to Shoal-water Bay, and that they could easily get across to the settlement, and that there was a house on the beach, near Toke's Point, where they could stop over night.

It was nearly dark when they reached the house, but it was empty; however, they stopped there over night, having nothing for supper but the recollections of the nice chickens they had left with the children; "but," said the colonel, "I felt that I was much more able to go without my supper than the children were, so I went to sleep." The next morning they walked around the beach till they came in sight of the houses on the opposite shore of the Bay, and, building a great fire to attract the attention of the settlers, set off in different directions to procure something to eat.

The colonel tried to find some crabs, but it was too late in the season for them; and, as the Indian was a stranger, he did not know where to look for clams. They found a few berries, with which they kept off the cravings of hunger, and waited all that day, not patiently, but anxiously, for some signs of recognition from the other shore; but no notice was taken of the signals, and they had to pass another night without any thing to eat but berries.

The next morning they began to feel quite anxious, and started off to find something to appease their ravenous appetites. At last the colonel saw a " butter-duck" in a shallow creek, and immediately gave chase to it. These ducks are the black surf-duck (*Fuligula perspicillata*). They rise from the water at all times with difficulty, but in the fall of the year they get so fat that they at times can not fly at all, hence the common name of butter-duck. They are hard to shoot, being expert divers, nor are they good for much when killed, as their flesh is coarse and fishy. The colonel's hunger gave him speed, and knowing if he got the duck ashore it could not fly, he at once rushed into the creek between the bird and deep water. Here a most exciting chase commenced, the duck frequently diving, and the colonel frequently getting ducked by stepping into some unseen hole; but perseverance and hunger enabled him to overcome all obstacles, and he finally got the duck ashore and killed it with a stick. Puffing and blowing, he returned to the fire, when the Indian offered to pick the feathers off; but that was too slow a process for a hungry man, and the quicker method of singeing them in the blaze was adopted. The colonel was so hungry that he could scarcely wait to have it cooked; but, hastily dividing it, they devoured the half-raw meat with great satisfaction. While thus engaged they saw a boat approaching; but the colonel was determined to eat his *butter-duck* after the race he had for it, and when the boat reached the shore he presented a very greasy appearance to the party, who, it appeared, had come over for a few days' shooting. They said they had seen the fire, but supposed it was only Indians, and took no notice of it.

They soon furnished the colonel and his two men with something to eat and drink, and then carried them across the Bay, where, after taking the census, the colonel started for the Columbia; but a southeast rain-storm coming on, he concluded to go as far as the Palux River, and stop with Mr. Brown till fair weather. Here he met with another adventure, which was a common occurrence at that time, and I will let the colonel relate his own story.

" After I had passed three days with the oyster-boys," said he, " where each one tried to outdo the others in hospitalities, I left with Steve Marshall and Big Charley, who were to take me to the portage. As we rounded Goose Point, the wind blew so strong against us that we thought best to run up the Palux to Brown's house, and stop over night. Brown had recently put up a little eight by ten zinc house, and when we reached there he had just finished eating his supper.   It was raining violently, and all our clothes and blankets were wet.

"Brown and his men went to work and cooked us up some supper, while we tried to dry ourselves a little.   It was near nine o'clock when we had finished eating, and while we were preparing to go to sleep we heard through the din of the storm, which was now furious, the sound of voices, and directly a party of four men came in, half famished, and drenched through.   Brown immediately went to work and cooked them a supper, and when we were all again ready to turn in for the night it was nearly twelve o'clock, for we had been talking and smoking with the new-comers.   Well, we had not lain down when another halloo outside announced the arrival of more travelers.   Who can that be, this time of night?   The door opened, and in came old Captain Crocker and Captain Gardiner, who had just arrived from the Columbia, wet through and half starved.   By the time they had eaten and were ready for sleep it was half past two o'clock, and when we did lie down it was pretty close packing, and the heat of the stove, with the steam from our wet clothes, nearly suffocated us.   Sleep was impossible, for Captain Crocker began to relate sea-stories, which that ancient mariner was always ready to do, and kept us awake all the rest of the night.   The howling of the tempest, the rattle of the rain on the zinc house, and the captain's gruff voice, reminded me of Dante's Inferno.   But we survived, and the next afternoon, the weather having cleared off, we took the flood tide and went to the portage, and in a couple of days more, having finished my census-taking, I reached Astoria, where I was glad to lie by a little to get rested."

During the time Colonel Anderson held the office of United States marshal, he probably traveled through Washington Territory more than any other individual, and the anecdotes just related are to show how he, as well as the rest of us, had some rough times during the early settlement of the country.

CHAPTER XX.

The Whale.—Toke in the Whale's Belly.—Blubber Feast.—Doctor Johnson and myself as Counsel.—Higher Law.—Champ's Decision. —Loss of Schooner Empire.—Captain Davis.—Captain Eben P. Baker.—M'Carty's Child among the Indians.—Her Rescue.—Feelings of the Indians toward Whites.—Remarks on the Indian Character.— They can live peaceably with Whites.—Course adopted by the Hudson Bay Company toward Indians.—Suggestions about a System of Sub-agencies.—Correct Views of the Hudson Bay Company respecting Indians.—The Conduct of the Company toward Americans.— They do not wish Americans among them.—History of the Hudson Bay Company and their Proceedings toward Americans.—Cause of the Outbreak among the Indians.—Gold Mines.—General Palmer.— General Wool.—Remarks,. &c.

ABOUT a month after my return from the treaty, a whale was washed ashore on the beach between Toke's Point and Gray's Harbor, and all the Indians about the Bay went to get their share. I had a curiosity to see their method of proceeding, and, accordingly, went to the scene of operations. The whale was a small one, of the humpback species, and had come ashore at the top of high water, and was pretty high up on the beach. The Indians were camped near by, out of the reach of the tide, and were all very busy on my arrival, securing the blubber, either to carry home to their lodges, or boiling it out on the spot, provided they happened to have bladders or barrels to put the oil in. Those who were intending to transport the blubber were hiding it by burying it in the sand till they were ready to go to their homes. This capped the climax of all dirty, greasy, filthy sights I ever saw among Indians. Toke, who was

BLUBBER FEAST.

on the ground early, had taken up a claim near the whale's fore fin, and, having carved out a space to stand in, was securely housed, like Jonah of old, in the whale's belly, his head and arms projecting out between the fish's ribs, while the remainder of the body was hidden in the whale's carcass.   There he was, entirely naked, besmeared with blood and grease, and as happy as possible.   Other Indians were cutting and carving away at the blubber, which they would pack on the backs of their slaves and retainers in pieces of about fifty pounds each, to be carried by them to their respective tents.

Those who were trying out the blubber cut it into strips about two inches wide, one and a half inches thick, and a foot long.   These strips were then thrown into a kettle of boiling water, and as the grease tried out it was skimmed off with clam-shells and thrown into a tub to cool and settle.   It was then carefully skimmed off again, and put into the barrels or bladders for use.   After the strips of blubber have been boiled, they are hung up in the smoke to dry, and are then eaten.   I have tried this sort of food, but must confess that, like crow-meat, "I didn't hanker arter it."   I should as soon attempt making a meal off an old India-rubber shoe, dipped in train oil, as to attempt masticating dried whale's blubber; but the Indians like it, and the whole party, children and all, were besmeared with grease from head to foot, and had a most ancient and fish-like smell about them.

Carcowan's people were present, and Tleyuk had a deal to say about the treaty.   He was very valiant, and assured me that the Indians did not care for the Bostons, and meant to have a fight with them.   I paid no attention to his conversation, as I considered it a mere ebullition of his wrath at the governor for taking away his recognition as chief.

I did not remain many hours about the whale; the sight and smell for about fifteen minutes satisfied me that I had learned all that was worth knowing about the Indian method of procuring whale oil.

Doctor Johnson and myself had, about this time, our fiercest legal conflict before 'Squire Champ. The case was that of "Weldon *versus* Watkins." The doctor considered himself the legal representative of Captain Weldon, who had gone to San Francisco, and Mr. Watkins, who was present, had asked me to aid him in sustaining his case before the learned court. The facts were these: Weldon and Watkins were connected in business so far as related to a saw-mill which Watkins had built and had in operation, but refused to account for, or settle with Weldon. An injunction had been prayed for in the United States Court, but, for some reason unknown to me, had not been granted. Watkins continued to make and sell boards, and Weldon, like Giant Despair in Pilgrim's Progress, bit his nails and gnashed his teeth when he saw the rafts of boards float by his residence without the power either of getting his just dues or of converting the boards to his own use. But soon the fall came, and with it the "latter rain." The higher law prevailed; for, owing to an interposition of Providence and a rise in the creek, the mill was raised from its foundations and floated bodily down the river till it reached the Bay, where it was seized upon by Fiddler Smith and John Green, two men in Weldon's employ, and by them towed to the beach at Weldon's store, and safely made fast. Weldon now had the mill, and Watkins had a pile of lumber. So far, so good. But, at length, Watkins, desirous to move from the Bay, swapped off his boards for oxen, and it was when the raft of boards came down the river that Doctor Johnson and myself were called upon to lay the claims of the several parties before 'Squire Champ.

Every thing had prospered until the raft had nearly crossed the Bay, when, an adverse wind coming up, it was drifted ashore almost in front of the doctor's house, who immediately seized it in the name of his client.

I was requested to appear for the defense, and accordingly met the doctor at old Champ's the next day, when Watkins and all interested were requested to make their plea.

The doctor appeared with his old volume of Iowa statutes, which he read off with a marked emphasis and good punctuation; but Watkins, who had just returned from Olympia, where he had been as our representative to the Territorial Legislature, had brought with him the Laws of the Territory, which we considered of more importance than the Iowa statutes.

Champ heard both sides, and, after taking an hour to consult with himself, announced his decision that he had nothing to do with the case; so Watkins won the boards and paid me. But the doctor was not so well off; for he not only lost his case, but Weldon, on his return, refused to recognize him as counsel, and he got no pay for his trouble.

That made no difference, however, in our friendship, for we were always on the best of terms; and that fall we chose the doctor for our representative to the Territorial Legislature, a post which he filled to the satisfaction of all.

On the third of August, as the schooner Empire was going out of the harbor, on her way to San Francisco, with a load of oysters, she struck on the spit at the north side of the entrance, where she remained fast. It was nearly calm at the time, and the captain, who had traded in the Bay for many voyages, and was a good pilot, thought he could drop out with the tide; but the swell set him on the point, and the schooner was finally lost.

This wreck, and that of the brig Palos, before mentioned, were the only two vessels ever lost in going in or out of the harbor, and both were wrecked in a calm, smooth time, simply because their captains thought there was no danger. Captain Davis, the master of the Empire, then went to San Francisco, and returned on the 13th of September in the schooner Maryland, belonging to the same owners; but he betrayed the trust reposed in him, and on the 20th, after the schooner had her cargo on board, he absconded, taking with him the money he should have used to pay for his cargo. Those persons who had put the oysters on board the vessel then called a meeting, and appointed Captain Eben P. Baker to take the schooner to San Francisco, which he did, and afterward made several successful voyages; but at length, on a voyage from San Francisco to Shoal-water Bay in December, was washed overboard during a gale of wind, and drowned.

I have before remarked on the great value these Indians place in any document, either printed or written, and in one instance I made it of service. M'Carty's little girl, who had been at school with the children of Mr. Holman, and had acquired some knowledge of books, was, on the death of her father, placed with the family of Judge Weston, the probate judge of the county. Her mother did not like to have her there, and managed to get her away, and for many months she had been living with her grandfather's people at Gray's Harbor, and had become in all respects a perfect little squaw. The judge had offered rewards, and had sent people for her several times without effecting any thing. We all thought it a shame that the child should be left with the Indians, but could not do any thing except by force, which we did not feel authorized to attempt. A few days before my leaving the Bay for San Francisco, I found the family of old Carcowan, the grandfather of the child, camped near Russell's house, and the little girl herself playing with some Indian children in a brook near by. I then saw the mother, and asked her why she kept the child away from Mr. Weston, for she would never get any of her father's property if she was always with the Indians, for white people would steal all they could get. She told me that she was ashamed to have her child live with the whites unless she could pay them, but that she had nothing, and therefore kept the child. "The only way," said I, "for you ever to get any thing for the child is to send her back." This she promised to do if I would give her a *paper* or letter to the judge. I promised her I would; but, supposing she had no intention of doing any such thing, I did not write the note, neither did I see them for several days. But it appeared they had been talking the matter over; for when I next met them they asked for the letter, and informed me that they were all going with the child. Finding they were really in earnest, I wrote a letter to the judge stating the facts, and the next day they all went to Chenook. Colonel Stevens, who was going to Astoria, accompanied them, and afterward wrote me that they had given up the child as they had agreed to, and she had been sent to school somewhere up the river. She was a bright, intelligent little girl, and I was glad to learn that she was placed away from the influence of her Indian relatives.

The provisions of Governor Stevens's treaty which he wished to make with the Indians at Chehalis were good, if they could be carried out with the same views with which they were originated. They would have answered exceedingly well for a colony of white emigrants, and, with the intention of civilizing and Christianizing the Indians, they had a most laudable aim; but one great difficulty is, that an Indian is essentially different from a white man in all his habits, customs, feelings, and desires.

They like to have the white men come among them and cultivate lands, and they like to trade with the whites for their commodities, but farther than this they do not want. They neither wish to adopt the white man's style of living, or his language, or religion.

They feel as we would if a foreign people came among us, and attempted to force their customs on us whether we liked them or not. We are willing the foreigners should come, and settle, and live with us; but if they attempted to force upon us their language and religion, and make us leave our old homes and take up new ones, we would certainly rebel; and it would only be by a long intercourse of years that our manners could be made to approximate.

Because we always live in houses, and do our cooking and make our fires where a chimney will carry off the smoke, and always keep our feet and heads protected and our bodies well clothed, and believe in the Christian religion, we think that it is right and proper to teach the Indians to do the same, simply for the reason that we think it for their good.

But they have been educated differently, and believe in building their fires in the centre of their lodges, where the smoke can be of benefit to dry their provisions for the winter. And they think it best at times to go half naked, and for nearly half the year to live in the open air, protected only by rush mats, and to look upon the Christian religion, as taught them by the priest, with its images, and pictures, and symbols, as something very nearly resembling their own Tománawos style of religion; and to the Protestant form of worship, with its appeals to the intellect, instead of graven images of men, and birds, and beasts, as something they can not comprehend, and do not wish to understand.

Take the whole body of American Indians, and consider the immense amount of treasure and blood that has been expended to civilize, to say nothing of Christianizing them, then see how few, how very few have become actually benefited compared with what was to have been expected. The whole nature of the man must undergo a radical change before he can be made even to approximate in his feelings and views with those of the white man. That the Indian can be absorbed into the white race with advantage to the Indian can be shown by the present condition of the Creeks, the Choctaws, and Chickasaws, but it has been brought about by a long series of years, and by a large admixture of white blood with the Indian stock; and they always have been more or less accustomed to agriculture, from having depended upon their corn as a principal means of subsistence; and a change in those tribes to a sort of demi-civilization was much more easily effected than it can be with the buffalo-hunting, salmon-catching, or blubber-eating natives of the Northwest.

It has been supposed by many that the whites and Red Men of the western frontier can not live together in one community in peace; but this is not so, as the course of the Hudson Bay Company will tend to show. That immense monopoly has spread itself all over that great region of the north, from the Pacific to the Atlantic, and for many years has been in constant intercourse with the savage tribes throughout that country, a territory larger than the whole of the United States, and, instead of wars of extermination or constant border raids and feuds, a lasting friendship has been maintained, which appears to grow stronger every day. And the cause of this is very evident, and seems to me to point out a way by which the Americans can live in peace with these tribes, for we must recollect that we are now on the Pacific shore, and

Q 2

there is no farther retreat to the west to which the Indian can be removed.   The secret of the success of the Hudson Bay Company in its friendly attempts with the Indian is that they have always impressed him with the belief that he is of some importance to them.   He procures for them their furs, and they, in return, give him such articles of barter as he may wish, and each, feeling the benefit the other is to him, wishes to be at peace. It is undoubtedly a very selfish kind of friendship, but it is no less a true one.   We, of course, can not expect every American settler to be a fur-trader or a shopkeeper, for the great body of emigrants across the Rocky Mountains are farmers; but the idea of making the Indians useful can be carried out, I think, with success.

It is erroneously supposed by some that an Indian is only fit to labor, and that labor to be agricultural; but constant labor of any kind is entirely repugnant to his nature; and, although I have always found them ready to work for the whites when they are paid, yet they can not and will not work like a white man; every thing they do, from paddling a canoe to hunting an elk or building a canoe, is done by sudden fits and starts.   An Indian, if put in a field to work, will do so with the greatest energy for ten or fifteen minutes, and then must sit still an hour to rest himself.   White men, who do not understand them, call them lazy, and wish nothing to do with them; say they are of no account, and not worth keeping.

Still, much work can be got out of an Indian by encouragement and praise.   Show them how you wish a piece of work done, and praise them when they have finished, and they are, just like children, very easily induced to try again; but scold, find fault, or blame an Indian, and he is done; you get no more work from him till his temper is sweetened.

Agricultural labor is not that kind best suited for an Indian; he likes something which taxes his ingenuity. He will spend whole days in fashioning a paddle or a spear, or taking the lock of his gun to pieces, just for the amusement of cleaning it and screwing it together again. Those that I have seen were fond of using tools, and readily learned the use of axe, and saw, and plane; and, whenever they had an opportunity, were fond of forging knives and daggers from files and rasps, and could easily do many simple kinds of blacksmith work.* But, although they are ready to work for the whites, I never saw them willing to work for themselves, and it is folly to place a body of Indians on a reservation with the expectation that they are going immediately to work as white men. They do not seem to appreciate the benefit of a division of labor. Each one works by himself and for himself. If he is making a canoe, no one but his slaves will help him, unless he pays them; so if he wishes to plant potatoes or make a net. This peculiar feeling was exhibited to us in their method of dealing for their oysters. Instead of several joining together and filling a canoe, and equally dividing the proceeds, each one works for himself, and must be paid for what he may have procured; so with their salmon. I have frequently had a canoe containing three or four Indians, and perhaps a hundred salmon in one pile: and when they were taken out, each man knew his own by some mark he had put upon it, and they would first have to

---

* I have noticed one peculiarity in an Indian's method of using tools. They never cut *from* them while using a knife, as we do while whittling, but invariably cut *toward* themselves, holding a stick as we would a quill while making a pen; or, when the wood is too large to hold in that manner, they will work with a knife as we would with a draw-shave. They also prefer to sit upon the ground while at work rather than stand up, and invariably do so when engaged in any kind of work which will permit them to be seated.

be assorted into separate heaps, and a trade made with each owner for his respective share. They would not, if placed in villages or communities by themselves, be any other than what they now are, without the presence of whites among them to give encouragement to their labors.

The Hudson Bay Company, in their treatment of the Indians, have combined and reconciled policy with humanity. Their prohibition to supply them with ardent spirits appears to have been in all cases rigidly enforced; and, although many of the employés of the company have furnished the Indians at times with spirits, yet such servants have invariably been dismissed or degraded when found out. Encouragement is also held out by the Company to induce their people, who are mostly French Canadians, to intermarry with the native women, as a means of securing the friendship and trade of the different tribes.

As there are, or rather were, few or no white women in those Territories, it will be easily seen that a great many half breeds are now growing up, who will in time form an important part of the population. The Company afford means for the education of these half-breed children, and, as far as possible, retain them among the whites ; and, wherever found capable, give them employ in the service of the Company.

Many of the former employés of the Company, who have retired from service, have taken farms, where they have successfully reared the half-breed children, and some of them have good educations and are well accomplished. These people are generally surrounded by the Indian relatives of their wives, and the force of their example is seen gradually to operate on the savages. Their natural shyness and distrust of the white man has been in a great degree removed. They have abandoned

the use of all their former arms, hunting and fishing implements, and the use of skins and furs for articles of
dress, and now depend entirely upon the guns and ammunition, fish-hooks, blankets, and calico which they receive in trade with the whites.   They have all been educated to look upon the Hudson Bay Company and its
officials as a great and powerful people, who are their
best friends, who treat them the best, pay them the best
prices for their furs, and who give them the best articles
in return; and the long intercourse they have had with
the Company, and the constant use of fire-arms, have
made them, what they really are, a formidable foe.   It
might be supposed that these Indians, who have acquired some habits of industry from their intercourse
with the whites, would be inclined to do something for
themselves; but I have always remarked that, when
they are removed from the white people and get together, they invariably return to their vagabond, wandering
life.

The conduct of the Hudson Bay people, in their treatment of the Indians, is certainly worthy of commenda-
tion.   But it should be remembered that their object is
not one of a missionary nature, and that, of the immense
territory placed under their authority, they care to devote
but a small portion to agriculture.   What they desire
to obtain are the furs; and as those articles can be procured in greater quantities and at a less cost by the Indians than by any other means, there is a direct and evident motive of interest to preserve and conciliate them,
and they certainly have employed the best methods to
attain those ends.   It is neither the policy or object of
our government to encourage a monopoly like the Hudson Bay Company, or to make a trade themselves, but I
think a system could be introduced by which the evidently excellent method of the Hudson Bay Company

and the Indian sub-agency, could be so combined as to produce the same effect. If the Indians are to be placed on a reservation, with the mill and blacksmith shop, and other adjuncts of civilization, as proposed by Governor Stevens, let there be a resident sub-agent at every reservation, and let that agent be allowed to keep a stock of such articles as the Indians need, and encourage them to bring in furs, or perform work, or learn to be mechanics, and always be ready to pay them for any work done. The mere paying the Indians an annuity, either in money or merchandise, amounts to nothing, so far as any good is expected to be derived toward civilizing them. In fact, it rather encourages idleness among them, and they are almost certain to barter off their annuities for such articles as they may prefer.

It is of little use to place Indians on reservations, and commence to civilize them by means of schoolmasters and missionaries, unless they can find that they are gaining something. Tell an Indian that he must go to work for himself, and it will be a good thing, and he simply will not believe a word about it; but if he knows that with the product of his labor he can go to the store and procure what he desires, he will not only go to work, but will then be ready to be taught some new ideas, with the hope that he can get more articles in trade. What he considers a good thing is something real, tangible, that he can take hold of and call his own. A good heart the missionary tells him of is very well, but a good blanket or a gun is better.

Some persons, and even members of Congress, think that whipping is a very good remedial means to apply to civilize the Indians; others, that the Indian is only fit for whisky-drinking. But there seems to be no particular necessity either for exterminating them by war or whisky just at present.

The course pursued by the Hudson Bay Company shows that they understand the Indian character to perfection; and if, by adopting some of their views, our government can bring about a state of feeling among our own Indians similar to those of the tribes in British North America toward the Hudson Bay Company, it would seem to be worthy the trial, and would be productive of good both to the Indian and our own people.

The Hudson Bay Company have no false, romantic ideas of Indians, or that bogus species of philanthropy which, looking upon an Indian or a negro as the brother and equal of a white man, thinks that he is capable of being treated in all respects like one, and thereupon wishes to teach him views and place him in positions for which he is not qualified. They look upon an Indian simply as he is—a wild savage, but a man who has rights which they take care to respect. That they do this for motives of gain is unquestionable; but the results have shown that they were correct, and that much good has been accomplished by their means.

But, though the course of the Hudson Bay Company toward the Indians has been commendable, their treatment of American citizens in the territory west of the Rocky Mountains, although equally politic, has not been equally unexceptionable. The British, represented first by the Northwest Company, and afterward by the Hudson Bay Company, have enjoyed the quiet and almost exclusive use of the Columbia regions from 1814 to 1840.

That the people of the United States did not participate in those advantages, doubtless arose from the circumstance that they could render their exertions more productive elsewhere, and also, probably, because their government, from its nature, could not afford them assurances and facilities for organization similar to those which have imparted so much vigor and efficiency to the operations of the British.

But when the tide of emigration began to turn toward the Columbia, it was viewed by the Hudson Bay Company with no very favorable eye. True, all the missionaries, and those who wished to settle for farming purposes, were hospitably received, and aided so far and so long as their objects were not of a commercial nature. Yet, if any one not connected with the Company attempted to hunt, or trap, or trade with the natives, then all the force of that body was turned toward him. Violent means were not used, for it was unnecessary on the part of the Company, from its great advantages of wealth and knowledge of the country by its agents. But, wherever the Americans attempted to establish a post or to engage in trade on the Columbia, an agent of the Hudson Bay has soon appeared in that quarter with a party of hunters, or with specie or merchandise to be given to the Indians in exchange for furs at rates so much less than the Americans could sell at, that they were soon driven off the field.

The Columbia River and its tributaries, and the rich country it drains, has always been regarded by this grasping monopoly as a country peculiarly their own, and, when the treaty between the United States and Great Britain, fixing the northwestern boundary, was concluded (June 15th, 1846), instead of retiring as they should, and as they have announced they intended doing, to their possessions north of the boundary-line, they are still remaining as an incubus on the prosperity of the Territory, waiting to extort from the American government a fabulous price for their old log forts and rotten trading-houses, and, through their employés, or those formerly in their employ, seeking to poison the minds of the Indians against the Americans, and with what success can be read in the annals of the Indian war.

Greenhow remarks that " the publications of the directors and agents of the Hudson Bay Company evince the most hostile feelings toward citizens of the United States, against whom every species of calumny is leveled in those works, as may be evinced in a History of the Oregon Territory and British American Fur Trade, by John Dunn (8vo, London, 1844); a compound of ridiculous blunders, vulgar ribaldry, and infamous calumnies. In blind and ferocious hatred of the Americans, Mr. Dunn, ex-storekeeper at Fort Vancouver, may claim equality with Lord Sydenham, formerly Captain General of Canada."

The governors and factors of the company are very ready to extend their hospitalities to any gentlemen visiting them, and are particular in their attentions to officials.

Wilkes, during his visit to Oregon, while on his exploring expedition, was very courteously received, and expresses his great astonishment how such generous people should be so unpopular among the settlers.

The principal objection against this Company remaining in Washington Territory is not that they are English or Scotch men, for any foreigner has the right to enter and trade in any part of the United States or its Territories, provided they obey our laws; but it is from the fact that this powerful company of British subjects should be able, by an English charter, to monopolize the whole Northwest trade; and that, while they are ostensibly American citizens, and take an interest in our political affairs in the Territory, they are, *de facto*, the subjects of the English government, considering themselves at all times responsible and amenable to the British laws, which are administered by their own officers either at their head-quarters in Montreal or London.

The Hudson Bay Company was first chartered by

Charles II., King of England, on the 16th of May, 1669, who granted to Prince Rupert and seventeen others, who were incorporated as *The Governor and Company of Adventurers of England trading into Hudson's Bay*, " the exclusive right and privilege of the whole trade and commerce of all those seas, straits, lakes, creeks, and sounds, in whatsoever latitude they shall be, that lie within the straits commonly called Hudson's Straits, together with all the lands, countries, and territories upon the coasts and confines of the seas, straits, lakes, bays, &c., &c., which are not now in possession of any of our subjects, or of the subjects of any other Christian prince or state." And the company were empowered to " send ships and to build fortifications for the defense of its possessions, as well as to make war or peace with all nations or people, *not Christian*, inhabiting those territories, which are declared henceforth " to be reckoned and reputed as one of his majesty's plantations or colonies in America called Rupert's Land."

This charter, it will be seen, gave the Hudson Bay Company almost sovereign powers over the vast portion of America drained by streams entering Hudson's Bay.

In July, 1821, an act was passed in Parliament " for regulating the fur-trade, and establishing civil and criminal jurisdiction within certain parts of North America." Shortly after the passage of this act, and in December of the same year, the king made a " grant of the exclusive trade with the Indians of North America to the Hudson Bay Company;" and about this time the Northwest Company had been merged into the Hudson Bay Company, and both were afterward known by the latter title.

In 1838 the company relinquished their charter and received a new one, entitled " Crown grant to the Hudson Bay Company for the exclusive trade with the Indians in certain parts of North America for a term of

twenty-one years, and upon surrender of a former grant."
This charter is the one under which the Hudson Bay
Company at present are operating, and which, it will be
seen, expires by limitation in 1858.   It is a source of
gratification to the people of Washington Territory to
know that the Canadian government are taking an active
part to have this odious monopoly broken up, and it is
to be hoped that, at the expiration of its present charter,
the English government will have the wisdom to throw
open the trade of that vast region to every one disposed
to enter into it.

I have before remarked on the influence this Company
have over the Indians, and I will now proceed to show
what were the causes of the Indian outbreak, and how
far the Hudson Bay Company may be said to have been
connected with it.*

It has been shown that, at the time of the commencement of the emigration of 1840, and for many years pri-
or, the almost sole occupants of the Columbia regions,
besides the Indians, were the Hudson Bay Company's
people, either those in actual service or their retired servants, who had made settlements in various places, but
principally in the Willamette Valley.   All these people,
and also the Indians, had been brought up in the belief
that the Hudson Bay Company was an actual independ-
ent government, as much so as the American government, and that the English were their powerful allies, to
whom at all times they could look for assistance in times
of need.   That they had powers over lands, and jurisdiction in civil and criminal cases, they knew from their
own experience; and, in fact, these people all looked up

* The reader is referred to the letter of General Gibbs, in the Appendix, for an exposition of his views on the subject of the Indian war.
General Gibbs's letter was addressed to me, but was not received in time
to be inserted in the text.

to the Company as their friends and protectors. On the other hand, the officers of the company looked upon the many advantages to be derived from the occupancy of the Columbia country, with a just appreciation of their merits, and were not at all anxious to have such rich possessions pass out of their hands. The treaty between Great Britain and the United States, by which all this territory was ceded to the latter, they cared nothing about so long as the United States assumed no jurisdiction over them, and they had seen how easy it had been for them to keep away American traders. The early emigrants across the Rocky Mountains were not of a character to impress them with any fear of opposition on their part, nor were they of a class calculated to inspire confidence or respect among the Indians. They were either farmers from the frontiers of Missouri, Iowa, or Wisconsin, who had no use for an Indian and never wished to see one, or else they were a set of lawless vagabond trappers and hunters, who, from their childhood, had been taught to look upon a savage as a wild beast to be shot down on every opportunity, and they were never slow to express their views on every occasion where their feelings were roused, both by words and action. It is very true that the colonies founded in 1834, in the Willamette Valley, and those afterward founded in the Walla Walla and Spokan countries, were composed of people who formed schools and churches, and tried to induce the Indian to become civilized and Christianized, and undoubtedly with many good results; but the Company did not care for these Christian emigrants, for they did not come to trade with the natives; the objection was not against them; but they came with the other emigrants who crossed the plains, and were classed by the Indians as belonging to them, and were all looked upon as *Bostons* in contradistinction to the Hudson Bay or *King George* people.

As the country became more settled, another class of men arrived, the trading, swapping representatives of the universal Yankee nation. These men had an entirely different style of trading from that of the Company's agents; for, while the latter have a regular, uniform price for their commodities, the former were accustomed to trade on the peddler system of each man for himself, and, of course, no two could be found to trade alike. Still, the Indians liked to trade with them, for they kept one article, in great demand, which the Hudson Bay people did not sell, and that was whisky. Reckless, worthless men, who are always to be found in a new settlement, would give or sell whisky to the Indians, and then, when drunk, abuse them. If the injury was of a serious nature, the Indian would be sure to have revenge, and, should he kill a white man, would be certainly hanged if caught; but, although the same law operated on the whites, I have never known an instance where a white man has been hanged for killing an Indian. The ill feeling thus engendered against the Americans by this and other causes was continually fanned and kept alive by the half-breeds and old servants of the Company, whose feelings were irritated at what they considered an unwarrantable assumption on the part of these settlers in coming across the mountains to squat upon lands they considered theirs by right of prior occupancy. The officers of the Company also sympathized with their old servants in this respect, and a deadly feeling of hatred has existed between these officers and the American emigrants for their course in taking possession of the lands claimed by the Puget Sound Agricultural Company, and other places on the Sound and the Columbia River; and there is not a man of influence among them who would not be glad to have had every American emigrant driven out of the country. Although they had too much policy to openly avow their sentiments in such a manner as to be traced home to them, their mouth-pieces, their servants and menials, but too well sounded forth the sentiments of their masters.

This state of angry feeling has been the occasion of speeches in Congress, violent denunciation by the Territorial press, and tedious and vexatious lawsuits.* Every man among the Company's people has looked upon the advent of the Americans as a horde of barbarians

* The following extract from the proceedings of the Legislature of Washington Territory in 1855, will show the state of feeling to which reference has been made:

"Memorial of the Legislature of Washington Territory to Congress, in relation to the Hudson Bay and Puget Sound Agricultural Companies, passed January 19th, 1855.

" *To the Honorable the Senate and House of Representatives of the United States, in Congress assembled:*

"Your memorialists, the Legislative Assembly of the Territory of Washington, respectfully represent, that the claims to portions of our Territory set up by the Hudson Bay and Puget Sound Agricultural Companies, under the treaty of 1846, are seriously retarding the growth and prospects of our Territory, and doing great injustice to our citizens.

"Your memorialists do not desire to argue the validity of the claims of either of these companies; all they are entitled to they wish them to have. But they most earnestly desire that their claims shall be settled, rendered definite and certain; for, as they now stand, with their claims extending over an indefinite extent of country, unmarked by any boundary, and those claims not asserted until some emigrant locates and improves, they hang like an incubus upon the best interests of the Territory. Your memorialists would therefore most respectfully pray that some steps may be taken, and that speedily, by which our Territory shall be freed from this deadly Upas, beneath whose branches every thing in our midst withers and dies.   *   *   *   *

"The best interests of the Territory, as well as the peace and quietude of the citizens, demand that something should be done upon this subject. Suits are now pending, and more in readiness to be brought in our courts, for trespasses by the citizens upon the unmarked, undefined, and unoccupied lands of these companies. Thus they prevent the valuable improvement of the country by others, and fail and refuse to make it by themselves.

"Your memorialists might cite numerous private and individual instances of injury and hardship caused by the uncertainty of the claims of these companies among us, but they deem it unnecessary."

who have come to rob them of their just rights; for it must be observed that almost all the Company's employés are ignorant men, who do not or will not understand by what right the Americans can settle in *their* territory and drive them away, or else make them become American citizens. Hence the feeling evinced by such men as Captain Scarborough, and others of influence among the Indians and lower order of whites.

The constant comparison was made that the Bostons, as the Americans are called, were *cultus tillicums*, mean, common, or trifling people; while the *King George*, or English, were *hyas tyee*, or great chief people, or persons of importance. Even articles of trade, blankets, calicoes, and other things, were the objects of invidious comparison. Whoever has traded with an Indian in the Territory must have often heard the remark, "*Wake close okoke Boston mámoke, wake car'qua King George, quánisum close kon'away icktas King George mámoke—* This is not good, this American manufacture; it is not like the English; that is always good."

But, although these people took good care to talk civilly to the Americans, they seldom failed, when by themselves, to curse the Yankees, and compare the state of things with the good old times when the Company held absolute control.

Some of them were active in advising the Indians not to make treaties with Governor Stevens, telling them the most fabulous tales of the designs of the Americans to drive them all out of the country. Although there was no positive proof that could be had against such persons (for an Indian's evidence is not taken), yet there exists no doubt upon the minds of all well-informed persons of the fact that the advice of these people to the Indians has operated very unfavorably toward the treaties of Governor Stevens.

It soon became apparent to the Hudson Bay Company that it was useless for them to attempt to withstand the tide of American emigration. They saw that, with the advent of the Americans, their trade with the Indians was interfered with, and that themselves were in very bad odor with a majority of the settlers. Many of their servants also deserted to get higher wages, which were readily obtained in all the American towns and settlements; so it was concluded to sell out to the United States, and retire north of the boundary-line so soon as a settlement could be effected. The fact that the Company were about to remove from the Territory, and intended closing up their affairs there, was well known and talked about by the Indians and by those of the former servants who had permanently settled themselves on farms. To all these people, the idea of the Company's removing seemed like the breaking up of old associations, and the severing the bonds of an ancient friendship. Nor did they like the idea of having the Indians placed on reservations. They wanted the Indians to remain with them, and consequently were busy in circulating their reports unfavorable to the Americans and favoring the English. The Indians also were, as a general thing, opposed to going on the reservations, both from a natural repugnance and from the advice of those who wished them to remain in their old homes.

Neither had they any faith in the treaties, as they had seen how little reliance was placed on all that had been before attempted to be concluded with them, a fact also constantly brought up by these servants of the Company in drawing their comparisons between the actions of the "Bostons" and "King George" people. They were undoubtedly correct in that respect, for all former treaties had been repudiated by Congress, the stupidity of the agents rendering them incompetent either to draw up a proper document or to negotiate one when drawn.

After my return from the treaty on the Chehalis, in February (1855), I was constantly hearing these tales from the Indians.   Carcowan and his people always had plenty of them to tell, and frequently that old savage has remarked that the King George people would help them to drive off the Bostons.

That the Company did furnish them with guns and ammunition is notorious to every one; but, in justice to them, I must add, that after the war actually commenced they stopped the sale of fire-arms and powder to the Indians within the limits of the Territory.

I was astonished at the regularity with which the Coast Indians received information of the occurrences taking place in the interior; but, as I placed no dependence on what the Indians reported (for we had not heard, except by them, of any trouble among the miners), I took but little notice.   But after my leaving the Bay, in October, 1855, I learned that all the stories told me by the Indians were true, and I was satisfied that a regular communication had been kept up by all the tribes of the Territory for a long time.   This state of feeling between the Hudson Bay servants, half-breeds, and Indians, and the Americans, had existed, as I have shown, for several years, but the immediate cause of the outbreak was the discovery of the gold at Fort Colville, and the consequent rush of the miners to that point.   Fort Colville is near the forty-ninth parallel, and consequently close to the Company's territorial possessions north of that boundary.

The news of this discovery was brought by some Nez Percé Indians, who every year visit the Dalles and Lower Columbia to sell horses.   A number of the retired servants of the Hudson Bay Company who had

R

intermarried with this tribe had settled in the Willamette Valley, and to these persons the Indians communicated the intelligence of the gold discovery. These settlers, who were mostly French Canadians, immediately left their farms and stock, and went off for the mines. The news soon spread, and a general rush took place. Thousands—some with tools and provisions, and some without either—left for the new El Dorado, and at one time it seemed as if there was a new California about being established.

The Hudson Bay Company did not at all like this movement on the part of the Americans. They did not object to French or English people, but the trading, swapping Yankee, who has always a stock of goods with him to "operate" with, was what they could not brook. They had always, before this, found no difficulty in keeping the Yankee traders at bay, but they now came like a swarm of locusts, and, instead of wishing to trade at the fort, almost every man was a trader. It is folly for any one to say that the Company did not want the trade and consequent gold of that multitude of miners; for, if they did not wish for trade, why do they remain in the Territory, like the dog in the manger, and prevent those from trading who wish?

Therefore what few expressions they did let fall served as sparks to powder, to induce the Indians, who were all ready to commence for themselves, to begin hostilities.

"The first blood that was shed in Washington Territory," says Colonel Anderson, in his speech before the House of Representatives, in Congress, on the 6th of August, 1856, "was that of a miner, who, in August, 1855, was on his way from Puget Sound to Fort Colville, having with him a good deal of money, provisions, etc. Soon after passing beyond the limits of the Yakamas, he was pursued by a party of Indians, massacred, and robbed of every thing he had with him.   Shortly after, other murders were reported to have been committed in the Yakama country.   In September, Indian Agent Bolon went into that country to ascertain something about these outrages, and he too was not permitted to return.   He was murdered in the most cruel manner.   When this occurred, there was no escaping the conviction that a general outbreak had been determined on by the Indians."

General Palmer, Superintendent of Indian affairs for Oregon, who went to the Dalles shortly after the death of Bolon for the express purpose of collecting reliable information in relation to the causes of the outbreak, says, in an official communication to the Indian Department, on the 25th of October, 1855, " The evidences of a deep-rooted prejudice against our citizens prevail among all our tribes in Middle and Upper Oregon, the Nez Percés excepted.   How far that feeling may be fanned and kept alive by *aliens* from other countries and their descendants, we are not able to judge, but *that it does extend to the entire exclusion and occupancy of the country by our own citizens is a fact undeniable.*" Captain Cain also wrote to the Commissioner for Indian Affairs, on the 22d of November, " There is abundant evidence to my mind that this war has been contemplated by the Indians for the last three or four years, and I will take the proper steps to obtain the testimony, and submit it to your consideration at the earliest moment."

I think I have shown the causes that have produced a state of feeling that would prompt the Indians to take the field against us ; and I think the officers of the Hudson Bay Company in the Territory, although no *proof* can be adduced to show that they, as a *Company*, have induced this state of things, yet they knew the feelings of the Indians toward the Americans, and they are morally responsible for not using the great influence they possess over the savages not only to have prevented this trouble at its incipiency, but to have advised the Indians to agree to Governor Stevens's propositions for treaties. It is a very significant fact that not a single English or Frenchman, or any one having to do with the Company, was murdered; it was invariably the Americans; and a party, on their way from the mines, were saved from massacre by having with them a couple of French half-breeds, who passed them off as English or King George people.*

My conclusions as to the existence of the bad feeling toward the Americans have been drawn from my own observations during my residence at Shoal-water Bay for three years. All the Indians I met with there had been accustomed to trade with the Company's agents until the oystermen of the Bay wished their services; and the conversations I have had with them at various times invariably showed a preference for the Company's people. There were also, at the mouth of the Columbia and about the Bay, persons who had been in the employ of the Hudson Bay Company in various capacities, and who were always ready to draw comparisons favorable to their former employers. It is perfectly natural such feelings should exist, and it is to be wondered at why this primary cause of difficulty should have been overlooked by General Wool, the commander of the forces on the Pacific, and the whole trouble be charged to a rapacious spirit of the settlers, who were accused by him of bringing about the war for the purpose of supplying forage to the

---

* It should be remembered that the exemption of the French and English from attack by the Indians was at the *beginning* of the Indian troubles. Since that time the Indians do not appear to be very particular whose scalp they get, provided it is a white man's.

United States troops.   Had he been as ready to search into facts as he was to become a "swift witness" against a whole community, far different results might have ensued.

At the time of the commencement of hostilities, Governor Stevens, with his party, was among the Black Feet Indians, east of the Rocky Mountains, and by the outbreak was cut off from all communication with Olympia, the seat of government.   The duty then devolved on Mr. Mason, the Secretary of the Territory, who was officiating as acting governor.   Mr. Mason informed the government at Washington of the existing state of affairs, and of his want of men and means, and orders were immediately issued to General Wool, then at San Francisco, to proceed at once to the scene of difficulties.

General Wool, with a lamentable ignorance of the topography of the country, issued a proclamation, in which he states that he intends "making his saddle his headquarters," and at once set off with a most commendable zeal for Fort Vancouver, on the Columbia River.   But on his arrival he found matters far different from his expectations.   A very severe winter had set in—in fact, the coldest that had been known for years, and the communication with the interior of the Territory and its more remote borders was for a time suspended.   There was no trouble in the immediate vicinity of Fort Vancouver, and but very few Indians, and those friendly, were to be seen.

General Wool now took the advice of parties who did not state to him the real condition of affairs; but he saw that he could be of no service by camping out on his saddle, so he returned to San Francisco, where he commenced writing his letters against the governors and people of both Oregon and Washington Territories.

The fact seemed to be entirely lost sight of that this

Indian trouble was commenced on the border between ourselves and a foreign state, and that the same influences were brought to bear that were used in all our border trouble with our northern neighbors—that of inciting a feeling among the Indians invidious to the Americans.   It would have been possibly a part of wisdom to have secured the good feeling and hearty co-operation of the Hudson Bay officials, who, by their influence, would have been far more effective than the troops which were kept quartered at Fort Vancouver.   It certainly is unfortunate that General Wool did not consult and advise with Governors Curry and Stevens, who, from their official positions and vastly superior knowledge, both of the country and the character of the Indians, could have given him sound and sensible advice.   Be that as it may, one thing is now certain: that no lasting, permanent peace can be maintained with those Indians until they are thoroughly subdued.   What was intended to have been effected by treaties must now be done by force; nor am I alone in this opinion.

General Gibbs, in a letter to me dated at Fort Steilacoom, Washington Territory, July 31, 1856, writes: "There is still no hope of a permanent peace here till one is concluded on the other (eastern) side the Cascade Mountains, and *you* know enough of Indians to know that a peace can not be made permanent till they are subdued.   *   *   *   The incompetency, or willful and obstinate inefficiency of General Wool paralyzed all operations in the country east of the Mountains during the past winter."   General Lane, of Oregon, in his remarks before Congress on the 7th of May, 1856, says: "The general (Wool) is mistaken in his information.   He has not examined the geography of the country.   He has been grossly deceived."

It is not my purpose to enter into a dissertation of

occurrences of this war since its commencement, but to record my own belief that the charges brought against the Oregon and Washington people having originated this war for their own selfish ends are wholly and unqualifiedly false; and that, as Colonel Anderson remarked in Congress (August 6th, 1856), "there is not the first shadow of a foundation or the first scintilla of evidence to substantiate them."

But while I thus record my views in the one case, I am no apologist, on the other hand, for any acts committed by settlers which have served to widen the breach between the Americans and Indians. That such acts have been committed does not admit of doubt; neither is it untrue that many persons have been glad of the war, that they "might furnish forage to the troops, and looked upon such an opportunity as a God-send." There always are people in every country glad of such chances to enrich themselves, but such things are an effect, not the cause, of the war; and General Wool has certainly been very much mistaken when he denounces a whole people as originating the unhappy state of affairs in Oregon and Washington for the purpose of plundering the Treasury of the United States.

These disturbances have been very prejudicial to the interests of the Territory, and have set back the improvements for years; but with the coming season and active operations, it is to be hoped that a solid and lasting peace will be established.*

* See General Gibbs's letter to me on the Indian War, in the Appendix.

CHAPTER XXI.

Description of Washington Territory.—Face of the Country.—Mountains, Minerals, Rivers, Bays, and Lakes.—Objects of Interest to the Tourist.—Falls of the Snoqualmie.—Colonel Anderson's Description. —Anecdote of Patkanim.—He forms an Alliance with Colonel Mike Simmons.—Constructive Presence of Colonel Simmons at a Fight.— Productions of the Territory.—Governor Stevens's Remarks.—Northern Pacific Rail-road.—Military Roads.—Public Spirit.—Appropriations by Congress.—Judge Lancaster.—Population.—Advantages to Emigrants.—Whale Fishery.—Russian Trade.—Amoor River.—Vancouver's Views on Climate.—Winter of 1806 in Latitude 56° North.— Salmon, 1807.—Closing Remarks.—Letter from Colonel Anderson. —Advice to Emigrants.

WASHINGTON TERRITORY is the extreme northwest domain of the United States, and is bounded by the Straits of Fuca and the 49th parallel of latitude on the north, the Pacific on the west, the Rocky Mountains on the east, and by Oregon on the south, from which it is separated by the Columbia River to near Fort Walla Walla, and from thence by the 46th parallel. Its form is nearly that of a parallelogram, with an area of some 123,022 square miles.

The approach to Washington Territory from the Pacific is not so abruptly mountainous as that of Oregon. The coast from Cape Disappointment to Cape Flattery is nearly north and south, and can be traveled almost its entire length on a beautiful sand-beach, with the exceptions of the openings of Shoal-water Bay, Gray's Harbor, the Copalis, Queniūlt, and one or two other small rivers. Only a few points jutting into the sea render a portage over them necessary, but the whole distance is easily traversed with the occasional aid of a canoe.

Vancouver noticed the difference of the appearance of

the coast north of the Columbia, and writes (April, 1792), while about two leagues off shore, Cape Disappointment bearing north 32° east: "The country now before us (Shoal-water Bay) presented a most luxuriant landscape, and was probably not a little heightened in beauty by the weather that prevailed. The more interior parts were somewhat elevated, and agreeably diversified with hills, from which it gradually descended to the shore, and terminated in a sandy beach. The whole had the appearance of a continued forest, extending north as far as the eye could reach, which made me very solicitous to find a port in the vicinity of a country presenting so delightful a prospect of fertility."

It is emphatically a mountainous country, and contains within its limits some of the highest mountains of the Coast range. The principal peaks of the Cascade range are Mount St. Helen's, Mount Adams, Mount Ranier, and Mount Baker. Mount Olympus, which is the highest of the Coast range, has an elevation of 8197 feet, Mount St. Helen's 13,300, and Mount Ranier 12,000. These peaks are clothed with perpetual snow.

The Indian disturbances have, in a great measure, retarded the developing of the resources of the Territory; and, with the exception of the operations in the coal mines at Bellingham's Bay, and the sandstone quarries on the Cowlitz, and the gold mines at Fort Colville, but few minerals have been worked.

Dr. Evans, the geologist of Oregon, who has obtained from personal experience more reliable information than any one else, states that there is coal in abundance, gold in rich diggings, marble in vast quarries, and an inexhaustible supply of lead.

The Columbia River, which separates the two Territories of Oregon and Washington, is the principal stream, and from Fort Walla Walla continues wholly within

Washington Territory till it enters the British territory near the junction of the Rocky Mountains and the 49th parallel. There are numerous and valuable tributaries to the Columbia in Washington, of which the principal are the Okinakane, Yakama, Snake, Walla Walla, Cathlapoodl, and Cowlitz. Shoal-water Bay, which is directly north of the Columbia, and which is a most excellent harbor, receives the waters of several small streams, of which the Whil-a-pah, Palux, and Nasal are the principal.

Gray's Harbor, eighteen miles north of Shoal-water Bay, receives the waters of the Chehalis, a fine stream of 130 miles in length, and also the Satsop, and other smaller rivers. The Queniült River, which runs into the Pacific five miles north of Point Grenville, has its rise in a fine lake of the same name, about twenty miles from the ocean, but can not be entered from its mouth, and is, consequently, of no commercial use. There are many streams running into Fuca Straits, and into the waters of Bellingham's Bay, Admiralty Inlet, Hood's Canal, and Puget Sound, and of these the Dungeness, Skokomish, Nisqually, Duwamsh, Snoqualmie, and Nooksahk are the principal.

Besides the Queniült Lake, there are several others of importance, as the Duwamsh, Sammamish, Whatcom, and Cushman, to the west of the Cascade range; and to the east are Lake Pend'oreilles, Chelan, Kullerspelm, Osoyoos, Okinakane, Grand Coulee, Lake Elias, Salt Lake, and many others of smaller size.

The only island of note on the Coast is Destruction Island, but in the waters of the Straits of Fuca and Admiralty Inlet are many of importance. The principal ones are Whidbey's Island in Admiralty Inlet, which is about forty miles long, and noted for its deer. East of Whidbey's Island is M'Donough's, and south are Bainbridge, Vashons; and in Puget Sound are Fox, M'Neil, Anderson's, and Hartstein's; and in Bellingham's Bay and the Rosario Straits are others of less importance.

Washington Territory shares with Oregon the grand scenery of the Columbia, the Cascades, the Dalles, and other interesting points. The lofty peaks of St. Helen's, Ranier, Adams, and Baker, of the Cascade range, and Mount Olympus on the Coast, rear their snowy heads. Mount St. Helen's is a volcano, and has been in active operation as late as 1842; and the appearance of many parts of the Territory shows that the volcanic action has not been uncommon.

The rivers of Washington, having their rise in the mountains, have magnificent scenery, and on many of them falls of magnitude may be found. Colonel Anderson, while marshal of the Territory, visited many of them while traversing the country taking the census. He writes me from Washington City, January 25th, 1857, as follows:

"During the month of July, 1852, I visited the celebrated Snoqualmie Falls, the second white party that had ever visited them. Lieutenant Floyd Jones, of the 4th Infantry, United States Army, was with me. We measured the falls with a thread, and found them to be 260 feet high *perpendicular*. They are truly grand. The Snoqualmie Falls are in about 47° 40′ north, and 121° 30′ west. The Snoqualmie River is the south branch and main tributary to the Snohomish, and empties into the latter about twenty miles below and west of the falls, and about thirty miles above and east of the mouth of the Snohomish, which makes it about fifty miles from the falls to the mouth of the Snohomish, which is nearly opposite the south end of M'Donough's Island, in what Vancouver called 'Possession Sound' (for there he took *possession* of the country in the name of his sovereign).

" The Snohomish is navigable by small steamers as far up as the mouth of the Snoqualmie, which is about the head of tide-water. Canoes ascend within a mile of the falls at all seasons. About ten miles below the falls," adds the colonel, " is the residence and head-quarters of the celebrated chief *Patkanim*, who had a brother hung at Fort Steilacoom in 1850 (by order of the court, Judge Strong) for murdering a soldier. Since that time Pat was supposed to harbor feelings of revenge against the *Bostons*, and, in consequence, was narrowly watched. He was known to be shrewd, designing, cunning, and crafty. But in 1852 he took a trip on a lumber vessel to San Francisco, and when he returned he said his *tum-tum* had *killapied*, or his heart had changed ; that the *Bostons* were too strong for the Indians to contend with ; they had too many ships, houses, men, &c. So, in this last war, he tendered the services of himself and a company of braves to the governor to assist in whipping Leschi, Nelson, and other Indians on White River. At first he was repulsed, but he importuned the governor, and protested the strongest friendship for the *Bostons*. At the solicitation of old Mike Simmons (the Daniel Boone of Washington Territory), the governor consented, and accepted Pat and his braves as *allies*.

" Simmons and a young man named Fuller accompanied Pat on his first and only expedition. They surprised the enemy on White River, routed them, killing nine and losing five *braves*. Pat brought the *heads* of his slain as trophies to Colonel Simmons, who did not participate personally in the fight, except by being *constructively* present, that is, in his tent near by. Of course, this was a feather in Pat's cap. He returned to Olympia with his *braves* to receive the crown of laurel that always awaits the conqueror, which in this case took the form of the *hiyu ickters*—many things in the shape of presents which the governor had promised him if he should be successful. *Pat and his company are the only ones who have ever yet received a dime for their services in this disastrous war.*"

Besides the Snoqualmie Falls, there are hundreds of others of various heights, and all worthy the attention of the tourist; but, as I have not received any description except the one just related by Captain Anderson, I am unable to give any more particular account.

The climate, which has already been alluded to, is similar to that of Oregon, with some variations caused by difference of latitude and local peculiarities. It is, however, in all parts of the Territory, much milder than in the same parallels of latitude east of the Rocky Mountains.

The soil of all the prairie lands, with the exception of those directly around Puget Sound, is exceedingly fertile. Those of the Sound are of a sandy, gravelly nature, not readily cultivated, but producing enormous fir and cedar trees. The soil on the mountains, wherever I have seen any attempt at a clearing, is generally very rich; but the dense growth of forest deters the emigrant from attempting clearings on a large extent, as the fine, fertile plains and prairie offer far greater inducements. Fruit of various kinds, particularly apples, can be cultivated very readily, and in the greatest perfection. Indian-corn does not thrive well, as the seasons are not hot enough; but wheat, barley, oats, and potatoes yield the most abundant crops, of the finest quality. The potatoes, in particular, are the best I have ever met with in any part of the world. The wheat grown on the Columbia, called Oregon wheat, is too well known for its superior excellence to need further remark at this time.

Although the Territory is a very mountainous country, yet there are many immense plains and prairies; and, by reference to the map, it will be seen that innumerable streams, like veins, permeate the whole region, and each of them, from the largest to the smallest, flows in its course through rich and fertile plains, of various sizes, lying between the mountains. Governor Stevens, in January, 1854, writing of the Territory, says of the waters of Puget Sound, and the adjacent ones of Hood's Canal, Admiralty Inlet, and Fuca Straits, "that their maritime advantages are very great, in affording a series of harbors almost unequaled in the world for capacity, safety, and facility of access, and they are in the immediate neighborhood to what are now the best whaling grounds of the Pacific. That portion of Washington Territory lying between the Cascade Mountains and the ocean, although equaling, in richness of soil and ease of transportation, the best lands of Oregon, is heavily timbered, and time and labor are required for clearing its forests and opening the earth to the production of its fruits. The great body of the country, on the other hand, stretching eastward from that range to the Rocky Mountains, while it contains many fertile valleys and much land suitable to the farmer, is yet more especially a grazing country—one which, as its population increases, promises, in its cattle, its horses, and, above all, its wool, to open a vast field to American enterprise. But, in the mean time, the staple of the land must continue to be the one which Nature herself has planted, in the inexhaustible forests of fir, of spruce, and of cedar. Either in furnishing manufactured timber, or spars of the first description for vessels, Washington Territory is unsurpassed by any portion of the Pacific coast."

Washington Territory abounds in fine timber, and the enormous growth of its spruce and fir excites the admiration of every one who sees them. The trees in the region about Puget Sound are especially large, comprising the spruce, hemlock, yew, cedar, fir, oak, ash, maple, and alder.   There are now about thirty-seven saw-mills in the Territory, the largest of which is that of Pope, Talbot & Co., under charge of Captain J. P. Kellar, at Teekalet (Port Gamble), on Hood's Canal.   The internal improvements of Washington Territory are progressing as fast as can be expected in a new and sparsely-populated country, situate so remote from the general government.   In 1853, Governor Isaac I. Stevens, the first governor of the Territory, surveyed a route for a Northern Pacific Rail-road, and discovered a pass near the sources of Maria's River suitable for a rail-road, estimated to be 2500 feet lower than the south pass of Fremont.   It is generally admitted that Governor Stevens's route is the best one for a rail-road that has yet been discovered, although the great, and, in fact, the principal objection urged against it is that it is too far north, and, consequently, will not suit the views nor accommodate the inhabitants of the more southern states and California.

Colonel J. P. Anderson, to whom I am under great obligation for valuable information, writes me from Washington City, January 30th, 1857, as follows: "In February or March, 1853, Congress made an appropriation of $25,000 to construct a military road from Fort Steilacoom to Walla Walla, over and across the Cascade Mountains.   Captain George B. M'Clellan (late of the Crimean Commission, now resigned) was charged with the work, in connection with the survey of that region for the Northern Pacific Rail-road.

" He assigned Lieutenant Arnold to the immediate duty of superintending in person the construction of the road.   However, before the government officers commenced this work, while they were getting ready, the citizens of Thurston and Pierce Counties, knowing the necessity of getting a road over the mountains that

summer (1853), in order to accommodate the expected
emigrants in the fall, set to work, raised private sub-
scriptions, and put on a strong force to look out a practicable pass and make a wagon-road.

"This company of citizens marked out the road, and so
opened it as to admit of travel by pack-animals all the
way, and wagons a great part of the way, before the government officers arrived.   Then Captain M'Clellan, with
that good judgment and liberality for which he was distinguished, adopted the citizens' road almost entirely,
reimbursed them out of the appropriation for much of
the work they had done, and spent the balance of the
$25,000 very judiciously in making a *good wagon-road
over the mountains.*

"There was about $8000 worth of work done by the
citizens which Captain M'Clellan could not pay for, but for
which I have at this Congress (January, 1857) procured
an appropriation (on his recommendation); also $10,000
more to finish the road.   I have also an appropriation
of $45,000 for a road from Fort Steilacoom to Belling-
ham's Bay; also $35,000 for one from the mouth of the
Columbia River to Fort Steilacoom, both of which have
passed the House, and only wait the action of the Senate, which, I doubt not, will be favorable; also an additional appropriation to complete the road from Fort Vancouver to Steilacoom.   When these are completed, *you*
will be able to see their importance, all radiating from
Fort Steilacoom, which is about the centre of the population."

During the Congress of 1854, the Honorable Columbia Lancaster, the then delegate from Washington Territory, procured, among other appropriations, one for placing buoys to mark the channel to Shoal-water Bay, and
another to erect a light-house at Cape Shoal-water, which,
however, has not, as yet, been done.   There is a light-

house on Cape Disappointment in operation, but, with this exception, there is no other one at present in the Territory, though many are needed.

Besides the military road already mentioned, there are various county and Territorial roads, the principal of which is the Cowlitz, leading from the Cowlitz Landing to Olympia, a distance of about fifty miles. This road is the principal mail-route.

The population of the Territory is composed of whites and Indians, and of the latter, the census taken by Governor Stevens in 1854 gives a total of 7559. Of the whites I have no recent reliable statistics.

Colonel Anderson, while Marshal of the Territory, took the first census, and finished in November, 1853, at which time he reported to the governor that the white population of the Territory was 3965, which would make the whole number of whites and Indians 11,524. Since that time there has been no official census taken, but the present white population has been estimated at about 8000, and the Indian at about 7400, which estimate is probably nearly correct.

The first Federal officer who reached the Territory after its separation from Oregon was the United States Marshal, Colonel J. Patton Anderson, who arrived at Olympia on the evening of the 3d of July, 1853, and proceeded at once to take the census. Governor Stevens arrived in the Territory about November of the same year, and immediately issued his proclamation for an election of members of both houses of the Legislature, and assigned the three judges, Lander, Munroe, and M'Fadden, their several districts.

The first court was held at Cowlitz Landing, in Lewis County, on the first Monday in January, 1854, and the first Legislature met the last of the same month at Olympia, and elected Seth Catlin President of the Council, and F. A. Chenowith Speaker of the House.   The Honorable Columbia Lancaster was the first delegate sent from the Territory to Congress, and was succeeded by Honorable J. Patton Anderson.   Both these gentlemen have exerted themselves with success for the good of their constituents while in Congress, and have ably assisted the governor in all his measures for the good of the Territory; and the present rapid increase of Washington, and its many inducements to encourage emigration, contrasting so favorably with some of our other territories, show skill and good management on the part of the executive and delegates, and the good sense of the local population.

To the emigrant Washington Territory presents great attraction.   The great diversity of its surface, whether mountain, valley, or plain, gives prospect of success to the farmer, the grazier, and the lumberman; and its numerous and inexhaustible mines of bituminous coal, its quarries of marble and sandstone, its rich gold and lead deposits, and its unrivaled water privileges offer great inducements to the capitalist, whether as manufacturer, trader, or ship-owner.

There is no state in the Union that has so vast a communication by water as Washington Territory—the Columbia River on its south, the Pacific on the west, and the Straits of Fuca, Hood's Canal, Admiralty Inlet, and Puget Sound on the north.   There is not a safer entrance from the ocean in the world than Fuca Straits; and the deep waters that flow through the whole of the inlets, bays, and sounds enable ships of the largest class readily to approach Olympia, the seat of government, at the head of Budd's Inlet, Puget Sound.   For a whaling station, the harbors and bays of the Straits of Fuca present remarkable advantages for ships, while for vessels of smaller size Shoal-water Bay can not be surpassed.

By reference to Maury's Whaling Chart of the Pacific, it will be seen that Washington Territory lies directly in the latitude of the present whaling grounds, and vessels can be sent to sea either from Shoal-water Bay or Fuca Straits, and reach the cruising ground easier and quicker than from any other place.   All that the Territory now wants are men and means.   To bring the first will be easy when we have the wagon-road completed for which an appropriation has just been made by Congress. We do not ask for, neither do we require, a rail-road at present.   Let the *wagon-road first* be built, with a view of hereafter being used, as far as practicable, as a rail-road, and as soon as the population increases enough to demand it, there will be no difficulty in laying down rails and running engines.*   The present difficulties in China between the authorities of that country and the English, Americans, and French, and the recent commercial ad-

* *Wagon-road from Fort Kearney to California.*—The following is a copy of the act passed at the late session of Congress to construct a wagon-road from Fort Kearney to California:

" *Be it enacted,* That the sum of $300,000, or as much thereof as may be necessary, be, and the same is hereby appropriated, out of any moneys not otherwise appropriated, for the construction of a wagon-road from Fort Kearney, in the Territory of Nebraska, *via* the South Pass of the Rocky Mountains, to the eastern boundary of the State of California, near Honey Lake ; to be expended under the direction of the Secretary of the Interior, pursuant to contracts to be made by him ; said road to connect with and form an extension of the road already authorized from Fort Ridgely to the aforesaid South Pass.

Sec. 2. That the sum of $200,000, or as much thereof as may be necessary, be, and the same is hereby appropriated, out of any moneys in the treasury not otherwise appropriated, for the construction of a wagon-road from El Paso, on the Rio Grande, to Fort Yuma, on the mouth of the Gila River ; to be expended by the Secretary of the Interior, pursuant to contracts to be made by him.

Sec. 3. That the sum of $50,000 be, and the same is hereby appropriated, out of any moneys in the treasury not otherwise appropriated, for the construction of a wagon-road from Fort Defiance, in the Territory of New Mexico, to the Colorado River, near the mouth of the Mohane River.

vantages obtained in China by the Russians, seem to in-
dicate that, unless some speedy reconciliation takes place,
Russia will obtain control of a large portion of the tea
trade.   Already tea has been shipped to England from
St. Petersburg, and we may expect that it will not be
long before an export trade will be opened between the
Russians and Americans from the River Amoor. A trade
between San Francisco and that river has already opened; but it will be seen, by reference to any chart of the
Pacific, what great advantages Washington Territory and
the Columbia River possess over all other places for that
trade.

The mouth of the Amoor is at the head of the Gulf
of Tartary, and lies in about lat. 53° north, and lon. 140°
east.   The entrance to Fuca Straits lies in lat. 48° 30′
north, and lon. 124° 30′ west—a difference in latitude of
only 270 miles, and distant 4000 miles.   This shows the
great advantage in point of distance; for, while the Straits
of Fuca are about 10 degrees farther north than San Francisco, they have a still farther advantage of being to the
windward; and when it is recollected that for the principal part of the year the prevailing wind is from the
northwest, the point of advantage can readily be seen.
The Amoor River is the largest stream flowing into the
Pacific from the western side; it is navigable for boats
to Nertchinsk, which is said to be 1700 miles from its
mouth.   Already the Russians have strongly fortified
the entrance, and there is no doubt that a large city will
soon be built upon its shores.

One great objection urged against Washington Territory by persons desirous to emigrate is, that it must,
from its high latitude, be excessively cold; that it is as
bleak and barren as the shores of the Atlantic in the
same parallel.   But such is not the fact.   It has already
been shown that the whole Pacific region is much warm-

er than corresponding points on the Atlantic, and that there are never the sudden and excessive changes of climate so often experienced east of the Rocky Mountains. In addition to instances already cited of its mildness and the early spring, Vancouver writes that in May, 1792, on landing near New Dungeness, " our attention was immediately called to a landscape almost as enchantingly beautiful as the most elegant finished pleasure-grounds in Europe. The country presented nearly a horizontal surface, interspersed with some inequalities of ground, which produced a beautiful variety of extensive lawn, covered with luxuriant grass, and diversified with an abundance of flowers. While we stopped to contemplate these several beauties of nature in a prospect no less pleasing than unexpected, we gathered some gooseberries and roses in a considerable state of forwardness." At another point, farther along the Strait, he remarks, " The ground was covered with a coarse spiry grass, interspersed with strawberries, two or three species of clover, samphire, and a great variety of other plants, some of which bore the most beautiful flowers. On a few of the points were shrubs that seemed to thrive excessively, such as roses, a species of sweetbrier, gooseberries, raspberries, currants, and several other smaller bushes, which, in their respective seasons, produce, most probably, the several fruits common to this and the opposite side of America. These all appeared to grow very luxuriantly, and, from the quantity of blossoms with which they were loaded, there was great reason to believe them very productive."

That Vancouver was correct in his belief as to the production of fruit I can testify from personal experience. I never have seen any where such great quantities of the fruits he has enumerated, or of so excellent a quality, as in Washington Territory. William Tufts, Esq., of Boston, to whom I am indebted for compiling the interesting and very valuable list of vessels trading on the Northwest Coast, which may be found in the Appendix, and who was on the Coast as supercargo of the ship Guatimozin, of Boston, in 1807–8, writes me from Boston, February 6th, 1857, that he was on the Coast for eighteen months, from the 20th of March, 1806, to the 24th of September, 1808. During that time their trading extended from the Columbia, in latitude 46° north, to about 59° 30′ south, but most of the time was passed between latitude 54° to 57°. The weather during the eighteen months was mild, but with abundance of rain during the winter months, and but little snow. While in the latitude of 56° north, during the winter, they experienced the coldest weather, which *lasted but a few days*, and during that time the wind was north-northeast.

Mr. Tufts also adds, what may be here inserted as corroborating my former statement of the size of the salmon in the Columbia, " I was in the Columbia River from about the first to the middle of July, 1807. Our dinner on the 4th of July was roast moose and boiled salmon. We attempted to smoke a dozen or two of the salmon purchased at that time. The largest weighed about 75 pounds, and the whole averaged not far from 60 pounds each."

Mr. Tufts also procured, at the same time, a medal given to the Indians by Lewis and Clarke. It was of pewter, and with the inscriptions upon it shown in the following cut.

But enough has been already adduced from the writings of the early navigators on the Pacific coast, from the times of Meares, Vancouver, and Gray, in 1789 and 1792, to the time of my personal experience, from 1852 to 1855, to show that not only is the climate far preferable to that of the Northeast Coast of America, but that

the natural products of the country are in such profusion as to render the Territory a desirable place of abode.

For persons desirous of emigrating to Washington Territory, the routes either by land or water can be selected. By water, the most expeditious is to cross the Isthmus of Panama, and proceed to San Francisco, where passage can be obtained for the Columbia River direct, either in the regular mail steamers, or by the numerous sailing vessels constantly plying between the two ports, or by sailing vessels bound either to Shoal-water Bay, or any of the numerous ports on Fuca Straits, or the other waters bounding the northwest section of the Territory.

The overland route would be to take any of the old and approved roads till the Columbia is reached at Fort Walla Walla, and from thence the military road can be taken either to Fort Steilacoom or Olympia, the seat of government, or the various settlements about Puget Sound. The Territory only needs men and capital to insure its being one of the most thrifty of our possessions, and when its value is more generally appreciated, we may expect to see as rapid an increase in the population as ever California had in its palmiest days.

NOTE.

THE following letter from Hon. J. P. Anderson relative to the overland route to Washington Territory may be considered as giving the most reliable information to emigrants.   Colonel Anderson writes from personal experience.

"Washington City, Feb. 19, 1857.

" DEAR SWAN,—Yours of the 16th reached me in due time.

"Emigrants to Puget Sound ought to leave Fort Leavenworth or Council Bluffs between the 20th of April and the 15th of May, cross the Rocky Mountains at the South Pass, proceed by Forts Hall and Boisè to the Grand Ronde, thence on to Walla Walla.   There is a road all the way.   The distance to Walla Walla is something like 2200 miles.   Thence to the Sound, by the military road over the Cascade Mountains, through the Wachess Pass, is 210 miles.   From Walla Walla, or, rather, Whitman's Old Mission, thirty miles *this side* (east) of Walla Walla, those who desire to go down the Columbia River, say to Vancouver, Portland, Astoria, etc., should *turn off to the left*, taking the Indian Agency on the Umatilla and Fort Henrietta in their way to the Dalles.

" This is on the old established emigrant road.   It is a plain wagon-way from Missouri to Walla Walla. It leaves the California road in the vicinity of the Soda Springs, on the west side of the Rocky Mountains. Emigrants ought to buy Walker's (or some other) Guidebook before leaving the Missouri River, for the purpose of learning where the best *water* and *grass* are to be found. Dozens of these Guide-books are to be bought any where on the frontier. After the first few days out, they ought to *guard their stock every night.* Indians *will* steal them unless they are watched closely. As soon as the novelty wears off, emigrants are too apt to become careless, thinking there is no danger, and *just then* their cattle are stolen, and they are left *afoot.* Hence nearly all of the suffering on the Plains. They are always in too great a hurry. If an ox gets lame or a little sick, they will turn him out and leave him rather than be detained half a day. This should not be done. They ought to *wait* and watch him till he gets well. Stop the whole train; let no one *stay behind* to bring him up.

" In haste, yours truly,

" J. Patton Anderson."

S

APPENDIX.

THE following extracts from the treaty between the United States and Great Britain, relative to the limits of the territory west of the Rocky Mountains, and in reference to the rights of the Hudson Bay Company, will show that, while the United States government recognize the claims of the Hudson Bay Company as actual settlers, they do not agree to pay the Company any sum to extinguish their title to lands, except in case any of such land should become of public and political importance.

The extracts from the Donation law, and also of the present law of the Territory relative to the purchase of land, will show the inducements held out to emigrants by the government, and also the method to be adopted at present to purchase land. It will be seen that at present the donation law has ceased, but any person can purchase surveyed lands for one dollar and twenty-five cents per acre.

Extract from Treaty between the United States and Great Britain of Lands westward of the Rocky Mountains. Concluded June 15th, 1846.

ART. III. In the future appropriation of the territory south of the forty-ninth parallel of north latitude, as provided in the first article of this treaty, the possessory rights of the Hudson Bay Company, and of all British subjects who may be already in occupation of land or other property lawfully acquired within said territory, shall be respected.

ART. IV. The farms, lands, and other property of every description, belonging to the Puget Sound Agricultural Company, on the north side of the Columbia River, shall be confirmed to the said Company. In case, however, the situation of those farms and lands should be considered by the United States to be of public and political importance, and the United States government should signify a desire to obtain possession of the whole or any part thereof, the property so required shall be transferred to the said government at a proper valuation, to be agreed upon between the parties.

Donation Act of September 27th, 1850.

SEC. 4. *And be it further enacted,* That there shall be, and hereby is, granted to every white settler or occupant of public lands, *American half-breeds included,* above the age of eighteen years, being a citizen of the United States, or having made a declaration on or before the first day of December, eighteen hundred and fifty-one, now residing in the

Territory, or who shall become a resident before the said first of December, 1851, and who shall have resided on and cultivated the same for four consecutive years, and shall otherwise conform to the provisions of this act, the quantity of one half section, or three hundred and twenty acres of land, if a single man; and if a married man, or if he shall become married within one year from the first day of December, 1850, the quantity of one section, or six hundred and forty acres, one half to himself and the other half to his wife, to be held by her in her own right; and the surveyor shall designate the part enuring to the husband and that to the wife, and enter the same on the records of his office.

SEC. 5. Grants to all persons, as mentioned in the previous act, who arrive in the Territory to settle between December 1st, 1850, and December, 1853, to a single man, one quarter section, or 120 acres of land; and to a married man, 320 acres of land.

Donation Act of February 14th, 1853.

SEC. 1. Provides that persons may be permitted, after occupation for two years of land, to purchase the same at one dollar and twenty-five cents per acre.

SEC. 3. Limits the Donation Act to December 1st, 1855, at which time all persons must file notices of claims.

Since that period, any actual settler can purchase the land on which his claim is located, provided the land has been surveyed, at the rates mentioned in Section First.

The organic act by which Washington was created a separate Territory from Oregon was passed March 2, 1853. Among the first acts passed by the Territory of Washington was one for the preservation of oysters and other shell-fish, as Washington Territory is the only place from whence the supply of oysters is procured for the California market.

Another early act was to appoint pilot commissioners to select pilots for the Columbia River and Shoal-water Bay.

A VOCABULARY OF THE CHEHALIS AND CHENOOK OR JARGON LANGUAGES, WITH THE DERIVATION OF THE WORDS USED IN THE LATTER.

Chehalis.

A.

Aās'ah-wah, give it.

Aās'ah-wah kahl', get water.

Aās-er, come.

Aās-ĕr-lĕ, come quickly.

Aïlsh, to-morrow.

Ait'chote, a bear.

A-quail'shiltl, north wind.

Ar'yuk, small clams.

C.

Cam'mass, the edible root of the Cammassia esculenta.

Car'kar, girl.

Car'koo, female infant.

Car'mox, dog.
Che-cose', mussels.
Che-poo'chucks, beard.
Chett'low, oysters.
Chesp,. neck.
Chūtl, three.
Cla-ath'a-lum, east wind.
Cla'koo, snow.
Cla'koon, good.
Cla-wilmsh', Indian.

Clo'lum, quahaug clam.
Clūnge, mouth.
Co'lish, how are you — a salutation on meeting.
Co-mailth', daughter.
Con-nath in-nis-ku, an expression of derision.
Cuck'ko, a small viviparous fish like the perch.
Cū-shū', hog.

D.

Der-chee'to-che-ny, humming-bird.

E.

Eath'wil-ly, flesh.
E-kap'pa, hail.

E-lip, first.
El-le-caid', slave.

H.

Has'litch, liver.
Hone'gin, an expression of impatience.

Hu-litn', make.
Hur-leit'za, stop, be quiet.
Hur-sache', bad.

J.

Jo'quitl, get up.
Jo'quitl omtz ta kahl, get up and give me water.

Jo'quitl po-ko'ge-pah whid'tuck, get up and make a fire, quick.

K.

Kae'poor, needle.
Kaer'huch, crab.
Kaer-ux'o, crooked nose.

Kahl, water.
Kla'koon, good.

L.

Le-vore'litch, bottle.

M.

Mailte, no.
Me-tar' or sme-tar', large sea-clams.
Mis'chin, lice.

Mitch-ip, fire.
Mock'sa, nose.
Moo'ser, eyes.
Mose, four.

N.

Nar-whatl', yes.

Nookh', you.

O.

Oh-whitl', another.

Omtz, give.

Omtz ta kahl, give me water.

P.

Par'nich, ten.

Pe'cose, freckled.

Pow, one.

Q.

Quac'a-chose, forehead.

Qua-ho'no-ish, finger.

Queer'hos, to strike, to wound.

Quer-lo'e-chintl, bear-berry (Arbutus uva ursi).

Quer'que-lin, mouse.

Que'tark, elk.

Que-tone', son.

Qui-natch', get.

Quin'ish, brother.

S.

Saer'tich, six.

Sak-tolm, paddle.

Sarctl, the reply to Co'lish, as Co'lish te, How do you do? Sarctl, Thank you, very well.

Sartl, two.

Schoh, old man.

Schoue, ice.

Se-cartl', spruce-tree.

She-ee'sinch, shrimp.

She-o'quintl, cedar.

Shooks'quitl, to-day.

Shūg'war, get out of the way, move along.

Skaer'kut-tle, woman.

Ske'poor, rabbit.

Sme-tar', bowl.

Sme-tarx' or me-tarx', large sea-clam.

Smo'o-lum, carrots or parsnips.

Snatchm', old woman.

Soil'me, cranberries.

Squeo, squirrel.

Squil'lim, heart.

Squin-too', poultry, partridges.

Squin'tum, white man.

Squin'tum sme-tar', earthen or crockery bowl.

Stay-a-ough', man.

Sus'per-ter, hip.

Swin-ailsh', a large viviparous fish like the menhaden.

T.

Taerkh, bone.

Tah-lass', foot.

Tah'ness, knee.

Ta'hun-er, king-fisher.

Tam, what.

Tar-mo'hoks, beads.

Ta-squilms', heart.

Tat-kloke'tat-arles, God.

Teh'a-ner, blue jay.

Ten-a-man' chathl', my little daughter.

Ten-a-man' que-tone', my little son.

Ten-a-mart', head.

Ten-a-mose', eye.

Ten-a-muck'um, throat.

Ten-a-mux', nose.

Ten-a-quel-ah'koo, my wife.

Ten-arts'lits, veins.

Ten-chait', elder brother.

Tene-ai', elder sister.

Ten-kaer', my mother.

Ten-kah', my father.
Ten-kahmtn', breast.
Ten-künge, mouth.
Ten-la-houtch', windpipe.
Ten-mo'qua, face.
Ten-nisch', younger brother.
Ten-pake', back.
Ten-pa-pa-ar'ich, nail.
Ten-pesch, younger sister.
Ten-quel-lan', ear.
Ten-sarst', stomach.
Ten-shen', my husband.
Ten-squails', blood.
Ten-sta'ko-no'weesh, hand.
Ten-taok'-tse, tongue.
Ten-thle-quärt', hair.
Ten-tome', navel.
Ten-tsa'whait, bladder.
Ten-tse-kwok', thigh.

Ten-tseulth, leg.
Tents-ho'mish, arm.
Ten-yan-ness', tooth.
Thluck'nist, shoulder.
Tole, boy.
Tōl-neuch', west wind.
Tolo, infant boy.
Toö'lux, south wind.
Tsa'ilich, five.
Tsa'kuns, stick.
Tsa'mose, eight.
Tsoo'itl, feet.
Tsopes, seven.
Tsuck'oke, hip-joint.
Tsum, writing, printing, or pictures.
Tūck, salmon eggs.
Tuckh, shut.
Tuck'ho, nine.

U.
Unz, I.

W.

Wap'pa-loot'za, owl.
War'tich, who.
Wee'a-hun, turn round.
Whe'ark, eagle.

Whid'tuk, hurry.
Wohk'sa, go.
Wohk'sa cla-ag'e-pah, go get wood.

Y.

Yan-jan'ka, necklace.

Yel-loh', whale.

Chenook or Jargon.

The abbreviations are *Che.* for Chenook, *Fr.* for French, *Eng.* for English.

A.

Ab'bah, *Che.*, well then.
Ae'kik, *Che.*, fish-hook.
Aet'-choot or a'chote, *Che.*, a bear.
Al'ki, *Che.*, by-and-by.
Al-loy'ma, *Che.*, another.
Al'ta, *Che.*, now.
An'kar-ty, *Che.*, of old time, or time past.

An-nah', *Che.*, exclamation of astonishment.
Ap'pola, *Che.*, any thing roasted.
Ar-hue'yo, *Che.*, a chest.
Arts, *Che.*, sister.
Arts'poe, *Che.*, fleas.
A-to'ke-te-ni-ka ait'semar, *Che.*, I have a good heart.

B.

Bos-ton, *Eng.*, American.

C.

Cah, *Che.*, where.

Cah'tah, *Che.*, how, why.

Caim-tux or Kaim-tux, *Che.*, I have or did understand.

Ca-nim', *Che.*, canoe.

Ca'pote, *Fr.*, coat.

Cap-swa'la, *Che.*, to steal.

Car-de'na, *Che.*, fight.

Car-mo'sah, *Che.*, beads.

Car'mox, *Che.*, dog.

Car'qua, *Che.*, thus, the same.

Chā-ko, *Che.*, to come.

Chee, *Che.*, new.

Chin'ka-min, *Che.*, iron or silver.

Chitch, *Che.*, grandmother.

Chupe, *Che.*, grandfather.

Cla'il, *Che.*, black, dark colored.

Clap or Klap, *Che.*, to find.

Clat'ta-wah, *Che.*, to go.

Clax'ta, *Che.*, who.

Cle-men'ti-kote, *Che.*, to lie.

Clo-clo, *Che.*, oysters.

Clo-nās', *Che.*, don't know; perhaps.

Clone, *Che.*, three.

Close or Klosh, *Che.*, good.

Cō-cumb', *Che.*, a swan.

Cok'shut, *Che.*, break, hurt, or destroy.

Cold Il'lihe, winter.

Cole'ly, *Che.*, lively, sprightly, frolicksome.

Comb, *Eng.*, comb.

Co'pah, *Che.*, for, to, with, &c.

Cul'la-cul'la, *Che.*, birds.

Cul'tus, *Che.*, trifling, common.

Cum'tux, *Che.*, to know, to understand.

Cu'shu, *Che.*, hog.

D.

Da-go, *Che.*, gnats or musquitoes.

De-late' or Tlaite, *Eng.*, straight.

Dly, *Eng.*, dry.

Dly tup'soe, *Che.*, hay.

E.

Ea'suk, *Che.*, paddle.

Eat-in-will, *Che.*, ribs.

E-li-ar-ty, *Che.*, slave.

En-ah, *Che.*, a beaver.

En-a'poe, *Che.*, lice.

E'na-tie, *Che.*, the other side.

En-si'ka, *Che.*, our or we.

G.

Glass, *Eng.*, glass.

Gleece, *Eng.*, grease.

Gleece-pire, *Eng.*, candles.

H.

Hachr or house, *Che.*, house.

Hah'lick-ly, *Che.*, open.

Ha'lo, *Che.*, there is none.

Han'ker-chim, *Eng.*, handkerchief.

Hee-hee, *Che.*, laugh.

Hee-hee la'mar, *Che.*, to gamble.

Hi-ack, *Che.*, make haste, hurry.

Hi-as Cul'tus, *Che.*, worthless.

Hi-yu', *Che.*, plenty.

Ho'ey-ho-ey, *Che.*, to exchange.

How, *Che.*, look here.

Hrowl'kult, *Che.*, stubborn.

Hy-as', *Che.*, great, very ; as, for instance, Hy-as' ca-nim', great canoe ; Hy-as' close, very good.

Hy-as' Sunday, *Che.*, Christmas.

I.

Icht, *Che.*, one.

Icht stick, *Che.*, one yard.

Ick'ta, *Che.*, what, or thing; as, Ick'ta mi-ka tik-ke, what do you want? Cah mi-ka ick'tas, where are your things?

Ick'poee, *Che.*, to shut.

Il'lihe, *Che.*, earth.

In-nude, *Che.*, across.

Ip'soot, *Che.*, to hide.

Is'cum, *Che.*, to get or to receive.

K.

Kae'poor, *Che.*, needle.

Ka-li'ten, *Che.*, lead, shot.

Ka'po, *Che.*, a relative older, as an older brother, sister, or cousin.

Kat'suck, *Che.*, midway.

Kee'quil-ly, *Che.*, down, under.

Kettle, *Eng.*, a pot or kettle.

Ke-whap', *Che.*, a hole.

Ke'yu-tan, *Che.*, a horse.

Kil'la-pie, *Che.*, to overturn, or to return.

Kil-lic'soe, *Che.*, bottle.

Kim'ta, *Che.*, behind.

Ki-noose, *Che.*, tobacco.

Kla-ceece, *Che.*, stars.

Klack'han, *Che.*, a fence.

Kla'hai-yam, *Che.*, poor or unfortunate.

Kla-how'ya, *Che.*, how are you.

Kla-pote, *Che.*, thread.

Klas'ka, *Che.*, they.

Kla-wa', *Che.*, slow.

Klax'ta, *Che.*, who.

Kle'men, *Che.*, any thing ground to powder.

Kle'men-saplel, *Che.*, flour.

Klem'men - kle'mem il-lihe, *Che.*, sand.

Kleutch'man, *Che.*, woman.

Klip, *Che.*, deep.

Klock, *Che.*, untie. Mamoke klock-lope, untie that rope.

Ko'le-ko'le, *Che.*, mouse.

Kon'a-way, *Che.*, all.

Kon'sick, *Che.*, how much or how many.

Kow, *Che.*, to tie.

Kull, *Che.*, hard, tough.

Kull-kull stick, *Che.*, oak.

L.

La bis'cuit, *Fr.*, biscuit, hard bread.

La blee', *Fr.* (blé), wheat.

La bottaile', *Fr.* (bottaile), bottle.

La bouche', *Fr.* (bouche), the mouth.

La breed', *Fr.* (bride), bridle.

La cas-sette', *Fr.* (cassette), trunk or chest.

La chan-delle, *Fr.*, candle.

Lack'et, *Che.*, four.

La gomme, *Fr.*, pitch or gum.

La gomme stick, *Fr.*, pitch knots.

Lake, *Eng.*, lake.

La leem , *Fr.* (lime), file.

La'ley, *Che.*, long time.

La lupan, *Fr.* (ruban), ribbon.

La'mai, *Fr.* (la mere), old woman or the mother.

La mar', *Fr.* (main), hand.

La mo'lu, *Fr.*, wild or like a young colt.

La mon-taigne', *Fr.*, mountain.

La mu-ton', *Fr.* (mouton), sheep.

La pash-ma', *Fr.* (blanchet), saddle blanket.

La peep', *Fr.* (pipe), pipe.

La pell', *Fr.* (pelle), spade, shovel.

La pia'ge, *Fr.* (piége), trap or snare.

La pio'sge, *Fr.* (pioche), hoe.

La plash', *Fr.* (planche), boards.

La porte', *Fr.*, door.

La pou'ille, *Fr.* (poêle), fry-pan.

La queen, *uncertain*, a saw.

Larch, *Fr.* (l'orge), barley.

La selle', *Fr.* (selle), saddle.

La sou'ille, *Fr.* (soie), silk.

La tamle', *Fr.* (table), table.

La ween, *Fr.* (avoine), oats.

Lazy, *Eng.*, slow or lazy.

Le chaise', *Fr.* (chaise), chain.

Le coque, *Fr.*, cock.

Le creme, *Fr.*, cream.

Le dar, *Fr.* (dents), teeth.

Le glow, *Fr.* (clou), nails.

Le hache', *Fr.* (hache), the hatchet.

Le job, *Che.*, the devil.

Le kallot, *Eng.*, carrots.

Le klee, *Eng.*, key.

Lek'y, *Che.*, spotted.

Le lame', *Fr.* (rame), oar.

Le lang', *Fr.* (langue), tongue.

Le loo', *Fr.* (loup), wolf.

Le nez', *Fr.* (nez), the nose.

Le pied', *Fr.* (pied), foot.

Le plate', *Fr.* (pretre), priest.

Le poor', *Fr.* (pois), peas.

Le poulet, *Fr.*, hen.

Le saik', *Fr.* (sac), bag or sack.

Le tete', *Fr.* (tete), the head.

Lice, *Eng.*, rice.

Lip-a-lip, *Che.*, to boil.

Lis'quis, *Che.*, mat.

Lo'lo, *Che.*, bring or carry.

Lope, *Eng.*, rope.

Luck-wul'la, *Che.*, nut.

Lum, *Eng.*, rum.

Lu'pul-la, *Che.*, back.

M.

Ma'moke, *Che.*, work.

Ma-moke la pou'ille, to fry any thing.

Man, *Eng.*, man.

Mar'koke, *Che.*, trade.

Marsh, *Che.*, put off until, &c., as, Marsh mi-ka ca'pote, put off your coat.

Mar'tin-ly, *Che.*, at a distance off shore.

Mart'quil-ly, *Che.*, toward the shore or on shore.

Mem'e-lose, *Che.*, dead.

Mer'cie, *Fr.* (je vous remercie), thanks.

Me-si'ka, *Che.*, yours.

Mia'mi, *Che.*, down stream.

Mid'lait, *Che.*, stop, put, &c.

Mi'ka, *Che.*, you.

Mit'quit, *Che.*, stand up.

Mo'lack, *Che.*, elk.

Moo'la, *Fr.* (moulin), mill.

Moos-a-moos, *Che.*, beef.

Moo'sum, *Che.*, sleep.

Mo'wich, *Che.*, deer.

Mox, *Che.*, two.

Mox-poh, *Che.*, double barrel gun.

Muck'a-muck, *Che.*, food, to eat.

Mu-sa'chee, *Che.*, bad.

N.

Na-nar'mox, *Che.*, otter.

Nar'nitch, *Che.*, see.

Nar'tle-ly, *Che.*, is it not so?

Nar-wit'ka, *Che.*, yes.

Ne'whar, *Che.*, how is it?

Ni'ka or Nai'ka, *Che.*, I.

O.

Oi'cut, *Che.*, road.
Oiee, *Che.*, small clams.
Ois'kin, *Che.*, cup.
Oke, *Che.*, those or that.
O'koke, *Che.*, this.
Oli-kai'yu, *Che.*, seal.
O'lil-lies, *Che.*, berries.
O'lo, *Che.*, hungry.

O-luck', *Che.*, snake.
Oo'moor, *Che.*, large sea clams.
Ope'cher, *Che.*, knife.
Ope'quin, *Che.*, basket.
O'pooche, *Che.*, tail.
Ote'quei-mar, mussels.
Ow, *Che.*, brother.

P.

Par'tle, *Che.*, full.
Par'tle lum, *Che.*, full of rum, or drunk.
Pay or pee, *Che.*, but, with, and.
Pe-chuck', *Che.*, green.
Pel'ton, *Che.*, drunk or foolish.
Pe-sioux', *Che.*, French.
Pil, *Che.*, red.
Pil'pil, *Che.*, blood.
Pire, *Eng.*, fire.

Pire o'lil-lies, *Che.*, ripe berries.
Pi-she-ak', *Che.*, exhausted.
Pish-pish, *Eng.* (puss), cat.
Pi-thik', *Che.*, thick.
Po, *Che.*, gun.
Po'lak-a-ly, *Che.*, night.
Po'lal-ly, *Che.*, powder.
Po'lal-ly il'lihe, *Che.*, sand.
Pos-sis'see, *Che.*, blanket.
Pot'latch, *Che.*, give or gift.

Q.

Qua'nice, *Che.*, whale.
Qua'ni-sum, *Che.*, always.
Quass, *Che.*, afraid.
Queo'queo, *Che.*, finger-ring.
Qui'cer, *Che.*, porpoise.
Qui'etz, *Che.*, nine.

Quil'lan, *Che.*, ear.
Qui'nim, *Che.*, five.
Qui'pet, *Che.*, stop, finish, done.
Quit-chad'dy, *Che.*, rabbit.
Quit'tle, *Che.*, shoot, hunt, kill.

S.

Sa'hil-li, *Che.*, up.
Sail, *Eng.*, calico, cotton cloth.
Sal-mon, *Eng.*, salmon.
Sap'pe-lail, *Che.*, flour.
Scal'la-been, *Eng.* (carabine), rifle.
Se-ar'host, *Che.*, eye, face, countenance.
Sear'portl, *Che.*, cap, hat.
See'py, *Che.*, crooked.
Seix, *Che.*, friend.
Se-kar'lox, *Che.*, pantaloons, leggins.
Sen'na-mox, *Che.*, seven.
Shar'ty, *Che.*, sing.

Shet'sam, *Che.*, swim.
Si-ah', *Che.*, far off.
Sick-tum-tum, *Che.*, sorrow.
Si'lix, *Che.*, angry.
Sil-sil, *Che.*, buttons.
Sit'kum, *Che.*, half.
Sit'kum-sun, *Che.*, noon.
Si-wash', *Fr.* (sauvage), Indian.
Skad, *Che.*, a mole.
Ska-kairk, *Che.*, hawk.
Skoo'kum, *Che.*, strong.
Skoo-kum' or Sku-kum', *Che.*, evil spirits.
Skub'by-you, *Che.*, skunk.

Skud′so, *Che.*, squirrel.
Smock-smock, *Che.*, grouse.
Snass, *Che.*, rain.
Soil′me, *Che.*, cranberries.

Soo′tie, *Che.*, mouse.
Stope′kin, *Che.*, eight.
Swaa′wa, *Che.*, panther.

T.

Ta-co-mo′nak, *Che.*, one hundred.
Ta-hum′, *Che.*, six.
Ta-mo′lich, *Che.*, barrel.
Tant′ki, *Che.*, yesterday.
Tat-te′lum, *Che.*, ten.
Te-ar′wit, *Che.*, foot, leg.
Te-cope′, *Che.*, white.
Tee-he or hee-hee, *Che.*, laugh.
Te-nas, *Che.*, small.
Tick-air′chy, *Che.*, although.
Ti-ki, *Che.*, want.
Til-li-cum, *Che.*, man.
Tin-tin, *Che.*, music, bells.
Tlcul′, *Che.*, still.
Tli-cup′, *Che.*, to cut.

To′lo, *Che.*, to win.
To-man′a-wos or To-mah′na-wos, *Che.*, medicine, or medicine-man, magic.
Too-tooche′ *Che.*, breasts, milk.
Too-tooche′ gleece, *Che.*, butter.
Tsick-tsick, *Che.*, wagon.
Tsuck, *Che.*, water.
Tul or Til, *Che.*, heavy, tired.
Tum-tsuck, *Che.*, waterfall.
Tum′tum, *Che.*, heart, soul, mind.
Tup′so, *Che.*, grass, hair, leaves.
Ty-ee′, *Che.*, chief.
Tzae, *Che.*, sweet.

U.

Ul′ti-cut, *Che.*, long.

W.

Wagh, *Che.*, spill.
Wake, *Che.*, no.
Wake-kon′sick, *Che.*, never.
Wap′pa-too, *Che.*, the bulb of the saggittafolia or arrow-head, an edible root.

Wap′pa-too, *Che.*, potatoes.
Warm il′lihe, *Che.*, summer.
Waugh-waugh, *Che.*, ow.
Wa′wa, *Che.*, talk.
Wha′ah, *Che.*, an exclamation.
Wicht *Che.*, also, then, after.

Y.

Ya-chost′, *Che.*, belly.
Ya-ka, *Che.*, he, she, or it.
Ya′kol-la, *Che.*, eagle.
Yak′soot, *Che.*, hair.

Ya-qua′, *Che.*, here.
Ya′wa, *Che.*, there.
Youl′ti-cut or ūl-ti-cut, *Che.*, long.

NUMERALS.

	Chehalis.	Chenook.
One,	pow,	icht.
Two,	sartl,	mox.
Three,	chūtl,	clone.
Four,	mose,	lack′it.
Five,	tsai-litch,	qui′nim.

	Chehalis.	Chenook.
Six,	saer-tich,	ta-hum.
Seven,	tsopes,	sin'na-mox.
Eight,	tsa-mose,	stope'kin.
Nine,	tūck-ho,	qui'etz.
Ten,	par-nich,	tat-te-lum.
Eleven,	par-nich-ten-pow,	tat-te-lum pe icht.
Twelve,	par-nich-ten-sartl,	tat-te-lum pe mox.
Thirteen,	par-nich-ten-chūtl,	tat-te-lum pe clone.
Fourteen,	par-nich-ten-mose,	tat-te-lum pe lack'it.
Fifteen,	par-nich-ten-tsai-litch',	tat-te-lum pe qui'nim.
Sixteen,	par-nich-ten-saer-tich',	tat-te-lum pe ta'hum.
Seventeen,	par-nich-ten-tsopes,	tat-te-lum pe sin'na-mox.
Eighteen,	par-nich-ten-tsa-mose,	tat-te-lum pe stope'kin.
Nineteen,	par-nich-ten-tūck-ho,	tat-te-lum pe qui'etz.
Twenty,	par-nich-ten-par-nich,	mox tat-te-lum.
Thirty,	chutl-par-nich,	clone tat-te-lum.
Forty,	mose-par-nich,	lack'it tat-te-lum.
Fifty,	tsai-litch-ten-par-nich,	qui'nim tat-te-lum.
Sixty,	saer-tich-ten-par-nich,	ta'hum tat-te-lum.
Seventy,	tsopes-tat-par-nich,	sin'na-mox tat-te-lum.
Eighty,	tsa-mose-ten-par-nich,	stope'kin tat-te-lum.
Ninety,	tūck-ho-par-nich,	qui'etz tat-te-lum.
One hundred,	ten par-nich-tat-par-nich,	icht ta-co-mo-nack.
One thousand,		icht hy-as-ta-co-mo-nack.

List of Words in the Nootkan Language the most in use, from John R. Jewett's Narrative of the Massacre of the Crew of the Ship Boston by the Savages of Queen Charlotte's Sound, 1803.

Ar-smoo-tish check-up, a warrior.

Ar-teese, to bathe.

Cha-alt-see-klat-tur-wah, go off or away.

Cha-hak, fresh water.

Cham-mass, fruit.

Cham-mass-ish, sweet or pleasant to the taste.

Chap-atz, canoe.

Check-up, man.

Chee-chee, teeth.

Chee-me-na, a fish-hook.

Chee-poke, copper.

Che-men, fish-hooks.

Chit-ta-yek, knife or dagger.

Choop, tongue.

Coo-coo-ho-sa, seal.

Een-a-qui-shit-tle, to kindle a fire.

Ein-nuk-see, fire or fuel.

Em-me-chap, to play.

Hah-welhs, hungry.

Hap-se-up, hair.

He-ho, yes.

Hoo-ma-hex-a, mother.

I-yah-ish, much.

I-yer-ma-hah, I do not understand.

Kah-ah-coh, bring it.

Kah-ah-pah-chilt, give me something.

Kak-koelth, slave.

Kas-see, eyes.

Kat-lah-tik, brother.

Klack-e-miss, oil.
Klack-ko ty-ee, thank ye, chief.
Klat-tur-miss, earth.
Kle-war, to laugh.
Klick-er-yek, rings.
Klish-klin, feet.
Kloos-a-mit, herring.
Kloot-chem-up, sister.
Klootz-mah, woman.
Klu-shish, good.
Kom-me-tak, I understand.
Kook-a-nik-sa, hands.
Mac-kam-mah-shish, do you want to buy?
Mah-hack, whale.
Ma-mook, to sell.
Ma-mook su-mah, to go to fish.
Mar-met-ta, goose or duck.
Meit-la, rain.
Mook-see, rock.
Moot-sus, powder.
Moo-watch, bear.
Muk-ka-tee, house.
Naet-sa, nose.
Nee-sim-mer-hiss, enough.
Noot-che, mountain or hill.

Noo-wex-a, father.
Oo-nah, how many?
Oo-phelth, sun or moon.
Oo-wha-pa, paddle.
Par-pee, ears.
Pook-shit-tle, to blow.
Po-shak, bad.
Pow or po, the report of a gun.
Pow-ee, halibut.
Quart-lah, sea-otter.
Queece, snow.
Quish-ar, smoke.
See-ya-poks, cap or hat.
Sick-a-min-ny, iron.
Sie-yah, sky.
So-har, salmon.
Tan-as-sis, child.
Tan-as-sis check-up, son.
Tan-as-sis kloots-mah, daughter.
Tar-toose, stars.
Taw-hat-se-tee, head.
Toop-elth, sea.
Toop-helth, cloth.
Toosch-qua, cod.
Ty-ee, chief.
Wik, no.

Comparative Words in the Nootka and Chenook or Jargon.

Nootka.	Chenook.	
Klootz-mah,	klooch-man,	woman.
Tan-as-sis,	ta-nas,	child or any thing small.
Sick-a-min-ny,	chink-a-min,	iron.
Ma-mook,	ma-mook,	work.
Kom-me-tak,	kum-tux,	understand.
Klu-shish, or, as Meares writes, Cloosh,	klose,	good.
Ty-ee,	ty-ee,	chief.
See-ya-poks,	sear-portl,	cap or hat.
Klack-ko,	klac-koon,	good.
Pow,	pow or po,	report of a gun or cannon.
Klat-tur-wah,	clat-te-wah,	go off or go away.
Wik,	wake,	no.

ACCOUNT OF THE VESSELS ENGAGED IN THE SEA-OTTER FUR-TRADE
ON THE NORTHWEST COAST PRIOR TO 1808.

In the following account of American vessels, it will be perceived
that the latest date is 1807. From that time to the close of the War
of 1812 the fur-trade was rather to be considered as the Columbia
River trade, and the names of such vessels can be found in the text up
to the time when Astoria was sold to the Northwest Company. I
should have published a full list of the early traders to the Columbia,
but could get no authentic statement.

*List of American Vessels engaged in the Trade of the Northwest Coast
of America for Sea-otter Skins from 1787 to 1809, compiled by William
Tufts, Esq., from his own Memoranda, and from the very valuable
Notes kindly furnished by Captain William Sturgis, of Boston.*

Time of sailing.	Vessels' Names.	Masters.	Where owned.	Owners.	What Years on the Coast.
1787	Ship Columbia.	Kendrick.	Boston.	Barrell, Bulfinch & Co.	1788, 1789.
1787	Sloop Washington.	Gray.	do.	do. do.	1788.*
1788 1789	None.				
1790	Ship Columbia.	Gray.	do.	do. do.	1791, 1792.†
1792	Sloop Union.	Boyd.	do.	Not known.	1793.
1792	Ship Jefferson.	Roberts.	do.		
1792	Brig Hancock.	Crowell.	do.		
1792	Ship Margaret.	Magee.	do.		‡
1792	Brig Hope.	Ingraham.§	do.		
1795	Snow Sea Otter.	Hill.	do.		1796, 1797.‖
1795	Schr. ———	Newbury.	do.		1796.
1796	Ship Dispatch.	Bowers.	do.	Dorr and Sons.	1797.
1796	Ship Indian Packet.	Rogers.	do.	do.	1797.
1796	Ship Hazard.	Swift.	do.	Perkins, Lamb & Co.	1797, 1798.
1797	Not known.				
1798	Ship Eliza.	Rowan.	do.	Perkins, Lamb & Co.	1799.
1798	Ship Ulysses.	Lamb.	do.	Lamb and others.	1799.
1798	Ship Hancock.	Crocker.	do.	Dorr and Sons.	1799.
1798	Ship Dispatch.	Breck.	do.	do.	1799.
1798	Ship Dove.	Duffin.	Canton.	Not known.	1799.
1798	Ship Cheerful.	Beck.	do.	do.	1799.
1798	Sloop Dragon.	Cleaveland.	do.	Cleaveland and others.	1799.
1799	Ship Alert.	Bowles.	Boston.	Lamb and others.	1800.
1799	Ship Jenny.	Bowers.	do.	Dorr and Sons.	1800.
1799	Ship Alexander.	Dodd.	do.	Bass and others.	1800.
1799	Schr. Rover.	Davidson.	do.	Dorr and Sons.	1800.
1799	Ship Dove.	Duffin.	Canton.		1800.
1799	Ship Hazard.	Swift.	Boston.	Perkins & others.	1800, 1801.
1800	Ship Charlotte.	Ingersoll.	do.	....	1801.

* Remained on the Coast under Captain Kendrick for many years. Gray went
home in the Columbia; Kendrick was accidentally killed at the Sandwich Islands.
  † Discovered Columbia River.
  ‡ Time of sailing, time on the coast, and owners not known.
  § Discovered the Washington Islands, South Pacific.   ‖ Captain killed.

Time of sailing.	Vessels' Names.	Masters.	Where owned.	Owners.	What Years on the Coast.
1800	Ship Guatimozin.	Bumstead.	Boston.	T. Lyman and others.	1801.
1800	Ship Atahualpa.	Wildes.	do.	do.	1801.
1800	Ship Globe.	Magee.	do.	Perkins, Lamb and others.	1801, 1802.*
1800	Ship Carolina.	Derby.	do.	do. do.	1801, 1802.†
1800	Ship Manchester.	Brice.	Philadel'a.	....	1801, 1802.
1800	Ship Lucy.	Pierpont.	Boston.	Cobb and others.	1801.
1800	Ship Dispatch.	Dorr.	do.	Dorr and Sons.	1801.
1800	Ship Belle Savage.	Ockington.	do.	J. Cooledge.	1801.
1800	Ship Enterprise.	Hubbell.	New York.	Hoy and Thorn.	1801.
1800	Brig Lavinia.	Hubbard.	Bristol,R.I.	R. J. De Wolf.	1801.
1800	Brig Littiler.	Dorr.	Boston.	Dorr and Sons.	1801.
1800	Brig Polly.	Kelly.	do.	Thomas Parish.	1801.
1801	Ship Alert.	Ebbetts.	do.	Lamb and others.	1802, 1803.
1801	Ship Catharine.	Worth.	do.	J. Cooledge.	1802.
1801	Ship Jenny.	Crocker.	do.	Dorr and Sons.	1802.
1801	Schr. Hetty.	Briggs.	Philadel'a.	....	1802.
1801	Ship Vancouver.	Brown.	Boston.	Lyman & others.	1802, 1803.
1801	Ship Juno.	Kendrick.	Bristol,R.I.	De Wolf.	1802, 1803.
1802	Ship Mary.	Bowles.	Boston.	J. Gray.	1803.‡
1802	Ship Guatimozin.	Bumstead.	do.	Lyman & others.	1803, 1804.
1802	Ship Hazard.	Swift.	do.	Perkins & others.	1803, 1804.
1802	Ship Boston.	Salter.	do.	T. Amory.	1803.§
1803	Ship Atahualpa.	O. Porter.	do.	T. Lyman and others.	1804, 1805.‖
1803	Ship Caroline.	Sturgis.	do.	Lamb and others.	1804, 1805.
1804	Ship Mary.	Trescott.	do.	J. Gray.	1805.¶
1804	Ship Vancouver.	Brown.	do.	Thomas Lyman.	1805, 1806.
1804	Ship Pearl.	Ebbetts.	do.	Lamb and others.	1805, 1806.
1804	Ship Juno.	De Wolf.	Bristol.	De Wolf.	1805.
1804	Brig Lydia.	Hill.	Boston.	T. Lyman.	1805, 1806.
1805	Ship Hamilton.	L. Porter.	do.	do.	1806, 1807.
1805	Ship Hazard.	Smith.	do.	Perkins & others.	1806, 1807.
1806	Ship Derby.	Swift.	do.	do. do.	1807, 1808.
1806	Ship Guatimozin.	Glanville.	do.	T. Lyman.	1807,1808.**
1806	Ship Atahualpa.	Sturgis.	do.	do.	1807.
1807	Ship Pearl.	Suter.	do.	Perkins & others.	1808, 1809.
1807	Ship Vancouver.	Whittemore.	do.	do. do.	1808, 1809.

The number of sea-otter skins shipped from the Northwest Coast to
Canton in   1799 were 11,000
                  1800   9,500
                  1801   14,000
                  1802   14,000—48,500.

Mr. Tufts writes, under date of Boston, February 3d, 1857,

"The foregoing list is nearly correct as it regards the vessels engaged in the early trade in *sea-otter skins* by American enterprise. The
owners in all cases are not known. There may have been other vessels on the Coast during the time who were engaged in collecting the
smaller skins and less valuable furs, but the above are the regular
Northwest traders for sea-otter skins.

* Captain killed.   † Captain died.   ‡ Captain died.
§ All the crew killed by the natives at Nootka Sound except two men, and the
vessel afterward accidentally burned.
‖ The captain, officers, and many of the men killed by Indians at Millbank Sound.
¶ Wrecked on her passage home.
** Wrecked on the coast of New Jersey, Feb. 3, 1810.

"I have obtained the most of my information from Captain Sturgis, who very kindly gave me the information which his experience and notes rendered extremely valuable.

"We sailed from Boston (ship Guatimozin, Glanville) July 7th, 1806, arrived on the Coast March 20th, 1807, left the Coast September 24th, 1808, and were wrecked on the coast of New Jersey (on Seven-mile Beach) the 3d of February, 1810."

Mr. Tufts was supercargo of the ship.

It is a rather singular fact that some of the first furs ever carried to Canton direct from the Northwest Coast should have been by an American. Lieutenant John Gore, a native of Virginia, who was with Captain Cook, took charge of the expedition after the death of the captain at Karakoor Bay, Sandwich Islands, and Captain Clerke, who succeeded him, and who died at the Russian settlement of Peter and Paul, or Petropawlowsk. Gore sailed from Petropawlowsk, or, as the sailors call it at present, Peterpulaski, in October, 1779, and reached Canton in the beginning of December. While the ships had been on the Northwest Coast, the officers and men had purchased a quantity of furs from the natives in exchange for knives, old clothes, buttons, and other trifles, not, however, with any reference to their value as merchandise, but to be used on board ship as clothes or bedding. On their arrival at Peterpulaski, they found the Russians anxious to buy all these furs; but, having learned that they were of great value in Canton, concluded to take them there, where they sold for money and goods for more than ten thousand dollars.

These furs, and a few carried by Benyowsky in 1770, were the only ones that had ever arrived at Canton direct from the Northwest Coast.

GENERAL GIBBS'S LETTER ON THE CAUSE OF THE INDIAN TROUBLES IN WASHINGTON TERRITORY.

The following extracts from a letter received from General George Gibbs, dated "Fort Vose, on Port Townsend, W. T., Jan. 7, 1857," give the most reliable information on the subject of the Indian War that has been received.

General Gibbs, who was with Governor Stevens, as secretary to the commission, during the making of treaties with the Indians of Washington Territory in 1855, and who was afterward chosen as the Brigadier General of the Territory, has throughout the war been so situated as to be perfectly cognizant of every event that has transpired worthy of note, and his information may be relied on as entirely correct.

Although General Gibbs does not endorse Governor Stevens's policy, yet he substantially takes the same view of the difficulties that I do, but with this exception, that, while admitting the ill feeling of the Indians toward the Americans to have existed for several years—as in

the instance of Kamăiyáh-kan—he does not go to the root of the difficulty, and state *why* the Indians should have this ill feeling toward the
Americans, and not toward the Hudson Bay Company's people. I have
charged this state of disaffection directly on to the Hudson Bay Company and their employés.

General Gibbs writes:

" As to our Indian war, I have not time to go into a proper detail of
its causes. Of one thing you may be sure ; it did not spring out of any
outrages on the part of the whites. Its origin was the unwillingness
of the Indians to have their lands intruded on. Kamăiyáh-kan, the
head chief of the Yakamas, has always been opposed to the intrusion
of the Americans, and as early as 1853 had projected a war of extermination. Father Pandory, the priest at the Atahnam mission, in the
spring of that year wrote to Father Mesplié, the one at the Dalles, desiring him to inform Major Alvord, in command at that post, of the
fact, and Major Alvord reported it to General Hitchcock, then in command on this coast. Hitchcock censured him as an alarmist, and Pandory was censured by his superior, who forthwith placed a priest of
higher rank with him. For this reason, when Captain M'Clennan's
party passed through in the summer of that year, Pandory said nothing
to us about it, and Major Alvord's precautionary moves had disconcert-
ed Kamăiyáh-kan's plans. The Indians, however, were not satisfied.
The next year, Bolon, the agent, who was afterward killed, learned that
a council had been held in the Grande Ronde, at which several tribes
were represented, and the question of peace or war was discussed. Kamăiyáh-kan did not attend, but sent his brother Sklome instead, as his
representative. During all that summer Bolon was unable to meet
with Kamăiyáh-kan, who avoided him, but he saw Sklome on his return, who told him that there had been such a council, that he attended it, and spoke against war. Later still Bolon met the *Lawyer*, the
Nez Percé council chief, who also informed him of the meeting, and
said that his tribe were divided in opinion, and that nothing had come
of it. The project was still agitated during the whole summer of 1855,
Kamăiyáh-kan being the head of the war party, and using his great
and deserved influence, as the ablest head in all the tribes, to concentrate them. The plan was now communicated to all the bands on this
side of the mountains (west of them) who are connected with the Yakamas and Klikatats, that is to say, to all those lying from the Snoqualmie River southward to the Columbia. The upper bands upon
the Snoqualmie, Cedar River, Green River (or the Nooscope), White
River, the Puyallup, the Nisqually, and the Cowlitz, are all of Yakama and Klikatat blood, and speak both languages. On the Cathlapoodl the Klikatats have superseded the original tribe, now extinct.
Leshchi, one of the Nisqually chiefs, was a Yakama by the mother's
side, and related, I think, to Owhai. He has always been a busy in-
triguer and a great traveler, and was the principal agent in the matter

on the Sound side. Considerable portions of all these tribes entered into the confederacy. There was a large band of Klikatats who had crossed the Columbia River and gone down by way of the Willamette to the Umpqua. These, General Palmer, the Oregon superintendent, unfortunately, in the course of his treaty operations, sent back to their own country in this territory just as the war broke out, to swell the ranks of the enemy. All that summer, rumors came in of the intention of the Indians to break out. Indian women living with white settlers warned their husbands to take care of themselves; but these reports were disregarded, because we had so long slept on the volcano that we did not believe it could burn. In July, just as I was going over to Fort Vancouver, Patkanam, the Snoqualmie chief, came to Fort Steilacoom and desired me to interpret to the officers what he was about to say. He brought with him Father D'Harborney, whom I had known at the Yakama mission in 1853, and stated that he would say in Klikatat to the father what he had to communicate; that he would tell me in French, and I should translate into English. He wanted two witnesses. The substance of his statement was, that the Indians on the eastern side of the mountains were going to war, and perhaps others would join them; that he would remain neutral, and keep his own people at home, and the whites might trust him. Patkanam kept his word through the war, and behaved well—better than any one expected of him. On my arrival at Fort Vancouver, Yah-ho-tow-it, a Klikatat sub-chief, whom I knew, came with Umtrets, another old Klikatat of influence and standing in his tribe, and desired me to make a communication to the officers there. He said there was going to be war, and that it was good that the whites should fill the Dalles, Vancouver, and Steilacoom with soldiers—not a few, as they were then, but full—many soldiers. They promised to remain at home on the Cathlapoodl, and keep their men there. Other warnings of like character were given, but we placed but little confidence in them, believing that a combination of tribes who had many of them been hostile, the one to the other, and among all of whom jealousies and divisions existed, was impossible.

" It was during this summer that the gold was discovered near Fort Colville, and many persons went over to the mines, and the murders commenced upon them as they were returning. The history of the rest I have not time to give you. It has been stated that the first cause of the outbreak was an outrage committed on one of the women of Te-ái-yas, a chief of the upper or northern band of Yakamas, and elder brother of Owhai. That this was not so is sufficiently proved by the evidence of the party accused, who were men of sufficient character to be believed in the matter, as well as by the fact that Te-ái-yas never joined in the war. The story, indeed, was not stated till long after. But that the war was premeditated by the Indians is evidenced incontrovertibly. They had laid in large stores of powder, and it is said that Owhai's son, Kwaltchin, bought at the Dalles 300 lbs. some time before the war. The whole character of their preparations, and the number of men from different tribes who, as it were, in an instant took the field, showed long and well-arranged concert, but it is believed the trap was sprung too soon. Kamăiyáh-kan wished to wait until the Columbia was closed with ice before he commenced the attack, when the whites this side the mountains could not go up to aid their friends, but the impatience of Kwaltchin thwarted this judicious intention.

" On the Sound, the Indians waited until Captain Maloney, Lieutenant Slaughter, and their men had crossed the Cascades to co-operate with Majŏr Haller before they broke out, when they commenced murdering the citizens on White River.

" That the governor's treaties had a great deal to do in fomenting this war there is no doubt. Those on the Sound were too much hurried, and the reservations allowed them were insufficient; but his grand blunder was in bringing together the Nez Percés, Walla Wallas, Yakamas, and others into one council, and cramming a treaty down their throats in a hurry. Still, the treaties were only one item in the reasons for disaffection. Treaties had been made with the Willamette and Columbia River Indians, first by a board of commissioners, then by a superintendent, and none of them ratified, nor payments made under them. The Donation Law had very unjustly given to settlers the lands before the title was extinguished. The tribes whose country was occupied had visibly perished, and the bolder tribes of the prairies east of the mountains were determined that they would keep us out, at all events till they were paid. They saw that the troops were few, and scattered in distant and petty posts; that they were not mounted, and only one station in their country, which they could easily exterminate. The Sound Indians, encouraged by hope of support from the Yakamas, whom they feared themselves, thought that they, in like manner, could clear the Sound, and they came pretty near doing it. But for Captain Maloney's fortunate return, they probably would have raised all the tribes, taken the unguarded post at Steilacoom, supplied themselves with arms and ammunition, and whipped us out. It needed only one great success to have enabled them to do this. As to the conduct of the war on this side (that is, west of the Cascade range of mountains), it has been well managed. Captain Keyes and Colonel Casey, who succeeded him in command, acted with judgment and energy; but the war on the other side, directed by Colonel Wright, has been a perfect farce. He has proclaimed peace when it only exists because the whites have been driven from the country. He left his communications behind him unguarded, suffered the Cascades to be taken and burned, ran back, gave up an expedition on which he started, undertook another, sent back for more troops, and finally, at the head of eleven companies of regulars, after talking and feeding the hostiles on sugar and flour, marched back without taking a single one of the murderers, without killing an enemy in the field, without dictating terms, or doing any thing whatever to chastise or subdue those who were in arms. The result is, that all communication by way of the Plains is abandoned; that other tribes, encouraged by the inefficiency of the troops, or, rather, of their commander, have joined; and that the Indians hold undisputed control over the country.

"Here the principal difficulty will arise from the non-fulfillment of the treaties with the friendly tribes. The treaty with the Nisquallies, &c., who took up arms, was the only one ratified, and of course they will receive their annuities; while the Lower Sound tribes, who have remained peaceable, and have been compelled to suffer great though necessary inconvenience, remain neglected. Whether the treaties are good or not, they ought to be ratified, or at least provision made by law to pay their annuities as promised.

"The conduct of the government has been most extraordinary. They have suffered a regular and a volunteer war to go on for a whole year, and have neither authorized nor stopped the latter. Governor Stevens and General Wool have been quarreling, and they have not decided in favor of either. In fact, the inaction or want of decision shown at Washington has been most culpable. * * * * *

"I can not stop to correct the above, or add what may, perhaps, be necessary to give connection to the data. What I have meant to show was that the war sprung partly from ill-judged legislation, partly from previous unratified treaties, and partly from recent blunders. Much is due to the natural struggle between the hostile races for the sovereignty of the soil. The *land* is at the root of the war. Many outrages have been committed *since* it begun, it is true, but it was not private wrongs that led to it. The numerous outrages committed by Indians on whites have not been taken into account by those who bleat about the 'poor Indian.'"

INDEX.

Achaitlin, a river at Shoal-water Bay, page 26.

Active, United States surveying steamer, 263.

Adair, General John, collector at Astoria, 243.

Adams, Point, named by Gray, 129.

Adventure, schooner, 132.

Adventures with crabs, 82; serious adventure and narrow escape, 144; adventure with a bear, 257; capsize in the surf, 272.

Agassiz, Professor, 207.

Albatross, ship, 223.

Alden, Captain James, U. S. Coast Survey, reconnaissance of Shoal-water Bay, 21; his remarks about the Bay, 24; steamer Active at Point Grenville, 263.

ALIENS causing trouble among Indians, 387.

Amoor River, description of, 404.

ANDERSON, Colonel J. PATTON, his adventure while taking the census, 355; his chase after a butter-duck, 357; speech in Congress, 386, 391; his account of the Falls of the Snoqualmie, 395; his account of Patkanim and Colonel Simmons, 396; the first United States Marshal of the Territory, 401; second delegate to Congress, 402; letter of advice to emigrants, 408.

Animals, description of, 28.

Antiquities of America, 207.

Anwillik, an Indian girl, 199; her skill in making dresses, 200.

Armstrong's Point at Gray's Harbor, 252.

Arrival from Kodiak, 205.

Ashley's, General William H., expedition across the Rocky Mountains, 233.

Assumption Inlet, 126.

Astor, John Jacob, 223.

Astoria, description of, 223; when named, 225; sold to the Northwest Company, 228; restored to the Americans, 232; its present appearance, 238; military road, 229.

Awilkatumar, the bloody ground, on the Palux River, Shoal-water Bay, 151.

Aztec language, 313.

Baker, captain of brig Jenny, of Bristol, 129.

Baker, Captain Eben P., master of schooner Maryland, is drowned, 366.

Baker, Bay, description of, 100; named after the captain of brig Jenny, 129.

Baking bread, method adopted, 165.

Baldt, William, our visit to the Columbia, 97; our examination of Chenook, 109; our adventures on the Portage, 114; we make a bonfire on Pine Island, 133; our jury duty, 292; interview with Captain Johnson, 296; canoe adventure, 303.

Barnes, Miss Jane, the first white woman who arrived at the Columbia, 230.

Barrows, J. F., a settler at Shoal-water Bay, 284; receives me hospitably, 328; get in a ditch while endeavoring to find his house, 354.

Bartlett, George G., one of the first settlers at Shoal-water Bay, 25; he is called Tom by the settlers, 69; his bear-fight on Stony Point, 70; gives me some iron to repair my chimney, 142.

Battle Rock at Port Orford, 219.

Bear River, Shoal-water Bay, 26.

Bear-fight, 69.

Bear-shooting, 256.

Bear-skin, 273.

Beauties of Washington Territory, 67.

Beaver, description of, 93.

Beaver, ship, 224.

Beeswax found at Clatsop, 206.

Berries, 88.

Bird feast, 268.

Birds, description of, 29.

Black, captain of sloop of war Raccoon, 229.

Blodget, Lorin, quotation from, respecting climate, 45.

Blossom, H. B. M. frigate, 232.

Blubber feast, 360.

Bolin, hotel-keeper at Astoria, 238.

Bolon, Indian agent, 387.

Bonfires, 54.

Bonneville, captain of an expedition in 1832, 234.

Bowman, trial of, 279.

Brandywine, or M'Carty, 102.

Bread, method of making, 164.

Brown, Joel L., 64.

Brown's Point, Gray's Harbor, 253.

Bruce Company, 63; their great hospitality, 283.

Bruceville or Bruceport, 319.

Bryonia Alba, 178.

Bullard, Joel and Mark, early settlers, 64.

Burial, form of, 185.

Bush-tail rat, 28.

Cabbage, method of preserving from Indians, 149.

Cain's, Captain, report on Indian troubles, 387.

432   INDEX.

Callicum, an Indian, 213; his cannibal-ism, 307.
Camp at Gray's Harbor, 254; at Copalis, 255; at the treaty-ground on the Chehalis River, 337.
Cannibals, Meares's account of, 213.
Canoe River, one of the head-waters of the Columbia, 121.
Canoes, description of, 80; method of traveling in, 248.
Carcowan, chief of the Chehalis Indians, 251; his son, 329; his talk about the treaties, 363.
Carcumcum, a sister of Comcomly, 55; she tells about the first rum ever brought into the Columbia, 156.
Cartumhays or Tomhays, visit to his house, 35; a cure for the small-pox, 57; his goose trade, 319.
Caslah'han, a Chehalis Indian, 252; takes me and a party to the treaty-ground, 333; an adventure with him, 304.
Caswell, second mate with Captain Gray, murdered at Massacre Cove, 132.
Catlin Seth, 401.
Cedar of Port Orford, 219.
Celebration of 4th of July, 133.
Champ, John W., one of the first settlers, 25; visit to the Columbia, 97; his troubles on the Portage, 115; his election as justice of the peace, 278; the first trial before his court, 279; counsel before the squire's court, 320; his decision in Watkins's case, 365.
Charley, Big, the constable, 278.
Chatham, brig, Lieutenant Broughton, enters the Columbia, 129.
Chehalis—visit to Gray's Harbor among the Chehalis Indians, 254; visit to the treaty-ground on the Chehalis River, 330; description of Chehalis River, 333.
Chenook Indians, description of their village, 110.
Chenowith, Honorable F. A., 402.
Cherquel Sha, an Indian, 49.
Chetzamokha, chief of the Clalams, 17.
Children's games, 197; songs, 199.
Chinese among the Indians, 163.
Christianity as applied to Indians, 193.
Christmas dinner on crow, 325; on skunk, 326.
Chutes of the Columbia, 123.
Clark River, 121.
Clearing land, 50.
Cletheas, an Indian, 251; relates about the Klickatats, 324.
Climate, Ross Cox's and Vancouver's remarks respecting, 44; Greenhow's and Blodget's remarks, 45; further remarks, 395.
Clyoquot Bay, 226.
Cocke, Colonel H. D., 327; at the camp, 330.
Colote, an Indian, 322.
Columbia River, 18; visit to, 97; history and description of, 117, 124; cross the bar, 220; current of, 259.
Columbia, ship, 20; outfit and owners' names, 130.

Colville, Fort, discovery of gold at, 385.
Comcomly, 230.
Coon and Woodward, 319.
Cooper, Dr., 214, 327.
Copalis, camp at, 255; description of river, 258.
Counsel, argument of, at Chenook, 300.
Cox, Ross, extracts from his writings, 44, 53, 225.
Cradle, description of, 168.
Crocker, Captain, 359.
Crows, great flocks of, 149; dinner on crow, 325.
Cure for inflamed eyes, 179.
Curry stews, 44.
Cushman, Commissary, 340; his famous stories, 342.
Dædalus, ship, one of Vancouver's, 129.
Dalles of the Columbia, 123.
Dart, Dr., his treaties with the Columbia River Indians, 349.
Davis, Captain George, 366.
Dawson, George, 243, 297.
Debatable Ground, 292.
Denter, Charles W., or Big Charley, 25; elected constable, 278; takes Colonel Anderson to the Portage, 359.
Derby, Lieutenant, alias Phœnix, Squibob, and Butterfield, 238.
Deserted villages, 212.
De Smet's letters, 236.
Destruction Island, 125.
Devil's Walking-stick, 41.
Digger Indians burn their dead, 153.
Dikentra Formosa, an early flowering plant, 48.
Disappointment, Cape, first named by Meares, 23; Vancouver's remarks upon, 127.
Discovery, Vancouver's flag-ship, 129.
Doctors, Indian, 176.
Domestic utensils, 163.
Douglas, Dr., extracts from history of, 191, 193.
Dowler, Dr., of New Orleans, remarks on antiquities, 207.
Ducheney, Roc, Hudson Bay Company's agent at Chenook, 109, 313.
Dunn, John, 377.
Duponceau's, M., remarks on language of American Indians, 311.
Ebbetts, captain of ship Enterprise, 224.
Edinburg Review's remarks respecting emigrants to Oregon, 237.
Edmands, John, a settler on the Wallacut River, 240.
Election, first, at the Bay, 277.
Ellewa, a Chenook chief, and his wife, 55.
Elsie, schooner, the first vessel built in the Bay, 282.
Emigrants, remarks and advice to, 377, 402, 407.
Empire, schooner, wreck of, 365.
Enterprise, ship, 224.
Evans, Dr., state geologist, 393.
Eyes, cure for inflammation of, 179.

Falls of the Palux, 42.
Falls of the Snoqualmie, 395.
Feast at Point Grenville, 268.
Feister's Portage, 240.
Felice, ship, 20.
Fight on the Palux River, 151.
Fire, method of procuring, 248.
First emigrants to the Columbia, 235.
Fisherman's pudding, 326.
Fishing—on the Columbia, 103; on the Nasal, 135; on the Palux, 36; for sturgeon, 245.
Fitting out ship Columbia, 130.
Flattening heads, method of, 167.
Flowers, 48.
Ford, Judge Sidney, 330, 342, 355.
Fort George first named, 229.
Fort Hall, on the Snake River, 234.
Foster, Thomas J., 25.
Fremont, 313.
Frondoso, Cape, 126.
Furs, 96, 425.

Gales, description of one which caused great damage, 143.
Gambling, description of, 157.
Gardiner, Captain, 359.
Gaultheria Shallon, or Sallal, 48.
General Warren, steamer, 259.
George, an Indian, 49, 321.
Gibbs, General George, 205, 210, 308, 390, 425.
Gliddon on languages, 312.
Goose Point, 27.
Grand jury at Chenook, 293.
Gray, Captain Robert, 20, 124, 127, 138.
Gray's Harbor, 128; visit to, 265; feast at, 275; a rough place, 330; description of, 394.
Green, John, 364.
Greenhow, quotations from his work on California and Oregon, 44, 130.
Grenville, Point, 125, 206.
Grindstone, great quantities of, 259.

Hahness, the thunder bird, 203.
Haitlilth, an Indian, 79, 258.
Hancock, Cape, 129.
Hanson, Captain Alexander, 25, 283.
Hayemar, an Indian, 284.
Heceta, the Spanish navigator, 20.
Herkoisk, a Copalis chief, 259.
Heyalma, an Indian, 54.
Hiawatha, 205.
Hickey, captain of H. B. M. ship Blossom, 282.
Hill, captain of brig Oriental, 17.
Hillyer, Captain Richard, 25, 282.
Hinkley, 136.
History of the Chenooks, 202.
Holman, J. D., 242, 301.
Hudson Bay Company, 232, 349, 369, 372.

Imperial Eagle, ship, of Ostend, 125.
Indians—superstitions of, 42; arrival of Northern tribes of, 59; tradition of the doctor respecting, 68; food of, 86; reception of friends by, 169; marriage ceremonies of, 170; fasts of, 171; unbelief in

Christianity of, 174, 192, 196; Schoolcraft's remarks on, 152; manners and customs of, 154; gambling of, 157; medicines of, 177, 180, 181; games of children of, 197; songs of, 200; early history of, 202; General Gibbs's theory of, 205; other theories of, 206–210; deserted villages of, 212; treaties of, 327, 345.
Indian War, first blood shed, 386.
Ingraham, Joseph, 130.
Irish words, 310; anecdote of, 311.
Isaac Todd, ship, 228.
Isla de Dolores, 125.
Islands—Pine, 27; Long, 27; Round, 28; Destruction, 125; other islands, 394.

Jackson, Captain, 64.
Jargon, 316.
Jenny, brig, of Bristol, 129.
Jesuits, 236.
Jewett's, John R., narrative, 307.
Joe, the steward, 43; runs away from the small-pox, 56.
John, an Indian doctor, 183.
John Adams, sloop of war, 228.
Johnson, Captain James, 239, 296.
Johnson, Dr. J. R., 319, 364.
Johnson's Lake, 246.
Judges of the U. S. District Court, 401.
Junk, Chinese, at Clatsop, 206.
Jury duty at Chenook, 293.

Kaithlawilnu, an Indian, 151.
Kape, a Queniult chief, 78; visit his lodge, 264.
Keith, superintendent of the Northwest Company, 232.
Kellar, Captain J. P., 399.
Kellogg, Dr., of San Francisco, 178.
Kendrick, Captain John, 130.
Klickatat Indians, 323.
Kohpoh, an Indian, 320, 322.

Lake, Captain William, 242.
Lamley's, Job, trial at Chenook, 294.
Lancaster, Honorable Columbia, 400.
Lane, General Joseph, 390.
Language of Indians, 306, 316; other languages, 312.
Lark, ship, 227.
Laroque, M., 227.
Leadbetter Point, 21.
Leonard and Green, 238.
Lewis and Clarke, 156, 160, 210, 406.
Lime-kiln, 291.
Long Island, 27, 248.
Louisiana, great age of antiquities of, 207.
Lyell, Sir Charles, 207.
Lynde, Walter, 25, 68.

Mahar, an Indian doctor, 185.
Maquilla, an Indian chief, 213.
Marhoo River, 26.
Marshall, Stephen, 25, 358.
Martindill, William, 298.
Martyr's Point, 125.
Mary Taylor, schooner, 283.
Mason, Charles H., Secretary of the Territory, 389.

T

Mat manufacture, 161.
Maury, Lieutenant, 403.
M'Carty, William, 102, 293, 366.
M'Clellan, Captain George B., 399.
M'Tavish, 230.
Meares, Lieutenant John, 20, 126, 307.
Medicine and medicine-men, 34, 176, 177, 179.
Memelose Tillicums, or dead people, 147.
Mendell, Lieutenant, 238.
Method of coloring roots and grass, 164.
Military road from Astoria, 238 ; from Walla Walla, 399.
Milward, Richard J., 25.
Mischin or Louse Rocks, 175.
Missionaries, 194.
Mississippi River, great age of antiquities of, 207.
Monroe, James, Secretary of State, 231.
Morgan, John, 25.
Morton's, Dr., views of aborigines, 209.
Mountains, 393, 395.
Mount St. Helen's, 108.
Mummy of an Indian, 73.
Munchausen tales of old sailors, 220.

Names, meaning of, 189 ; of tribes, 210.
Narkarty, a Chenook chief, his speech to the governor, 345.
Nasal River, 26.
Necomanchee or Nickomin River, 26.
Needles for making mats, 162.
Neefus and Tichenor, 219.
Nemar River, 26.
Nertchinsk, a Russian city, 404.
Nets, description of, 104.
Nez Percé Indians, 385.
Nichols, Captain, 241.
Niebuhr, B. L., views of origin of mankind, 209.
Nootka language compared with the Chenook, 307.
Northwest Company, 232.
Nott and Gliddon's Types of Mankind, 207, 311.

Ontario, sloop of war, 231.
Oregon winters, 65, 67.
Orford, Port, 219.
Oriental, brig, 17.
Origin of Indian tribes, 203, 207 ; of mankind, 204.
Ornaments, 158.
Ossinobia, 232.
Otter, Sea, description of, 91.
Owners of ship Columbia, 130.
Oyster fishery, 50; statistics of oyster trade, 63 : noble conduct of oystermen, 66.
Oysterville, 241.

Pacific Fur Company, 223.
Palmer, General, 387.
Palos, brig, wreck of, 141.
Palux or Copalux River, 26 ; scene on, 35; falls of, 42.
Patkanim, an Indian, 396.
Paulding, Mrs., 241.
Peddler, brig, 228.
Peninsula, trip across, 247.

Pepper coffee, 146.
Peter, or Claclals, an Indian, 137, 149, 167, 251, 318, 323.
Peytona, steamer, 219.
Pilcher, journey from Council Bluffs in 1827, 233.
Pine Island, 27.
Pohks, an Indian fool, 265.
Point George, 225.
Point Grenville, 125, 260.
Polypodium Falcatum, 178.
Pope, Talbot and Co., saw-mills, 399.
Port Orford, 219.
Potato poultice, 179.
Prescott, note, 314.
Preservation of bodies, 73.
Printing-press, first established at Walla Walla, 236.
Provost, J. B., U. S. Commissioner, 231.
Pumpkin lantern, 149.
Punta de Martires, 125.
Purrington, Captain James S., 49, 141, 322, 325, 326.

Quadra, Lieutenant Juan Francisco de la Bodega y, 124, 129.
Queaquim, an Indian lad, 54; dies of small-pox, 57.
Quenainar, or strong men, 151.
Queniūlt Indians, 211; visit to Queniūlt, 251.
Querquelin or Mouse River, 74, 242.
Quootshooi, an ogress, 203.

Raccoon, sloop of war, 229
Rain, 65.
Red River, 232.
Religion, 196.
Return from Chenook, 114.
Rivers tributary to the Columbia, 121, 394.
Roberts, Robert, goes with me to Queniūlt, 251.
Roots eaten by Indians, 90.
Rotan, F., 97.
Round Island, 28.
Roundtree, Dr., 253.
Rubus spectablis, 47.
Russell, Charles J. W., 17, 25, 33, 144, 284.
Russia, trade with China, 403.

Sacodlye, an Indian doctor, 181.
Sallal, or Gaultheria Shallon, 47, 87.
Salmon-berry, Rubus spectablis, 47, 87.
Salmon fishing, 36, 103, 135.
Salmon hook, description of, 264.
Salve, Indian method of making, 180.
San Francisco, 215.
San Roque River, 20.
Scarborough, Captain James, 101, 298, 383.
Schoolcraft, H. R., 152, 171.
Schools at Walla Walla, 236.
Schooner Elsie, 282.
Schooner Northwest America, 163.
Sea-gull, steamer, 219.
Seal-fishery, 83.
Sea-otter, description of, 91.
Semple, Governor, of Ossinobia, 232.
Settlers in Shoal-water Bay, 25; first on the Columbia, 235.

Shaw, Colonel B. F., 309.
Sheriff, Commodore, 232.
Shoal-water Bay, 20, 25, 30, 211, 250
Shoal-water, Cape, 20.
Sickness of author at Queniült, 265.
Simmons, Colonel Mike, Indian agent, 250, 396.
Skulls, superstition about, 214.
Slavery among Indians, 166, 344.
Small-pox, 55.
Smith, captain of schooner Maryland, 215.
Smith, captain of ship Albatross, 223.
Smith, Fiddler, 239, 364.
Snohomish River, 395.
Snoqualmie Falls, 395.
Songs, 201.
Sonora, schooner, attack of, 125.
Sowles, captain of ship Beaver, 224.
Squier, remarks on language, 310.
Squintoo, 266.
Squintum, or old George, an Indian, 320.
Stevens, Colonel Henry K., 135, 242, 369.
Stevens, Governor, 309, 367, 383, 398.
Stewart, Charles, 64.
St. John, Augustus E., 25.
Stony Point, 68.
Storm, 143.
Strawberry frolic, 249.
Strong, Judge, 396.
Sturgeon fishing, 245.
Sturgis, Captain William, list of Fur-traders on the Northwest Coast, 423.
Suis, an Indian squaw, 33, 146, 151, 181.
Superstition, 42, 212, 214.
Swan, Doctor, 230.
Swing, Indian children's, 198.

Tappan, William B., Indian agent, 327.
Tarlilt River, 26.
Thorne, captain of ship Tonquin, 228.
Tichenor, Captain, 219.
Tide—high tide and great storm, 142.
Timber growth in Washington Territory, 398.
Tleyuk, a Chehalis chief, 251, 347, 363.
Toke, a Shoal-water Bay Indian, 33, 74, 247, 328, 360.
Tomanáwos, 146, 173, 175, 246.
Tomhays or Cartumbays, 35, 57, 319.
Tongue Point, 225.
Tonquin, ship, 224; massacre of her crew, 226.
Tower of Babel, 312.

Traditions, 68.
Treaties—with England, 231; of Ghent, 230; with Indians, 327, 343–350.
Trees, immense growth of, 53.
Trial of Bowman, 280; of Joe, 281.
Tribes, names of, 210.
Trout-fishing, 139.
Tufts, William, Esq., remarks on climate, 406; list of vessels, Appendix.

Uncle Ned, one of the Bruce Company of Shoal-water Bay, 283.
United States District Court at Chenook, 292.

Vail, Captain John, 43, 244.
Vancleave, 136.
Vancouver, Captain George, 23, 127, 129, 213.
Venison pie, aversion of Indians to, 213.
View from the ocean, 276.
Villages, deserted, 212.
Virgin Mary seen by an Indian lad, 236.

Wagon road from Fort Kearney, 403.
Walla Walla settlement, 236.
Wamalsh, a Queniült Indian, 79, 266.
Wappalooche or Chenook River, 243.
Wappatoo Island, 124, 234.
Washington, sloop, 131.
Washington Territory, 382, 392.
Weeks, Cale, of Astoria, 165.
Weldon, Captain David K., 64, 364.
Weston, Judge, of Chenook, 366.
Whil-a-pah River, 25.
Whitcomb, Henry, 64.
Wild-fowl, 143.
Wilkes, 206.
Willamet Valley, 237.
Willemantic, schooner, wreck of, 43, 275.
Wilson, James, 64.
Winant, Mark, 25, 283.
Winant, Samuel, 251, 283.
Woodward, Samuel, 64.
Woodward, Samuel, senior, 113.
Wool, General, 388.
Wreck—nearly wrecked, 216.
Wreck of steamer General Warren, 259.
Wyeth, Captain Nathaniel, 234.
Wy Yellock, a Queniült Indian, 79.

Yancumux, a Chenook Indian, 113; his disbelief in God, 295.

THE END.